RAGNARÖK

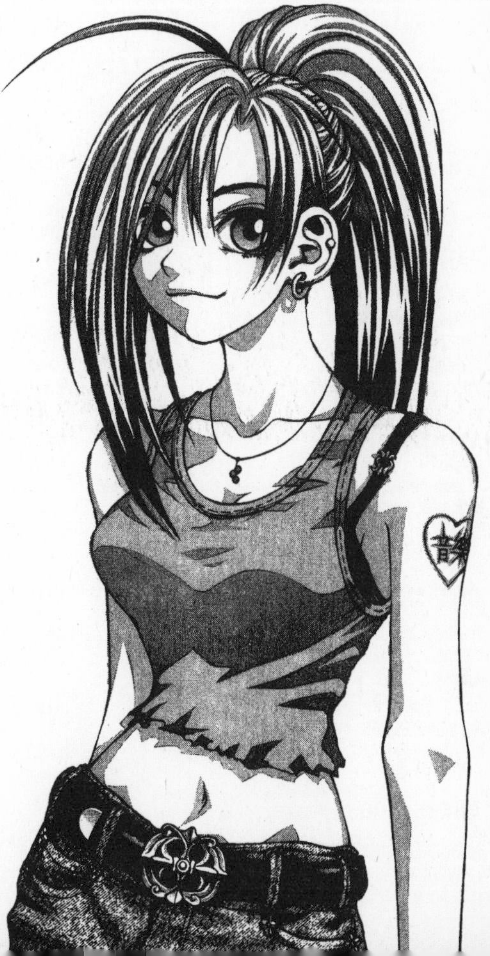

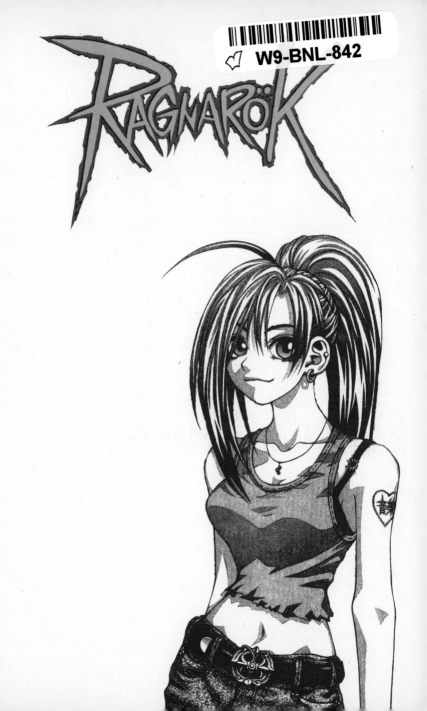

ALSO AVAILABLE FROM 🐢TOKYOPOP®

MANGA

ACTION

ANGELIC LAYER*
CLAMP SCHOOL DETECTIVES* (April 2003)
DIGIMON
DUKLYON: CLAMP SCHOOL DEFENDERS* (September 2003)
GATEKEEPERS*
GTO*
HARLEM BEAT
INITIAL D*
ISLAND
JING: KING OF BANDITS* (June 2003)
JULINE
LUPIN III*
MONSTERS, INC.
PRIEST
RAVE*
REAL BOUT HIGH SCHOOL*
REBOUND* (April 2003)
SAMURAI DEEPER KYO* (June 2003)
SCRYED*
SHAOLIN SISTERS*
THE SKULL MAN*

FANTASY

CHRONICLES OF THE CURSED SWORD (July 2003)
DEMON DIARY (May 2003)
DRAGON HUNTER (June 2003)
DRAGON KNIGHTS*
KING OF HELL (June 2003)
PLANET LADDER*
RAGNAROK
REBIRTH
SHIRAHIME:TALES OF THE SNOW PRINCESS* (December 2003)
SORCERER HUNTERS
WISH*

CINE-MANGA™

AKIRA*
CARDCAPTORS
KIM POSSIBLE
LIZZIE McGUIRE
POWER RANGERS (May 2003)
SPY KIDS 2

ANIME GUIDES

GUNDAM TECHNICAL MANUALS
COWBOY BEBOP
SAILOR MOON SCOUT GUIDES

ROMANCE

HAPPY MANIA* (April 2003)
I.N.V.U.
LOVE HINA*
KARE KANO*
KODOCHA*
MAN OF MANY FACES* (May 2003)
MARMALADE BOY*
MARS*
PARADISE KISS*
PEACH GIRL
UNDER A GLASS MOON (June 2003)

SCIENCE FICTION

CHOBITS*
CLOVER
COWBOY BEBOP*
COWBOY BEBOP: SHOOTING STAR* (June 2003)
G-GUNDAM*
GUNDAM WING
GUNDAM WING: ENDLESS WALTZ*
GUNDAM: THE LAST OUTPOST*
PARASYTE
REALITY CHECK

MAGICAL GIRLS

CARDCAPTOR SAKURA
CARDCAPTOR SAKURA: MASTER OF THE CLOW*
CORRECTOR YUI
MAGIC KNIGHT RAYEARTH* (August 2003)
MIRACLE GIRLS
SAILOR MOON
SAINT TAIL
TOKYO MEW MEW* (April 2003)

NOVELS

SAILOR MOON
SUSHI SQUAD (April 2003)

ART BOOKS

CARDCAPTOR SAKURA*
MAGIC KNIGHT RAYEARTH*

TOKYOPOP KIDS

STRAY SHEEP (September 2003)

RAGNARÖK

Volume 6:
Midnight's Masters

By
Myung-Jin Lee

English Version
by
Richard A. Knaak

Los Angeles • Tokyo

Translator - Lauren Na

Retouch & Lettering - Monalisa de Asis
Cover Layout - Anna Kernbaum

Senior Editor - Jake Forbes
Production Manager - Jennifer Miller
Art Director - Matthew Alford
VP of Production & Manufacturing - Ron Klamert
President & C.O.O. - John Parker
Publisher - Stuart Levy

Email: editor@TOKYOPOP.com
Come visit us online at www.TOKYOPOP.com

A 🐾**TOKYOPOP**® Manga
TOKYOPOP® is an imprint of Mixx Entertainment, Inc.
5900 Wilshire Blvd., Suite 2000, Los Angeles, CA 90036

ISBN: 1-931514-78-X

First TOKYOPOP® printing: March 2003

10 9 8 7 6 5 4 3 2
Printed in the USA

Bonus Supplement

Ragnarök

Players Handbook

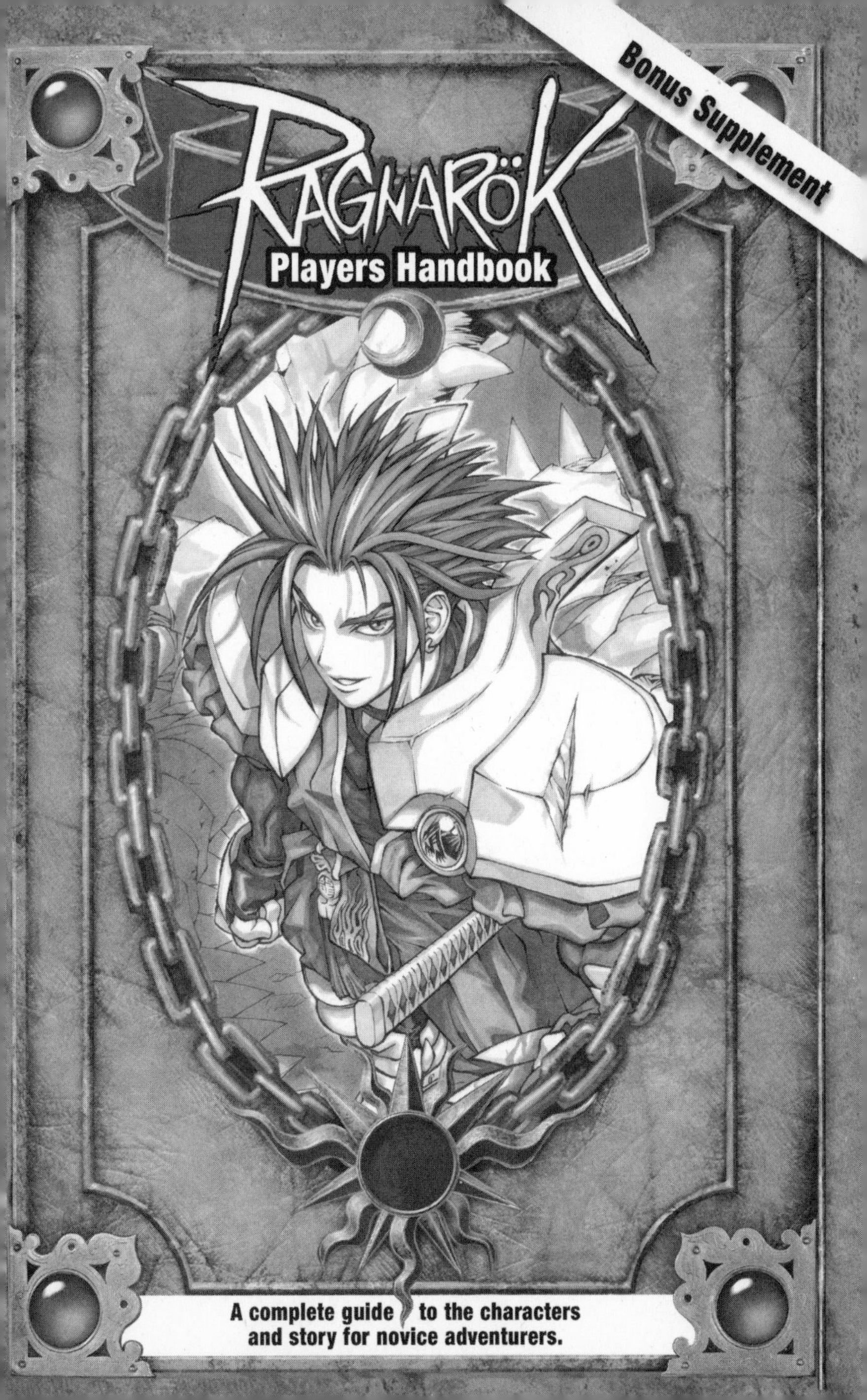

A complete guide to the characters and story for novice adventurers.

HEROES

NOTE: THE FOLLOWING STATISTICS ARE INSPIRED BY THE MANGA, BUT DO NOT REFLECT ANY OFFICIAL RAGNAROK RPG. – EDITOR

NAME: Chaos
Class: Rune Knight
Level: 9
Alignment: Chaotic Good
STR: 17
DEX: 10
CON: 15
INT: 12
WIS: 14
CHR: 16

Equipment:
Vision- Enchanted sword- STR +2

Rune Armor- AC -4, 20% bonus
saving throw vs. magical attacks.

Notes:
The reincarnation of the fallen god Balder, Chaos has been told by his divine mother, Frigg, that the fate of the world rests in his hands. He may also be tied to the legendary "Dragon Knights."

NAME: Iris Irine
Class: Cleric
Level: 5
Alignment: Lawful Good
STR: 7
DEX: 12
CON: 9
INT: 13
WIS: 16
CHR: 16

Equipment:
Chonryongdo- Enchanted dagger-
STR +1, DEX +1, 1D4 damage if
anyone but she touches it.

Irine Family Armor- AC -5, WIS +1

Notes:
Iris would have become the new leader of the city of Fayon... that is, if it weren't destroyed by her sister, the Valkyrie Sara Irine. She now follows her close friend Chaos.

HEROES

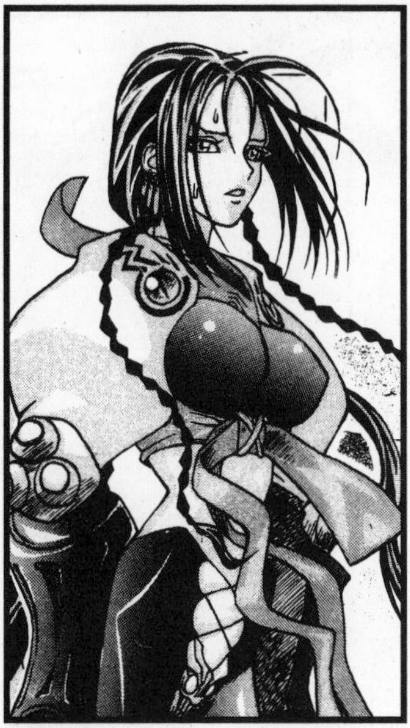

NAME: Fenris Fenrir
Class: Warlock
Level: 9
Alignment: Neutral Good
STR: 14
DEX: 15
CON: 13
INT: 16
WIS: 12
CHR: 14

Equipment:
Psychic Medallion: Magic compass which leads its bearer to whatever his or her heart most desires.

Laevatein, Rod of Destruction- STR+1, extends to staff on command.

Notes:
The reincarnation of the Wolf God, Fenris helped Chaos to realize his identity. She now follows him on his quest.

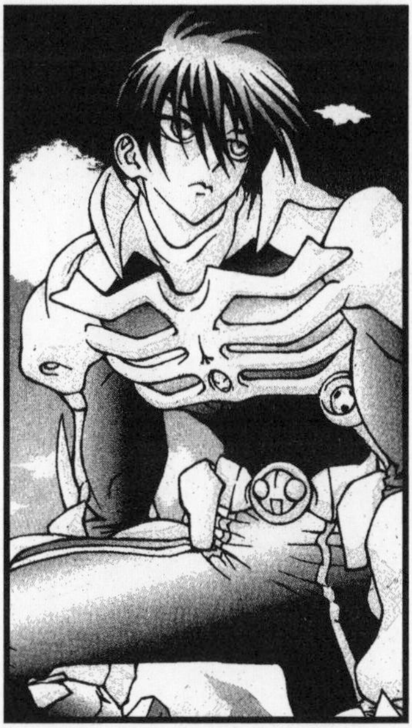

NAME: Loki
Class: Assassin
Level: 9
Alignment: Lawful Neutral
STR: 14
DEX: 18
CON: 12
INT: 12
WIS: 14
CHR: 10

Equipment:
Sword of Shadows: + 4 to hit, damage +2

Bone Armor: AC -5, STR +2

Notes:
Greatest of the Assassins, Loki's anonymity is a testament to his skill at going unseen. An enigma himself, his curiousity and respect for the even more mysterious Chaos caused him to join the Rune Night for as long as they follow the same road.

HEROES

ENEMIES

NAME: Lidia
Class: Thief
Level: 4
Alignment: Neutral Good
STR: 8
DEX: 15
INT: 13
WIS: 10
CHR: 15

Equipment:
Treasure Hunter's Bible: 50% chance of identifying magical items

Follower: Sessy, Cat o' Two Tails: +50% saving throw to pick pockets

Notes:
An "expert treasure hunter" by trade, Lidia "borrows" whatever she can get her hands on while she looks for bigger hauls. She was last seen leaving the city of Prontera. Her current whereabouts are unknown.

NAME: Sara Irine
Class: Valkyrie
Level: 7
Alignment: Chaotic Neutral
STR: 14
DEX: 12
CON: 13
INT: 14
WIS: 15
CHR: 17

Equipment:
Haeryongdo, Sword of Retribution-STR+2

Enchanted Parchments x 24

Notes:
One of the 12 Valkyries of Valhalla, Sara was once the heir to Fayon until the villiage elders cast her out in favor of her sister, Iris. Sara returned to Fayon and destroyed everything, including her parents. She now joins Himmelmez in her quest.

ENEMIES

NAME: Himmelmez
Dual Class: Necromancer/Valkyrie
Level: 10
Alignment: Lawful Evil
STR: 9
DEX: 16
INT: 18
WIS: 12
CHR: 14

Equipment:
Wand of Hela: damage +6; 70% chance
that those killed by it will become undead

Fortress- "Dark Whisper"

Notes:
One of Freya's strongest generals,
Himmelmez's arrogance is justified by her
effectiveness. All who stand against her
army have fallen, only to join her undead
legion. Perhaps her only weakness is her
overconfidence.

NAME: Bijou
Class: Witch
Level: 5
Alignment: Chaotic Evil
STR: 15
DEX: 10
INT: 13
WIS: 16
CHR: 7

Equipment:
Claw of the mantis: STR +4; CHR -3

Follower: Geirrod, the Troll:
HP: 120; damage- 2d6 +4; regeneration;
+60% saving throws against magic attacks

Notes:
A witch who began sacrificing her body
at a young age in order to increase her
occult powers. An abomination of her
former self, Bijou now serves Himmelmez,
lending her cruel and unorthodox tech-
niques to Freya's cause.

The Story so Far...

Darker things than storm clouds have gathered over the once-golden city of Prontera. The necromancer Himmelmez, one of Freya's generals, has brought her floating fortress, the Dark Whisper, to occupy Volsug's capital with her unholy army. Dark Whisper's snaking tendrils of bone and nail lay waste the peaceful city and her undead legions slaughter the populace in their search for Ymir's heart, life source of all Midgard.

Dark clouds these are indeed, but not without a silver lining. The fates have brought four young heroes who may have the strength to stand against Himmelmez. Faced by such an overwhelming foe, our fellowship has broken into two parties. Chaos, the Rune Knight, and his Assassin friend Loki take to Prontera's streets to face Himmelmez's forces directly. Meanwhile, Fenris the Sorceress and Iris the Cleric, sisters-in-arms, descend to the bowels of Prontera's keep to protect Ymir's heart from the invaders, and just in time. The witch Bijou, an abomination of stitchery, has already begun to release the heart, and sent her troll Geirrod to eliminate our heroes. Now, let us rejoin the tale in its darkest chapter, and witness the destruction of Midnight's Masters...

RAGNARÖK

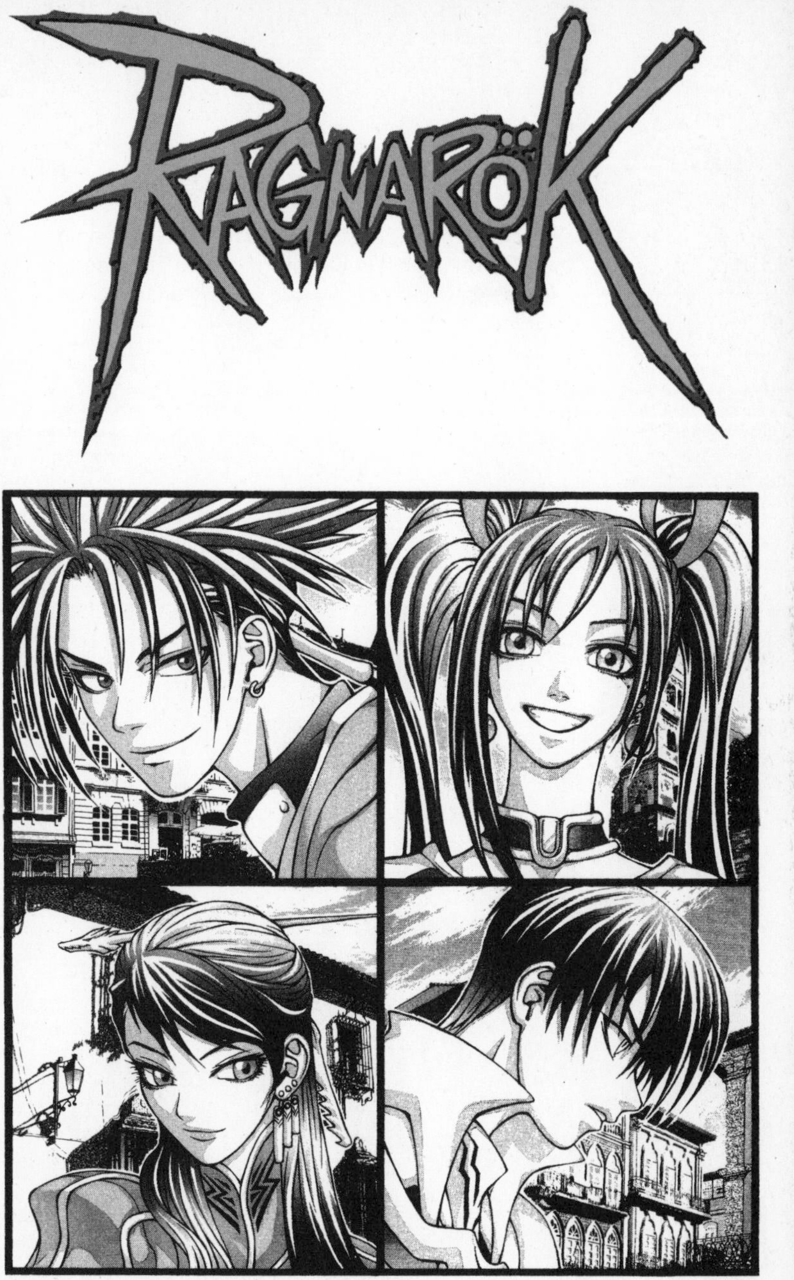

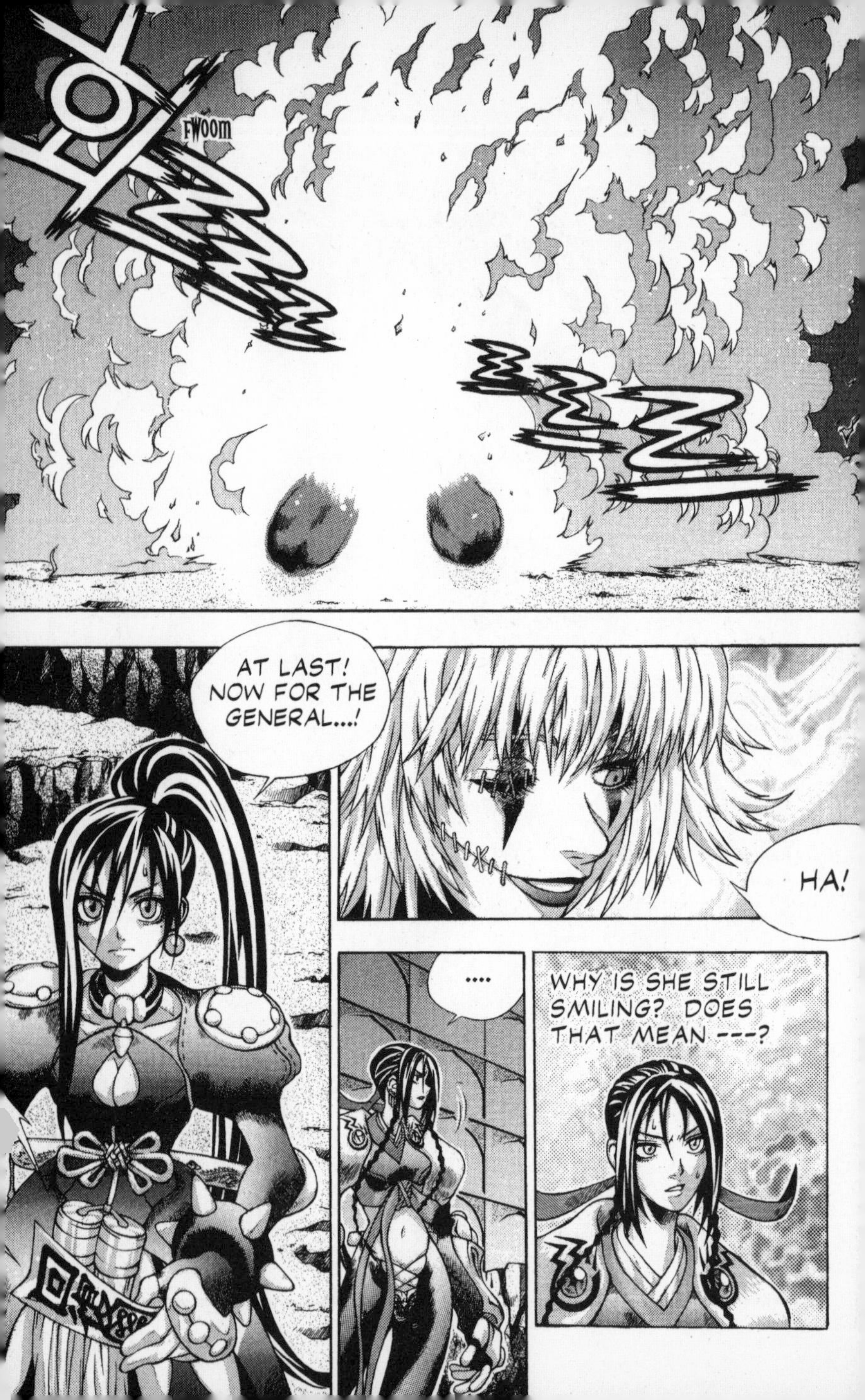
FWOOM
AT LAST! NOW FOR THE GENERAL...!
HA!
....
WHY IS SHE STILL SMILING? DOES THAT MEAN ---?

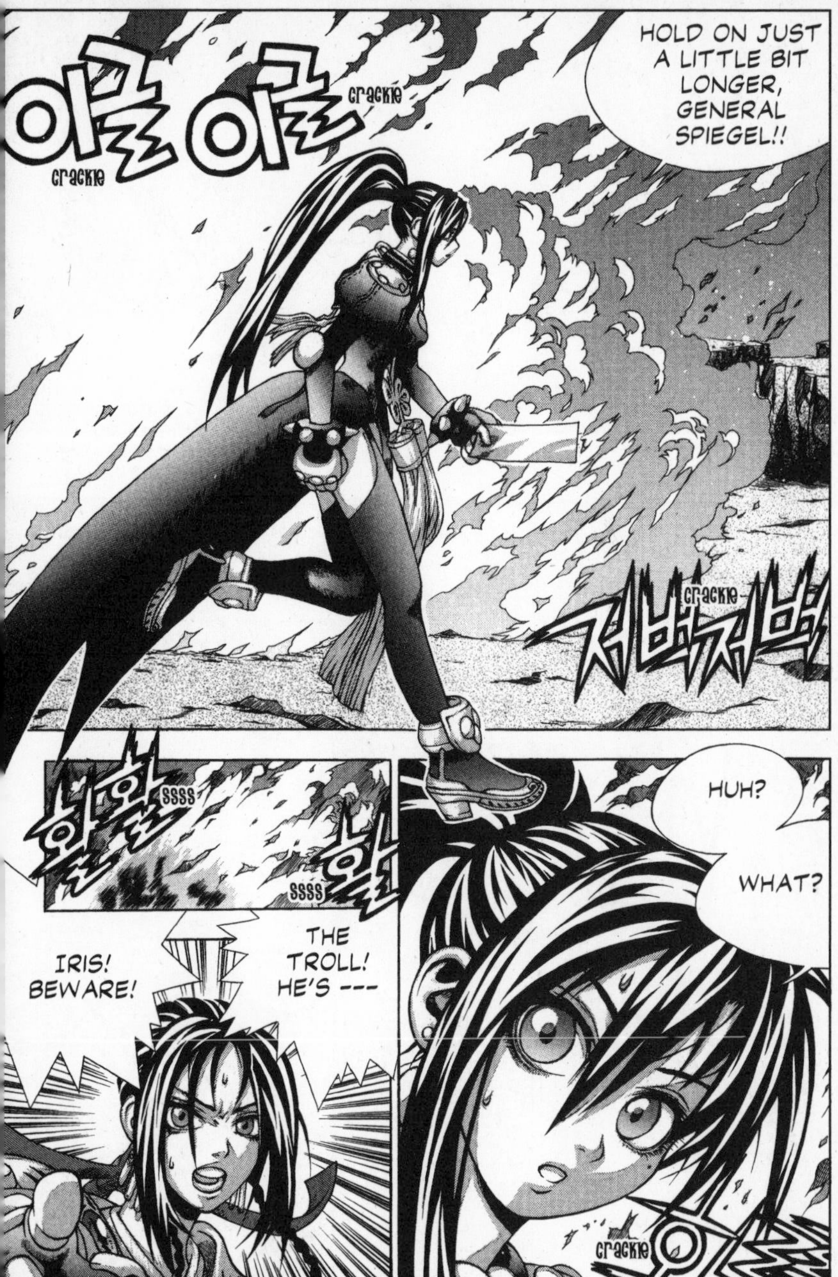
이글 이글
crackle
crackle
HOLD ON JUST A LITTLE BIT LONGER, GENERAL SPIEGEL!!
crackle
SSSS
SSSS
IRIS! BEWARE!
THE TROLL! HE'S ---
HUH?
WHAT?
crackle

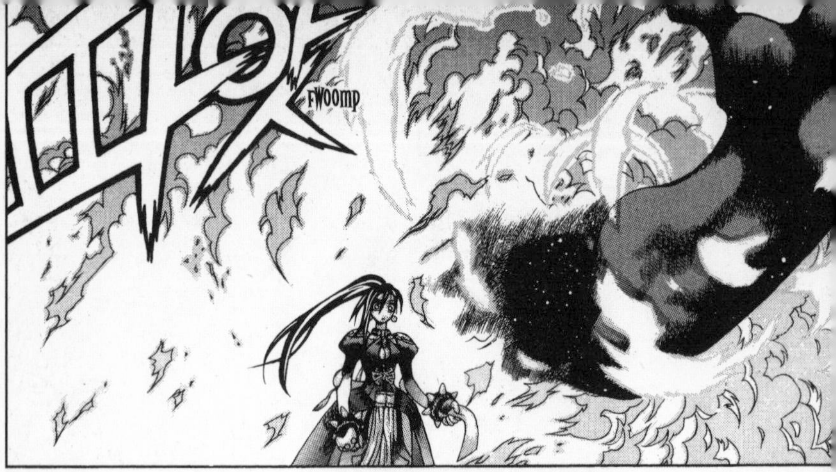
FWOOMP

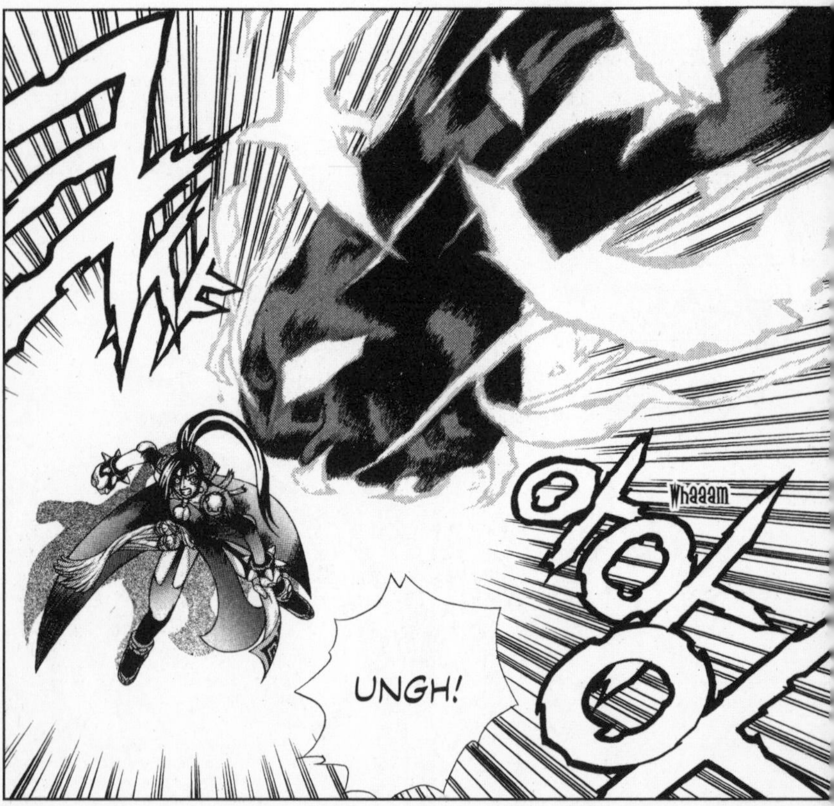
Whaaam
UNGH!

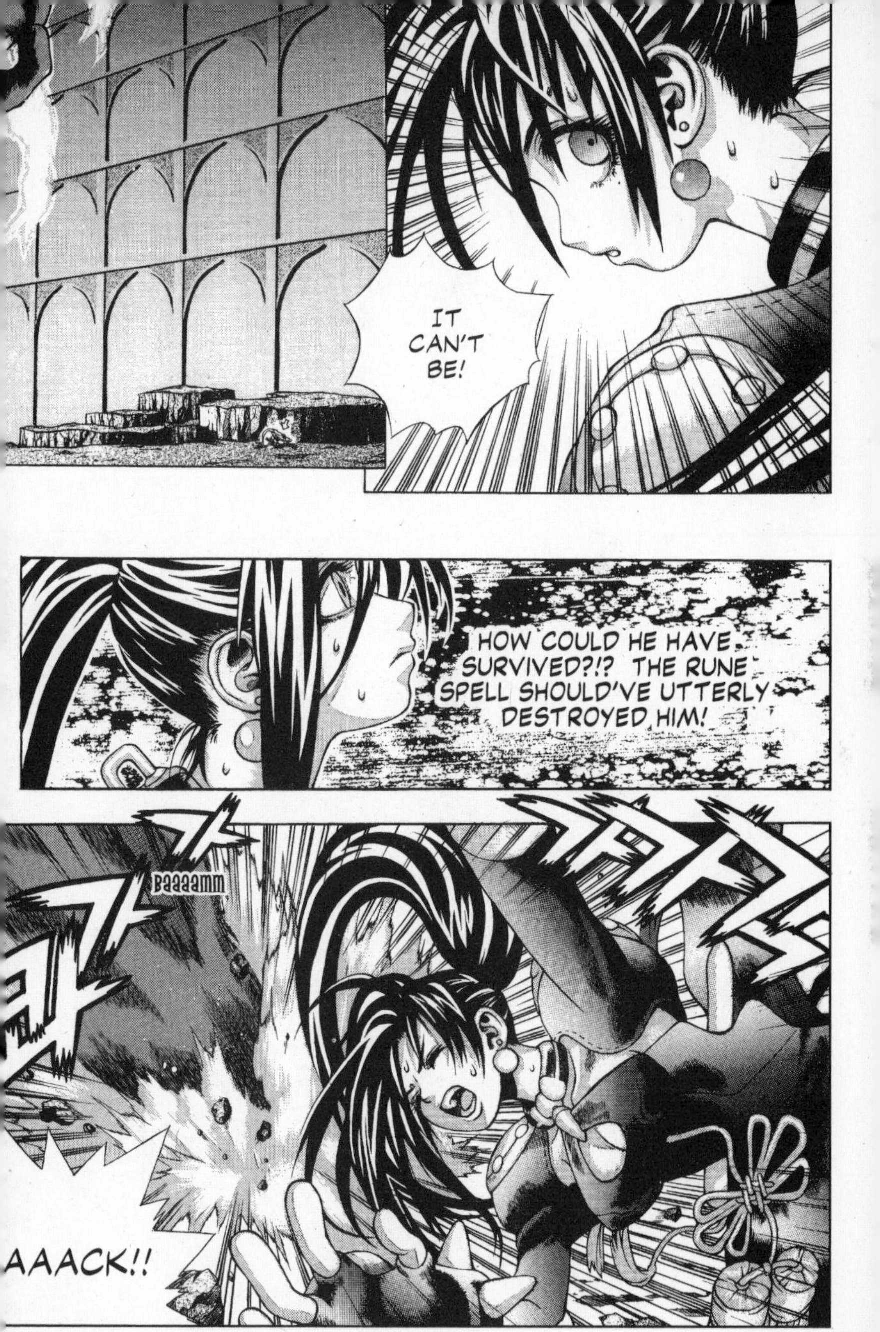
IT CAN'T BE!
HOW COULD HE HAVE SURVIVED?!? THE RUNE SPELL SHOULD'VE UTTERLY DESTROYED HIM!
BAAAAMM
AAACK!!

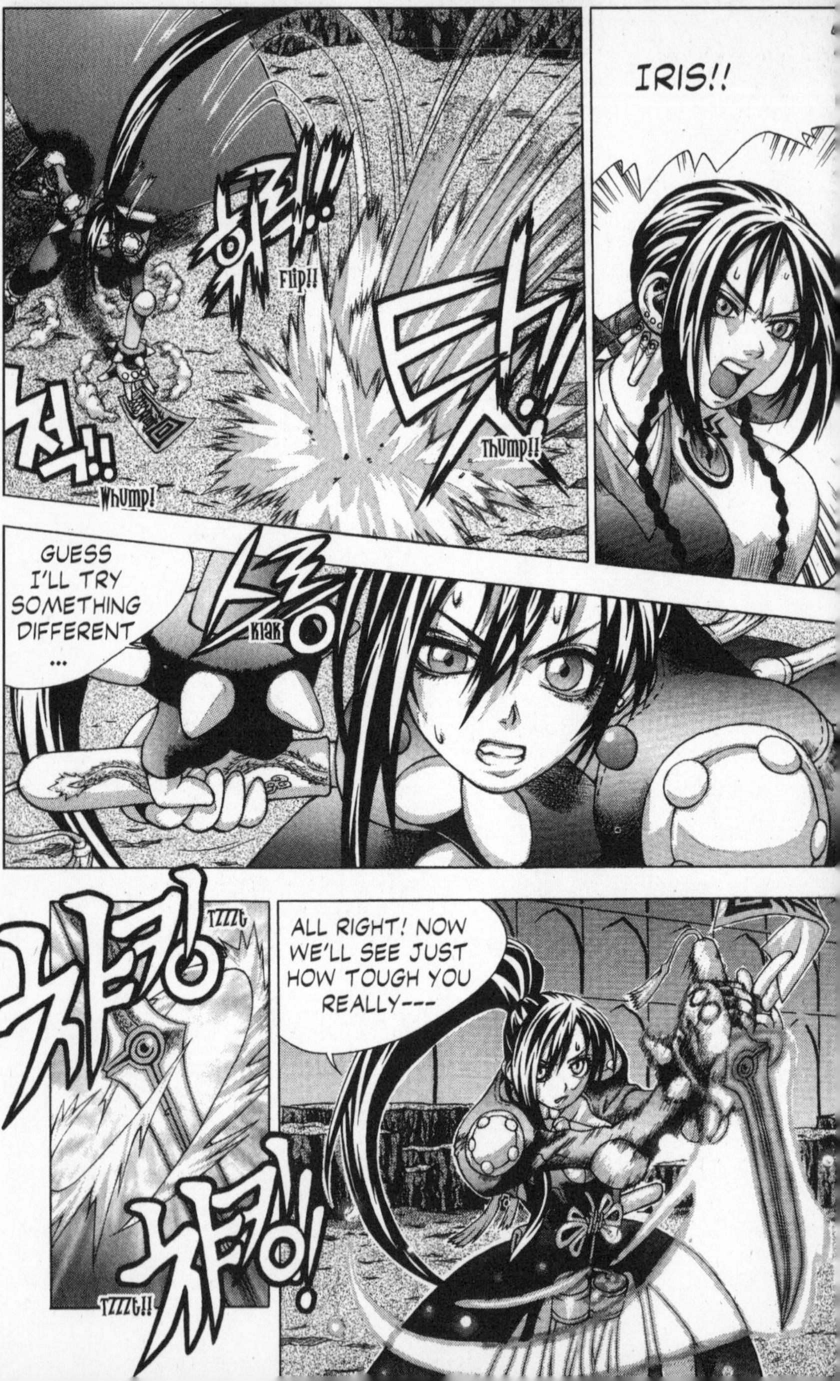
Flip!!
Thump!!
Whump!
IRIS!!
GUESS I'LL TRY SOMETHING DIFFERENT ...
KIAK
TZZZt
TZZZt!!
ALL RIGHT! NOW WE'LL SEE JUST HOW TOUGH YOU REALLY---

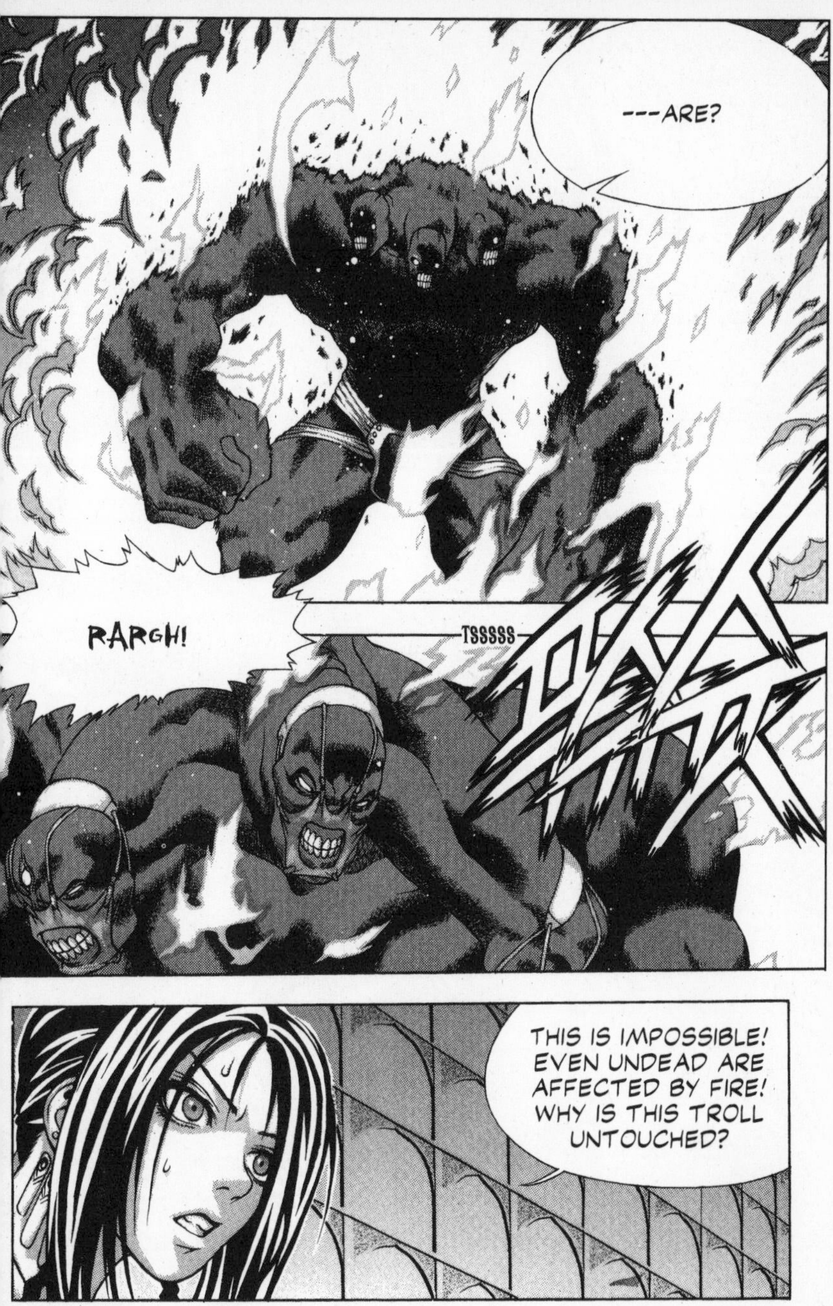
---ARE?
RARGH!
TSSSSS
THIS IS IMPOSSIBLE! EVEN UNDEAD ARE AFFECTED BY FIRE! WHY IS THIS TROLL UNTOUCHED?

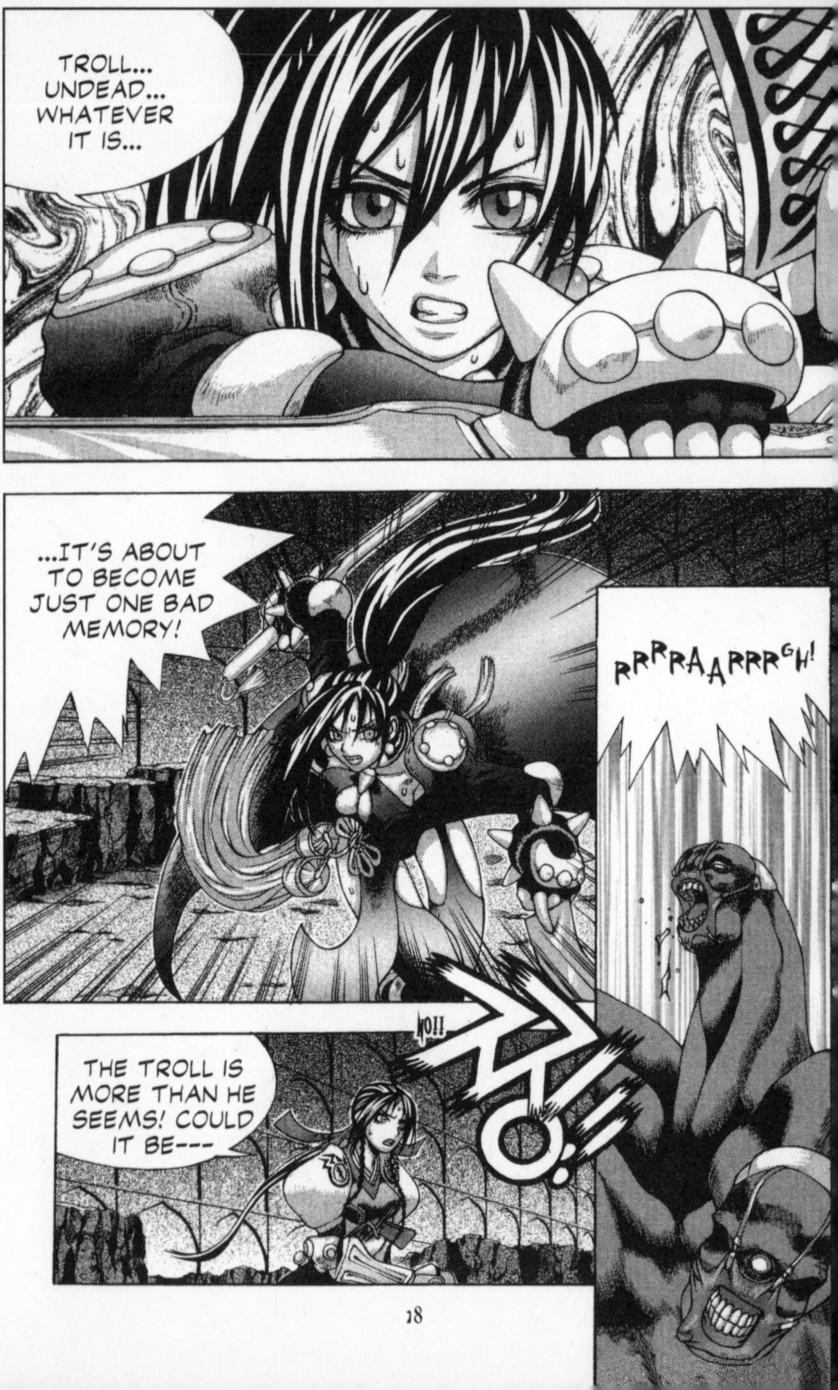
TROLL... UNDEAD... WHATEVER IT IS...
...IT'S ABOUT TO BECOME JUST ONE BAD MEMORY!
RRRRAAARRRGH!
NO!!
THE TROLL IS MORE THAN HE SEEMS! COULD IT BE---

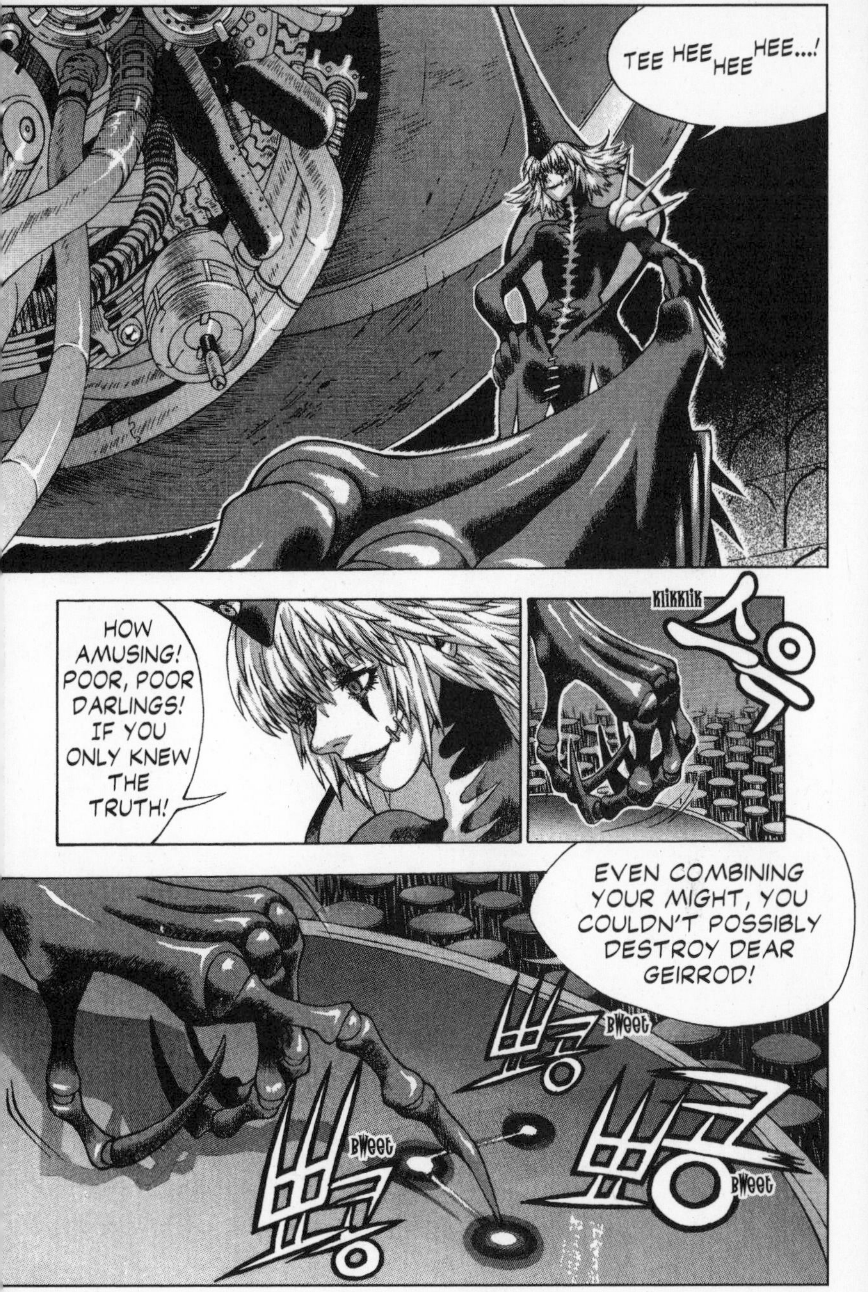
TEE HEE HEE HEE...!
HOW AMUSING! POOR, POOR DARLINGS! IF YOU ONLY KNEW THE TRUTH!
KLIKKLIK
EVEN COMBINING YOUR MIGHT, YOU COULDN'T POSSIBLY DESTROY DEAR GEIRROD!
BWEET
BWEET
BWEET

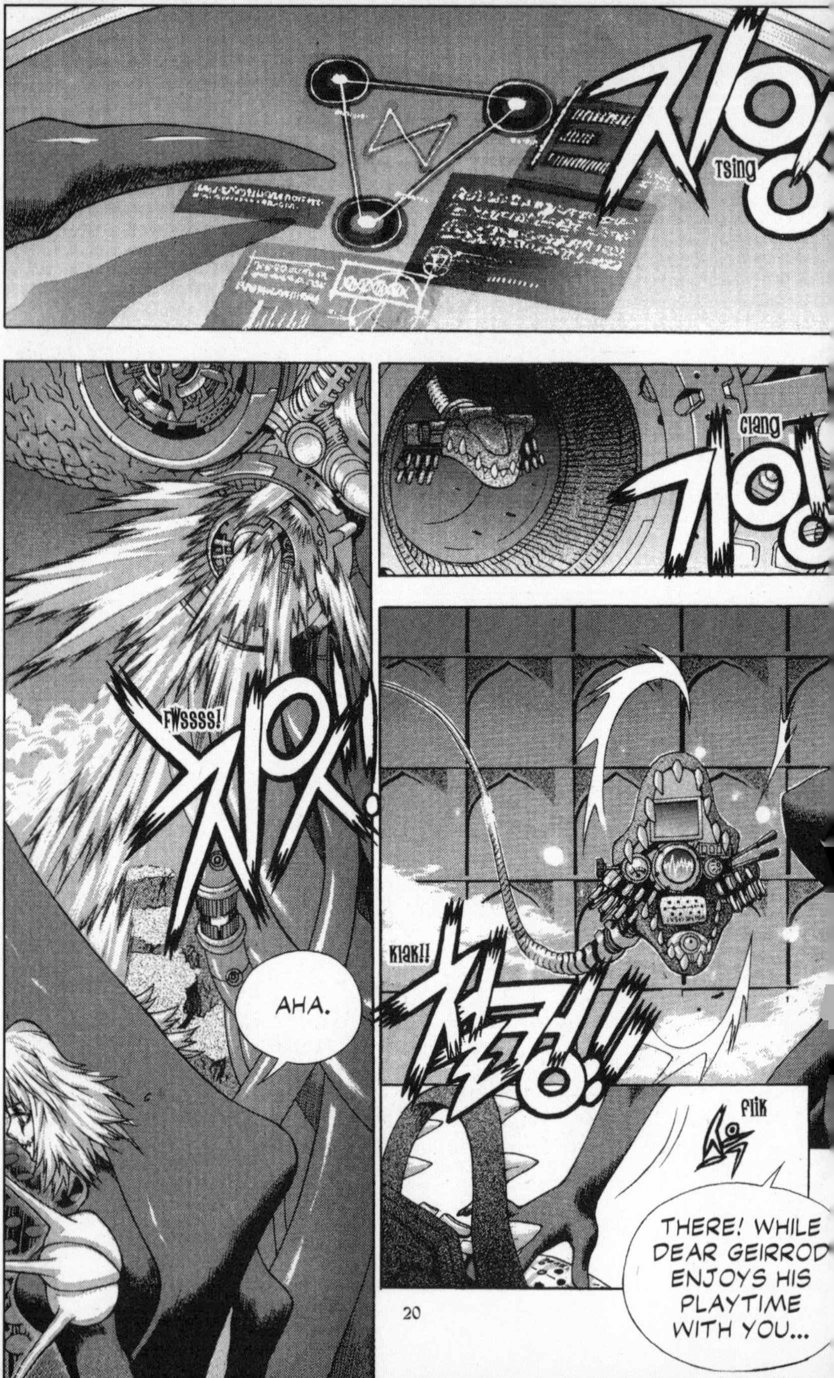
TSING
FWSSSS!
AHA.
CLANG
KLAK!!
FLIK
THERE! WHILE DEAR GEIRROD ENJOYS HIS PLAYTIME WITH YOU...

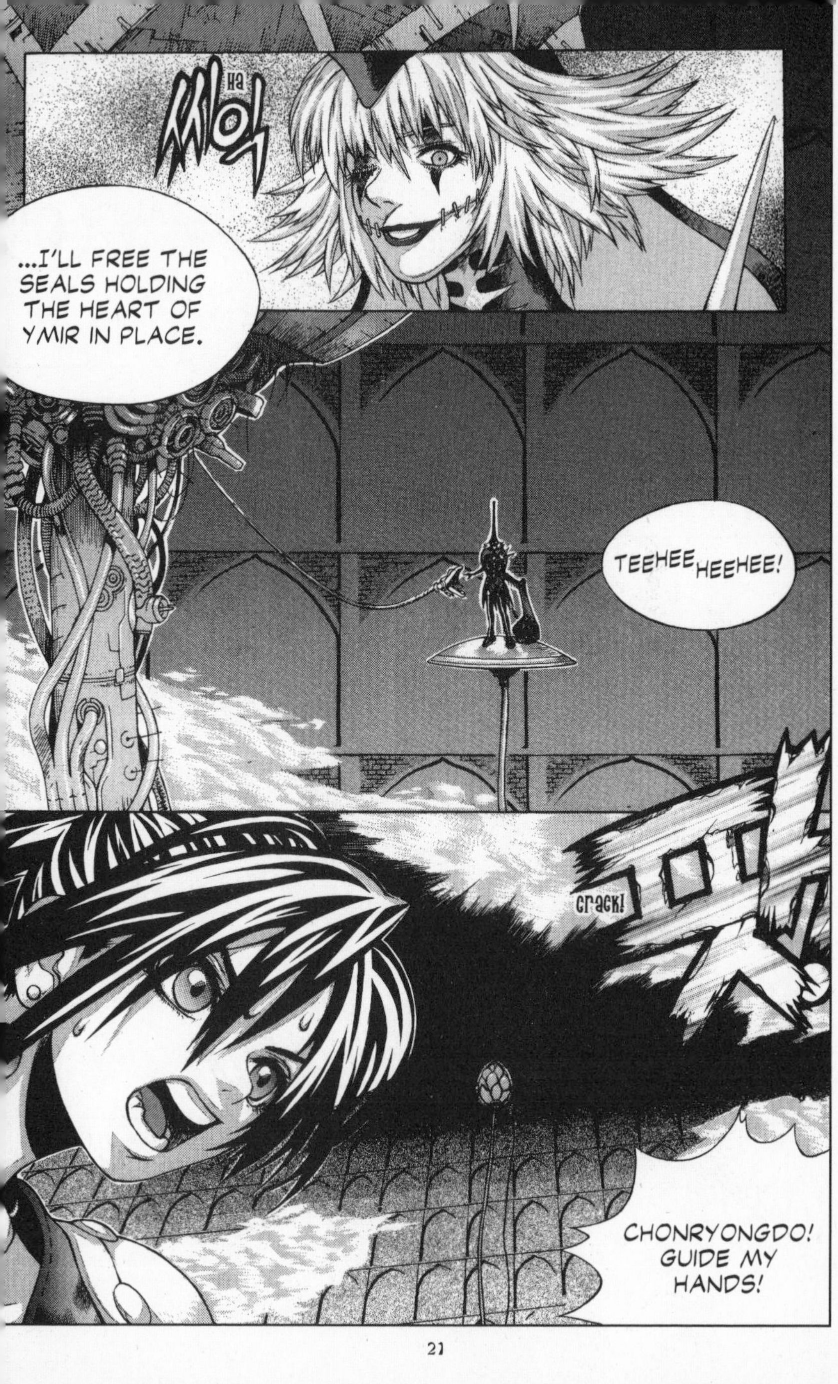
HA
...I'LL FREE THE SEALS HOLDING THE HEART OF YMIR IN PLACE.
TEEHEE HEEHEE!
CRACK!
CHONRYONGDO! GUIDE MY HANDS!

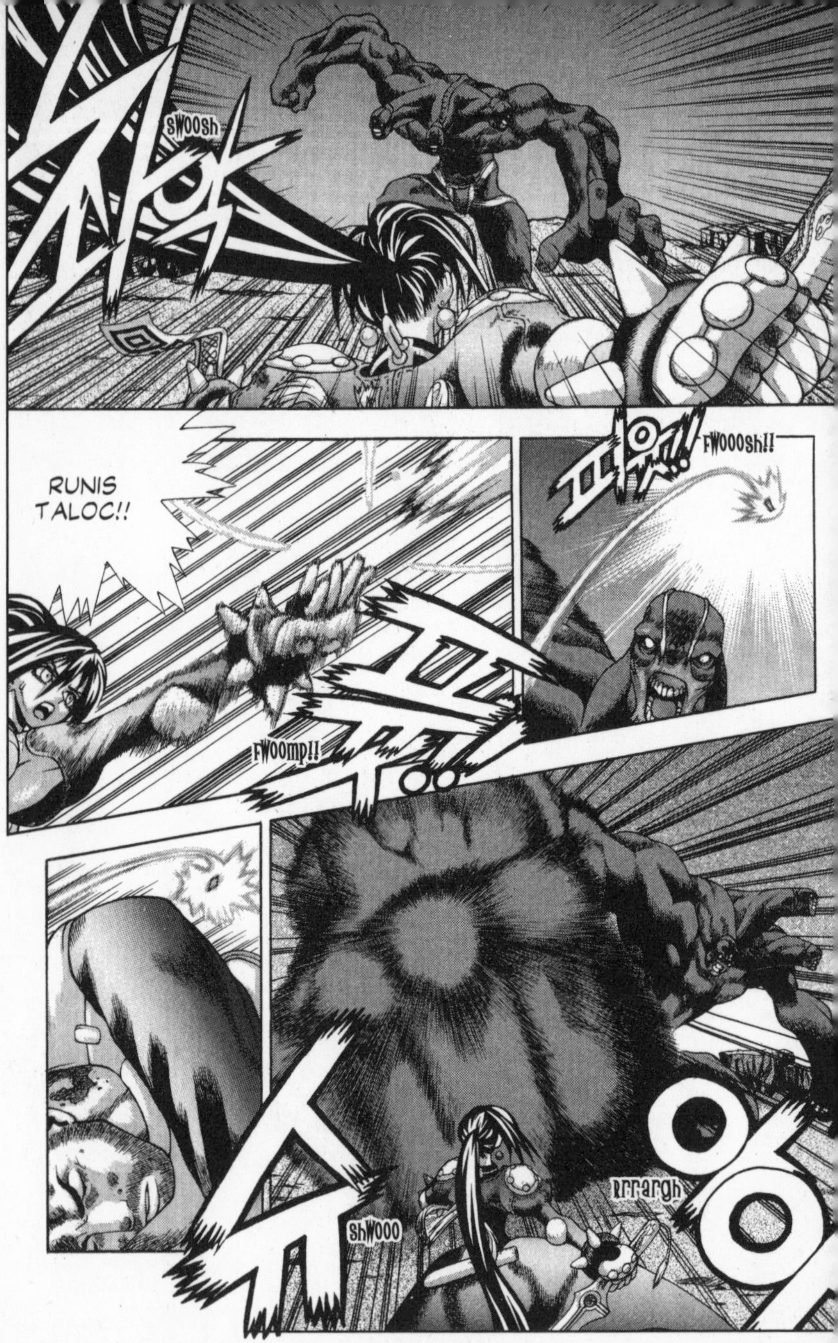
SWOOSH
RUNIS TALOC!!
FWOOOSH!!
FWOOMP!!
SHWOOO
RRRARGH

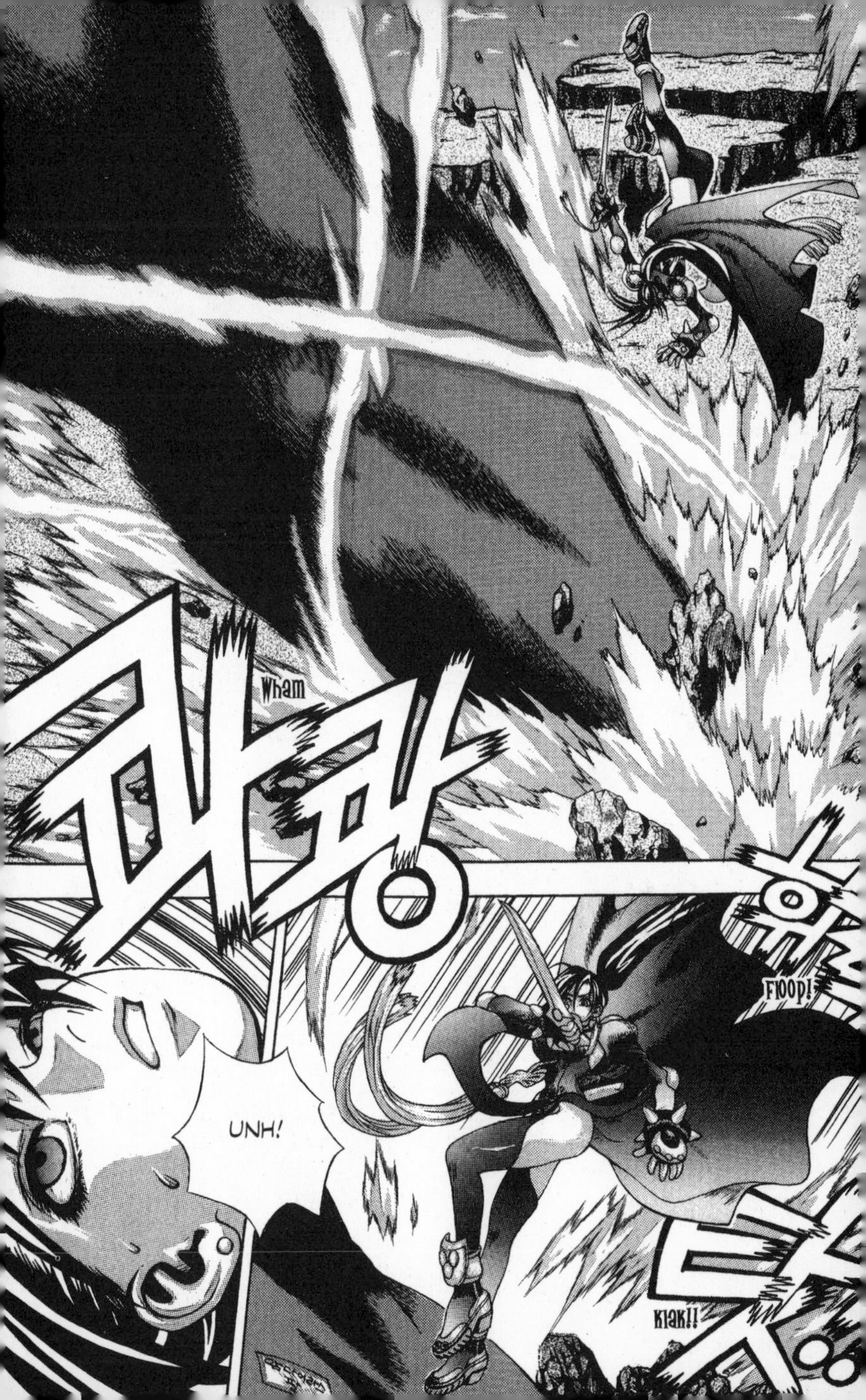
Wham
UNH!
Floop!
Klak!!

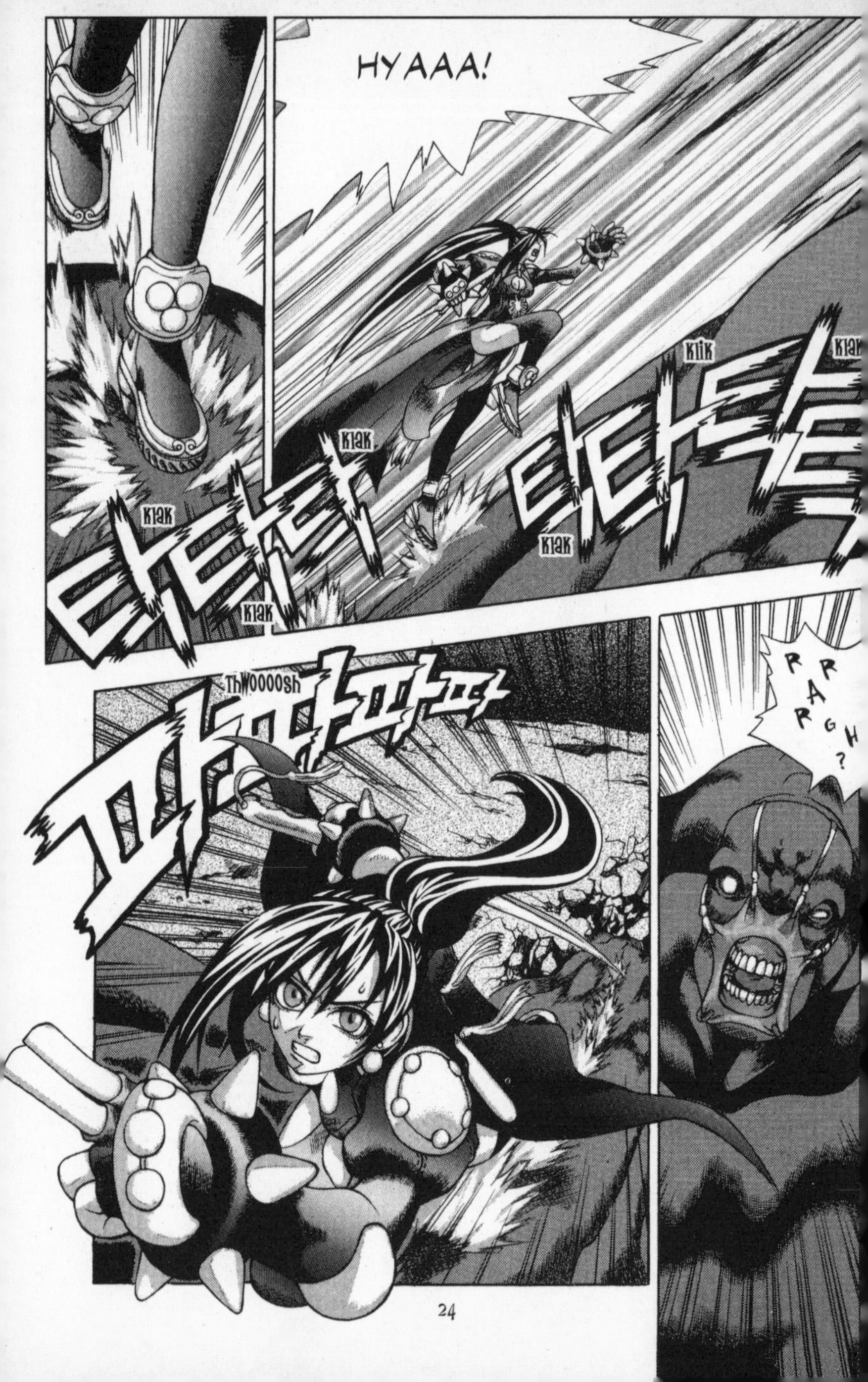
KLAK
KLAK
HYAAA!
KLAK
KLIK
KLAK
KLAK
ThWOOOOsh
RRARGH?

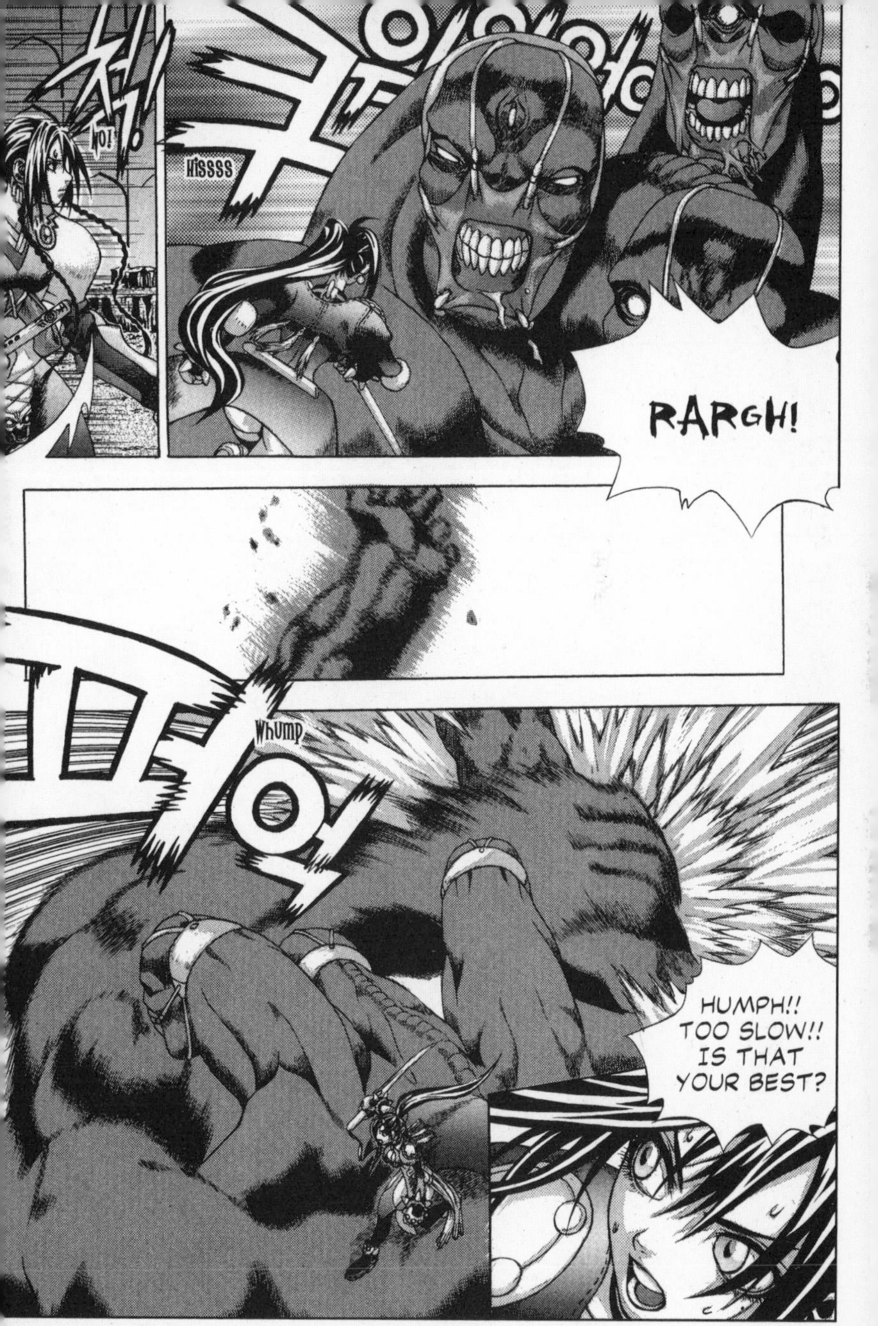
NO!
HISSSS
RARGH!
WHUMP
HUMPH!! TOO SLOW!! IS THAT YOUR BEST?

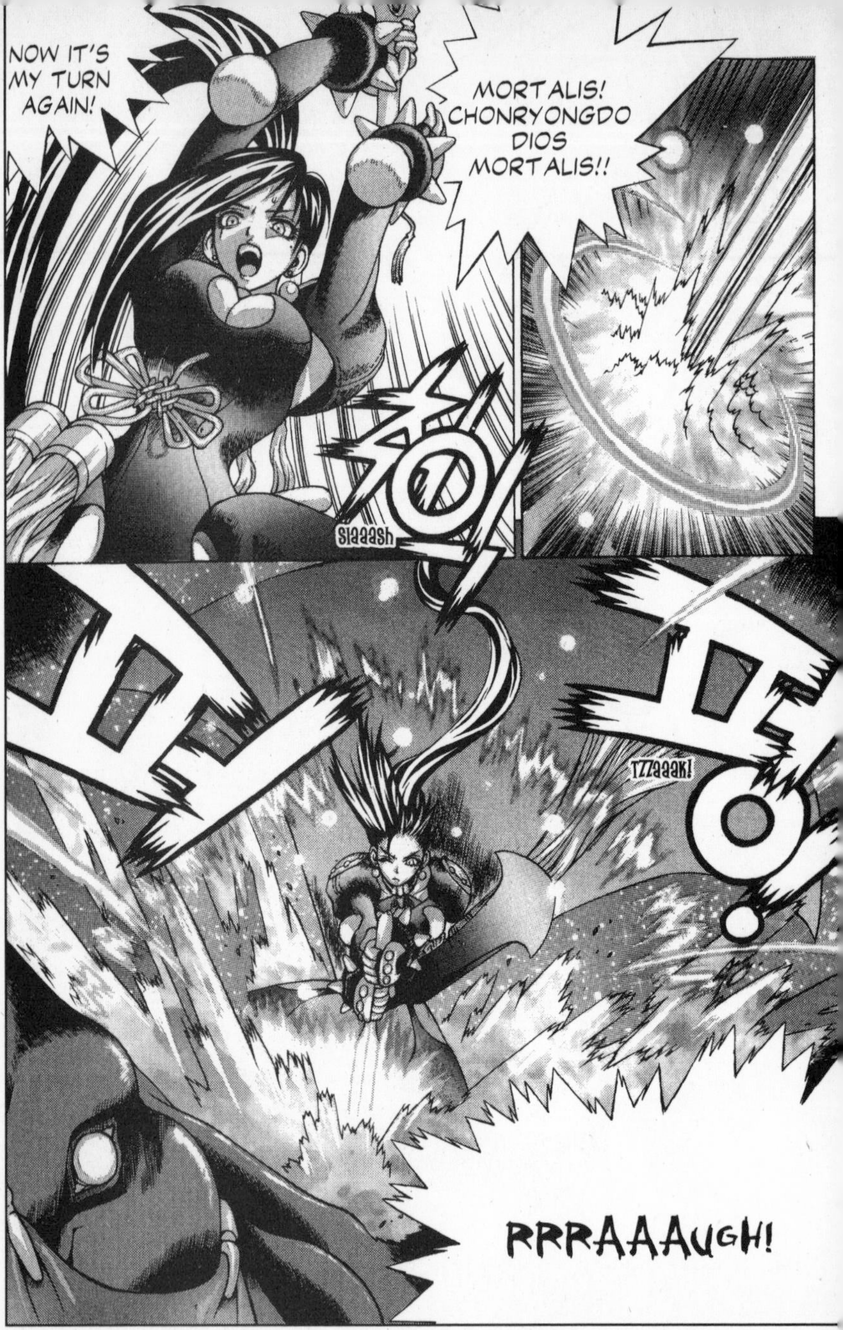
NOW IT'S MY TURN AGAIN!
MORTALIS! CHONRYONGDO DIOS MORTALIS!!
SIaaaSH
TZZaaak!
RRRAAAUGH!

RAGNAROK
라그나로크
IN TO THE ABYSS

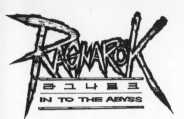

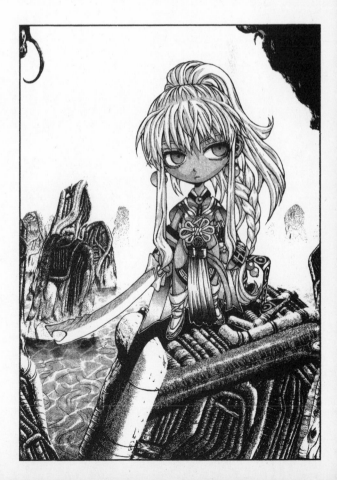

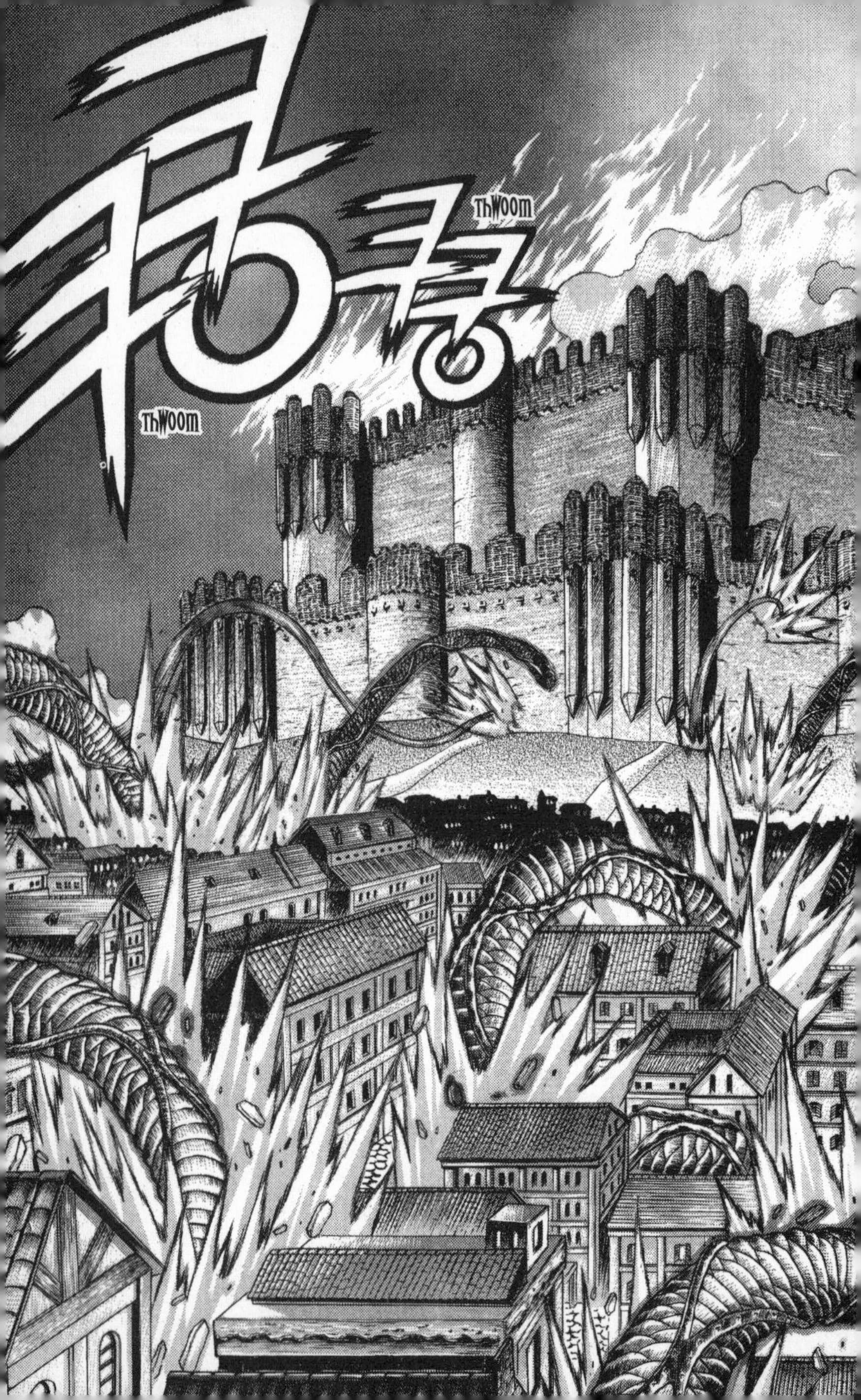
ThWOOM
ThWOOM

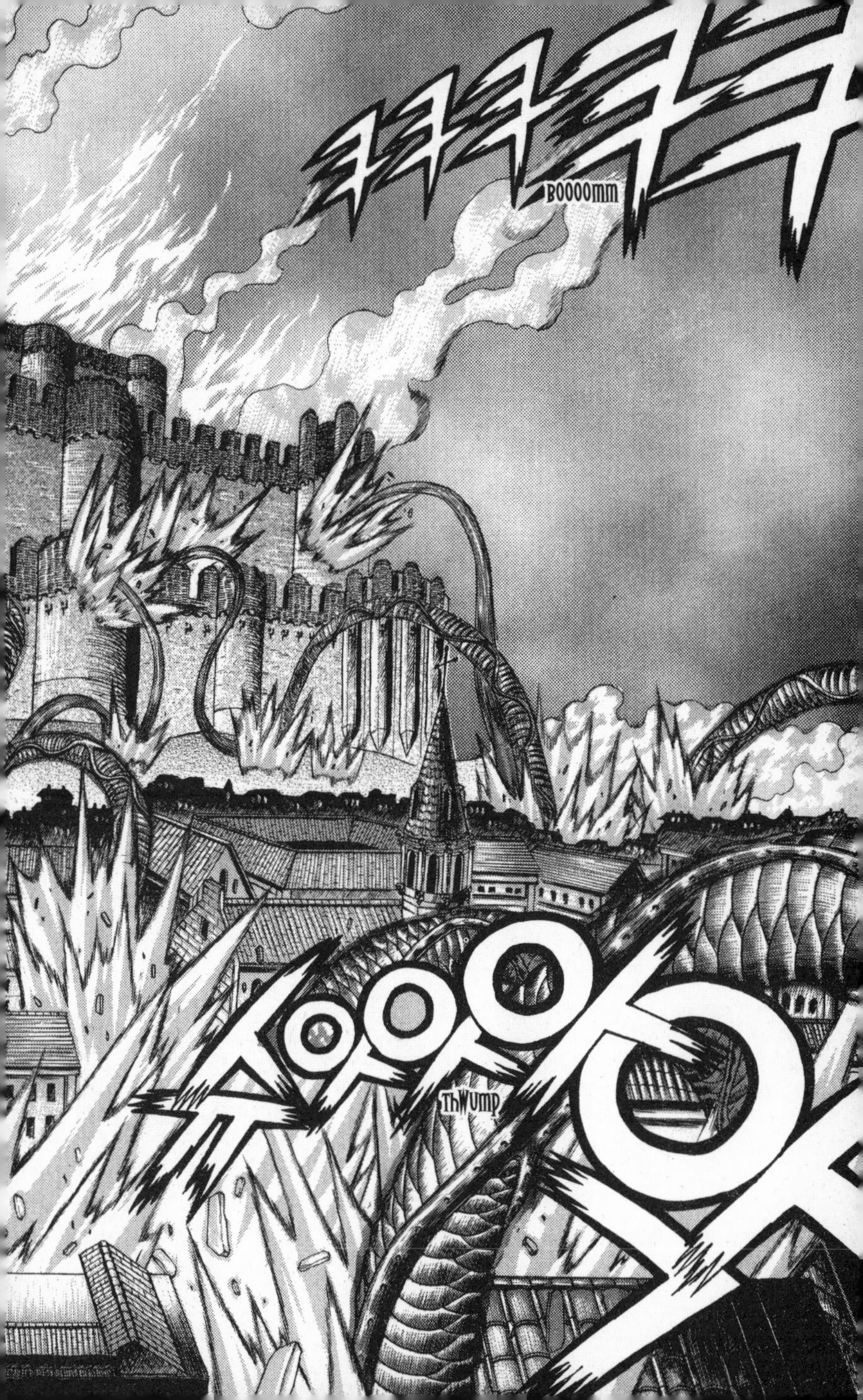
BOOOOMM
ThWUMP

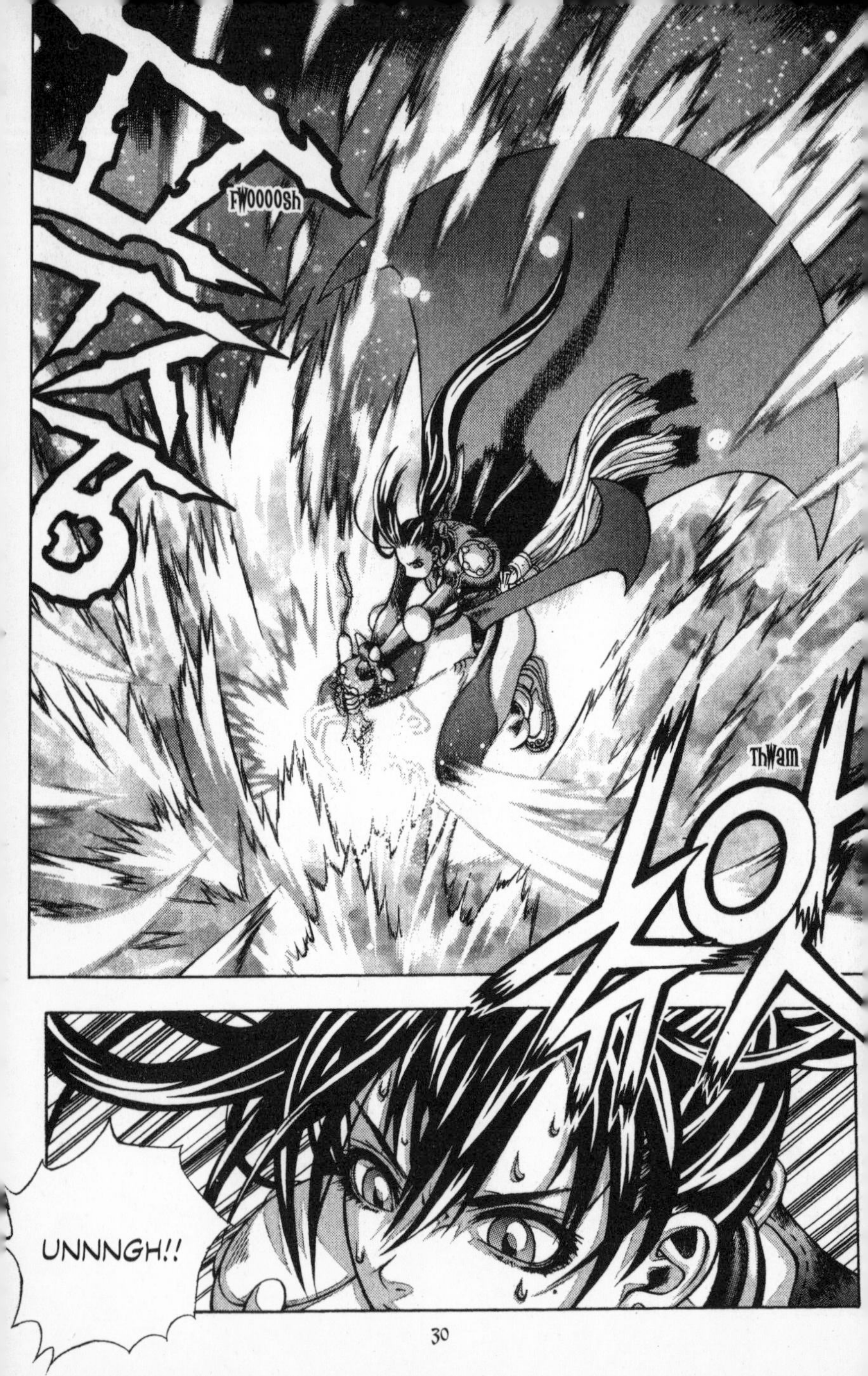
FWOOOOSH
THWAM
UNNNGH!!

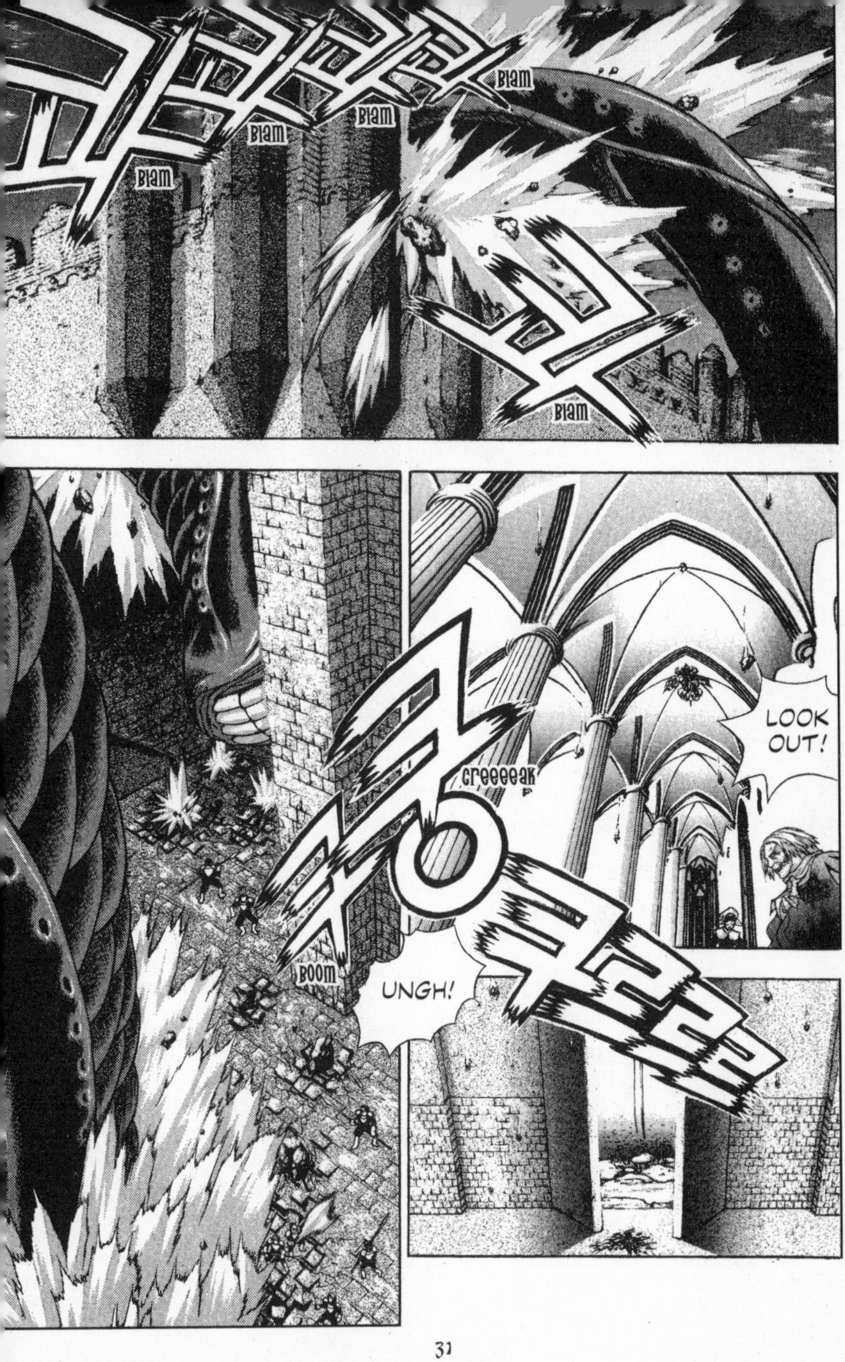
Blam
Blam
Blam
Blam
Blam
Boom
UNGH!
creeeeak
LOOK OUT!

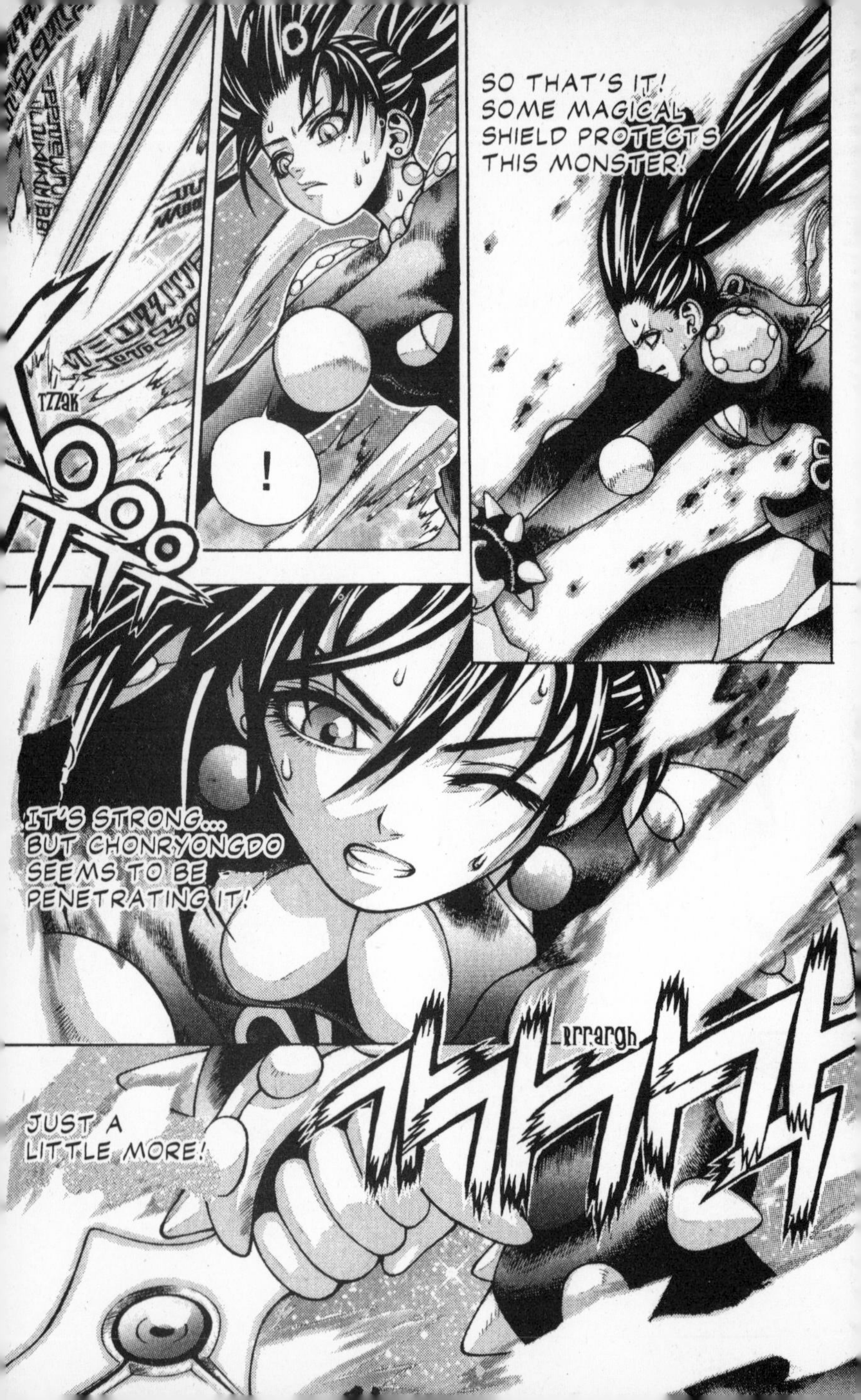
TZZAK
!
SO THAT'S IT! SOME MAGICAL SHIELD PROTECTS THIS MONSTER!
IT'S STRONG... BUT CHONRYONGDO SEEMS TO BE PENETRATING IT!
RRRARGH
JUST A LITTLE MORE!

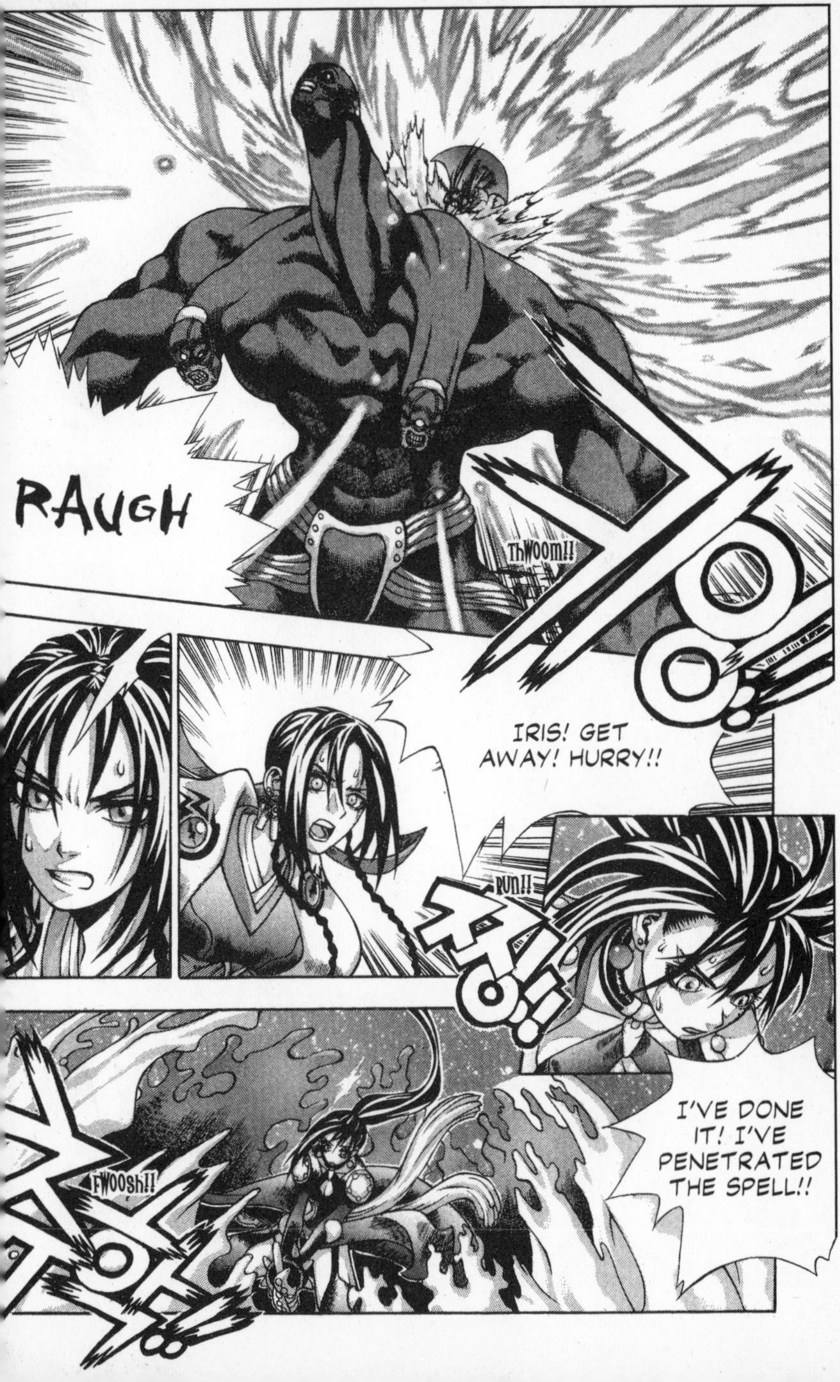
RAUGH
ThWoom!!
IRIS! GET AWAY! HURRY!!
RUN!!
FWOOsh!!
I'VE DONE IT! I'VE PENETRATED THE SPELL!!

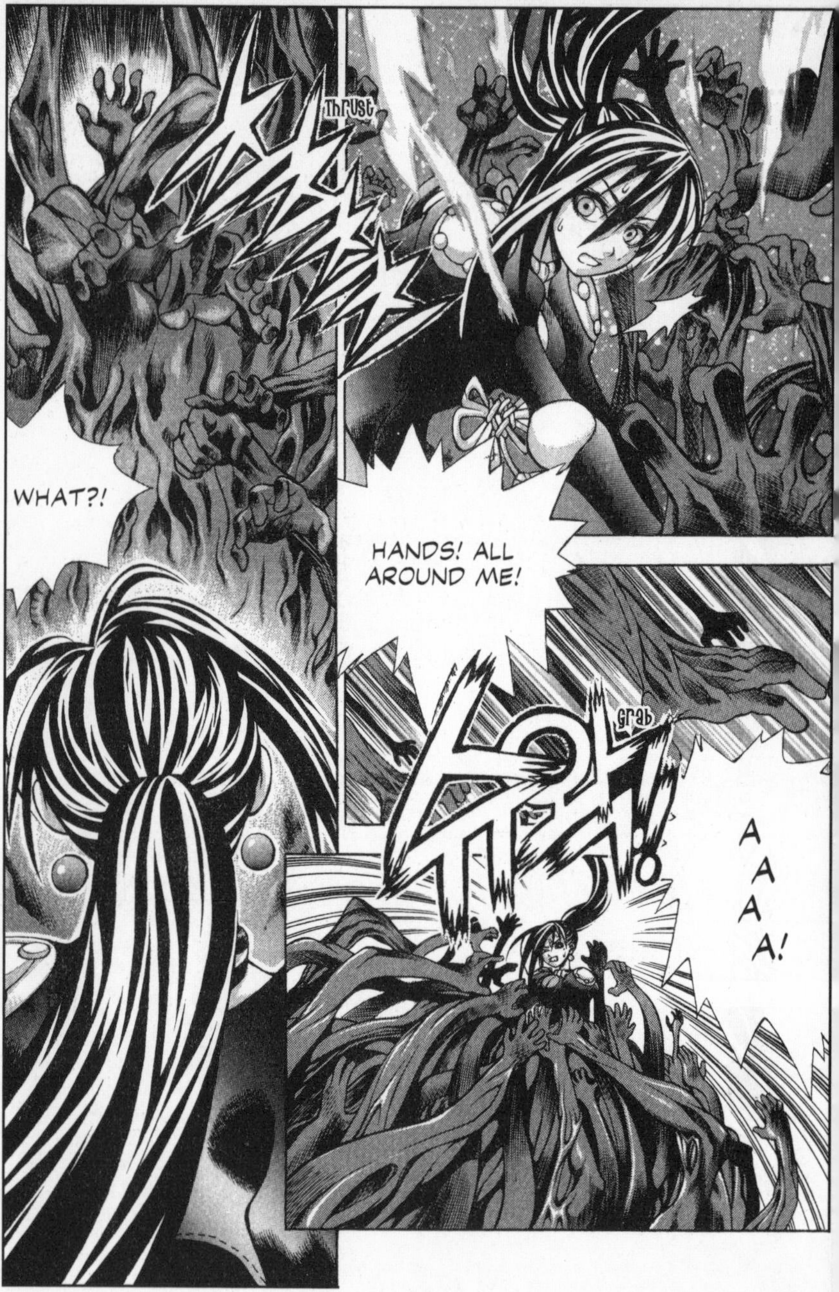
Thrust
WHAT?!
HANDS! ALL AROUND ME!
grab
AAAAA!

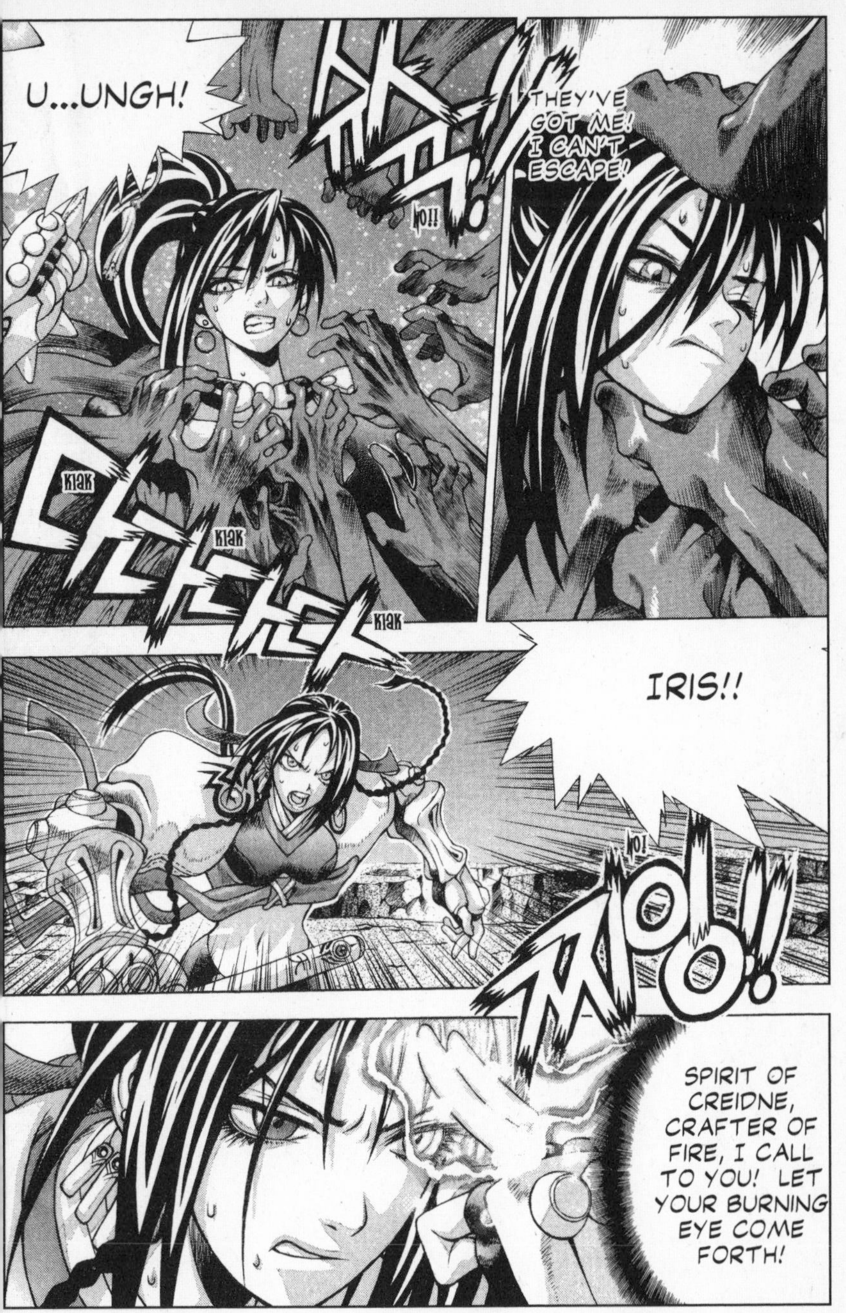
U...UNGH!
NO!!
KLAK
KLAK
KLAK
THEY'VE GOT ME! I CAN'T ESCAPE!
IRIS!!
NO!
SPIRIT OF CREIDNE, CRAFTER OF FIRE, I CALL TO YOU! LET YOUR BURNING EYE COME FORTH!

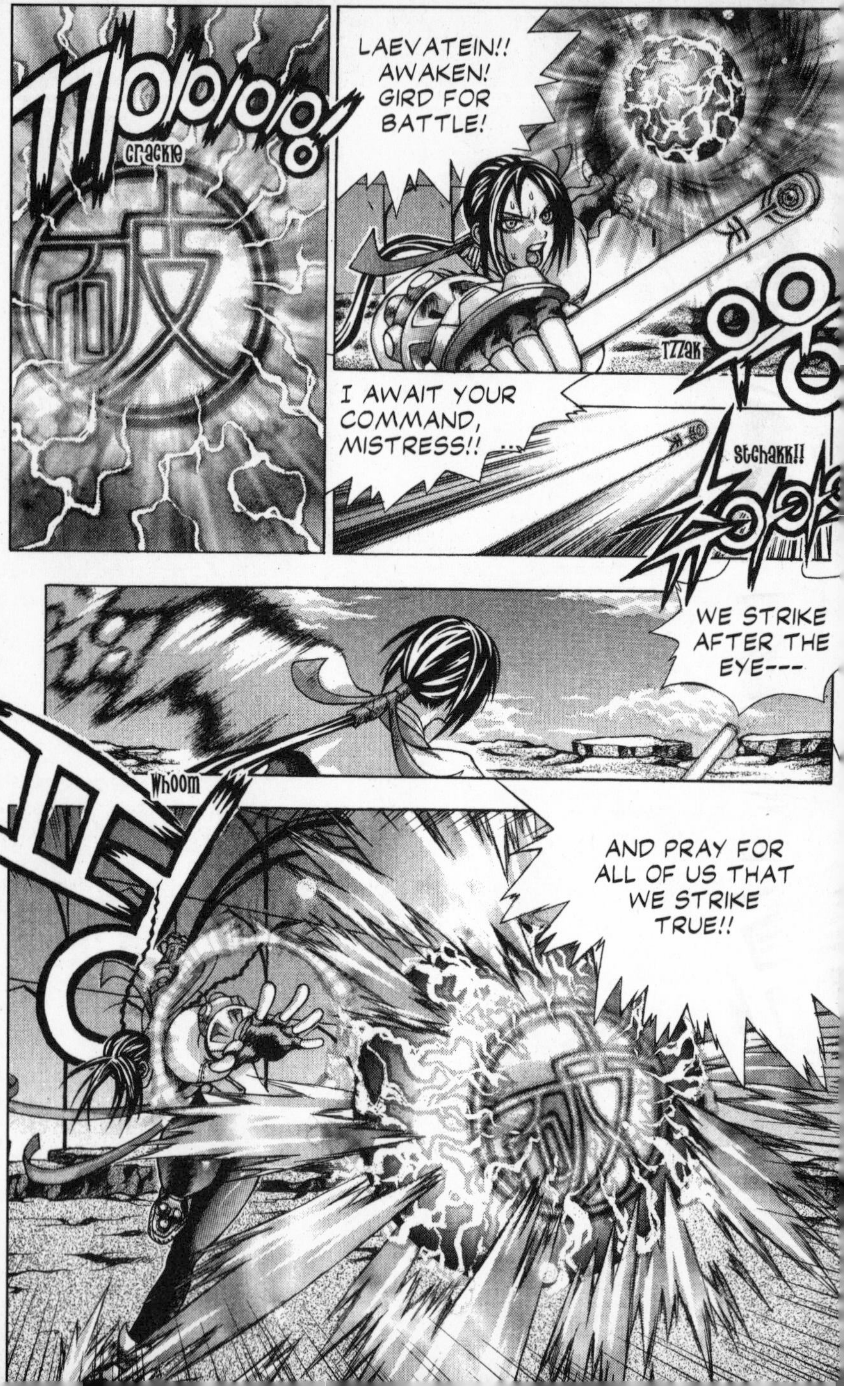
crackle
LAEVATEIN!! AWAKEN! GIRD FOR BATTLE!
TZZAK
I AWAIT YOUR COMMAND, MISTRESS!!
stchakk!!
WE STRIKE AFTER THE EYE---
Whoom
AND PRAY FOR ALL OF US THAT WE STRIKE TRUE!!

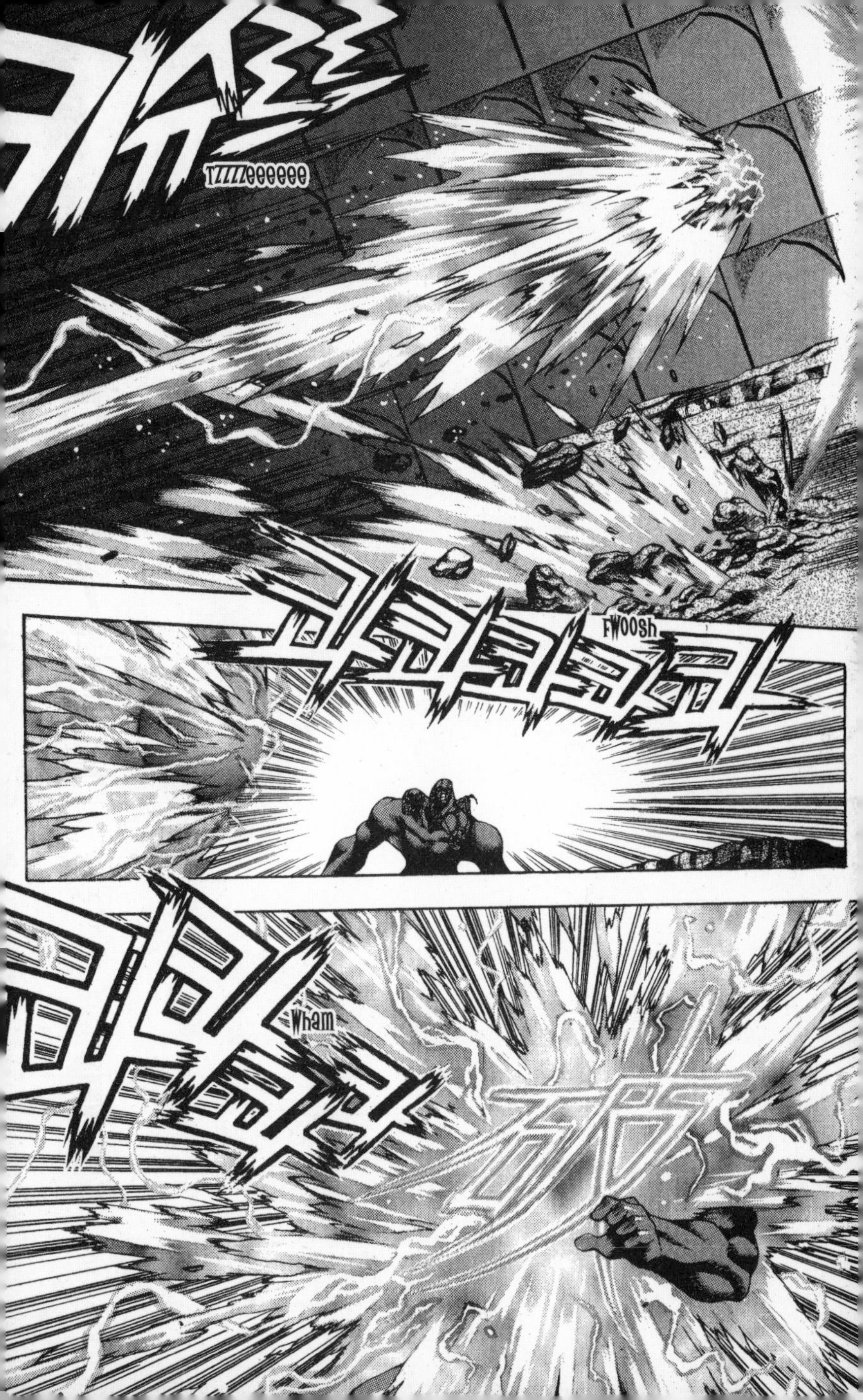
TZZZZeeeeee
FWOOSH
Wham

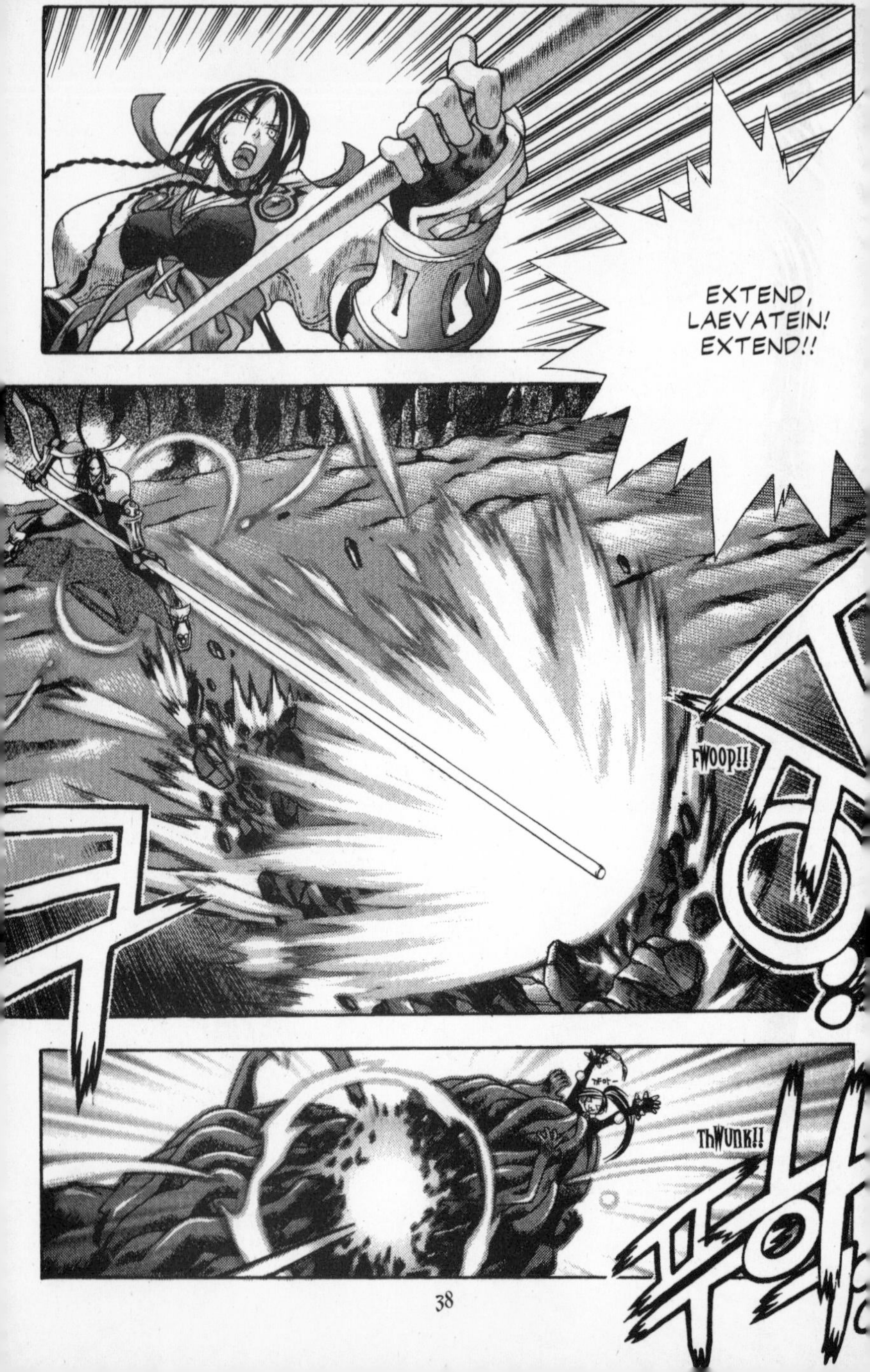
EXTEND, LAEVATEIN! EXTEND!!
FWOOP!!
ThWUNK!!

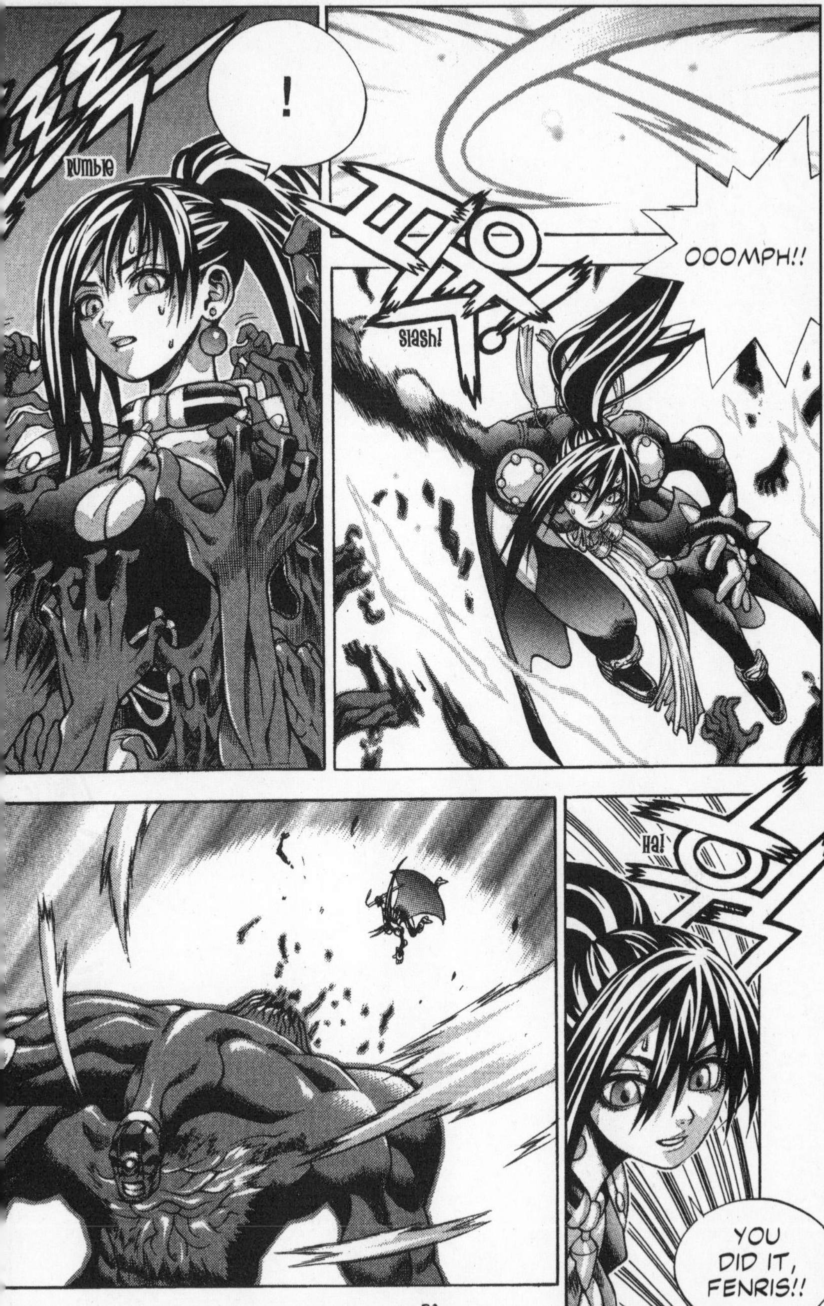
!
RUMBLE
SLASH!
OOOMPH!!
HA!
YOU DID IT, FENRIS!!

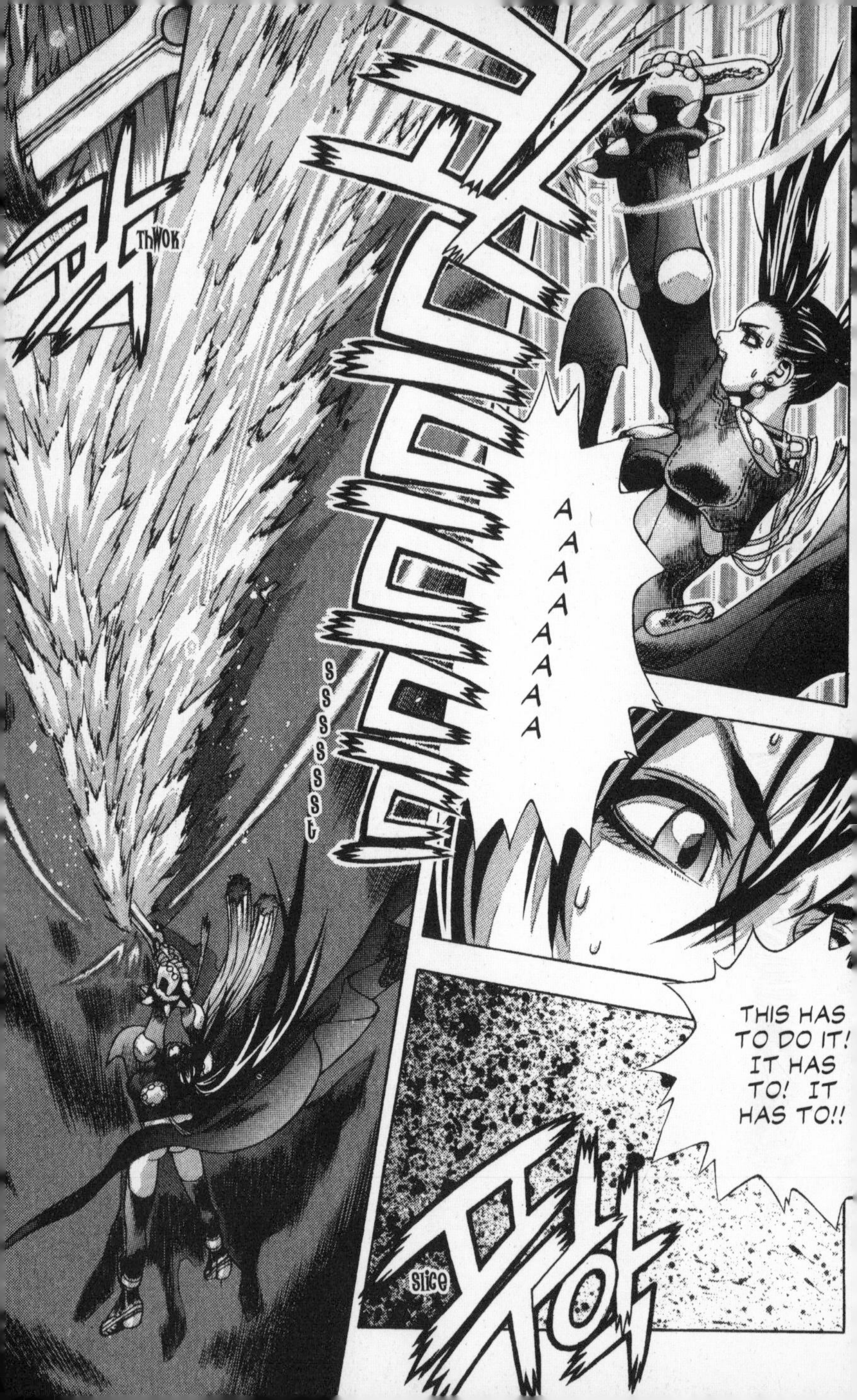
ThWOK
SSSSSSt
AAAAAAAA
THIS HAS TO DO IT! IT HAS TO! IT HAS TO!!
SLICE

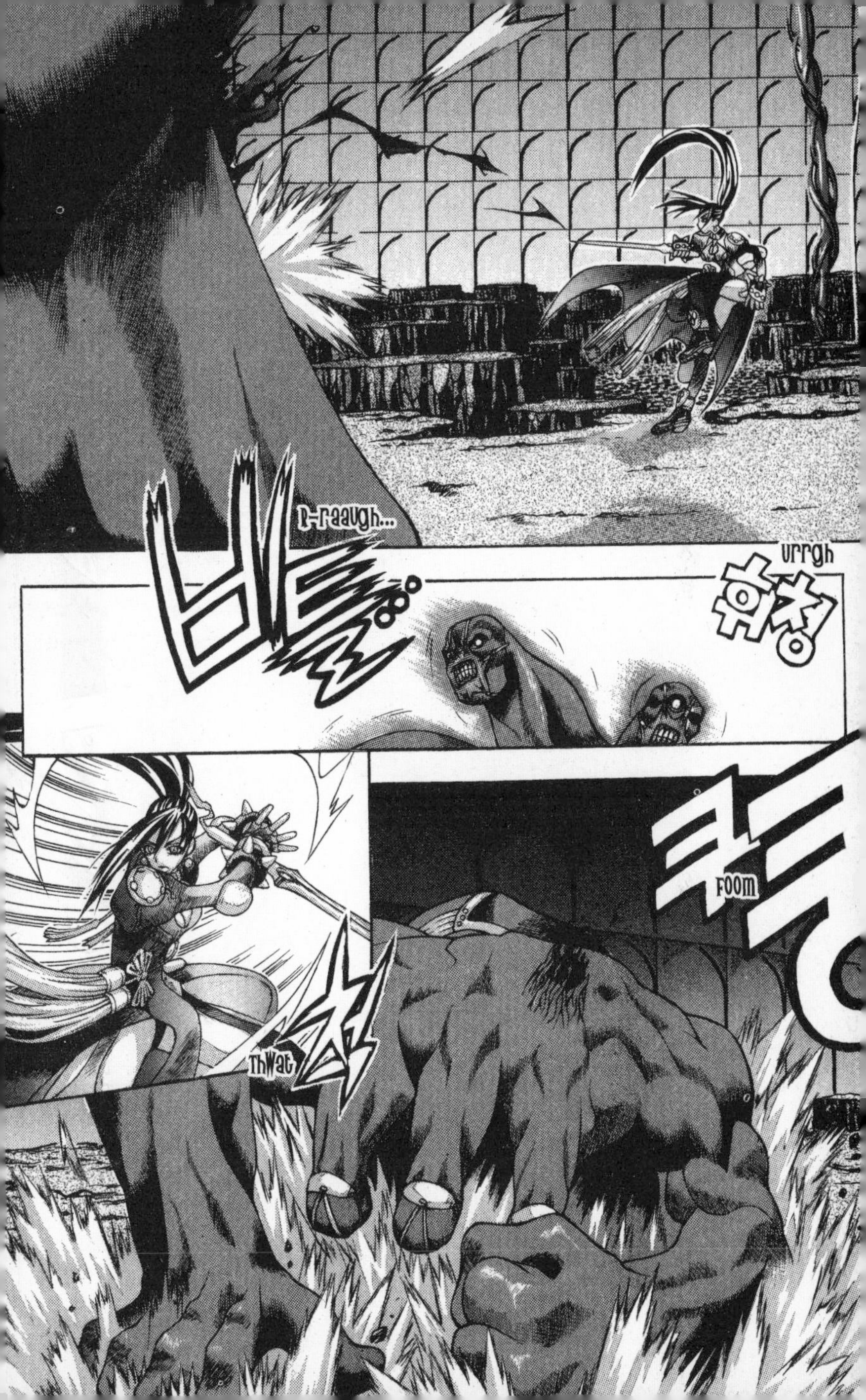
R-raaugh...
Urrgh
휘청
Thwat
FOOM

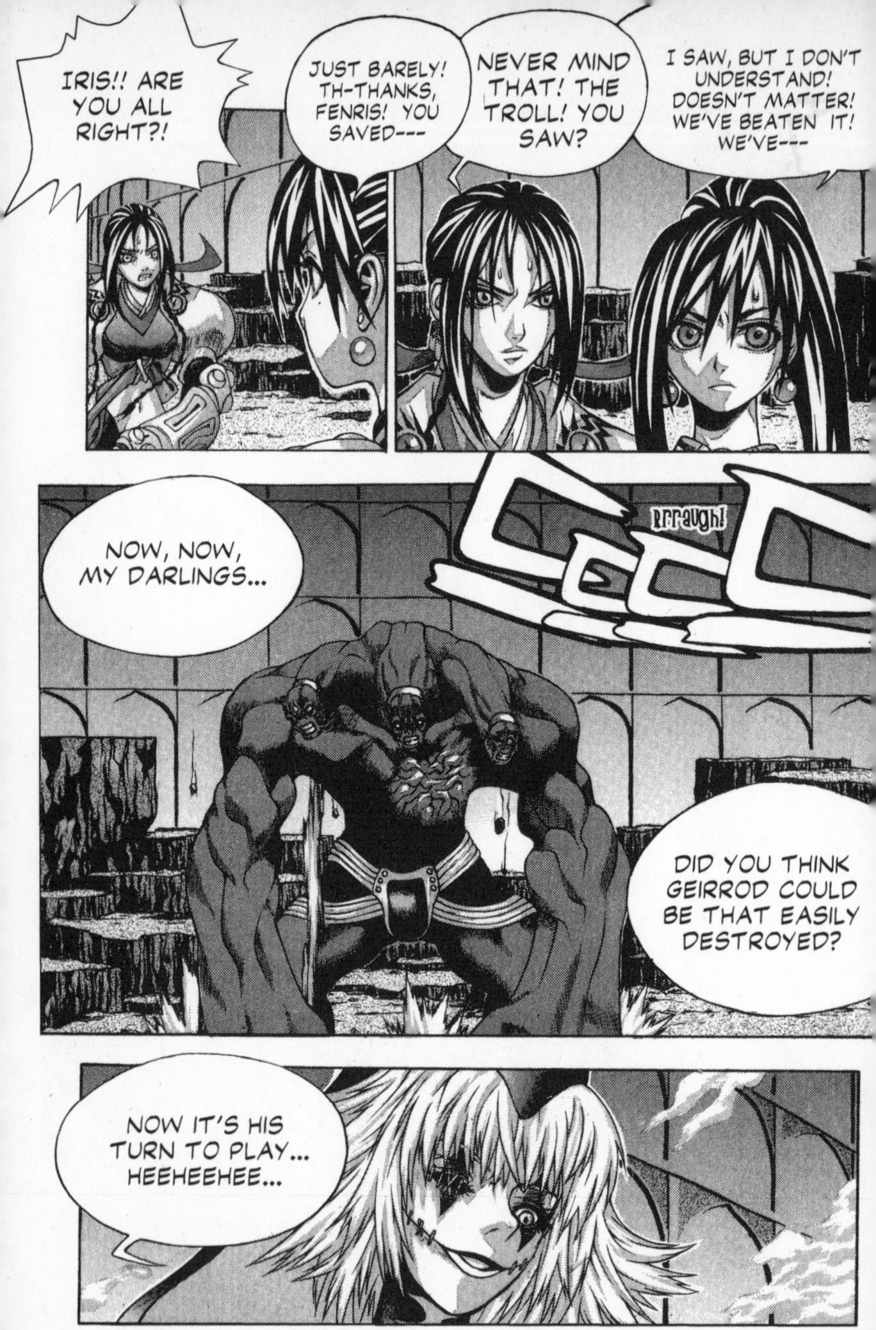
IRIS!! ARE YOU ALL RIGHT?!
JUST BARELY! TH-THANKS, FENRIS! YOU SAVED---
NEVER MIND THAT! THE TROLL! YOU SAW?
I SAW, BUT I DON'T UNDERSTAND! DOESN'T MATTER! WE'VE BEATEN IT! WE'VE---
NOW, NOW, MY DARLINGS...
RRRAUGH!
DID YOU THINK GEIRROD COULD BE THAT EASILY DESTROYED?
NOW IT'S HIS TURN TO PLAY... HEEHEEHEE...

RAGNAROK

라그나로크

IN TO THE ABYSS

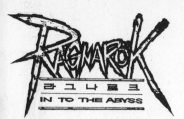

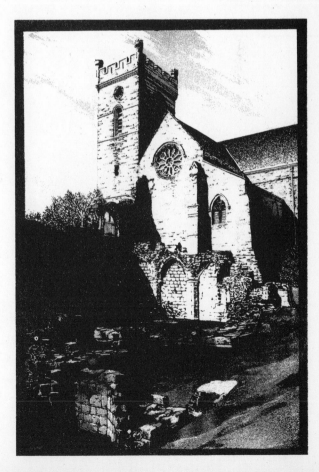

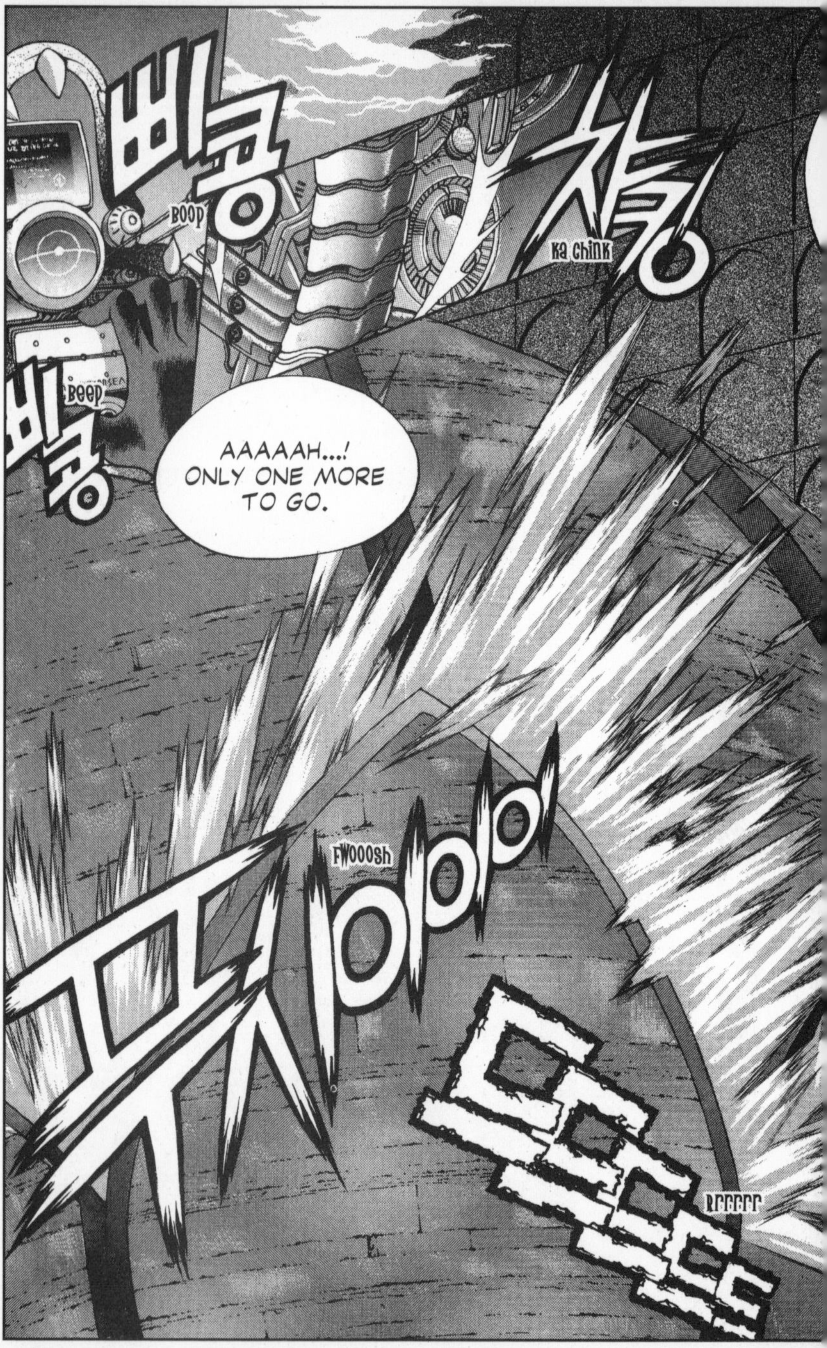
BOOP
KA CHINK
BEEP
AAAAAH...! ONLY ONE MORE TO GO.
FWOOOSH
BRRRRR

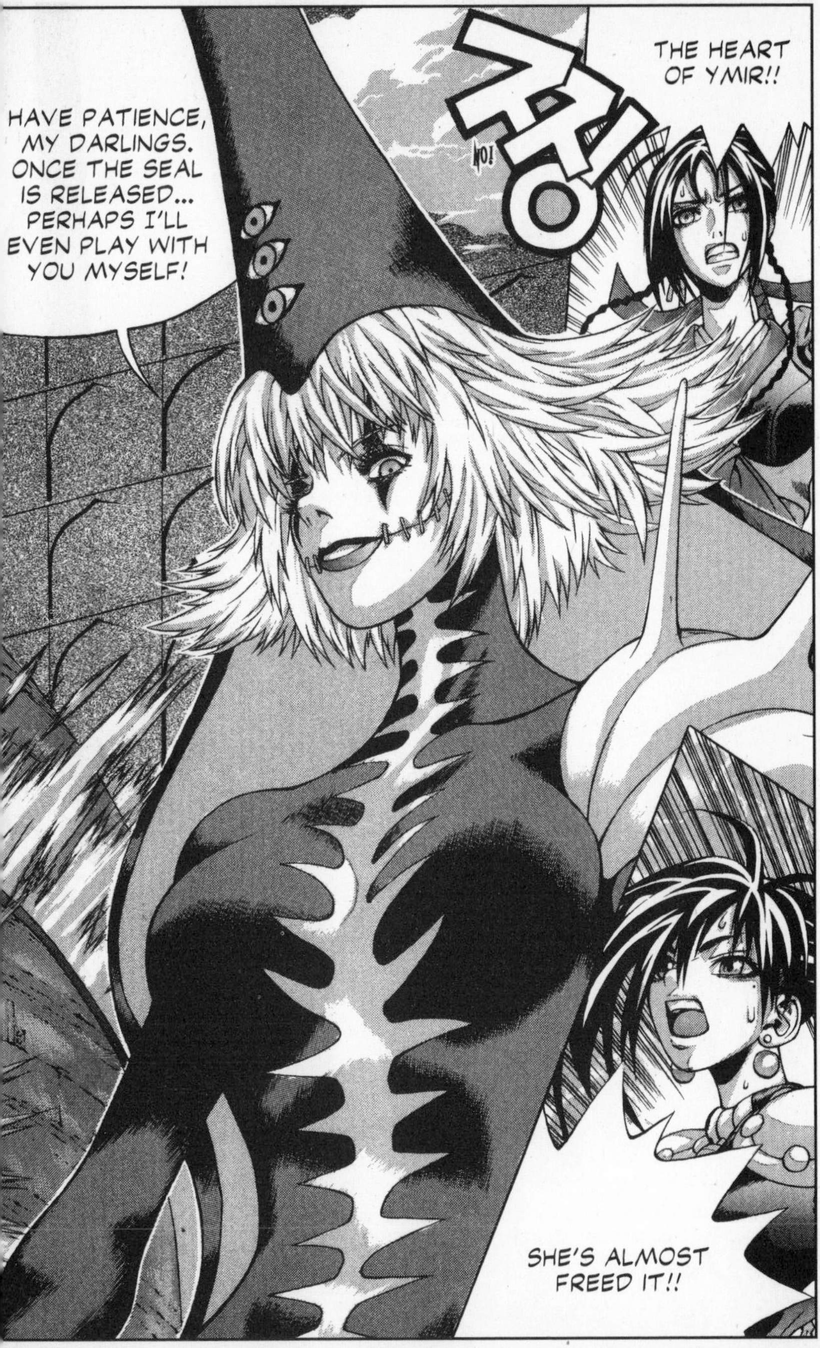
HAVE PATIENCE, MY DARLINGS. ONCE THE SEAL IS RELEASED... PERHAPS I'LL EVEN PLAY WITH YOU MYSELF!
NO!
THE HEART OF YMIR!!
SHE'S ALMOST FREED IT!!

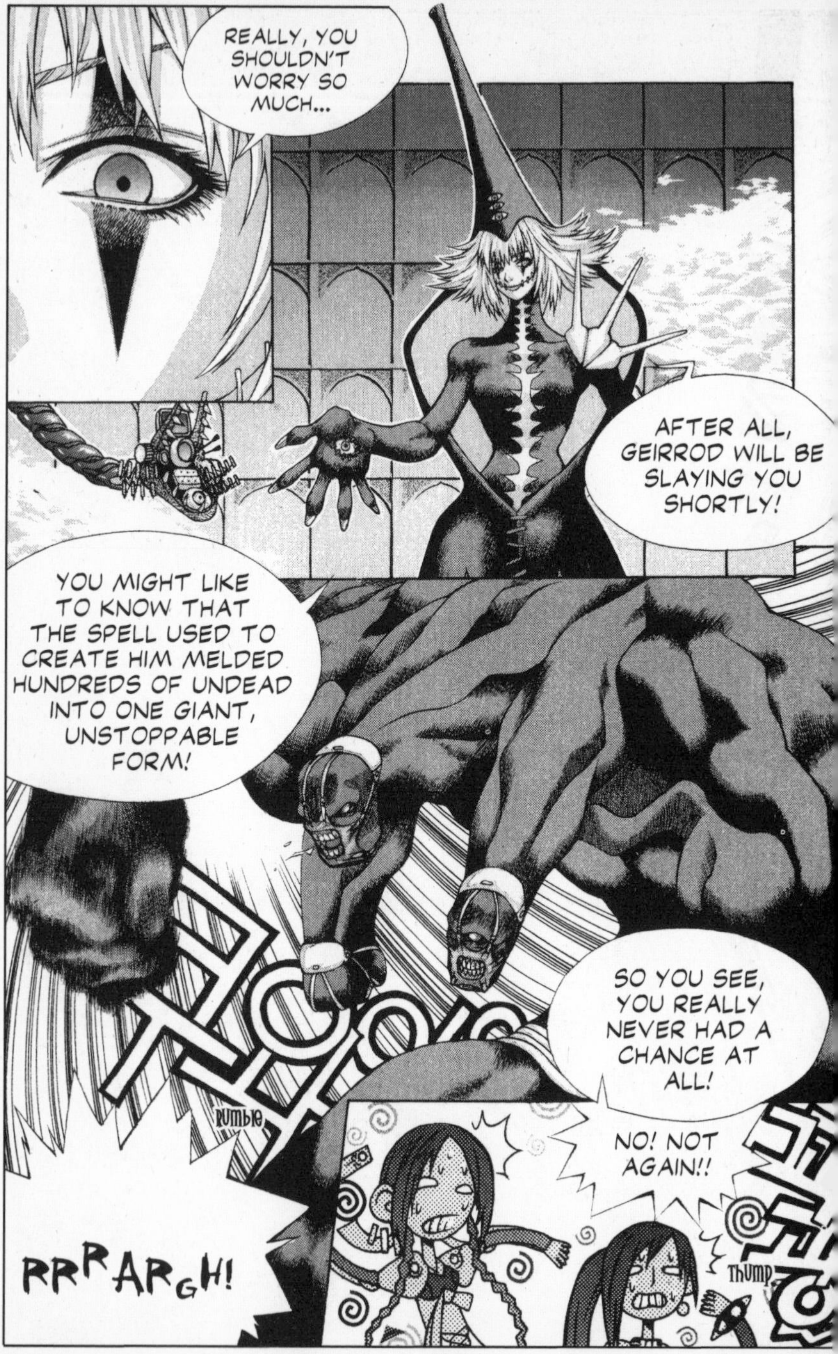
REALLY, YOU SHOULDN'T WORRY SO MUCH...
AFTER ALL, GEIRROD WILL BE SLAYING YOU SHORTLY!
YOU MIGHT LIKE TO KNOW THAT THE SPELL USED TO CREATE HIM MELDED HUNDREDS OF UNDEAD INTO ONE GIANT, UNSTOPPABLE FORM!
RUMBLE
RRRARGH!
SO YOU SEE, YOU REALLY NEVER HAD A CHANCE AT ALL!
NO! NOT AGAIN!!
THUMP

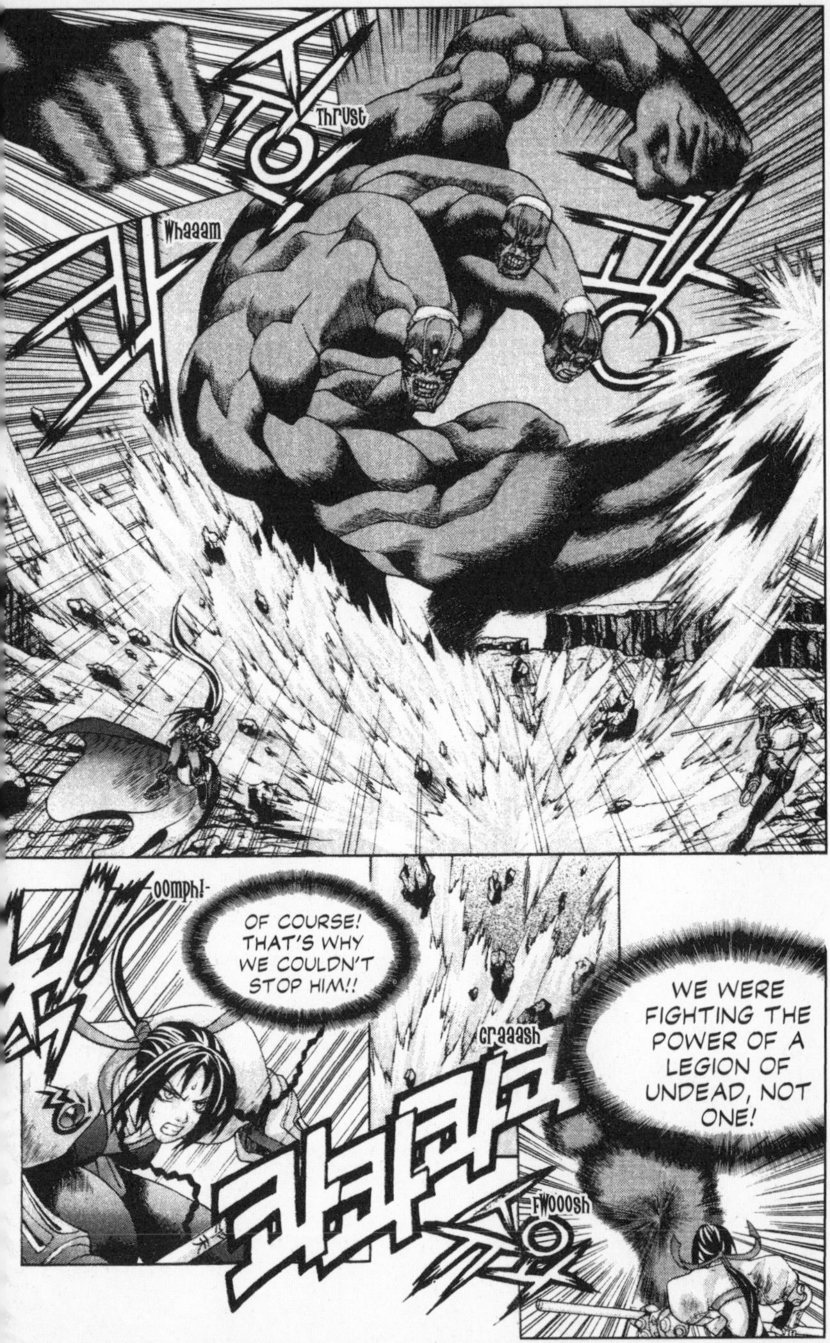
Thrust
Whaaam
-oomph!-
OF COURSE! THAT'S WHY WE COULDN'T STOP HIM!!
craaash
WE WERE FIGHTING THE POWER OF A LEGION OF UNDEAD, NOT ONE!
FWOOOSH

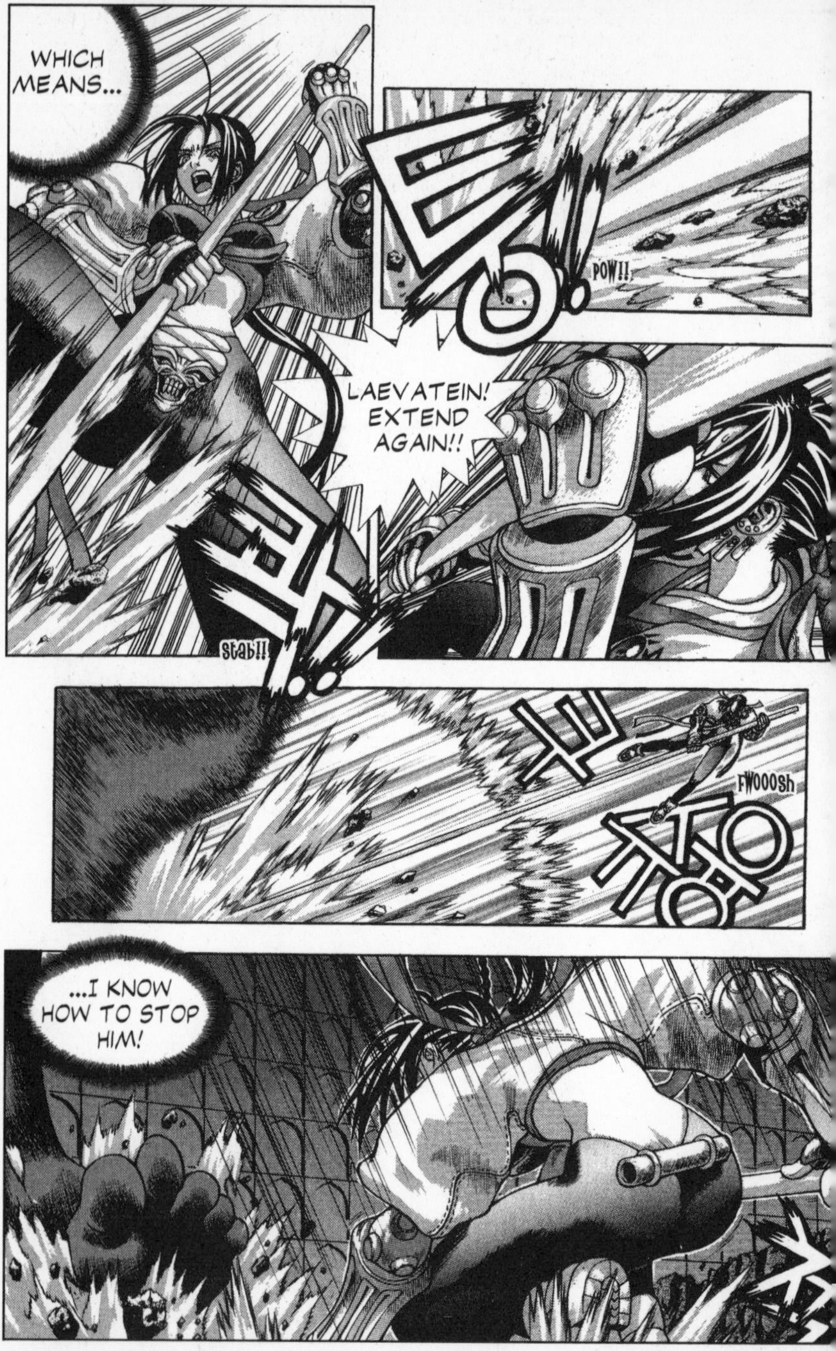
WHICH MEANS...
POW!!
LAEVATEIN! EXTEND AGAIN!!
STAB!!
FWOOOSH
...I KNOW HOW TO STOP HIM!

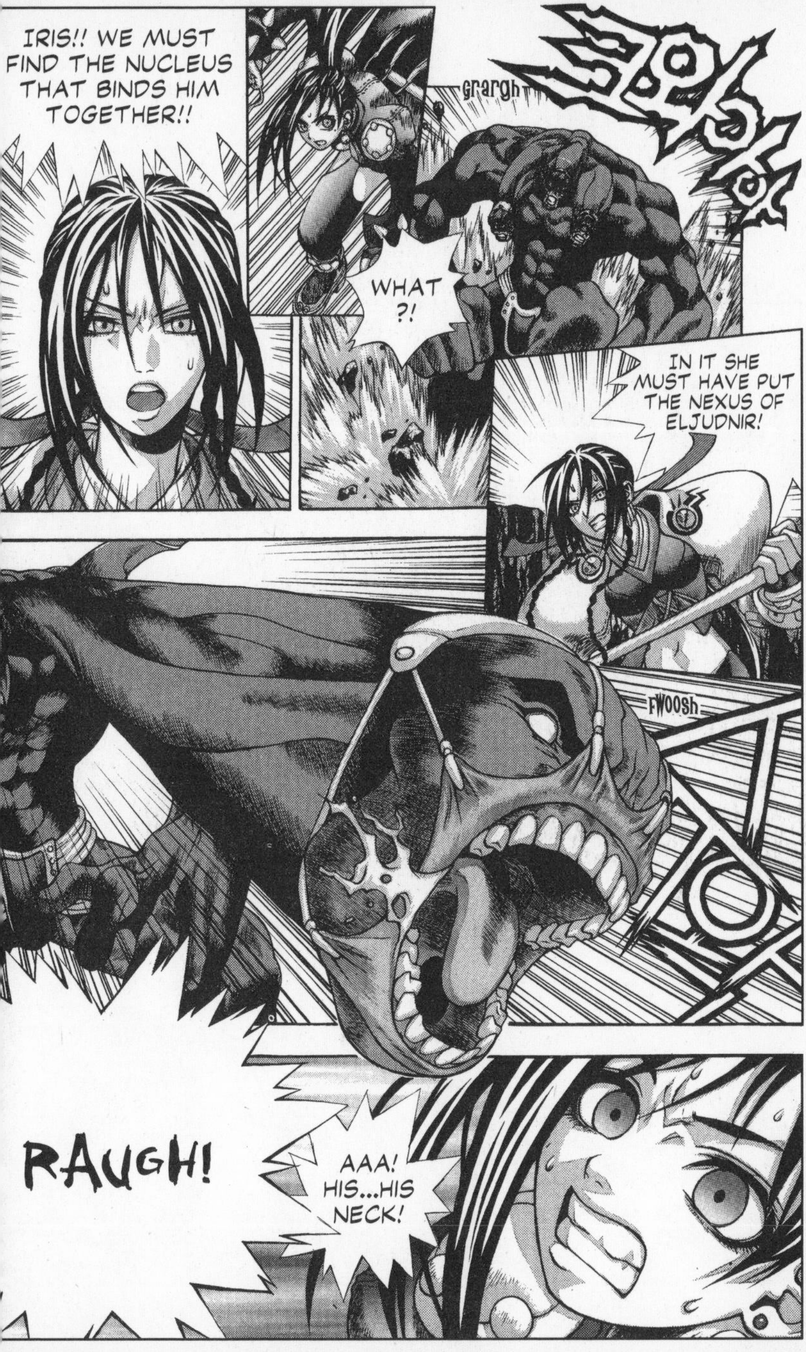
IRIS!! WE MUST FIND THE NUCLEUS THAT BINDS HIM TOGETHER!!
grargh
WHAT ?!
IN IT SHE MUST HAVE PUT THE NEXUS OF ELJUDNIR!
FWOOSH
RAUGH!
AAA! HIS...HIS NECK!

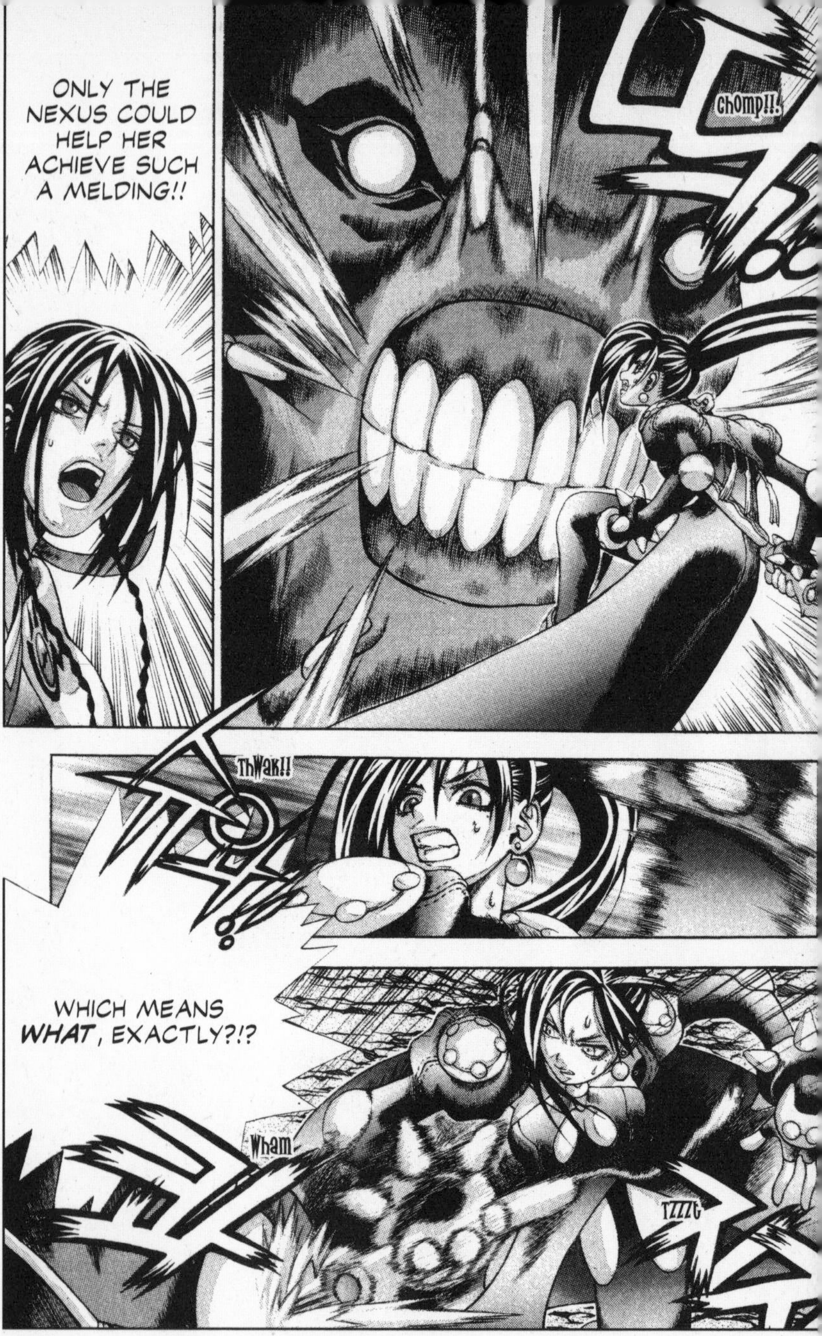
ONLY THE NEXUS COULD HELP HER ACHIEVE SUCH A MELDING!!
Chomp!!
ThWak!!
WHICH MEANS WHAT, EXACTLY?!?
Wham
TZZZt

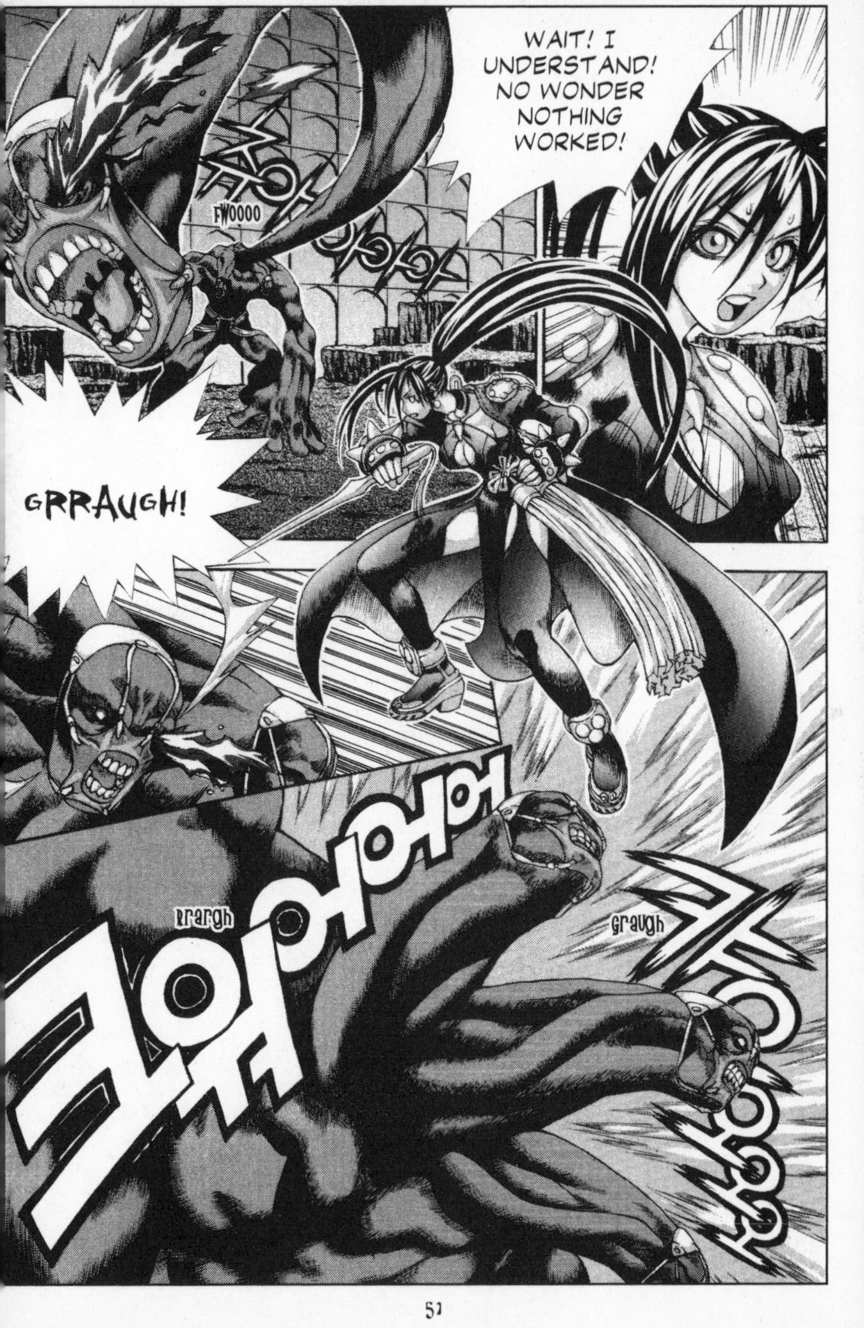
FWOOO
WAIT! I UNDERSTAND! NO WONDER NOTHING WORKED!
GRRAUGH!
Brargh
Graugh

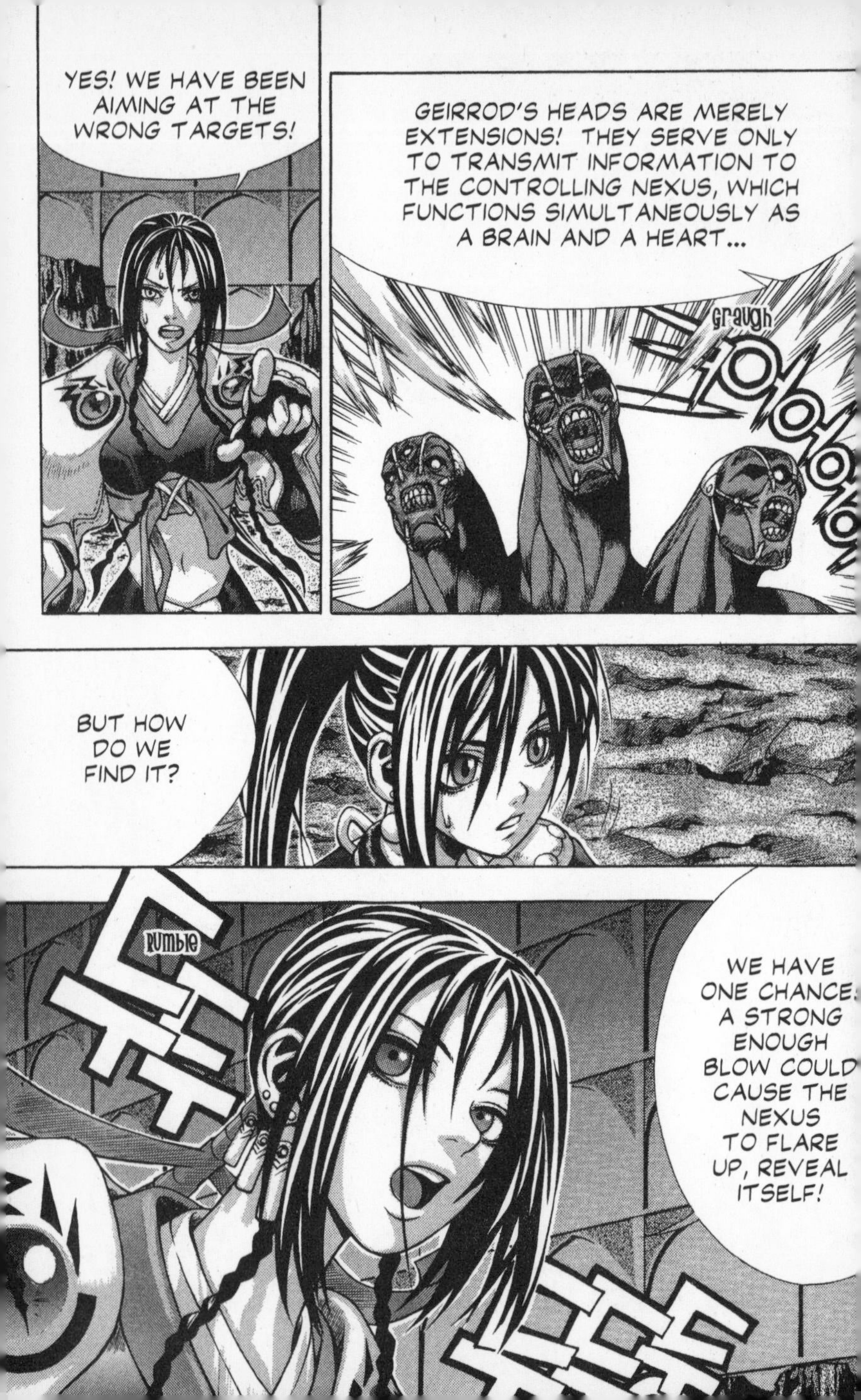

YES! WE HAVE BEEN AIMING AT THE WRONG TARGETS!
GEIRROD'S HEADS ARE MERELY EXTENSIONS! THEY SERVE ONLY TO TRANSMIT INFORMATION TO THE CONTROLLING NEXUS, WHICH FUNCTIONS SIMULTANEOUSLY AS A BRAIN AND A HEART...
GRAUGH
BUT HOW DO WE FIND IT?
RUMBLE
WE HAVE ONE CHANCE. A STRONG ENOUGH BLOW COULD CAUSE THE NEXUS TO FLARE UP, REVEAL ITSELF!

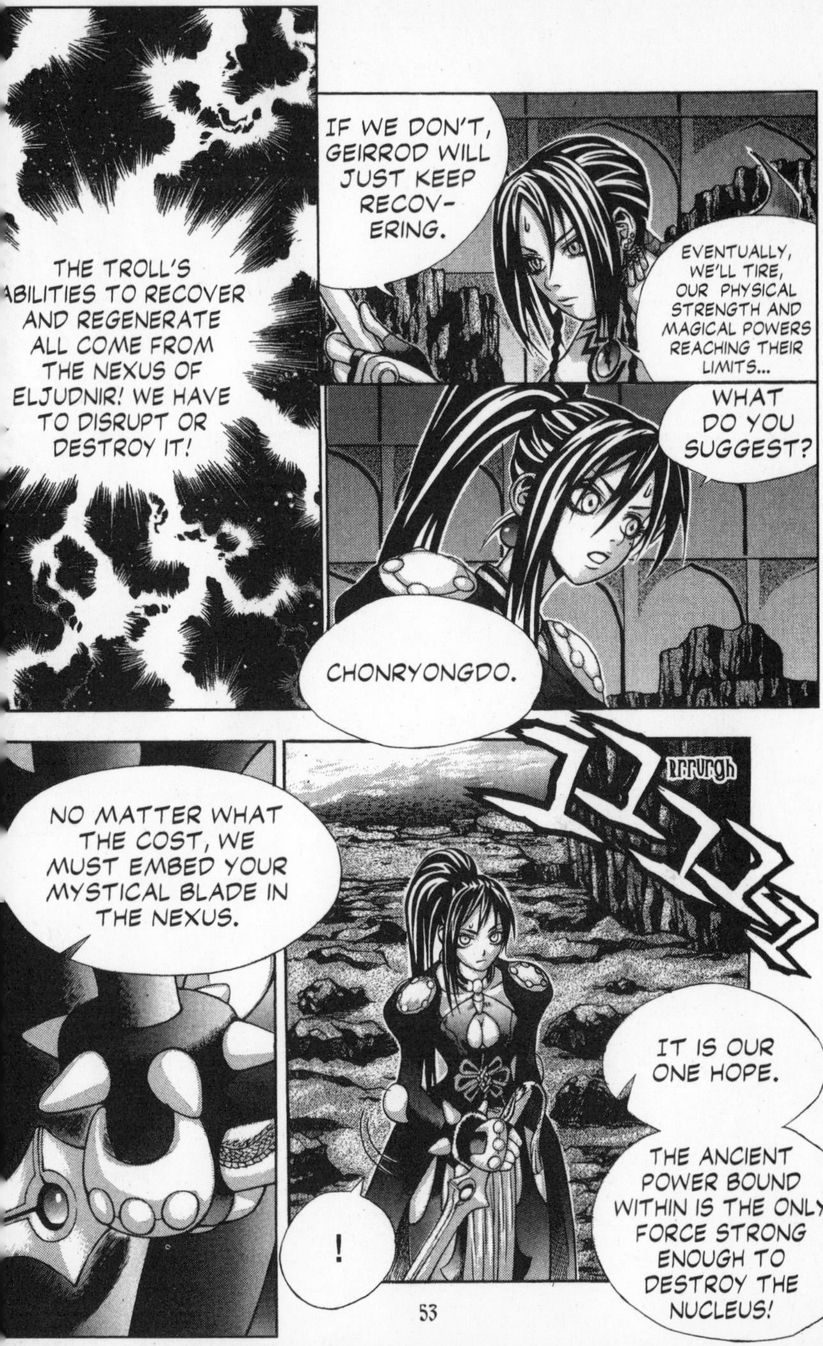
THE TROLL'S ABILITIES TO RECOVER AND REGENERATE ALL COME FROM THE NEXUS OF ELJUDNIR! WE HAVE TO DISRUPT OR DESTROY IT!
IF WE DON'T, GEIRROD WILL JUST KEEP RECOV-ERING.
EVENTUALLY, WE'LL TIRE, OUR PHYSICAL STRENGTH AND MAGICAL POWERS REACHING THEIR LIMITS...
WHAT DO YOU SUGGEST?
CHONRYONGDO.
NO MATTER WHAT THE COST, WE MUST EMBED YOUR MYSTICAL BLADE IN THE NEXUS.
RRRURGH
IT IS OUR ONE HOPE.
THE ANCIENT POWER BOUND WITHIN IS THE ONLY FORCE STRONG ENOUGH TO DESTROY THE NUCLEUS!
!

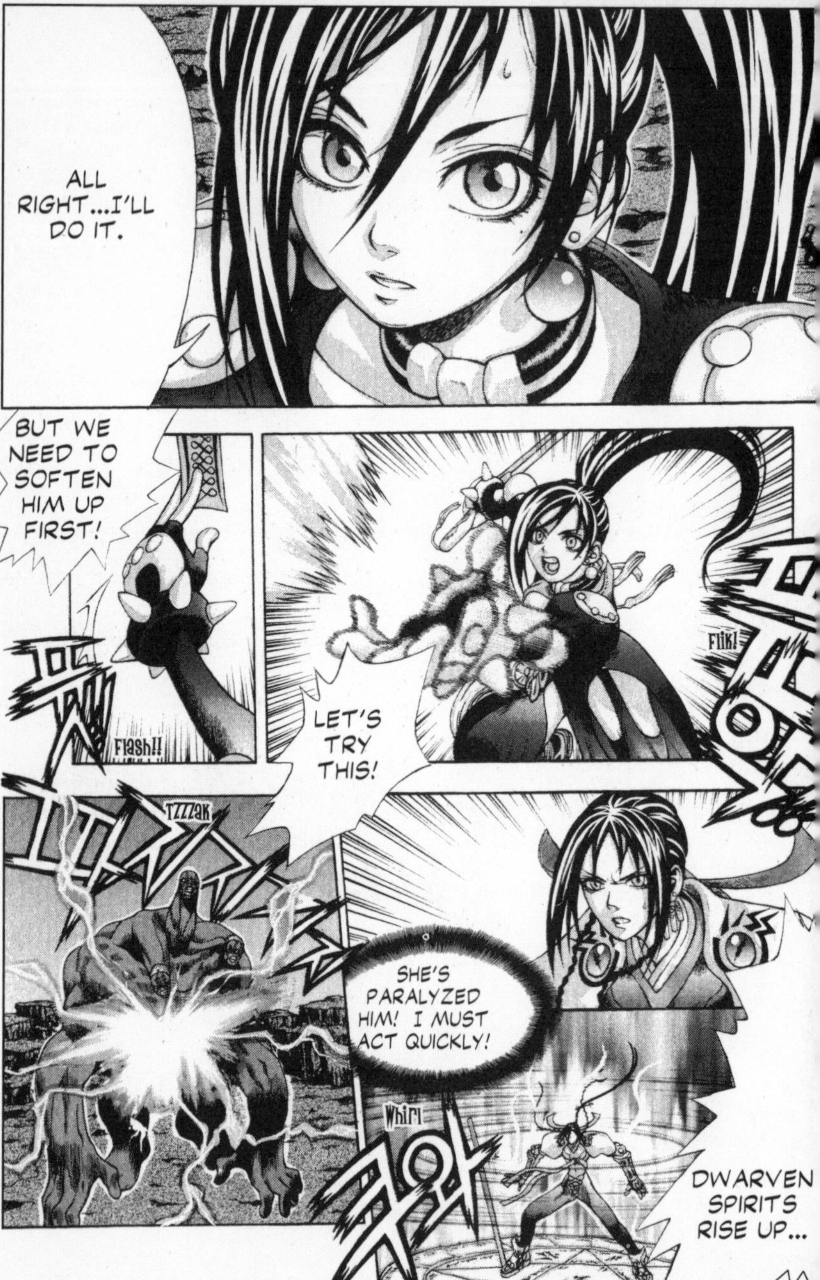
ALL RIGHT...I'LL DO IT.
BUT WE NEED TO SOFTEN HIM UP FIRST!
Flash!!
LET'S TRY THIS!
Flik!
TZZZAK
SHE'S PARALYZED HIM! I MUST ACT QUICKLY!
Whirl
DWARVEN SPIRITS RISE UP...

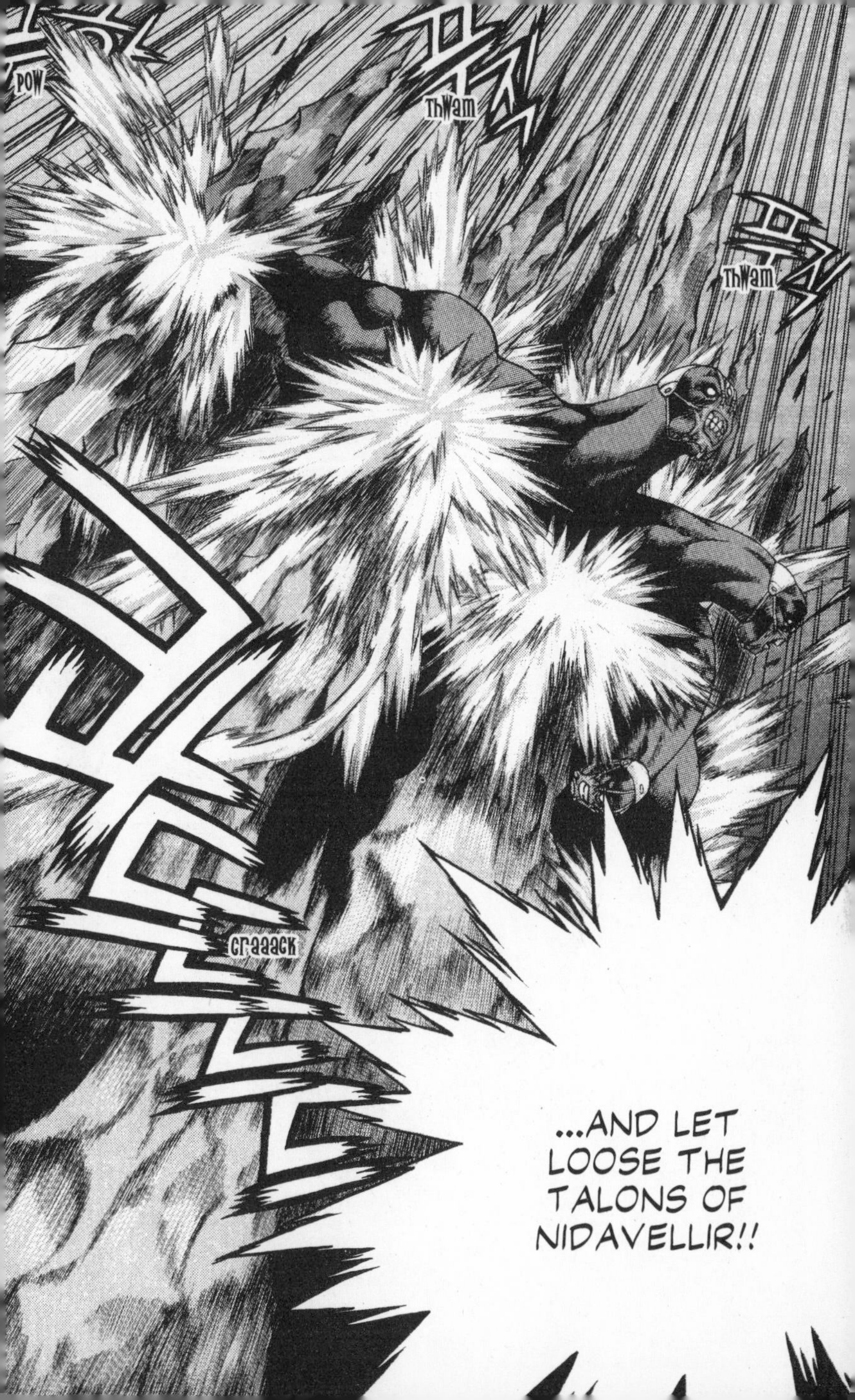
POW
ThWam
ThWam
craaack
...AND LET LOOSE THE TALONS OF NIDAVELLIR!!

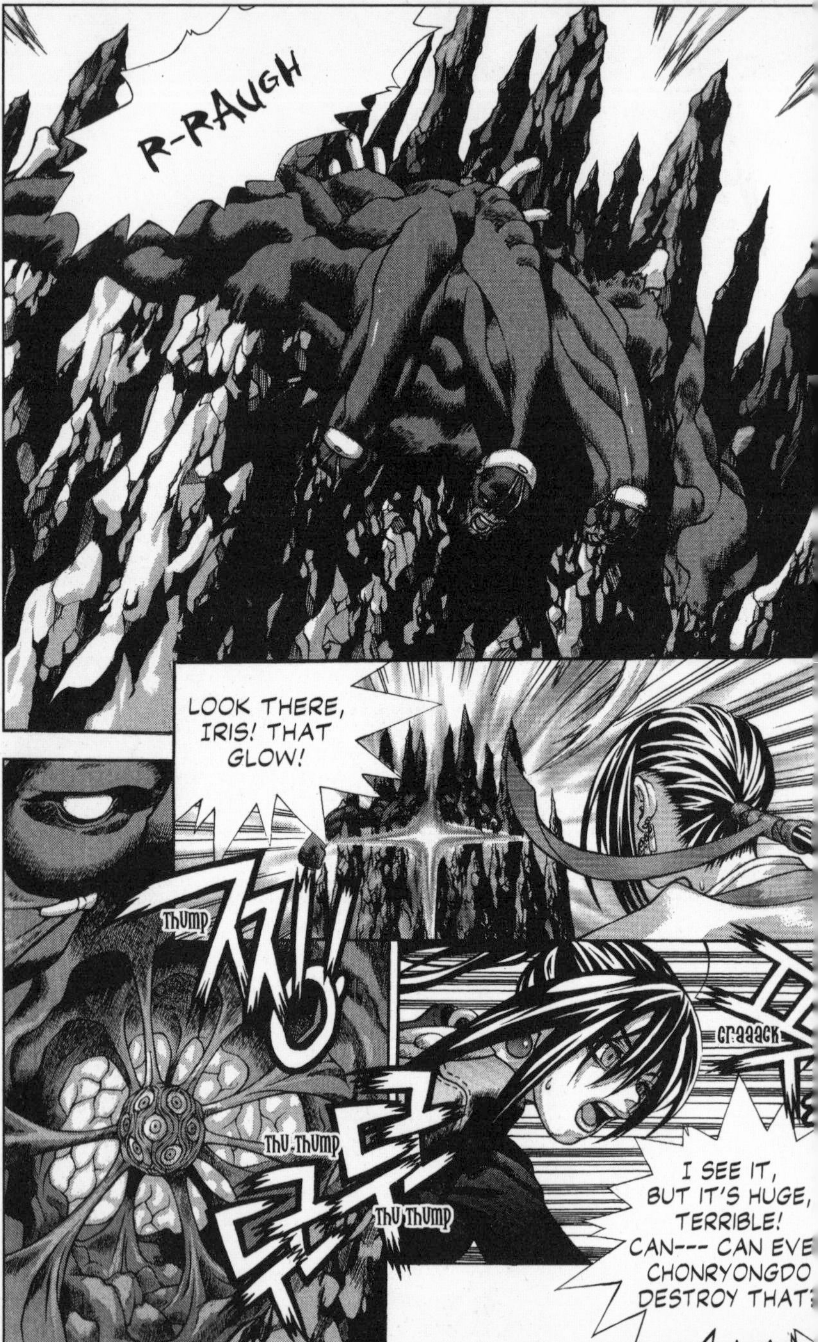
R-RAUGH
LOOK THERE, IRIS! THAT GLOW!
Thump
Thu Thump
Thu Thump
craaack
I SEE IT, BUT IT'S HUGE, TERRIBLE! CAN--- CAN EVE CHONRYONGDO DESTROY THAT

RAGNAROK
라그나로크
IN TO THE ABYSS

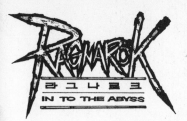

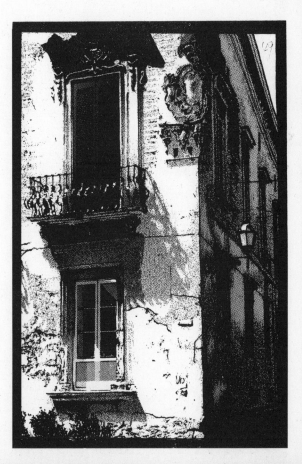

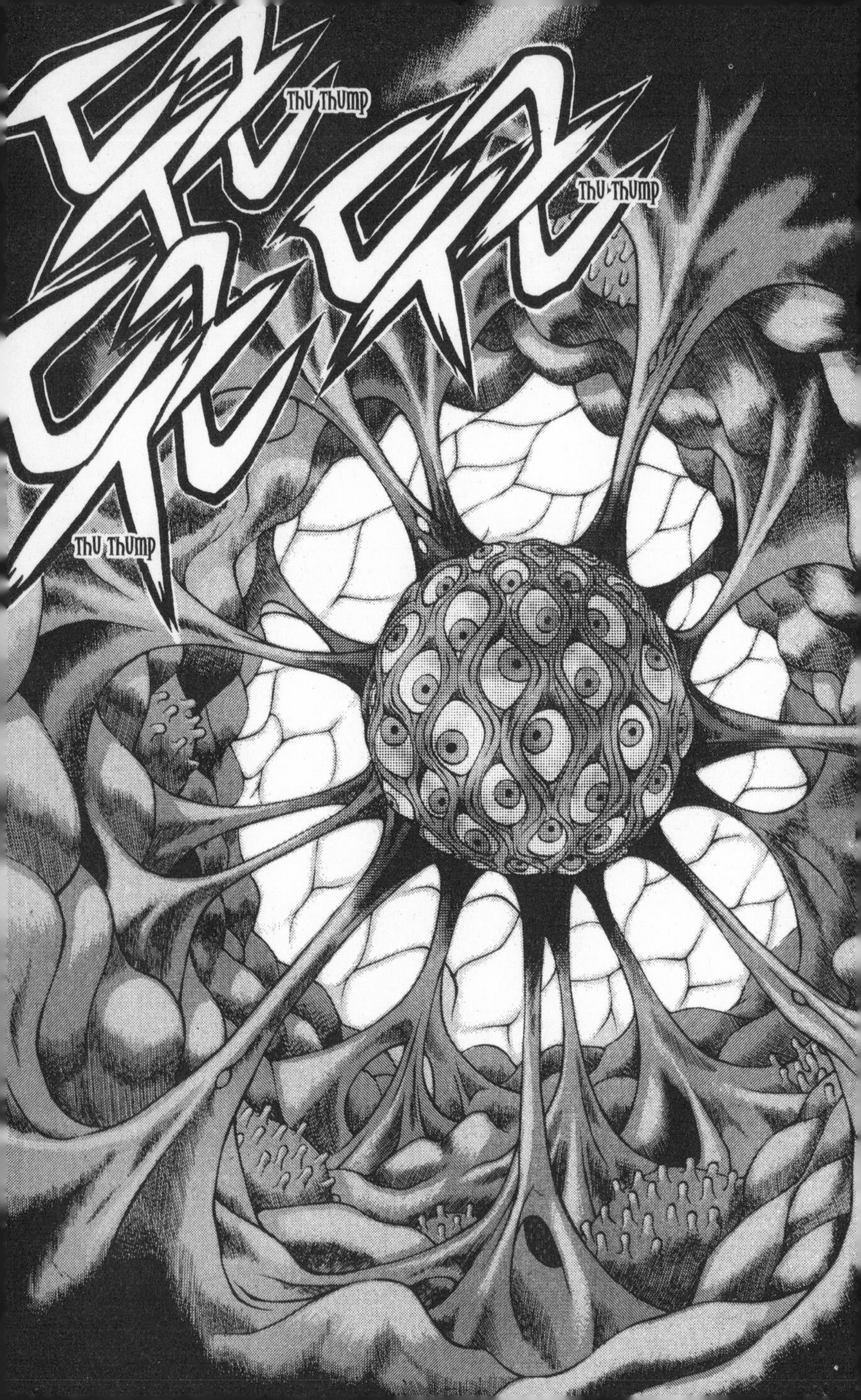
ThU ThUmp
ThU-ThUmp
ThU ThUmp

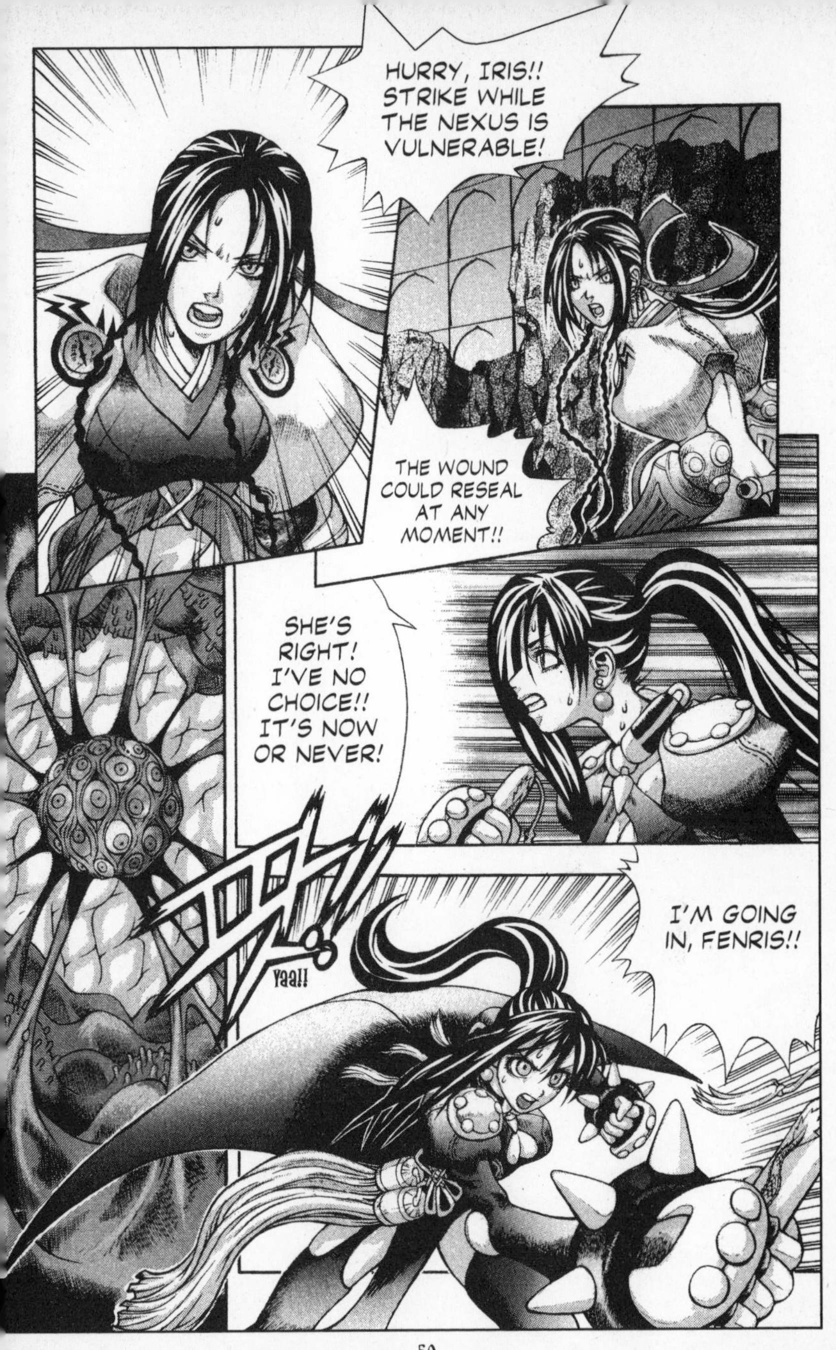

HURRY, IRIS!! STRIKE WHILE THE NEXUS IS VULNERABLE!
THE WOUND COULD RESEAL AT ANY MOMENT!!
SHE'S RIGHT! I'VE NO CHOICE!! IT'S NOW OR NEVER!
Yaa!!
I'M GOING IN, FENRIS!!

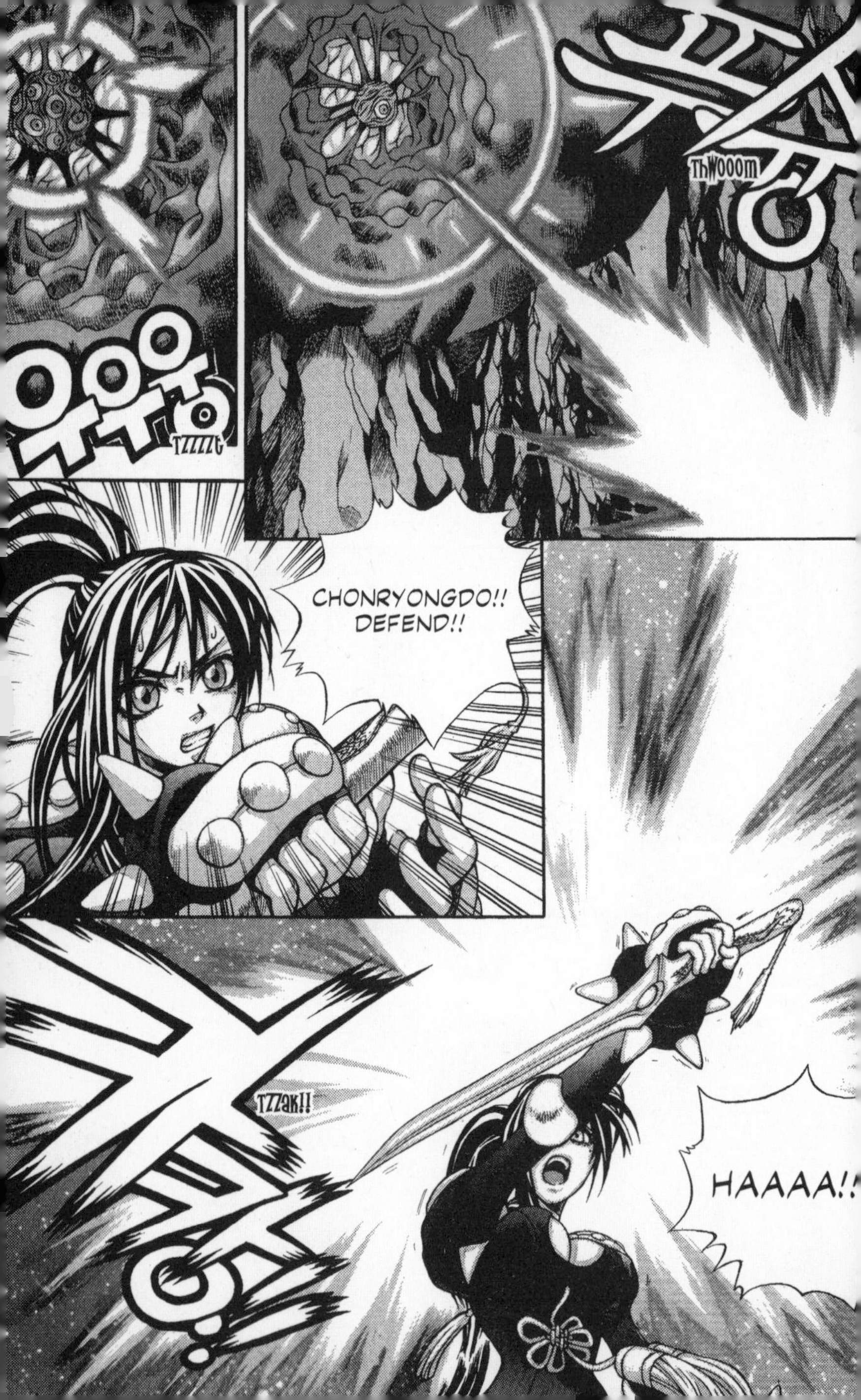
TZZZZt
ThWOOOm
CHONRYONGDO!! DEFEND!!
TZZAK!!
HAAAA!!

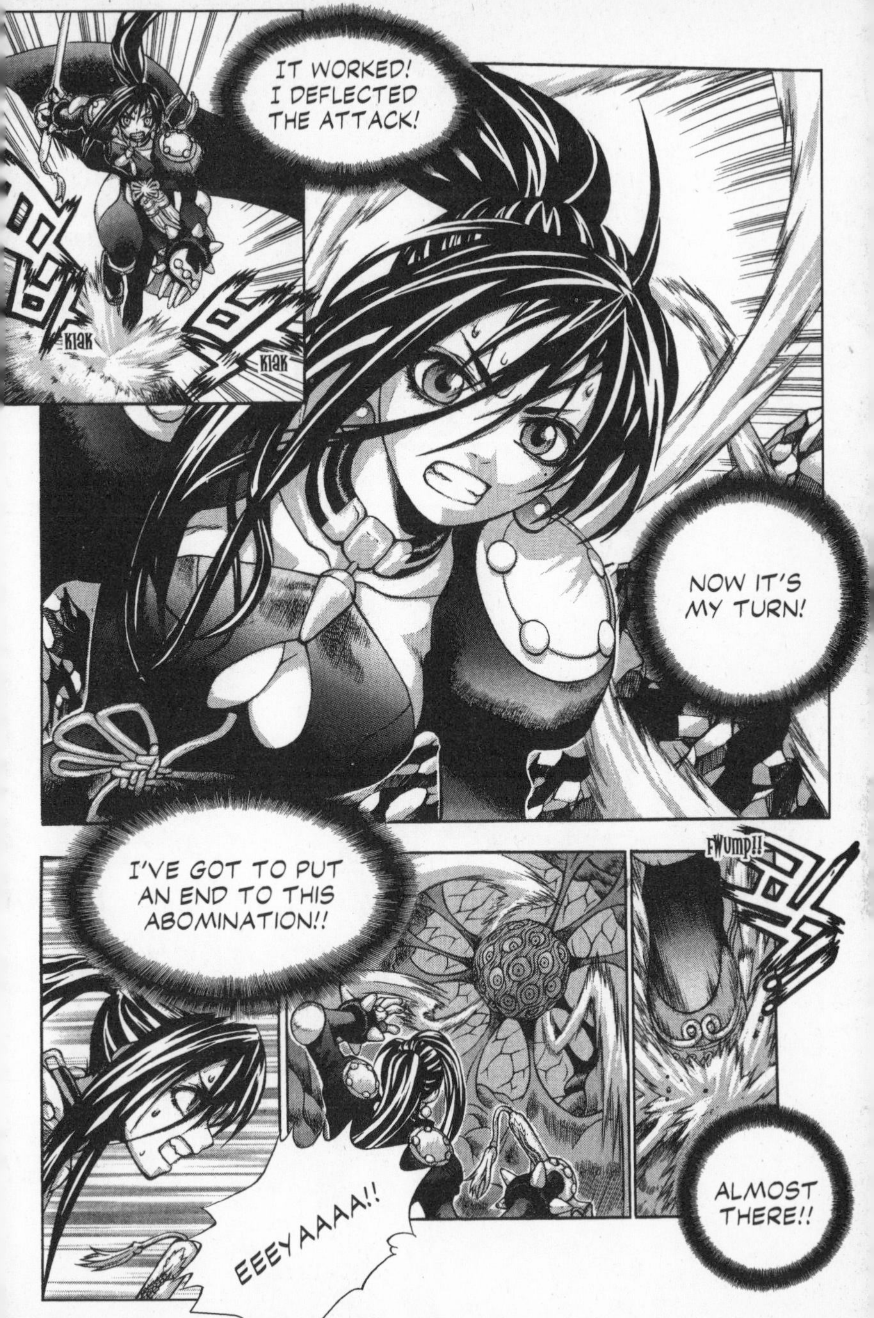
IT WORKED! I DEFLECTED THE ATTACK!
KIAK
KIAK
NOW IT'S MY TURN!
I'VE GOT TO PUT AN END TO THIS ABOMINATION!!
EEEYAAAA!!
FWUMP!!
ALMOST THERE!!

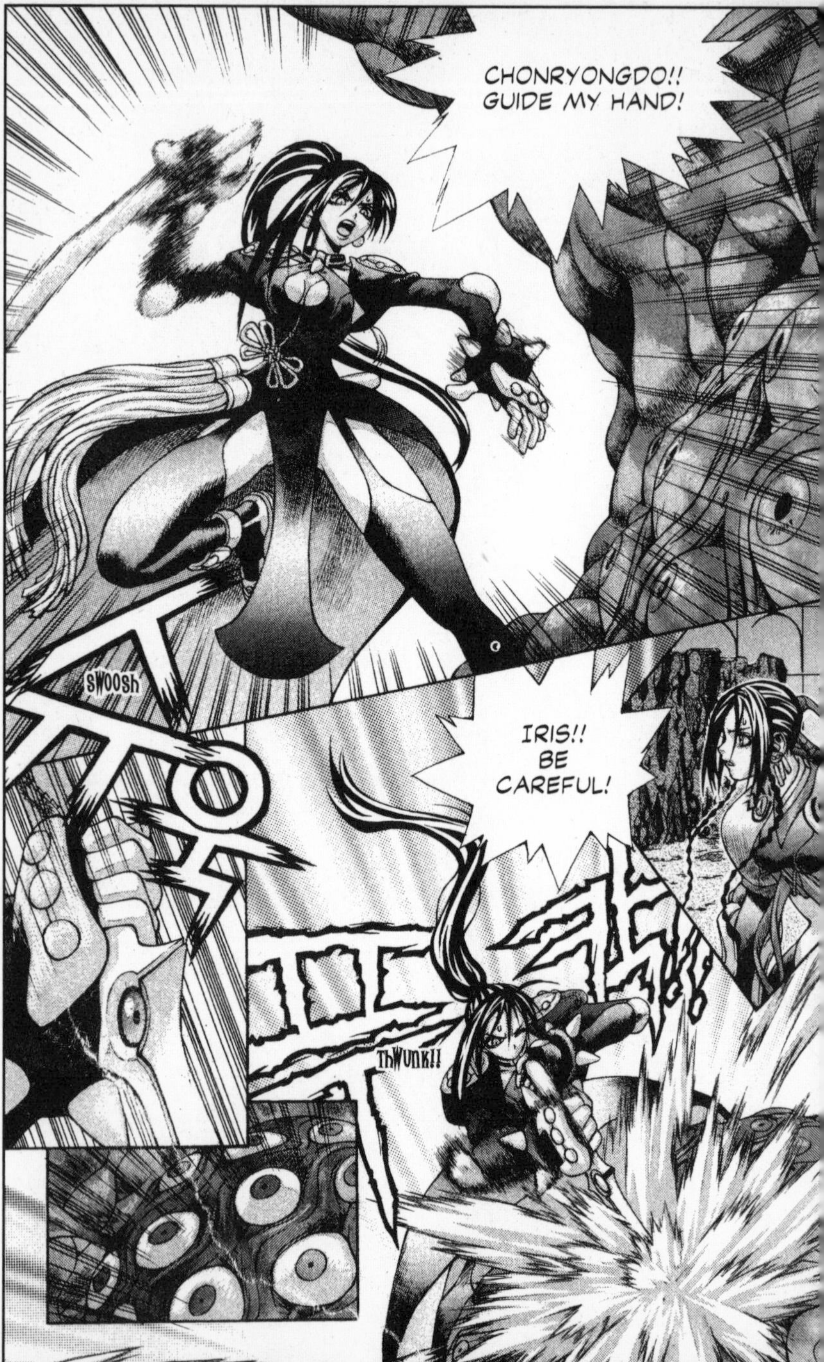
CHONRYONGDO!! GUIDE MY HAND!
SWOOSH
IRIS!! BE CAREFUL!
THWUNK!!

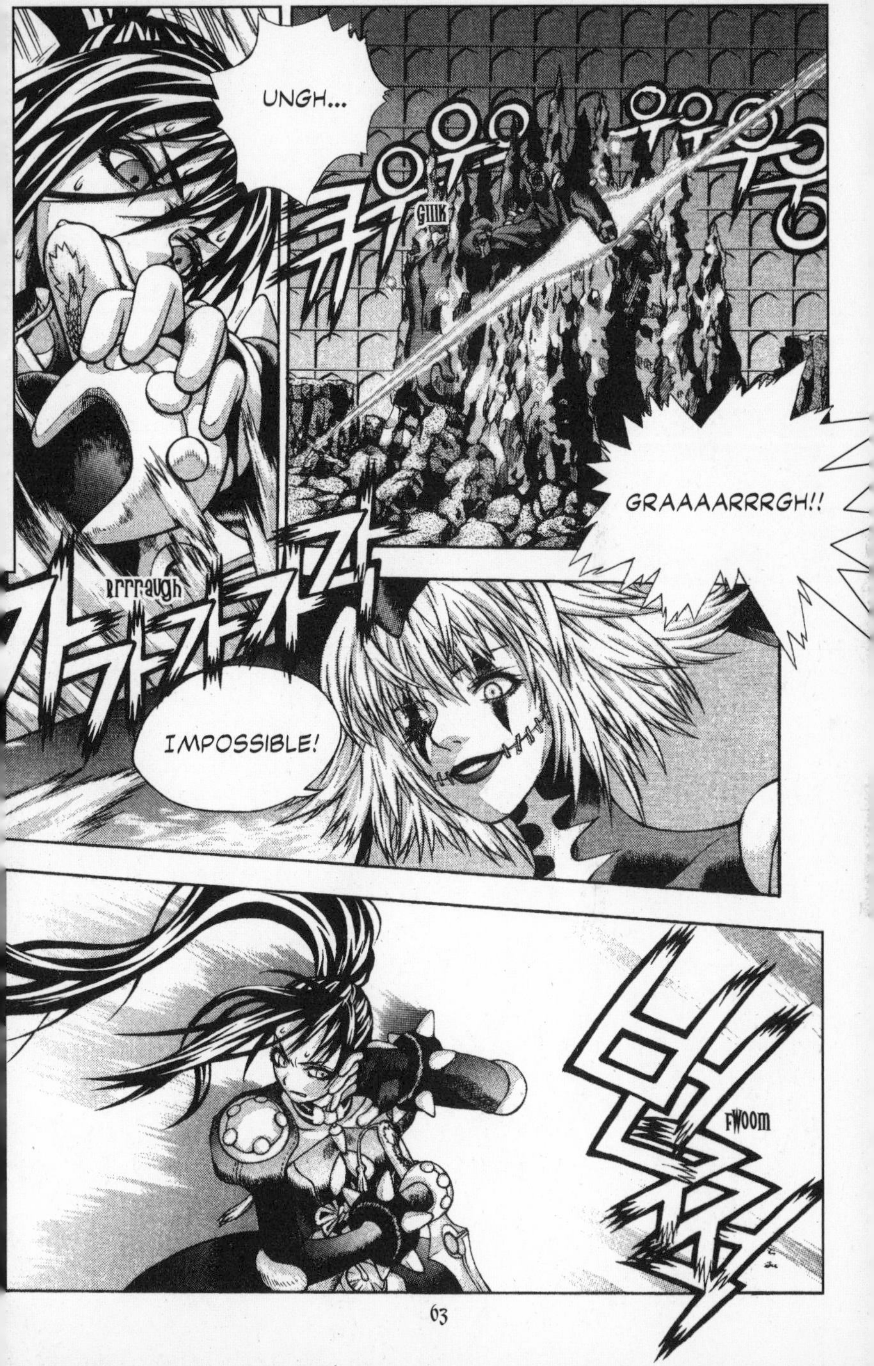

UNGH...
GIIIK
GRAAAARRRGH!!
RRRRAUGH
IMPOSSIBLE!
FWOOM

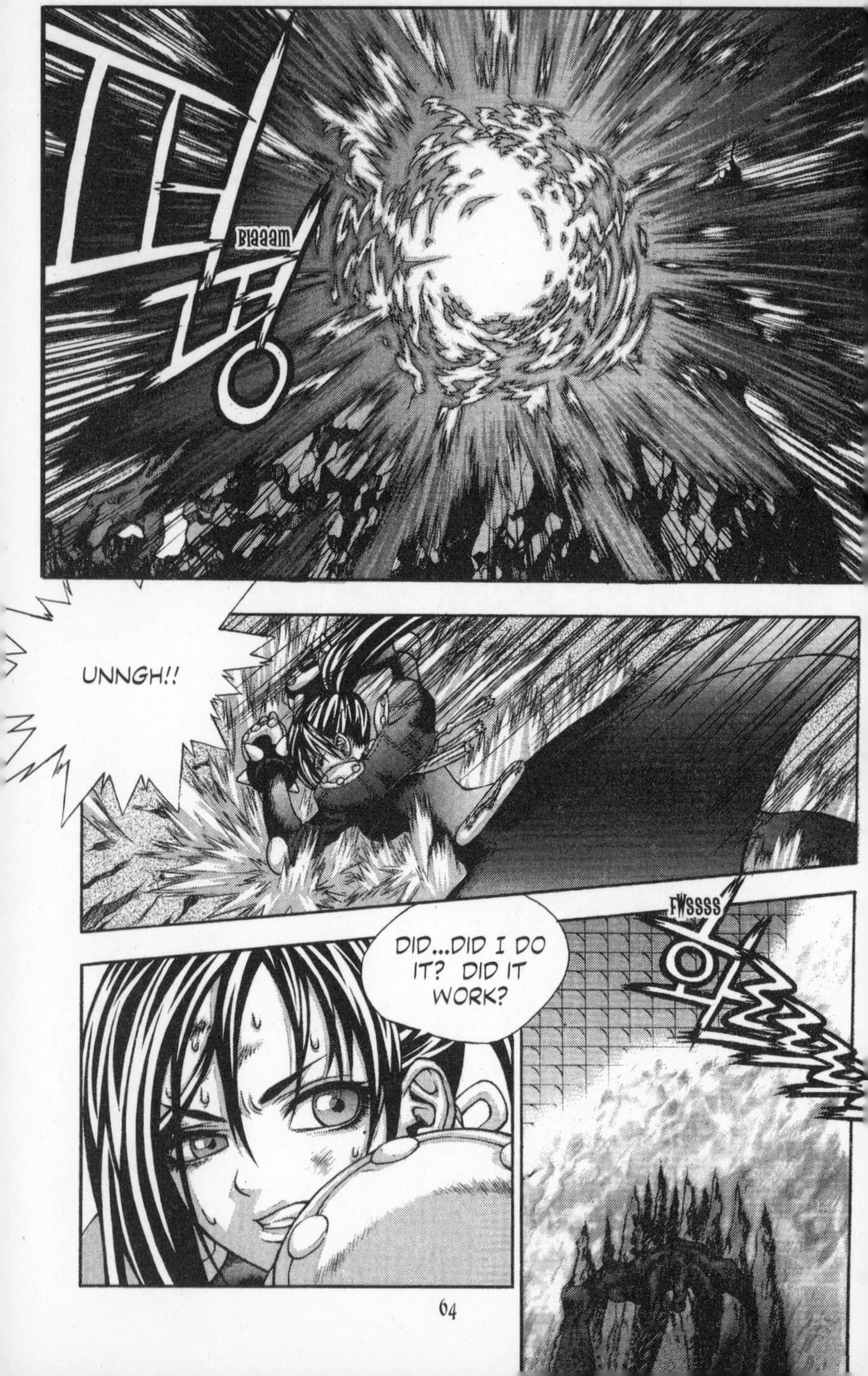
BLAAAM
UNNGH!!
DID...DID I DO IT? DID IT WORK?
FWSSSS

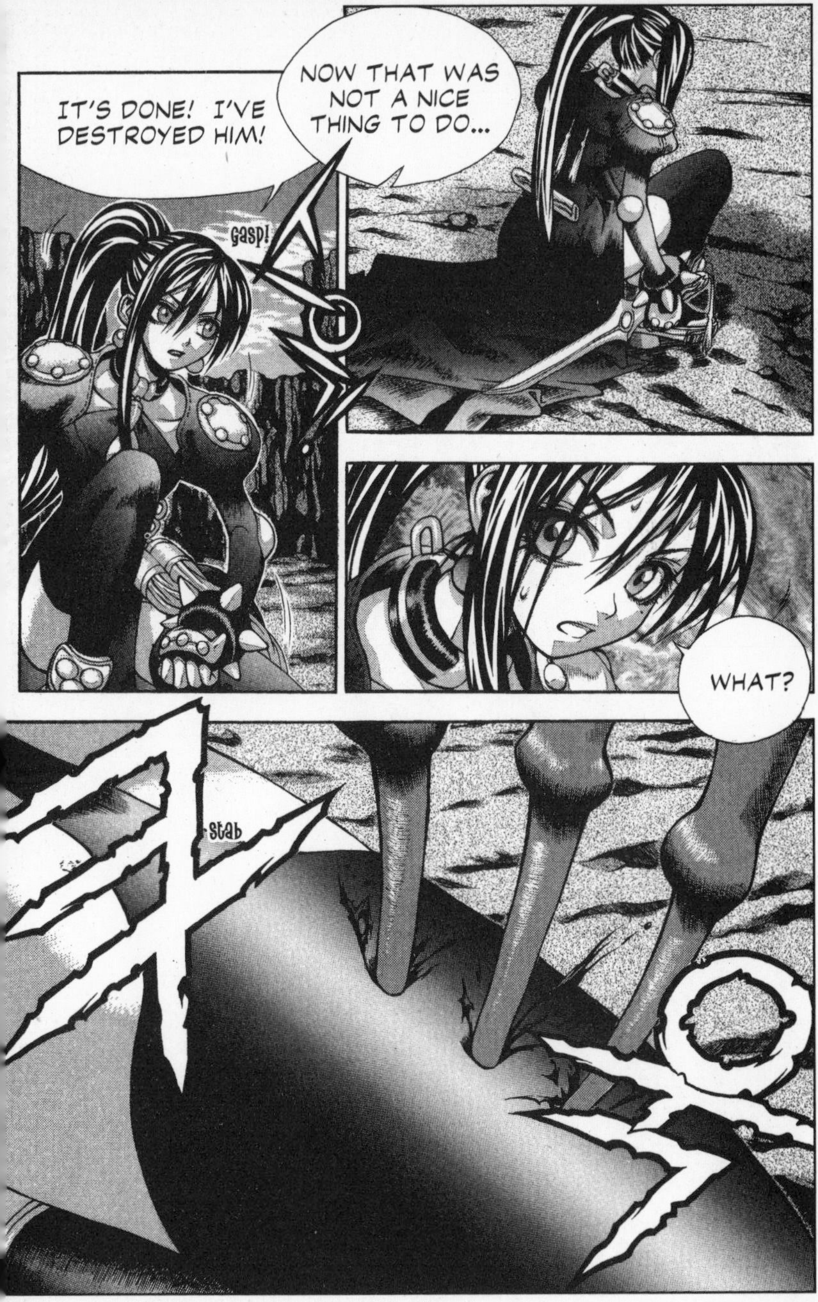
IT'S DONE! I'VE DESTROYED HIM!
GASP!
NOW THAT WAS NOT A NICE THING TO DO...
WHAT?
STAB

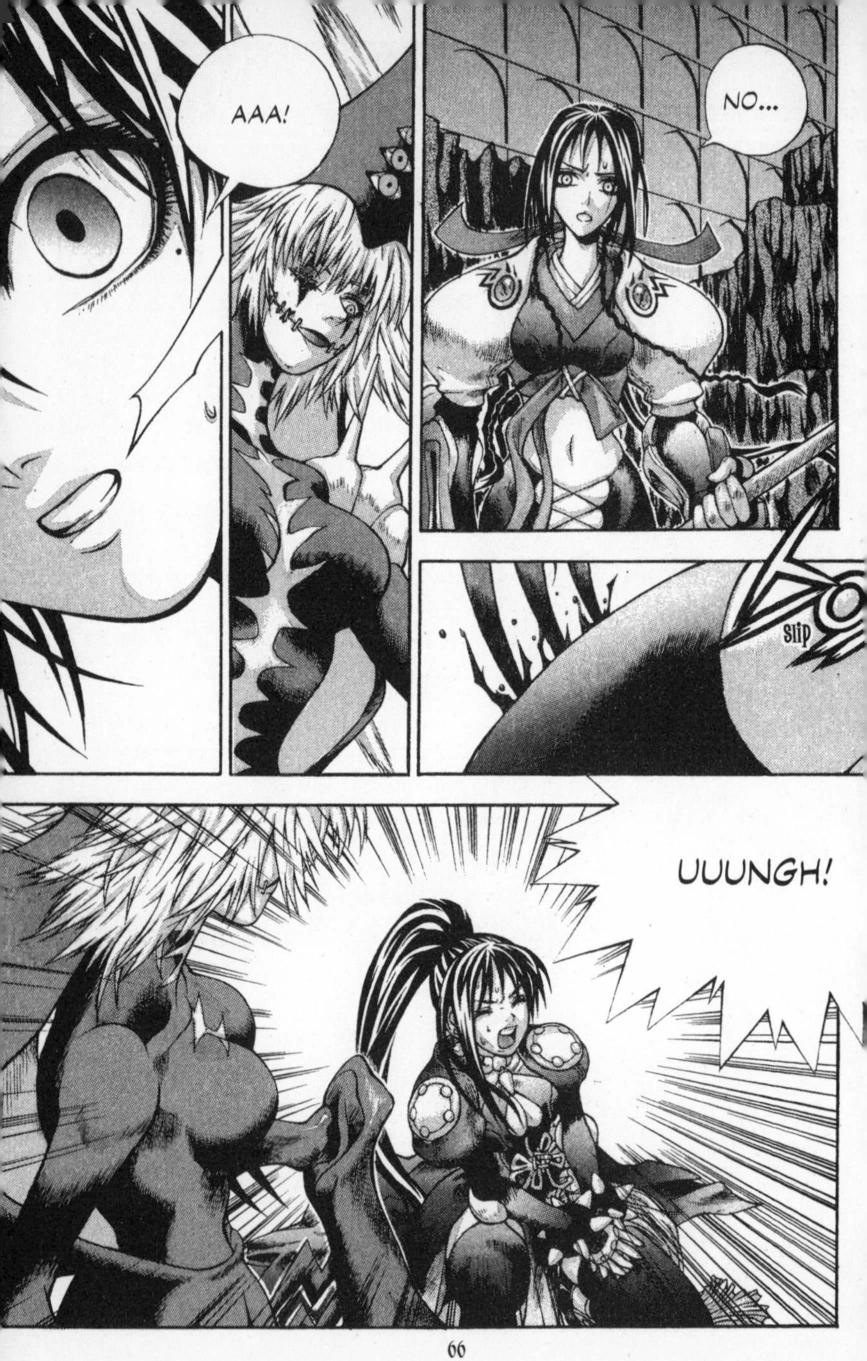
AAA!
NO...
slip
UUUNGH!

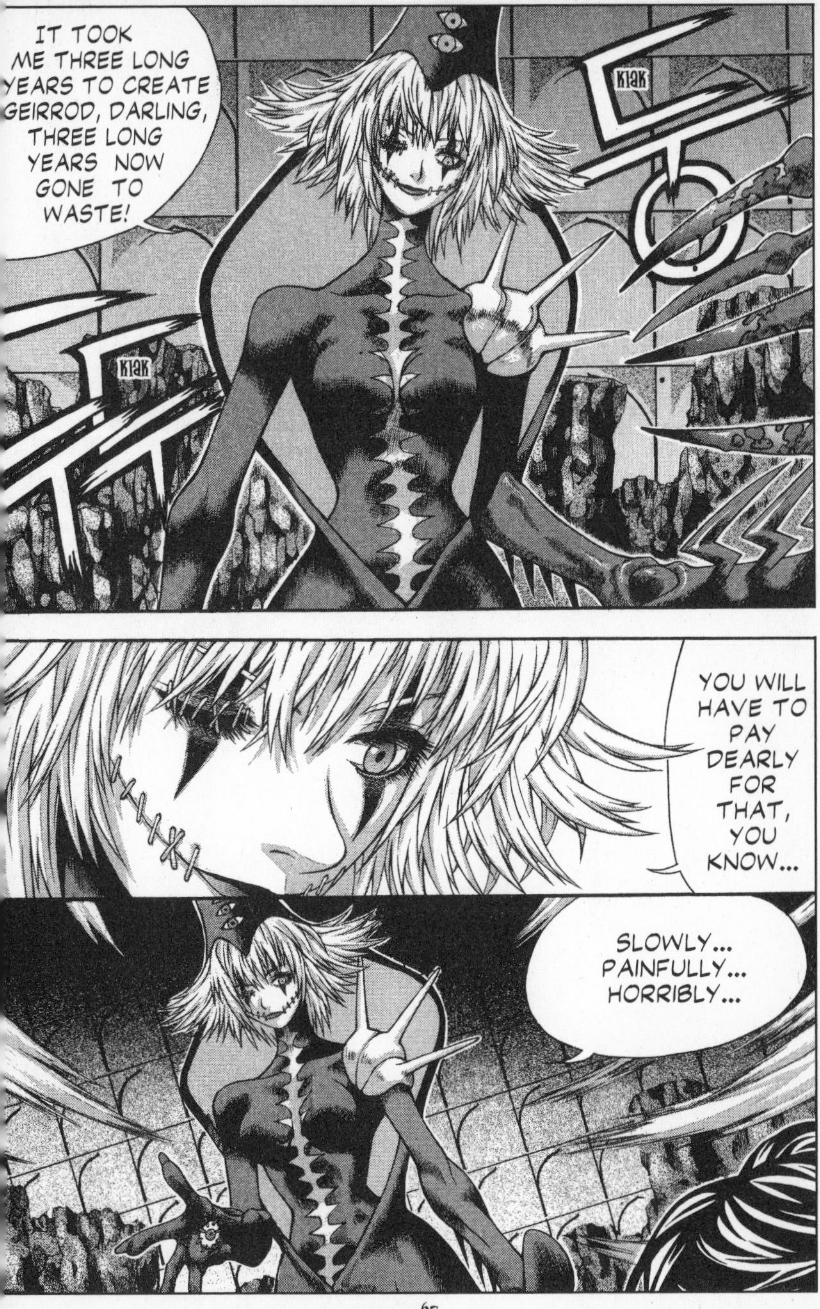
IT TOOK ME THREE LONG YEARS TO CREATE GEIRROD, DARLING, THREE LONG YEARS NOW GONE TO WASTE!
KIAK
KIAK
YOU WILL HAVE TO PAY DEARLY FOR THAT, YOU KNOW...
SLOWLY... PAINFULLY... HORRIBLY...

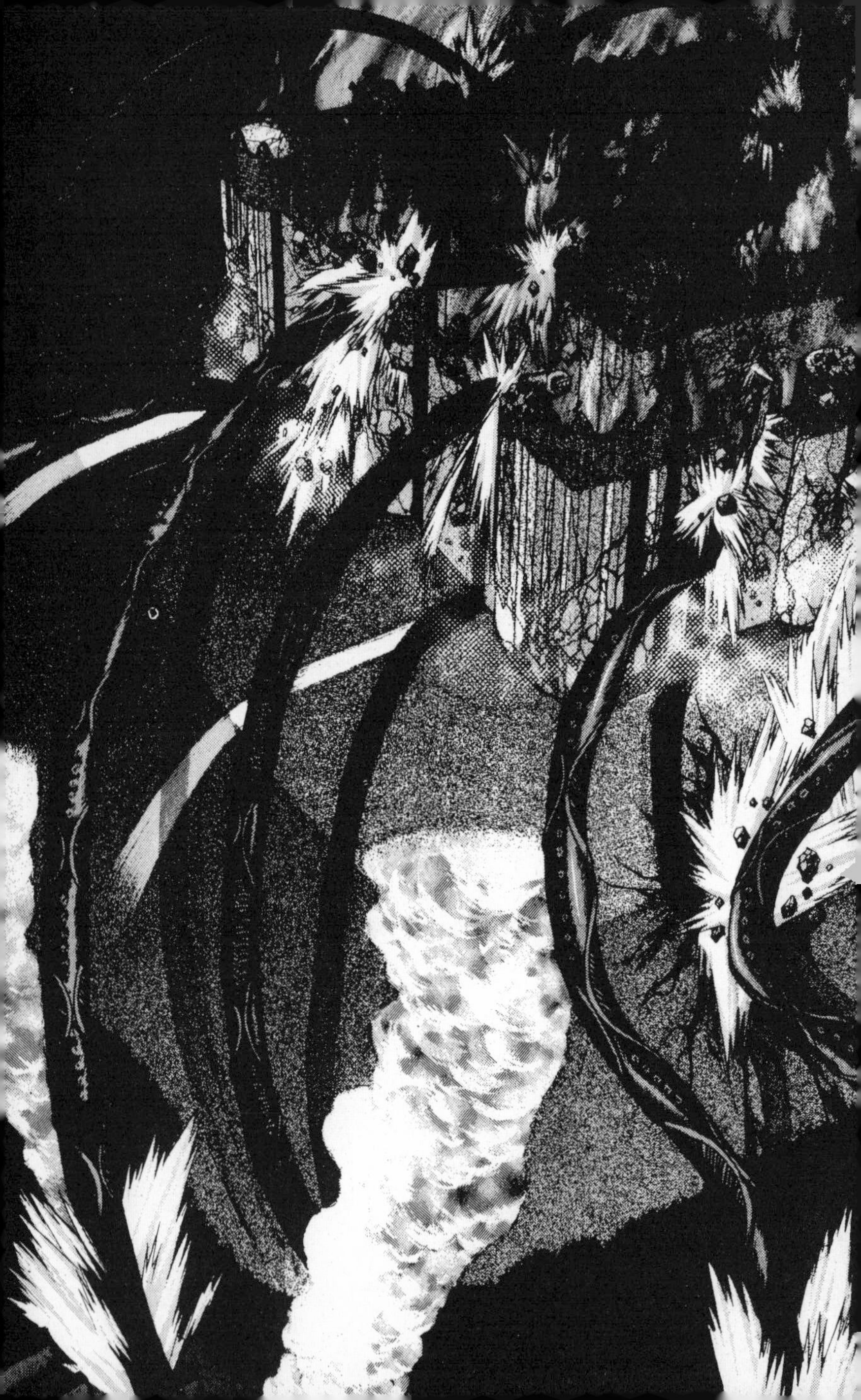

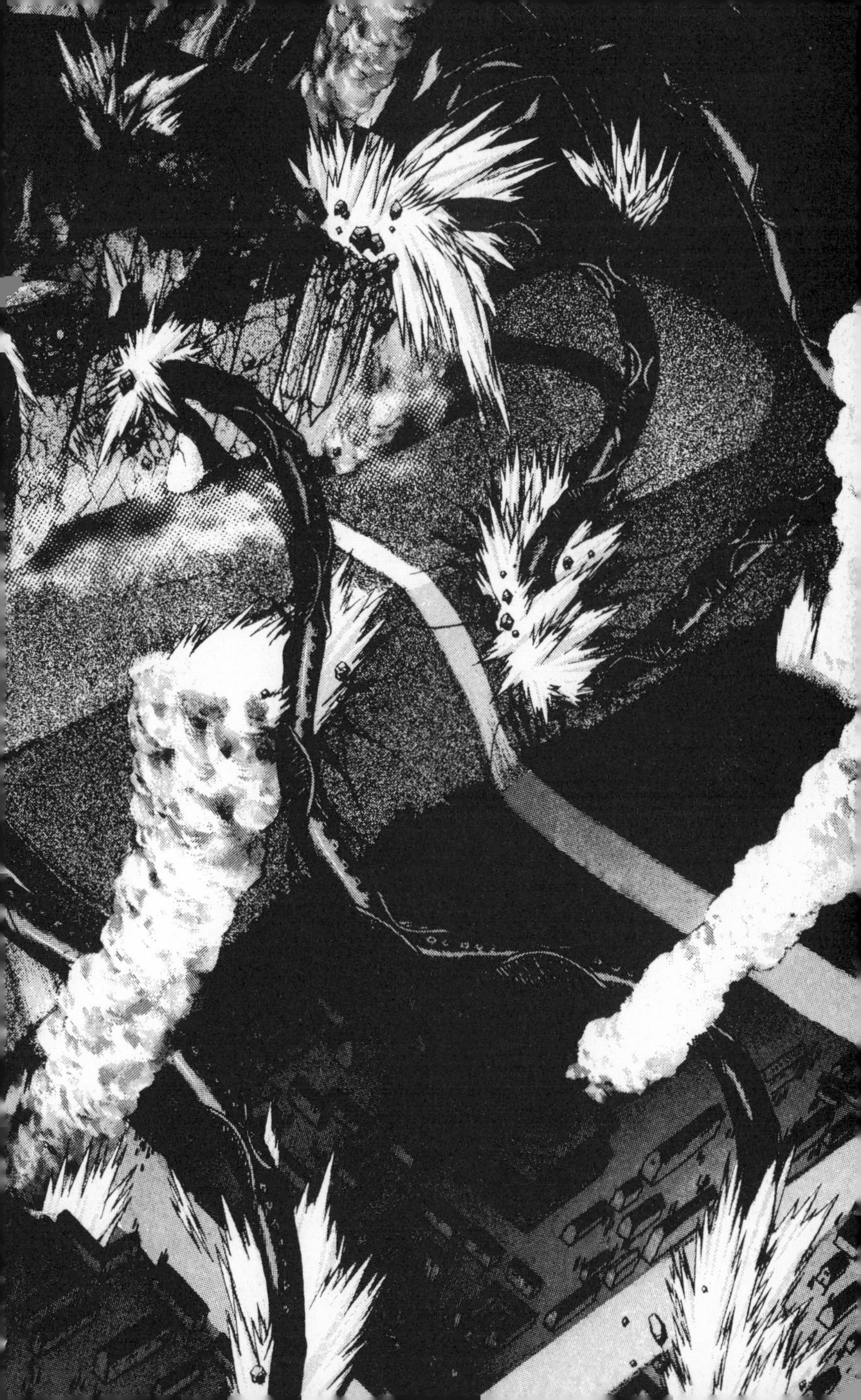

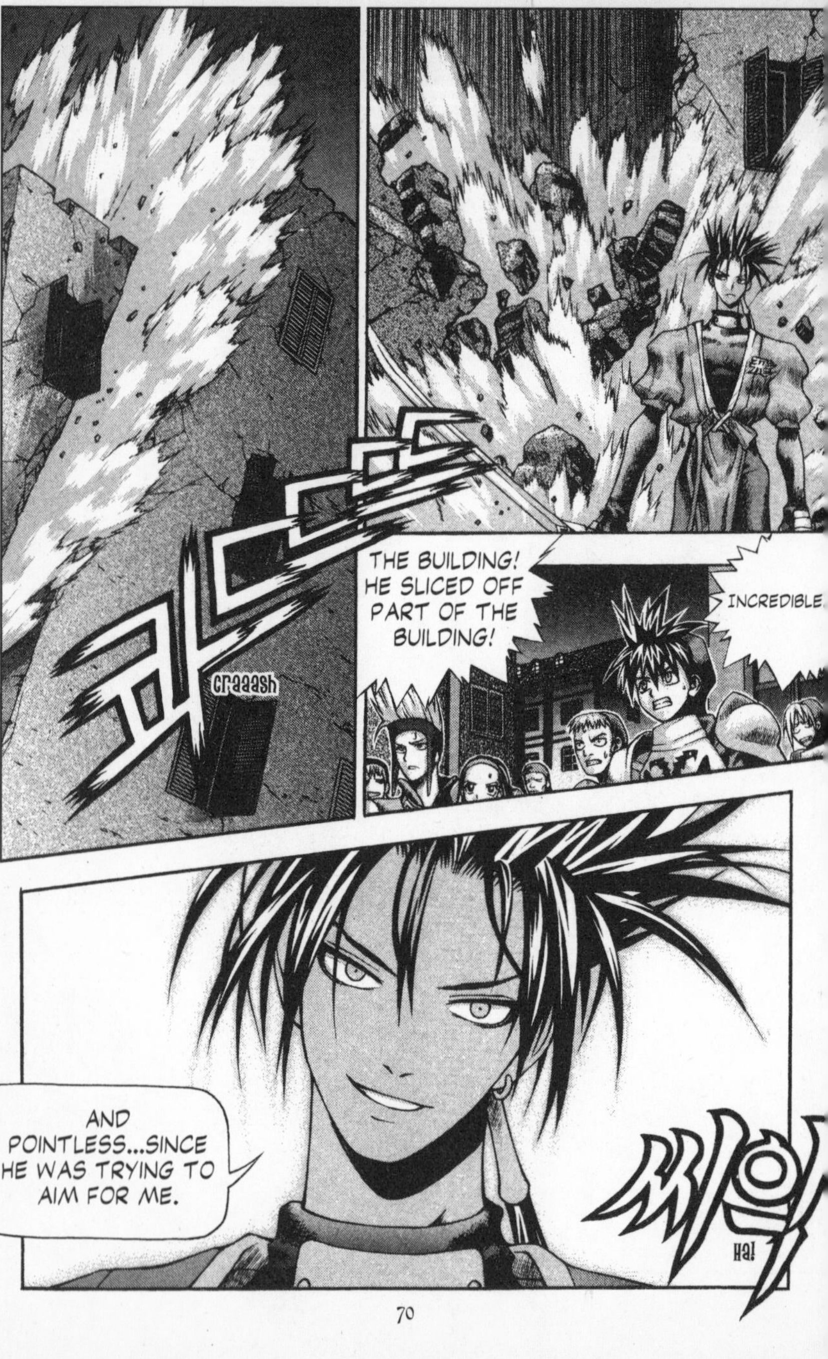
CRAAASH
THE BUILDING! HE SLICED OFF PART OF THE BUILDING!
INCREDIBLE.
AND POINTLESS...SINCE HE WAS TRYING TO AIM FOR ME.
HA!

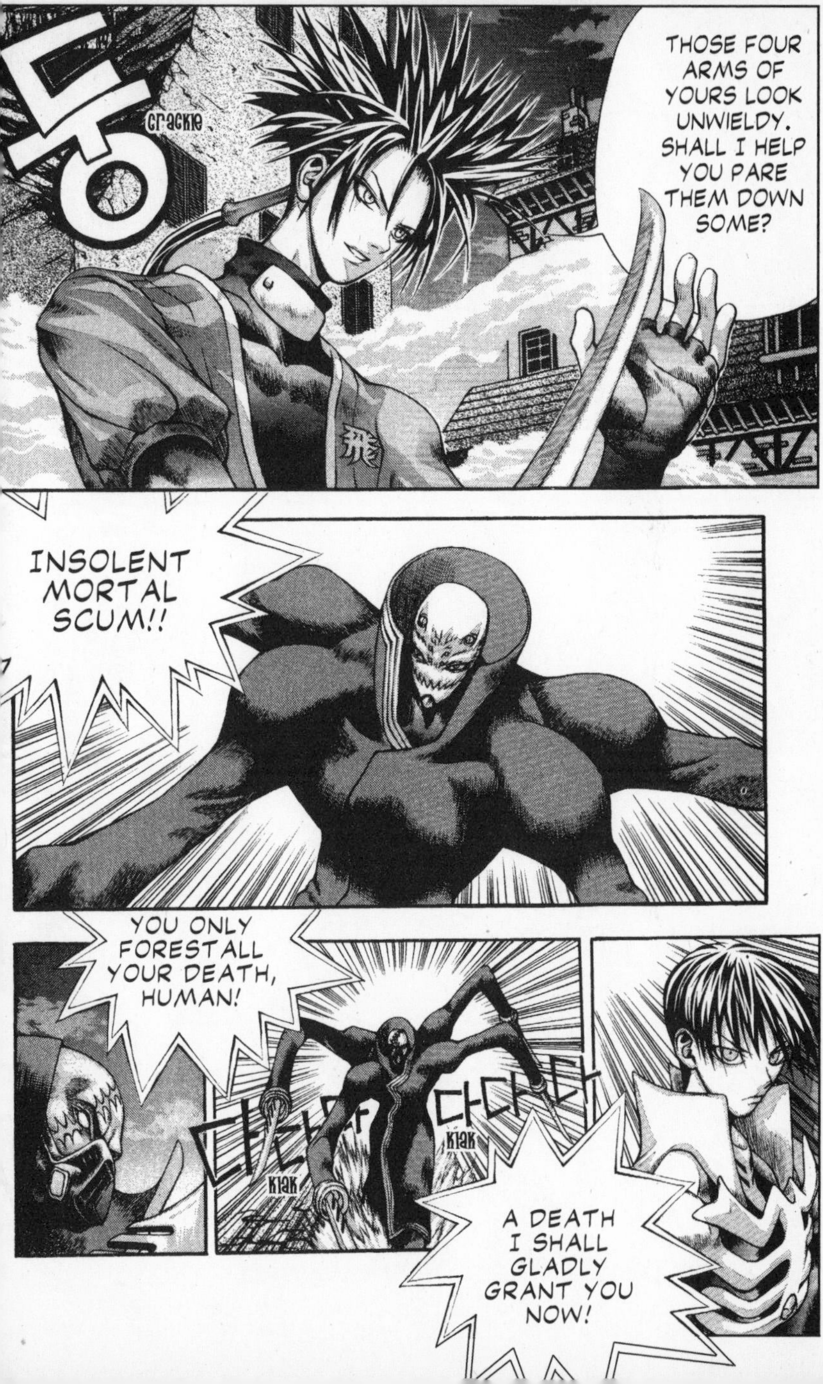

CRACKIE
THOSE FOUR ARMS OF YOURS LOOK UNWIELDY. SHALL I HELP YOU PARE THEM DOWN SOME?
INSOLENT MORTAL SCUM!!
YOU ONLY FORESTALL YOUR DEATH, HUMAN!
KIAK
KIAK
A DEATH I SHALL GLADLY GRANT YOU NOW!

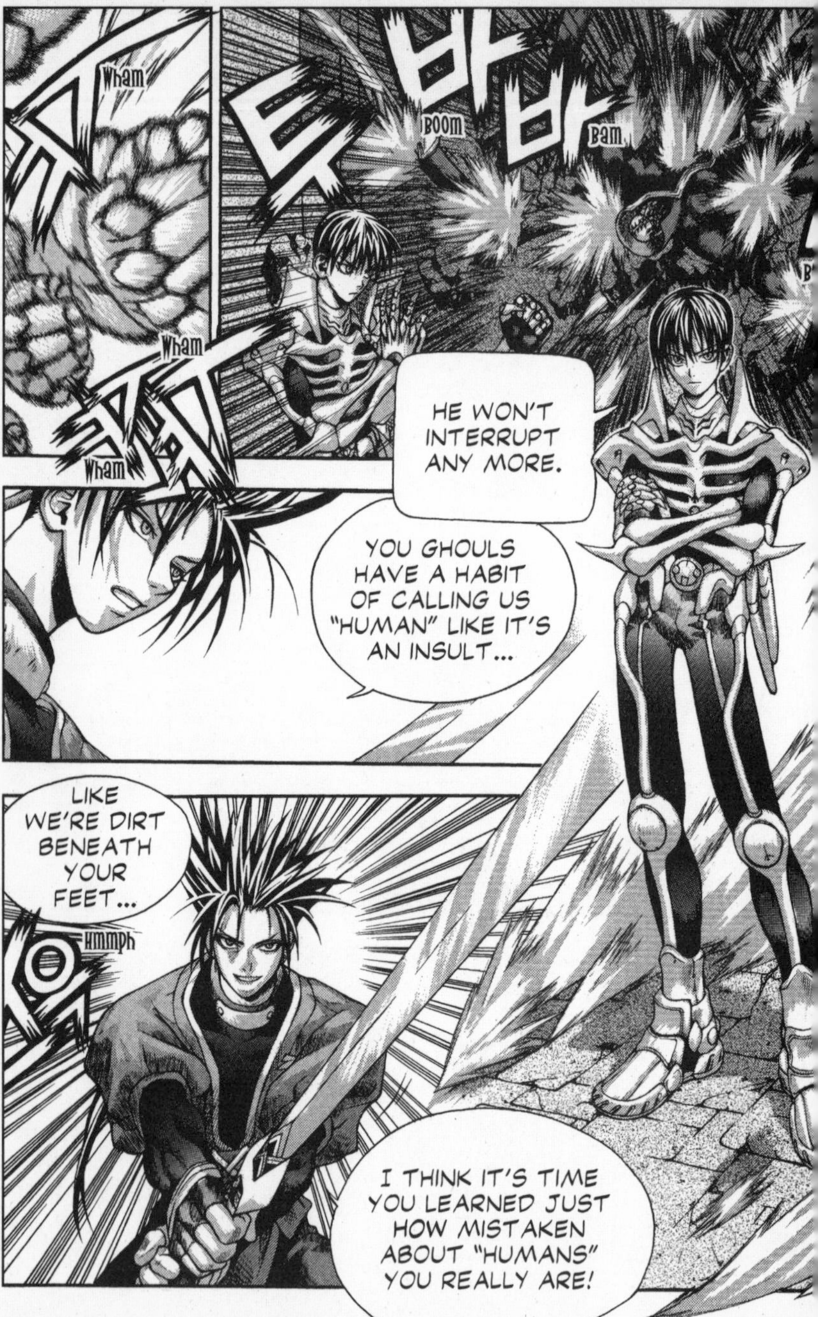
Wham
Wham
Wham
BOOM
BAM
HE WON'T INTERRUPT ANY MORE.
YOU GHOULS HAVE A HABIT OF CALLING US "HUMAN" LIKE IT'S AN INSULT...
LIKE WE'RE DIRT BENEATH YOUR FEET...
HMMPH
I THINK IT'S TIME YOU LEARNED JUST HOW MISTAKEN ABOUT "HUMANS" YOU REALLY ARE!

RAGNAROK
라그나로크
IN TO THE ABYSS

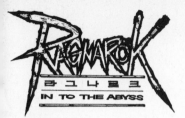

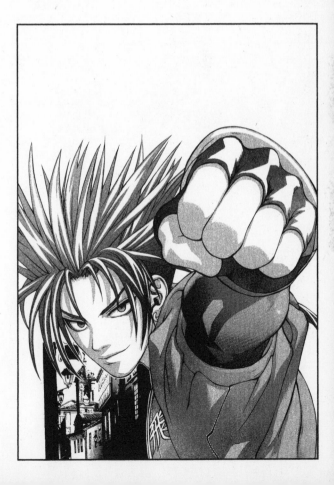

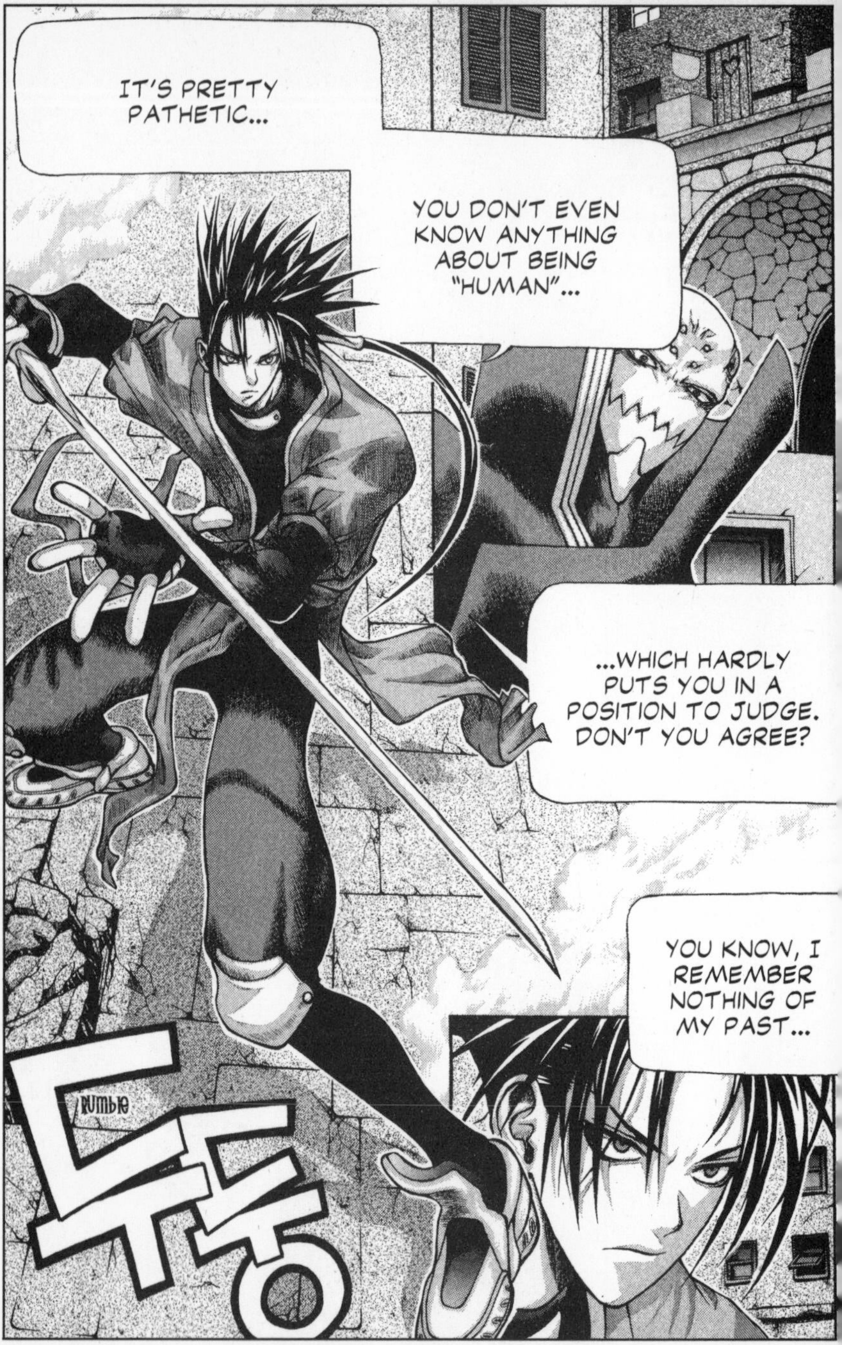
IT'S PRETTY PATHETIC...
YOU DON'T EVEN KNOW ANYTHING ABOUT BEING "HUMAN"...
...WHICH HARDLY PUTS YOU IN A POSITION TO JUDGE. DON'T YOU AGREE?
RUMBLE
YOU KNOW, I REMEMBER NOTHING OF MY PAST...

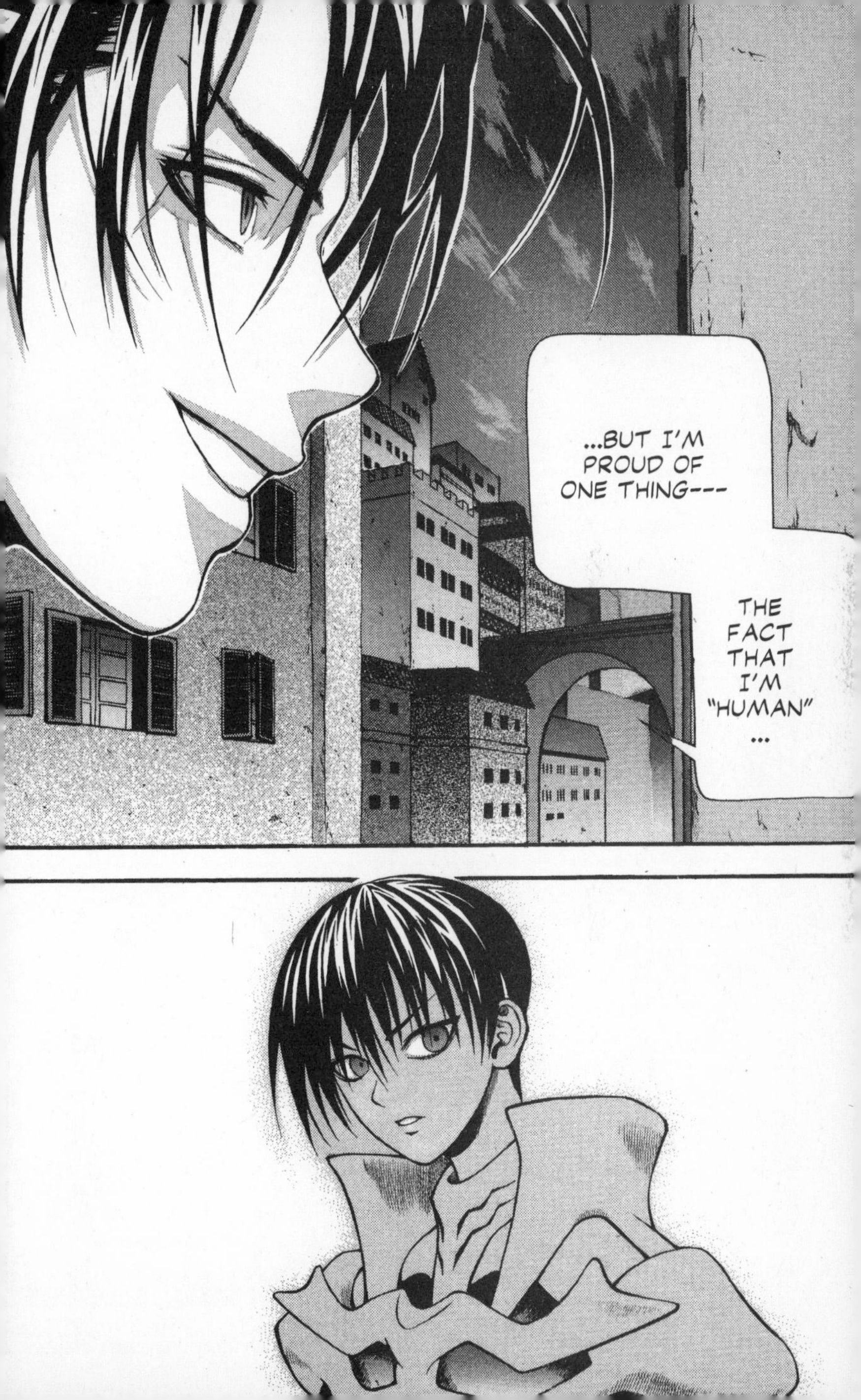
...BUT I'M PROUD OF ONE THING---
THE FACT THAT I'M "HUMAN" ...

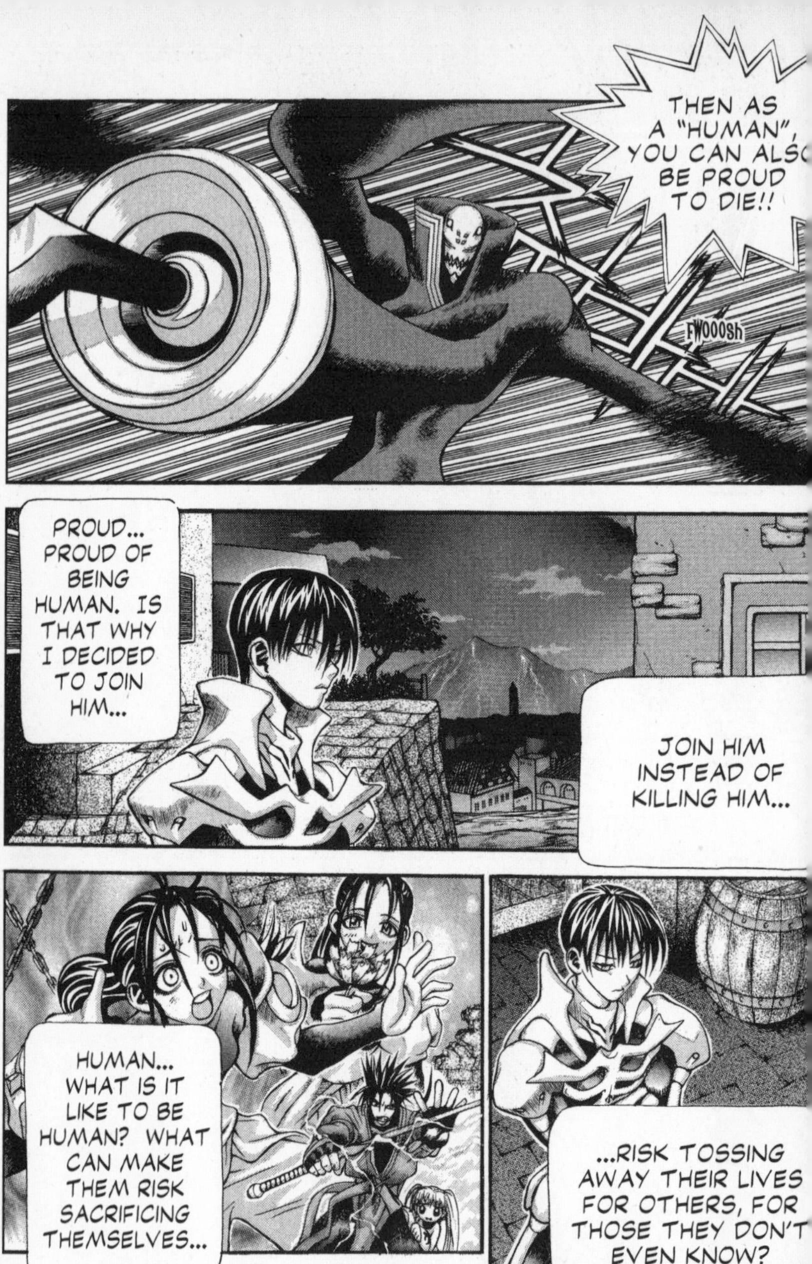
THEN AS A "HUMAN", YOU CAN ALSO BE PROUD TO DIE!!
FWOOOSH
PROUD... PROUD OF BEING HUMAN. IS THAT WHY I DECIDED TO JOIN HIM...
JOIN HIM INSTEAD OF KILLING HIM...
HUMAN... WHAT IS IT LIKE TO BE HUMAN? WHAT CAN MAKE THEM RISK SACRIFICING THEMSELVES...
...RISK TOSSING AWAY THEIR LIVES FOR OTHERS, FOR THOSE THEY DON'T EVEN KNOW?

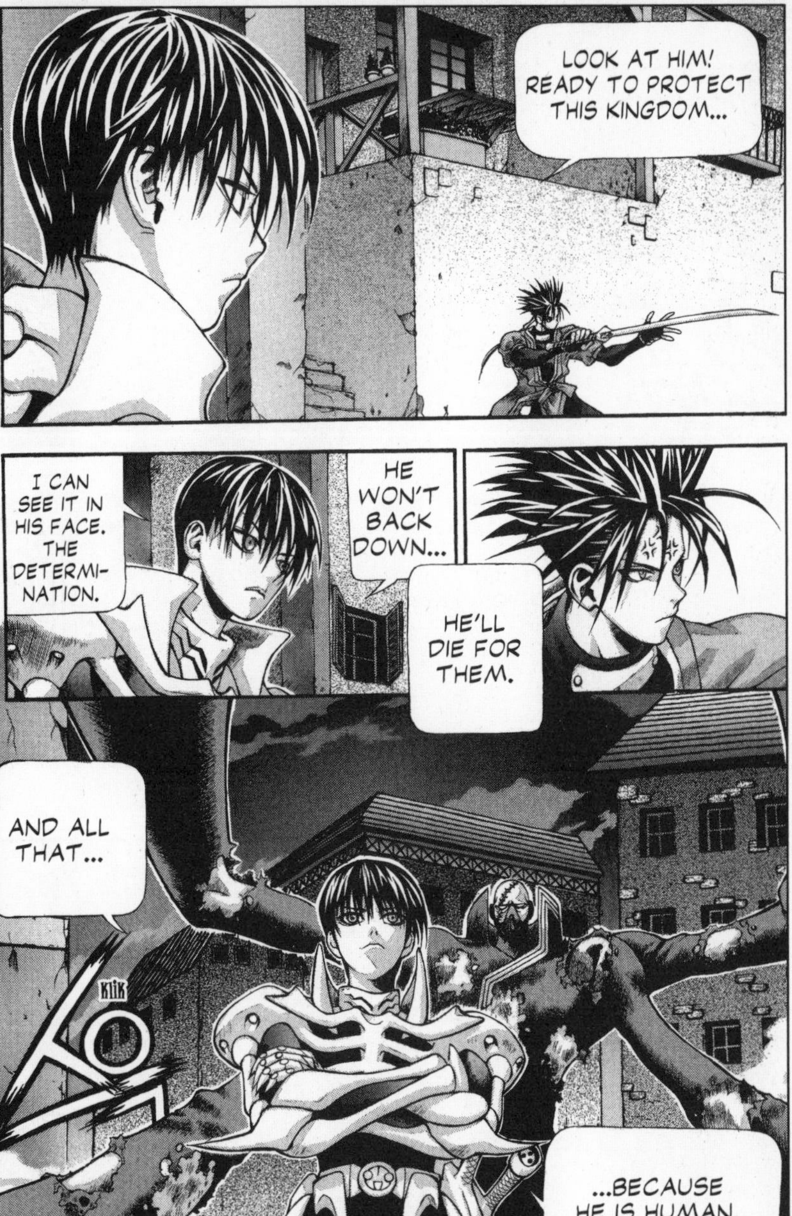
LOOK AT HIM! READY TO PROTECT THIS KINGDOM...
I CAN SEE IT IN HIS FACE. THE DETERMI-NATION.
HE WON'T BACK DOWN...
HE'LL DIE FOR THEM.
AND ALL THAT...
KLIK
...BECAUSE HE IS HUMAN.

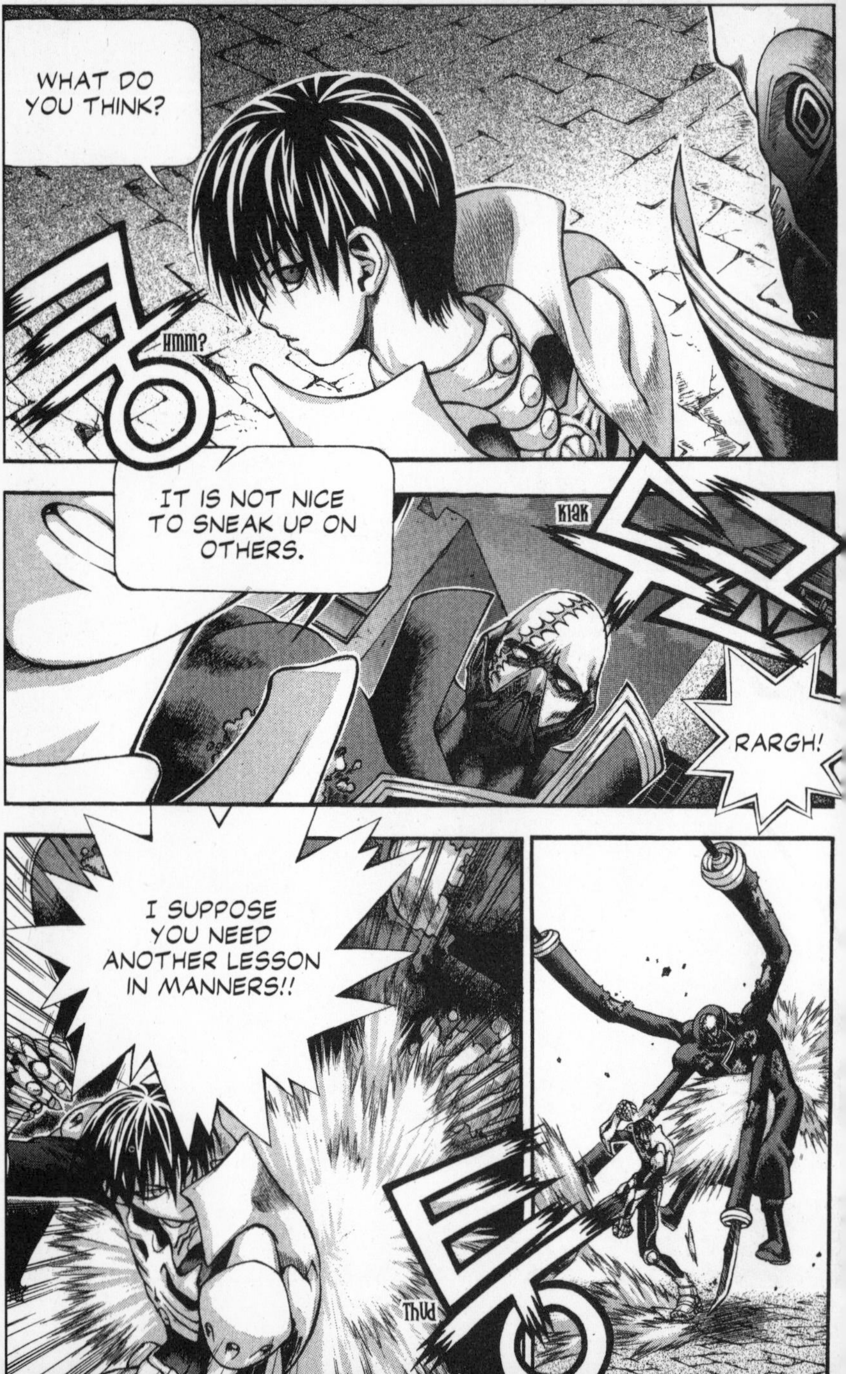
WHAT DO YOU THINK?
HMM?
IT IS NOT NICE TO SNEAK UP ON OTHERS.
KlAK
RARGH!
I SUPPOSE YOU NEED ANOTHER LESSON IN MANNERS!!
ThUd

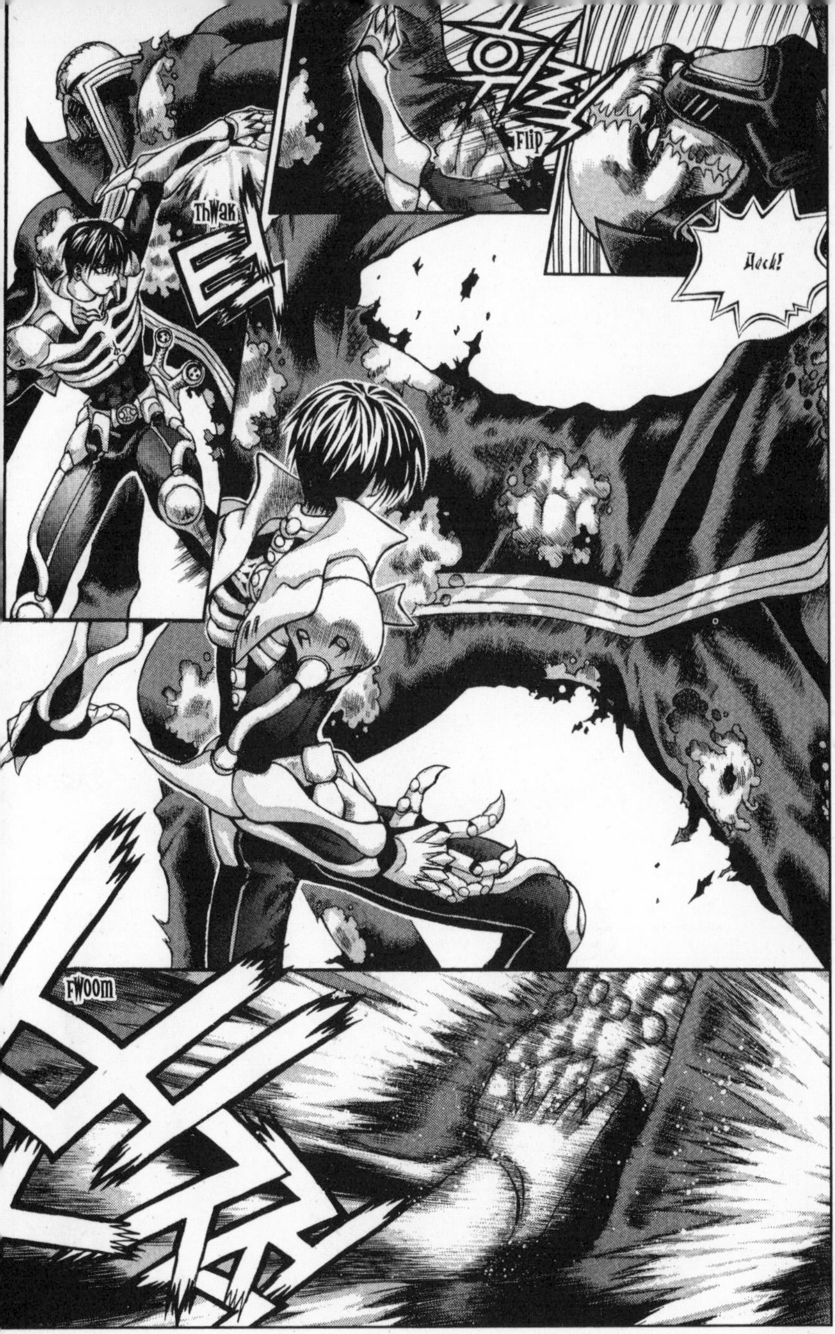
ThWak
Flip
Hack!
FWoom

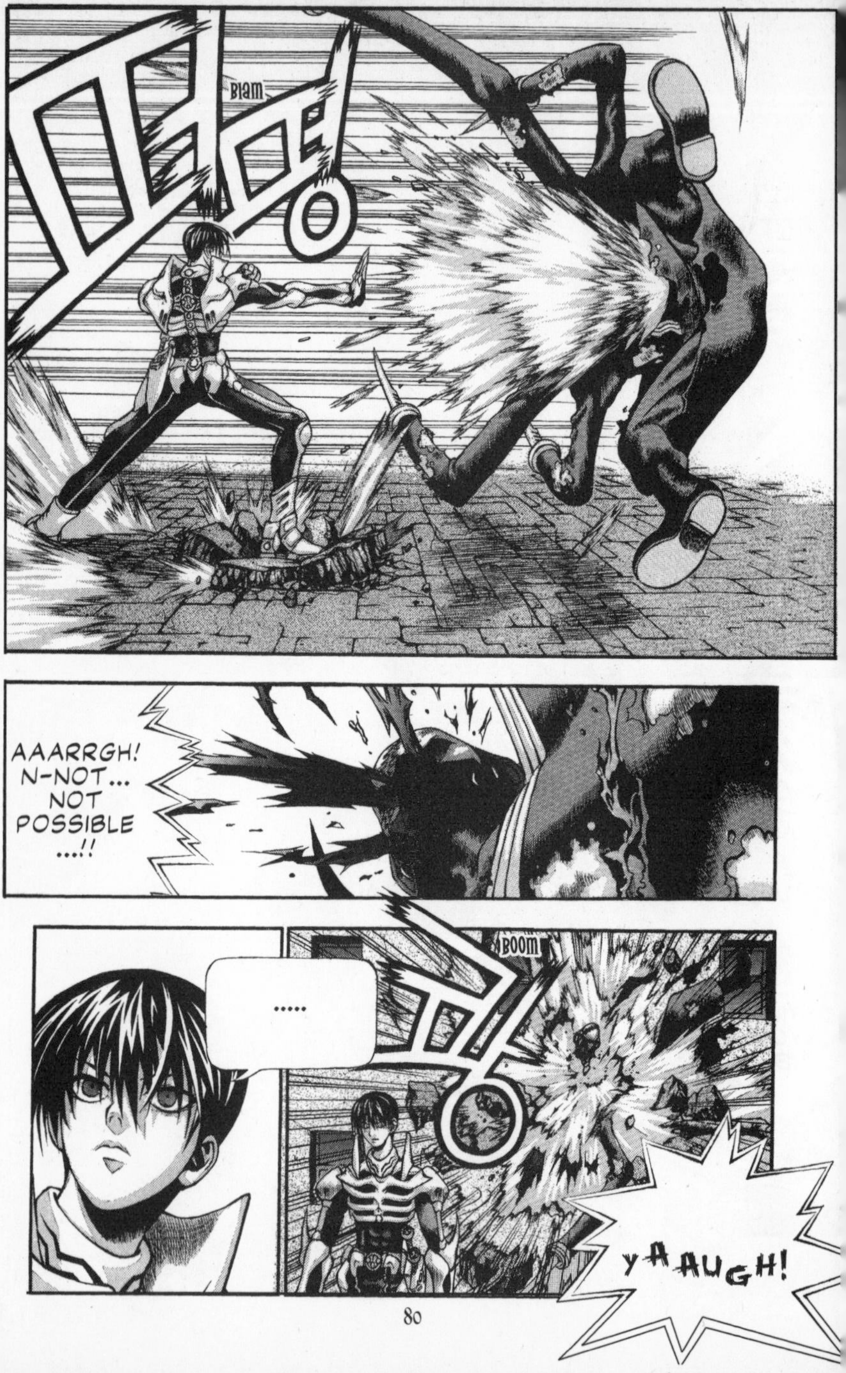
BLAM
AAARRGH! N-NOT... NOT POSSIBLE ....!!
BOOM
.....
YAAUGH!

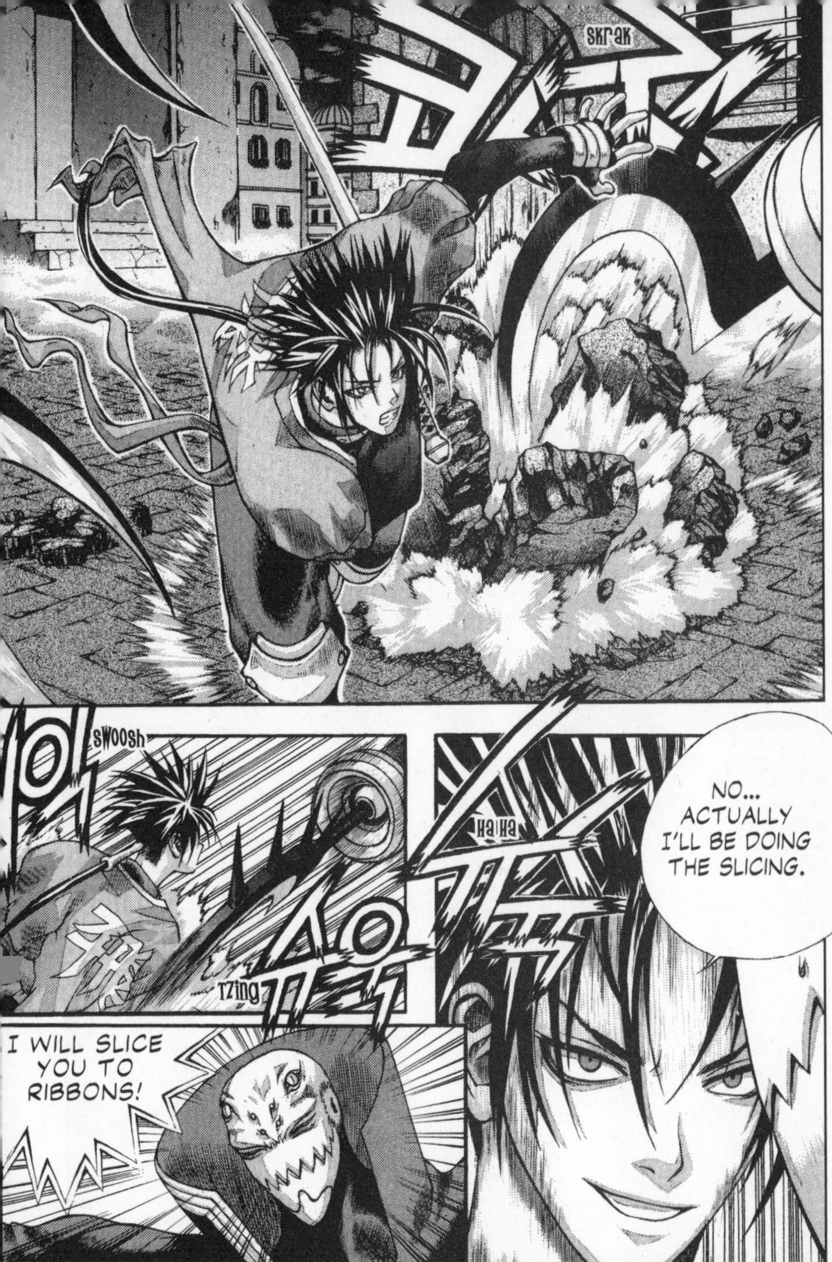
SKRAK
SWOOSH
TZING
I WILL SLICE YOU TO RIBBONS!
HA HA
NO... ACTUALLY I'LL BE DOING THE SLICING.

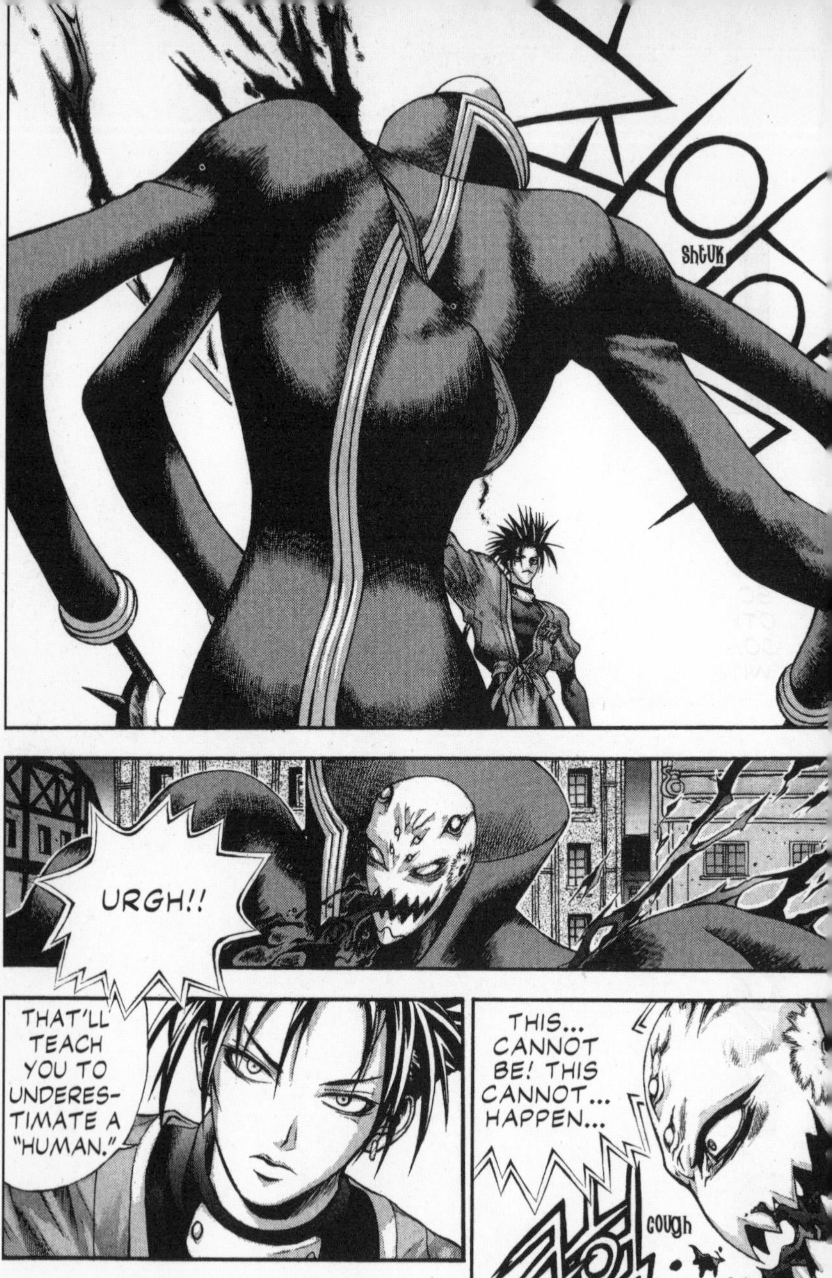
SHTUK
URGH!!
THAT'LL TEACH YOU TO UNDERES-TIMATE A "HUMAN."
THIS... CANNOT BE! THIS CANNOT... HAPPEN...
COUGH

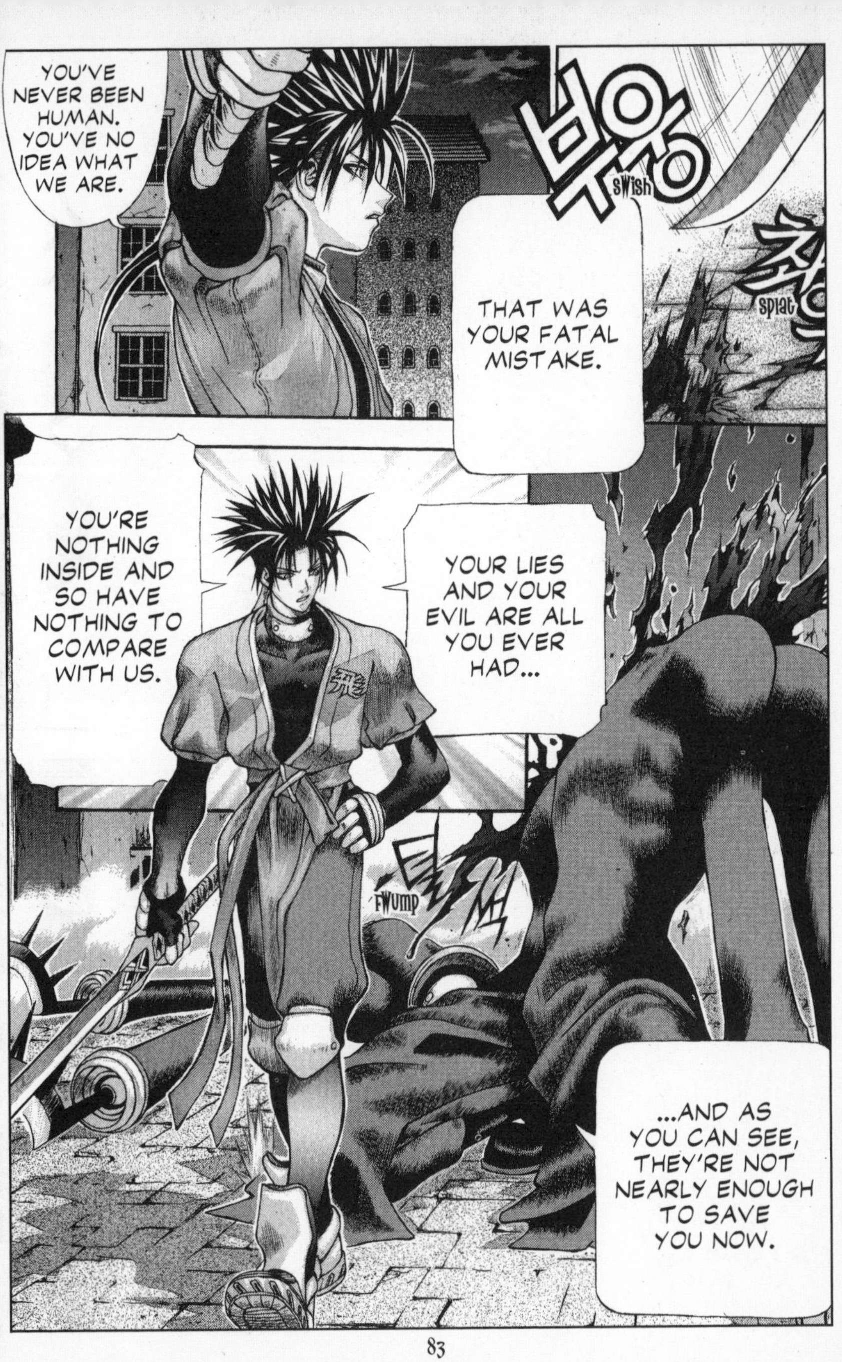
YOU'VE NEVER BEEN HUMAN. YOU'VE NO IDEA WHAT WE ARE.
sWish
splat
THAT WAS YOUR FATAL MISTAKE.
YOU'RE NOTHING INSIDE AND SO HAVE NOTHING TO COMPARE WITH US.
YOUR LIES AND YOUR EVIL ARE ALL YOU EVER HAD...
FWump
...AND AS YOU CAN SEE, THEY'RE NOT NEARLY ENOUGH TO SAVE YOU NOW.

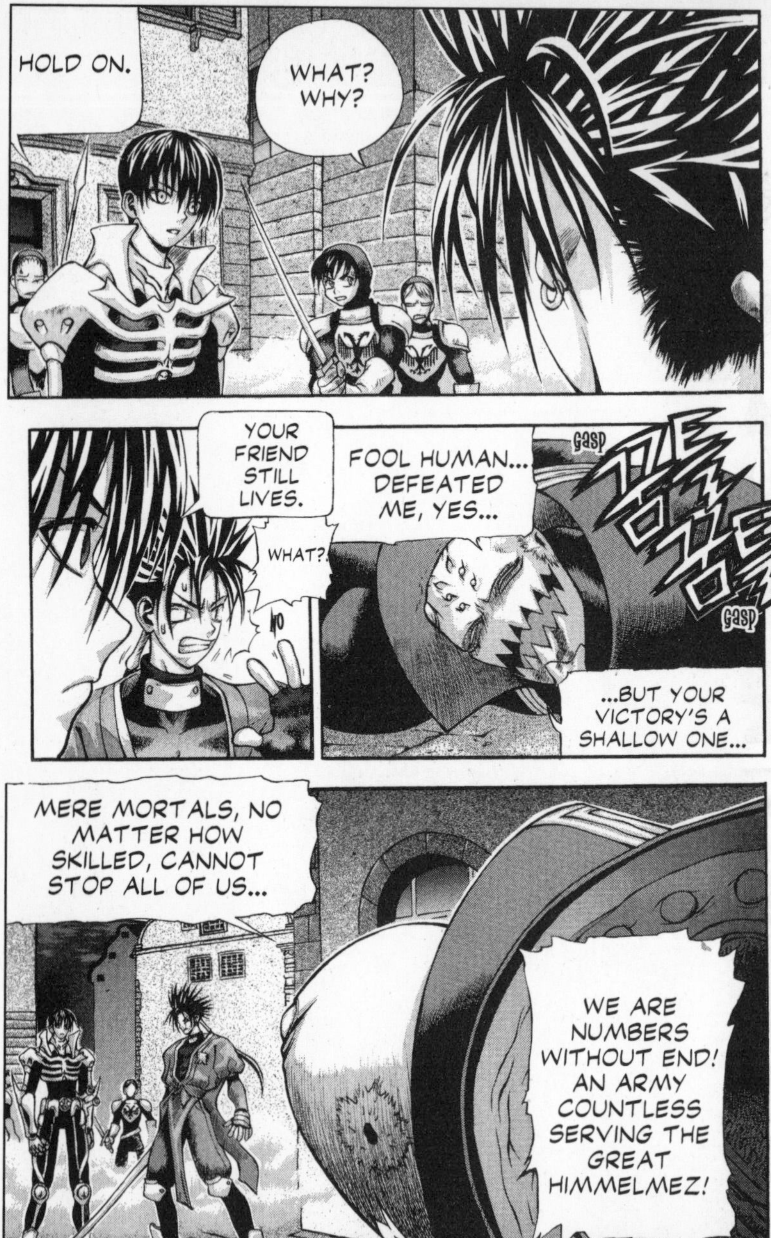
HOLD ON.
WHAT? WHY?
YOUR FRIEND STILL LIVES.
WHAT?
FOOL HUMAN... DEFEATED ME, YES...
GASP
GASP
...BUT YOUR VICTORY'S A SHALLOW ONE...
MERE MORTALS, NO MATTER HOW SKILLED, CANNOT STOP ALL OF US...
WE ARE NUMBERS WITHOUT END! AN ARMY COUNTLESS SERVING THE GREAT HIMMELMEZ!

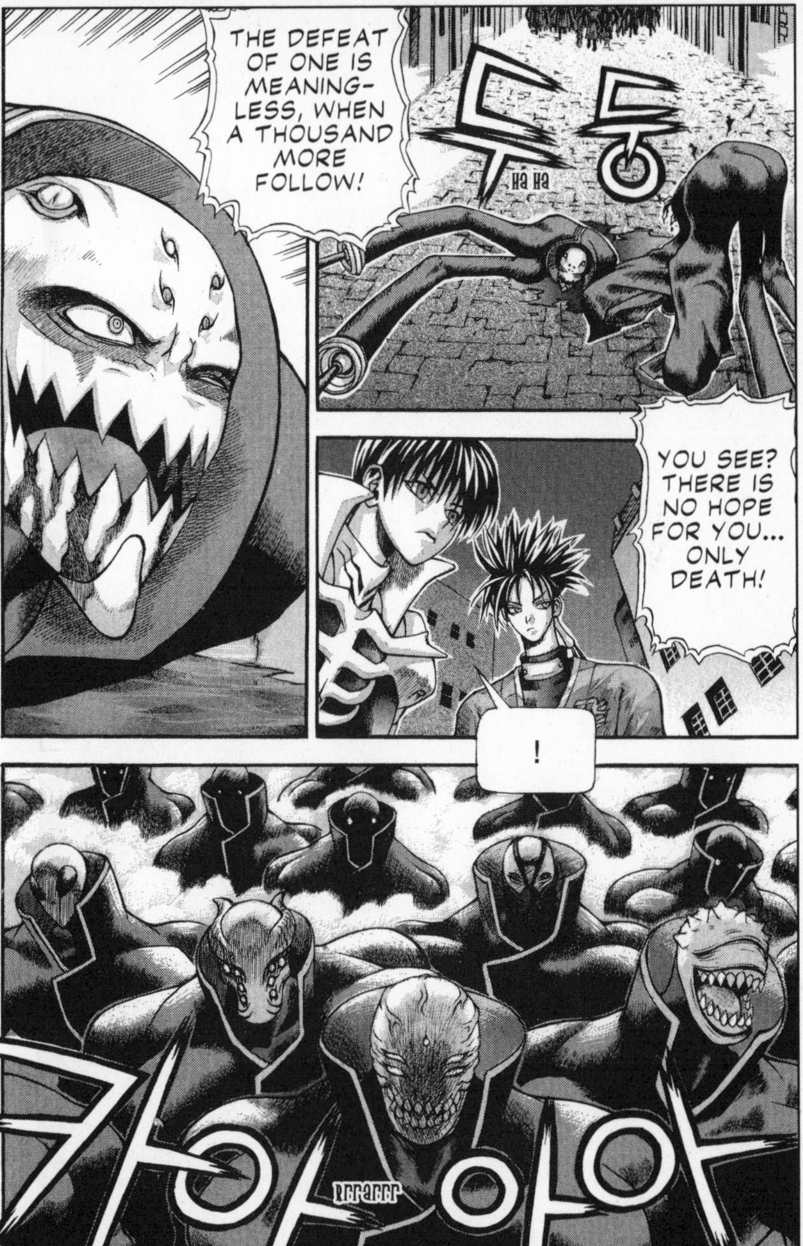
THE DEFEAT OF ONE IS MEANING-LESS, WHEN A THOUSAND MORE FOLLOW!
HA HA
YOU SEE? THERE IS NO HOPE FOR YOU... ONLY DEATH!
!
RRRARRR

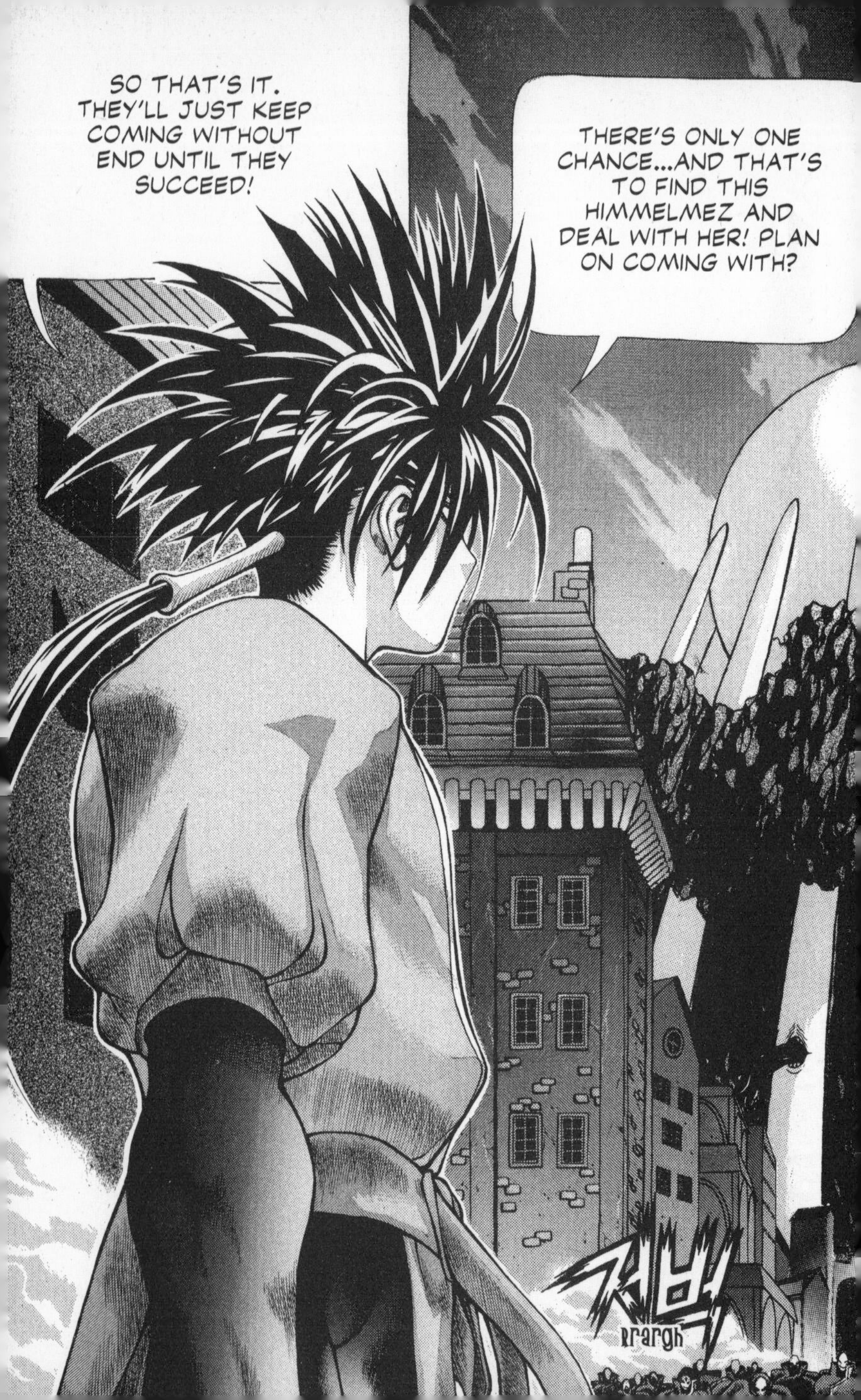
SO THAT'S IT. THEY'LL JUST KEEP COMING WITHOUT END UNTIL THEY SUCCEED!
THERE'S ONLY ONE CHANCE...AND THAT'S TO FIND THIS HIMMELMEZ AND DEAL WITH HER! PLAN ON COMING WITH?
Rrargh

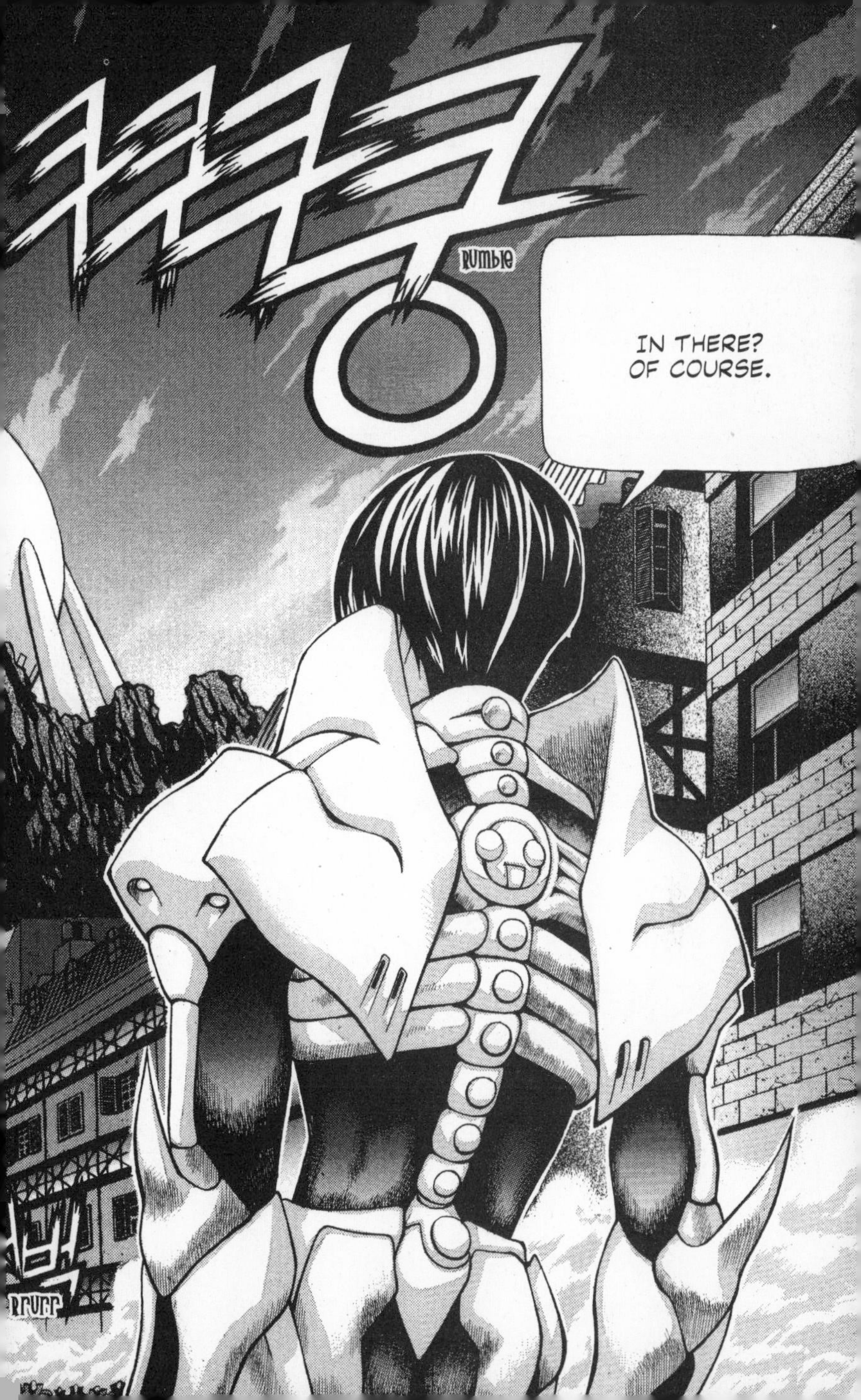
RUMBLE
IN THERE? OF COURSE.
RRURR

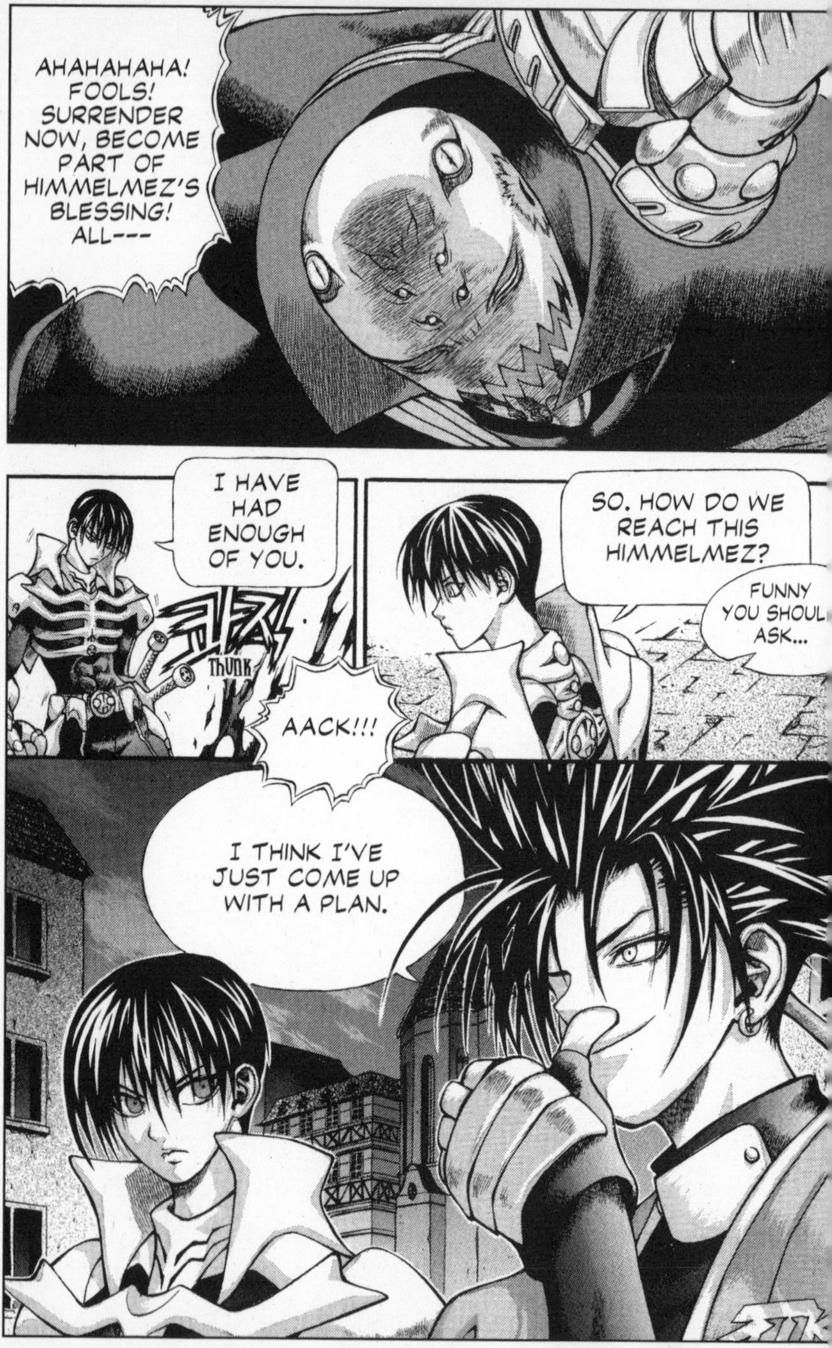
AHAHAHAHA! FOOLS! SURRENDER NOW, BECOME PART OF HIMMELMEZ'S BLESSING! ALL---
I HAVE HAD ENOUGH OF YOU.
THUNK
AACK!!!
SO. HOW DO WE REACH THIS HIMMELMEZ?
FUNNY YOU SHOUL ASK...
I THINK I'VE JUST COME UP WITH A PLAN.

RAGNAROK
라그나로크
IN TO THE ABYSS

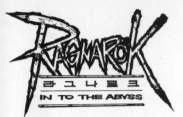

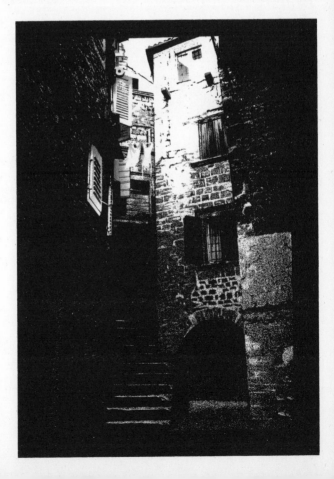

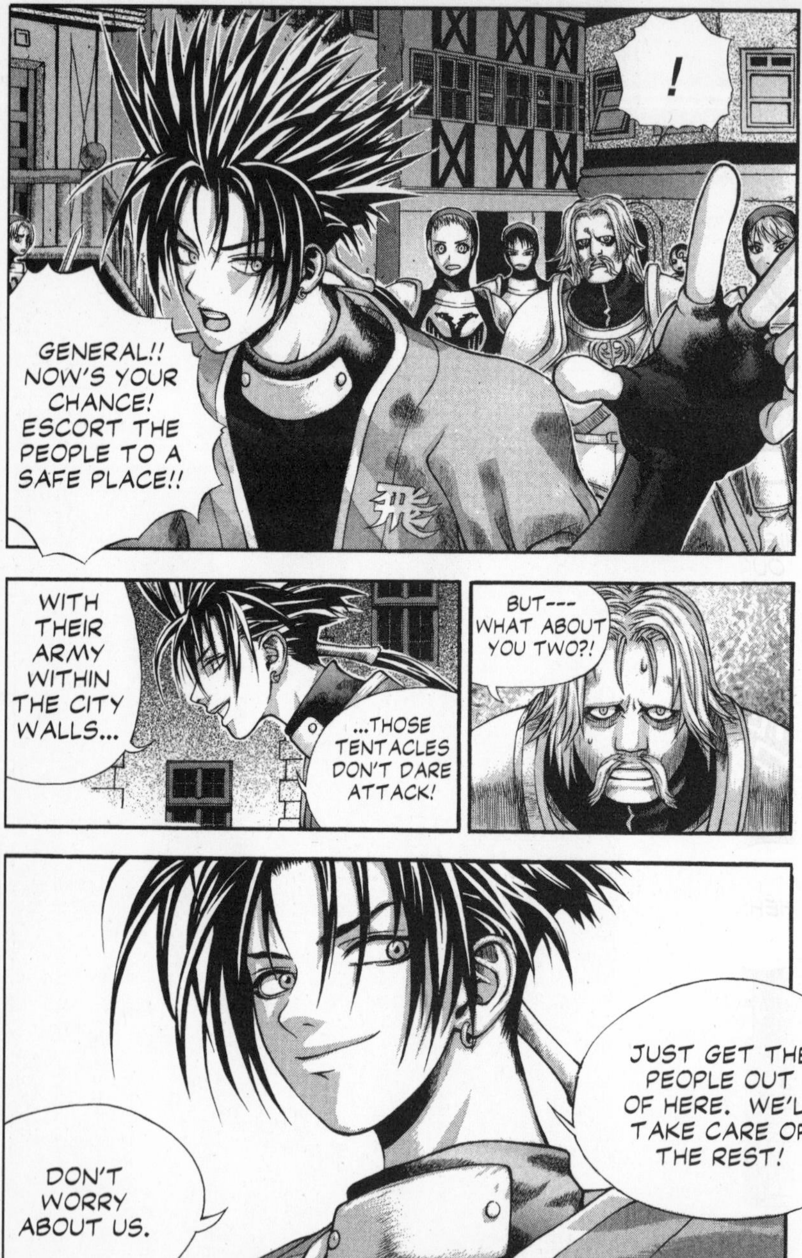
!
GENERAL!! NOW'S YOUR CHANCE! ESCORT THE PEOPLE TO A SAFE PLACE!!
WITH THEIR ARMY WITHIN THE CITY WALLS...
...THOSE TENTACLES DON'T DARE ATTACK!
BUT--- WHAT ABOUT YOU TWO?!
DON'T WORRY ABOUT US.
JUST GET THE PEOPLE OUT OF HERE. WE'LL TAKE CARE OF THE REST!

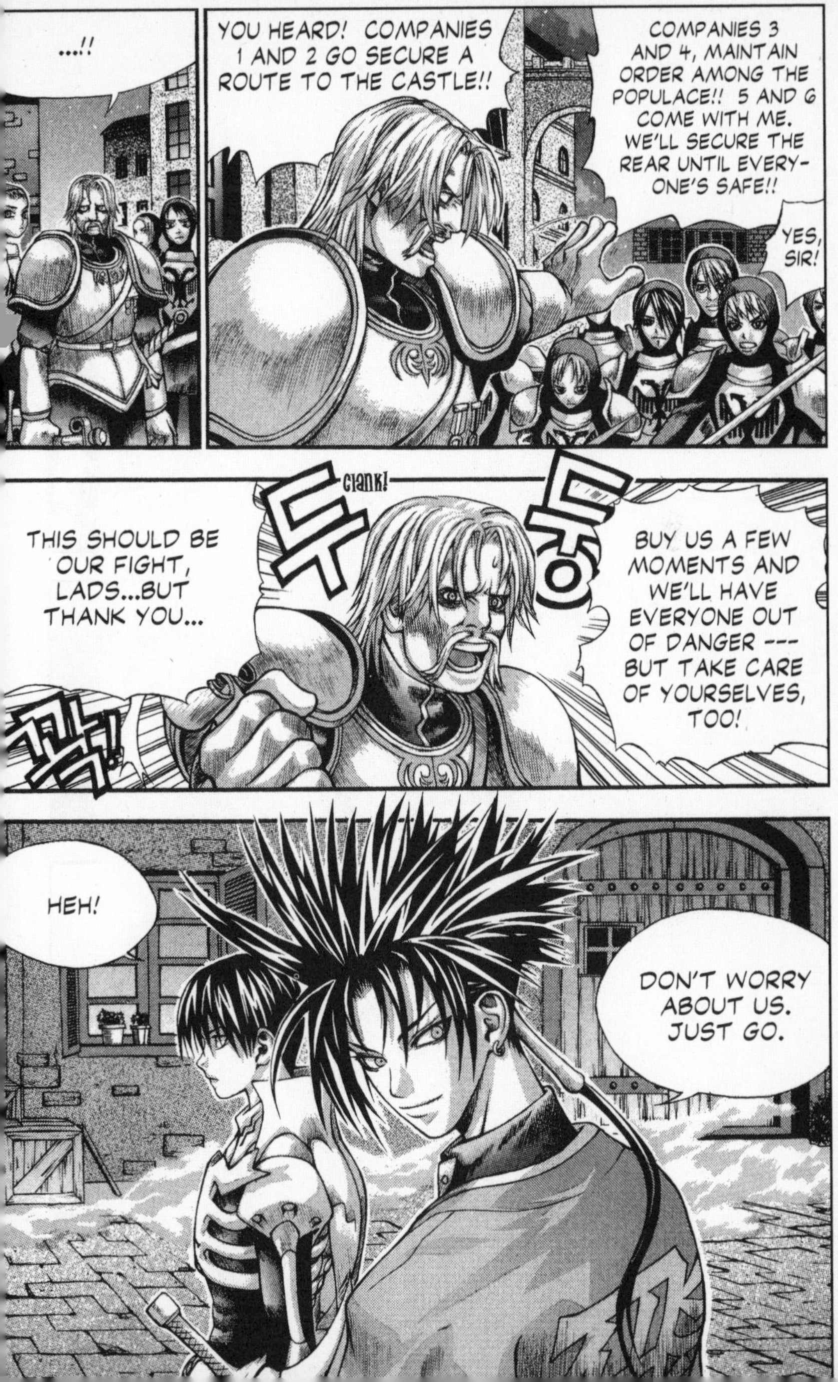
...!!
YOU HEARD! COMPANIES 1 AND 2 GO SECURE A ROUTE TO THE CASTLE!!
COMPANIES 3 AND 4, MAINTAIN ORDER AMONG THE POPULACE!! 5 AND 6 COME WITH ME. WE'LL SECURE THE REAR UNTIL EVERY-ONE'S SAFE!!
YES, SIR!
CLANK!
THIS SHOULD BE OUR FIGHT, LADS...BUT THANK YOU...
BUY US A FEW MOMENTS AND WE'LL HAVE EVERYONE OUT OF DANGER --- BUT TAKE CARE OF YOURSELVES, TOO!
HEH!
DON'T WORRY ABOUT US. JUST GO.

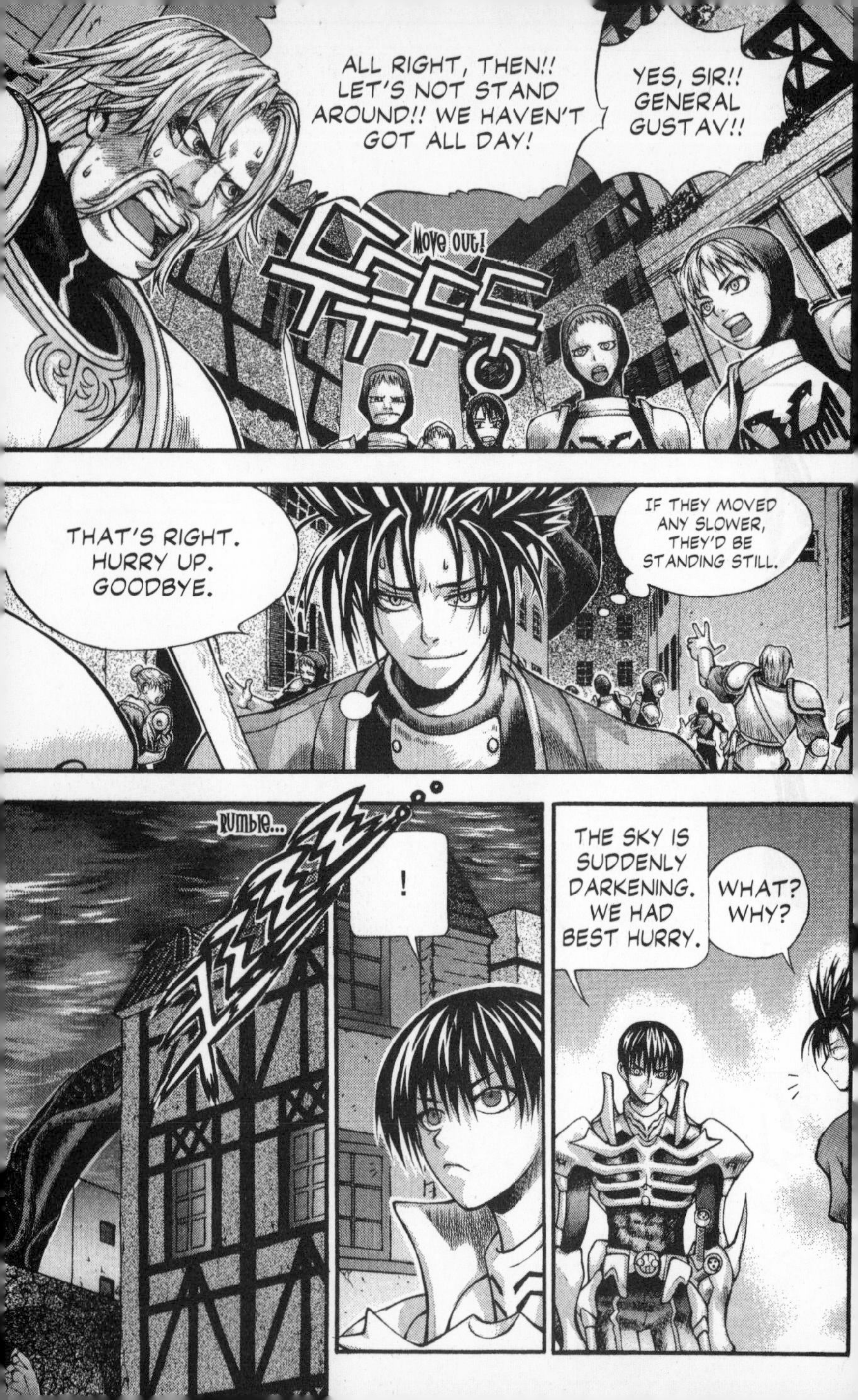
ALL RIGHT, THEN!! LET'S NOT STAND AROUND!! WE HAVEN'T GOT ALL DAY!
YES, SIR!! GENERAL GUSTAV!!
Move out!
THAT'S RIGHT. HURRY UP. GOODBYE.
IF THEY MOVED ANY SLOWER, THEY'D BE STANDING STILL.
Rumble...
!
THE SKY IS SUDDENLY DARKENING. WE HAD BEST HURRY.
WHAT? WHY?

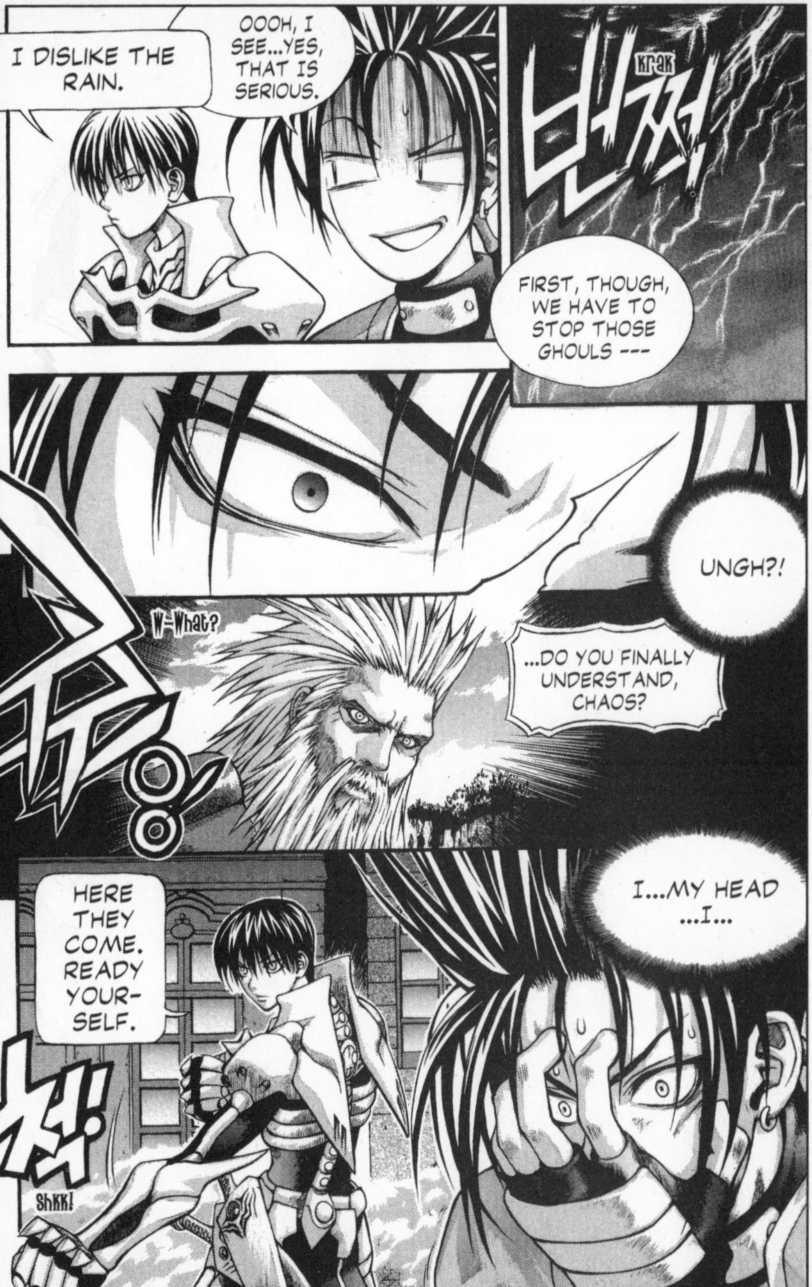
I DISLIKE THE RAIN.
OOOH, I SEE...YES, THAT IS SERIOUS.
KRAK
FIRST, THOUGH, WE HAVE TO STOP THOSE GHOULS ---
UNGH?!
W-What?
...DO YOU FINALLY UNDERSTAND, CHAOS?
HERE THEY COME. READY YOUR-SELF.
I...MY HEAD ...I...
Shkk!

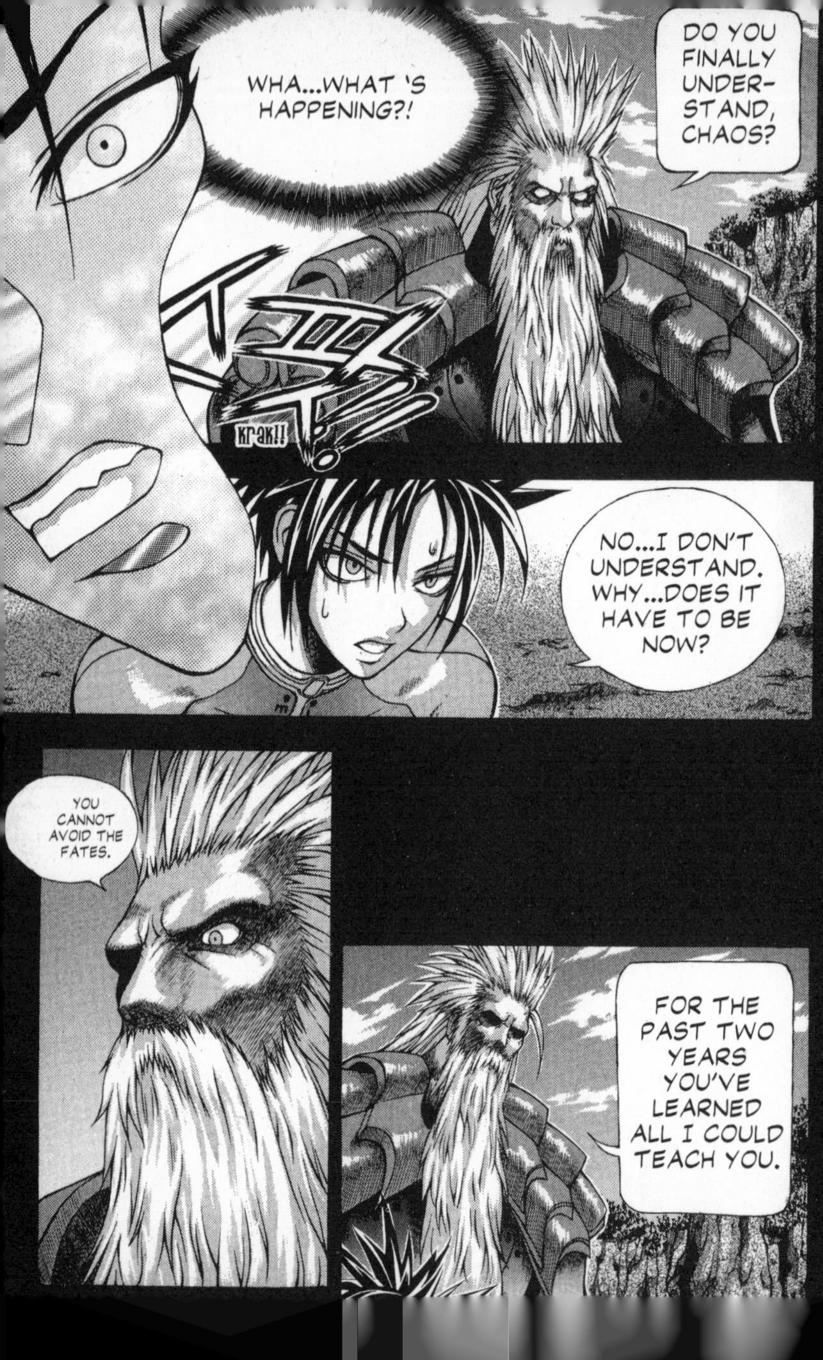
WHA...WHAT 'S HAPPENING?!
DO YOU FINALLY UNDER-STAND, CHAOS?
KRAK!!
NO...I DON'T UNDERSTAND. WHY...DOES IT HAVE TO BE NOW?
YOU CANNOT AVOID THE FATES.
FOR THE PAST TWO YEARS YOU'VE LEARNED ALL I COULD TEACH YOU.

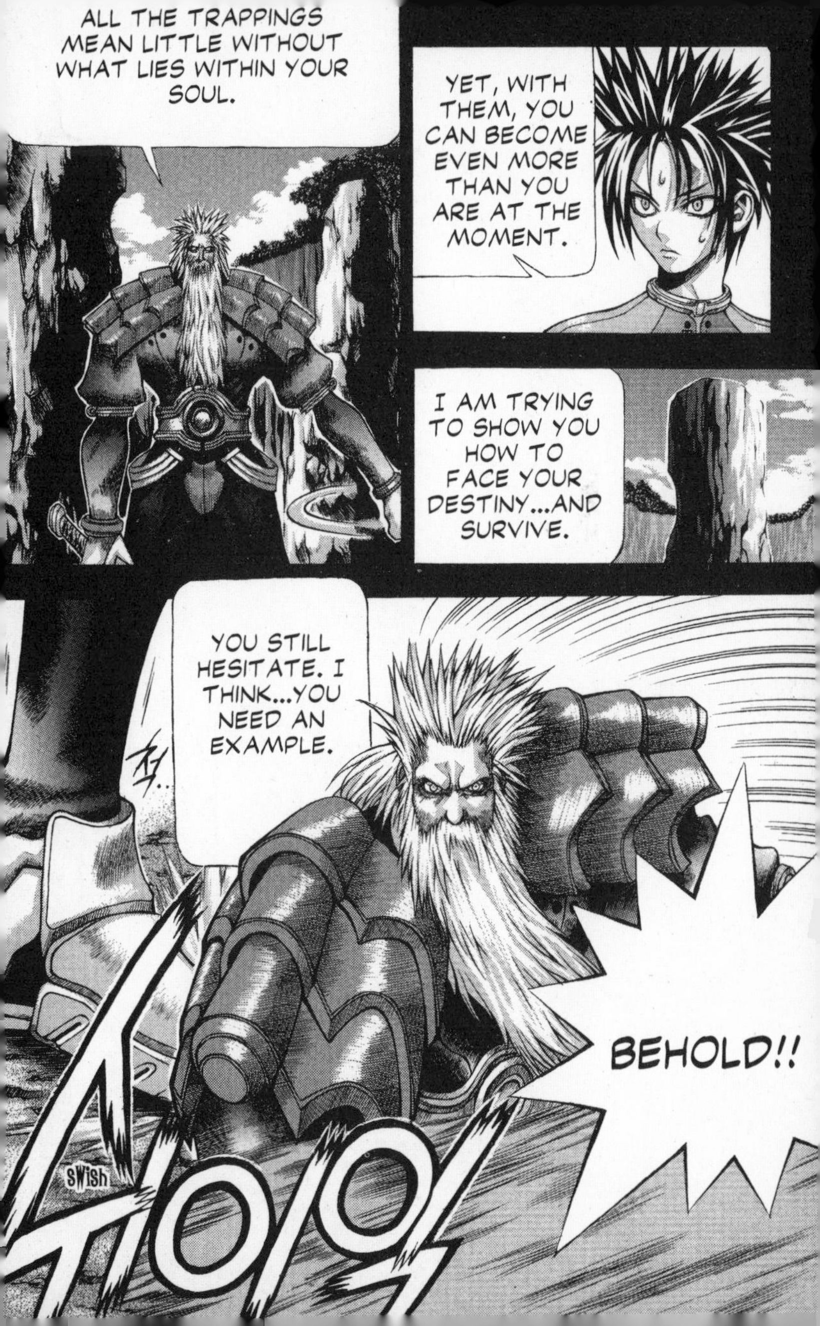
ALL THE TRAPPINGS MEAN LITTLE WITHOUT WHAT LIES WITHIN YOUR SOUL.
YET, WITH THEM, YOU CAN BECOME EVEN MORE THAN YOU ARE AT THE MOMENT.
I AM TRYING TO SHOW YOU HOW TO FACE YOUR DESTINY...AND SURVIVE.
YOU STILL HESITATE. I THINK...YOU NEED AN EXAMPLE.
SWISH
BEHOLD!!

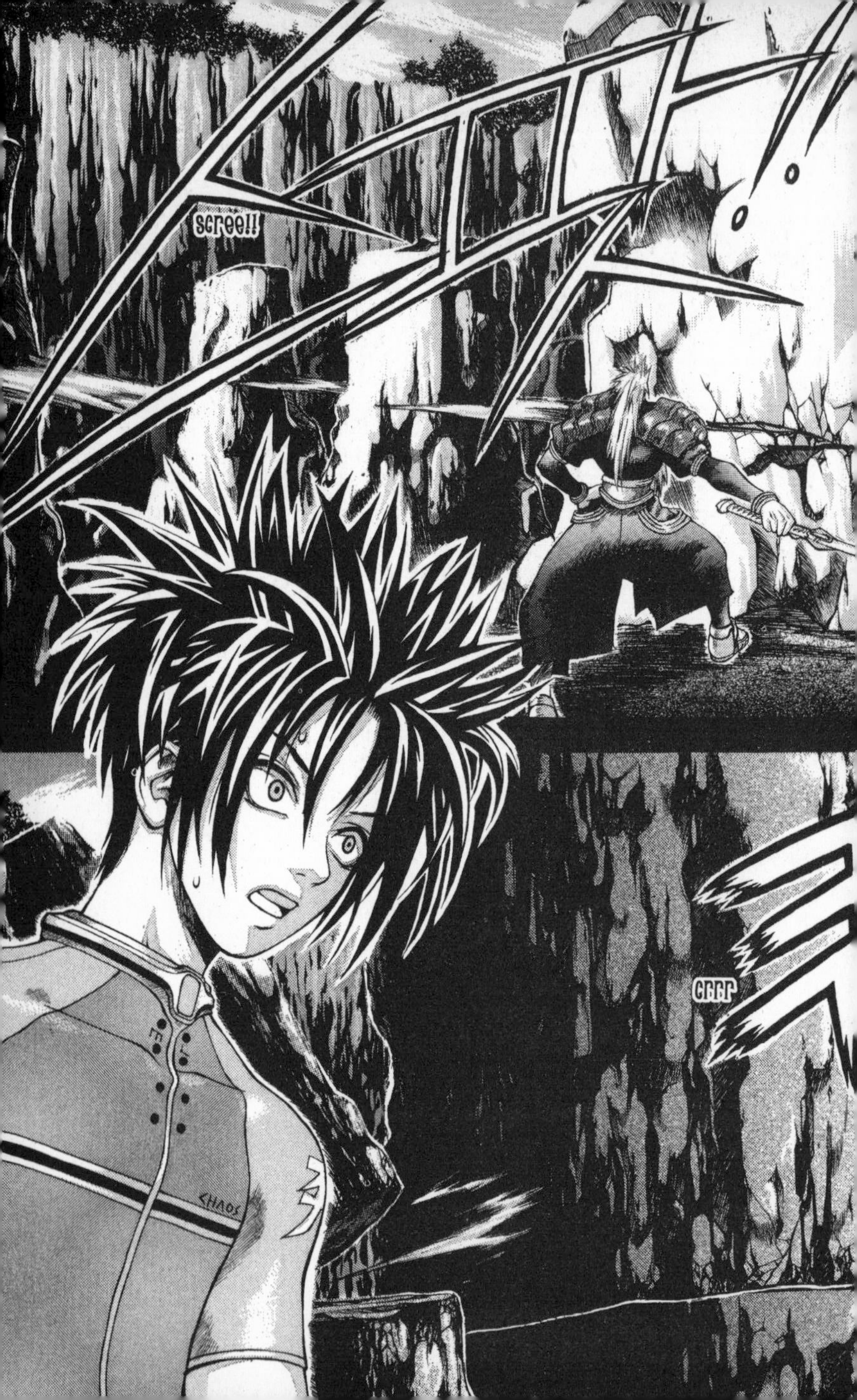
scree!!
crrr

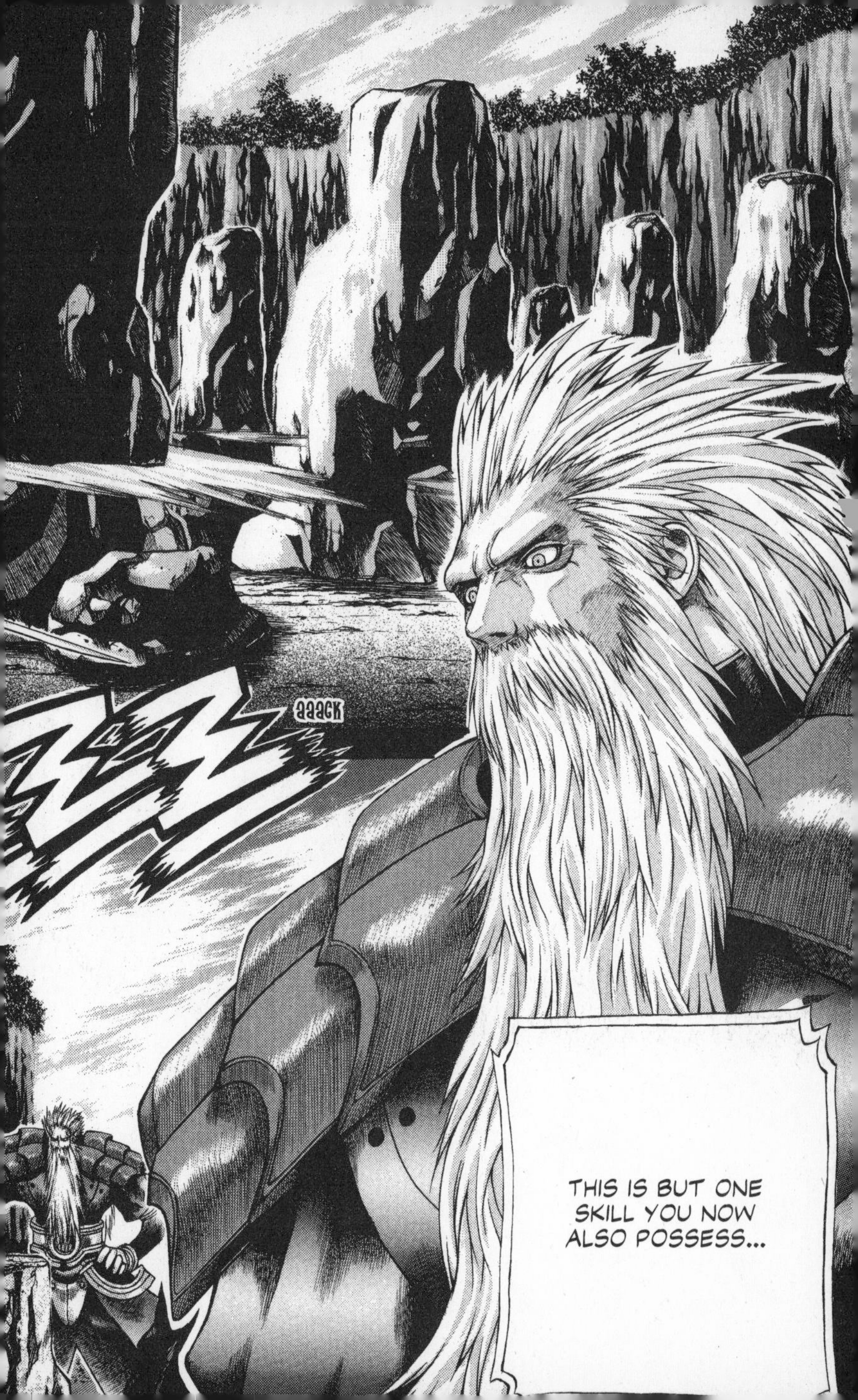
aaack
THIS IS BUT ONE SKILL YOU NOW ALSO POSSESS...

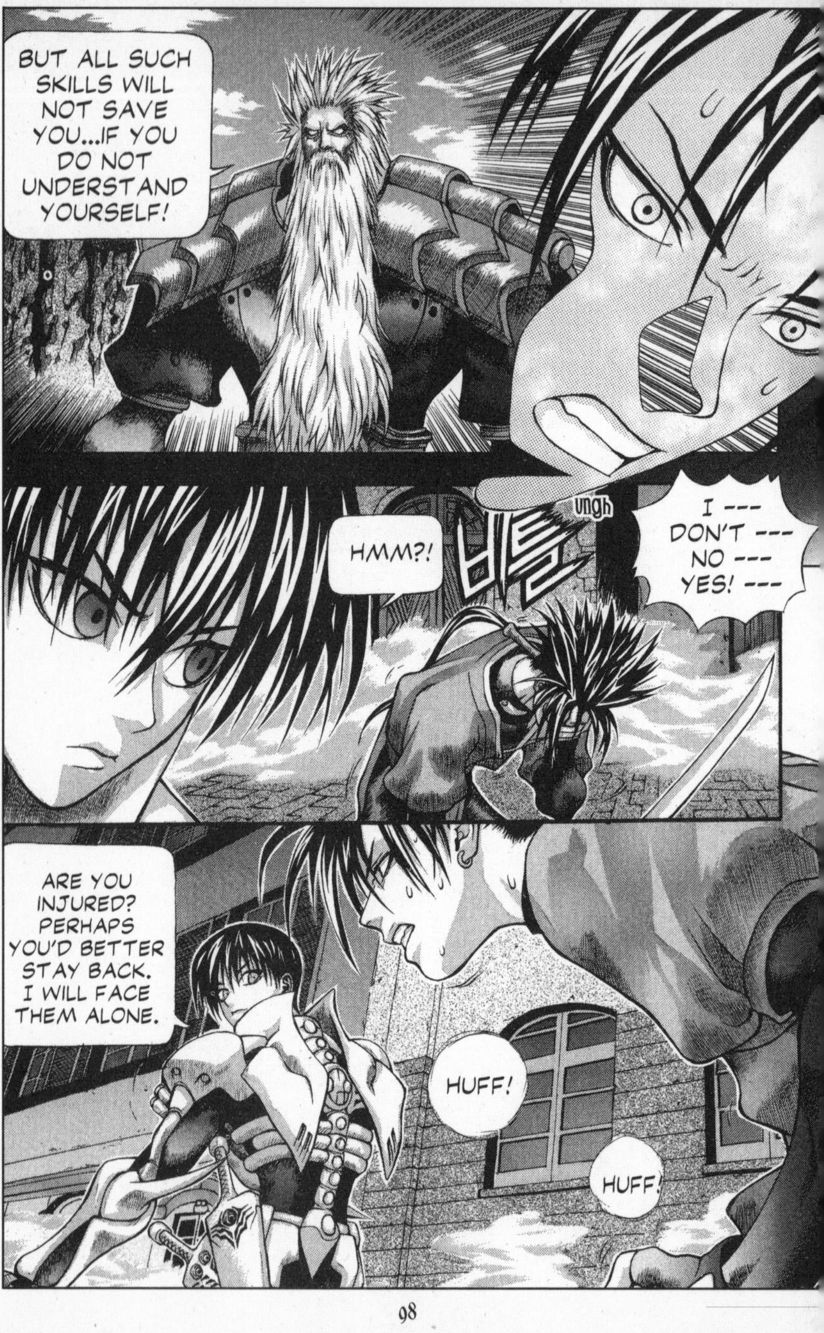
BUT ALL SUCH SKILLS WILL NOT SAVE YOU...IF YOU DO NOT UNDERSTAND YOURSELF!
HMM?!
비틀
ungh
I --- DON'T --- NO --- YES! ---
ARE YOU INJURED? PERHAPS YOU'D BETTER STAY BACK. I WILL FACE THEM ALONE.
HUFF!
HUFF!

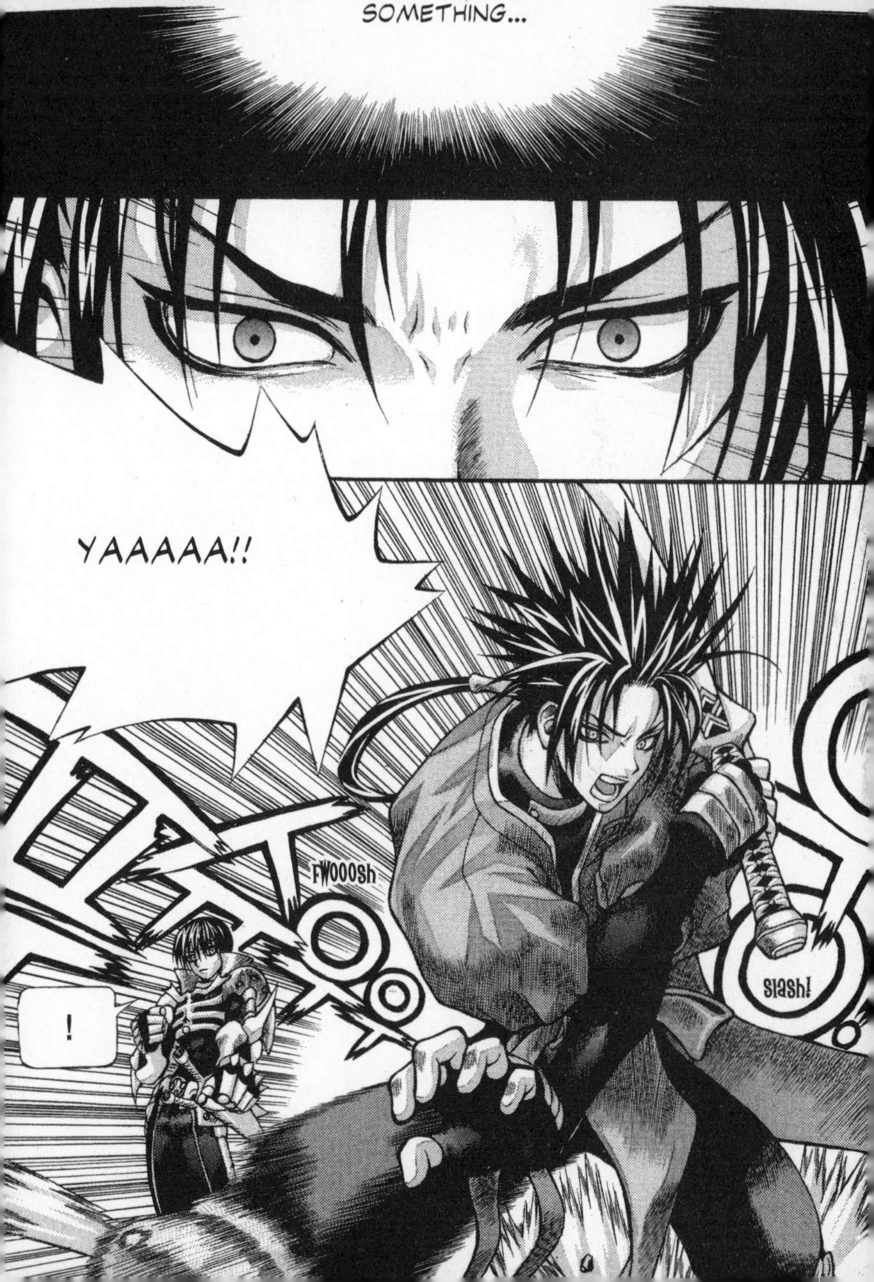
SOMETHING...
YAAAAA!!
FWOOOSH
SLASH!
!

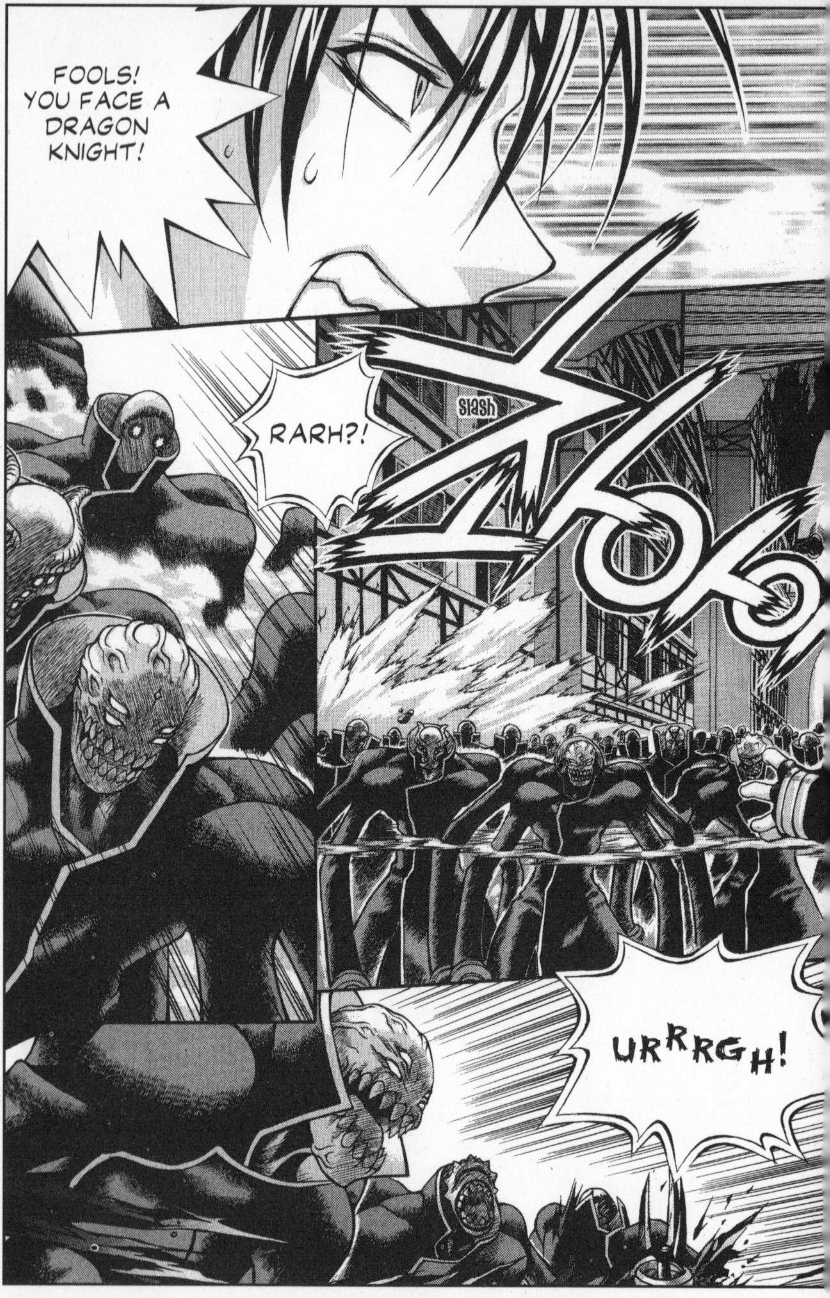
FOOLS! YOU FACE A DRAGON KNIGHT!
RARH?!
SLASH
URRRGH!

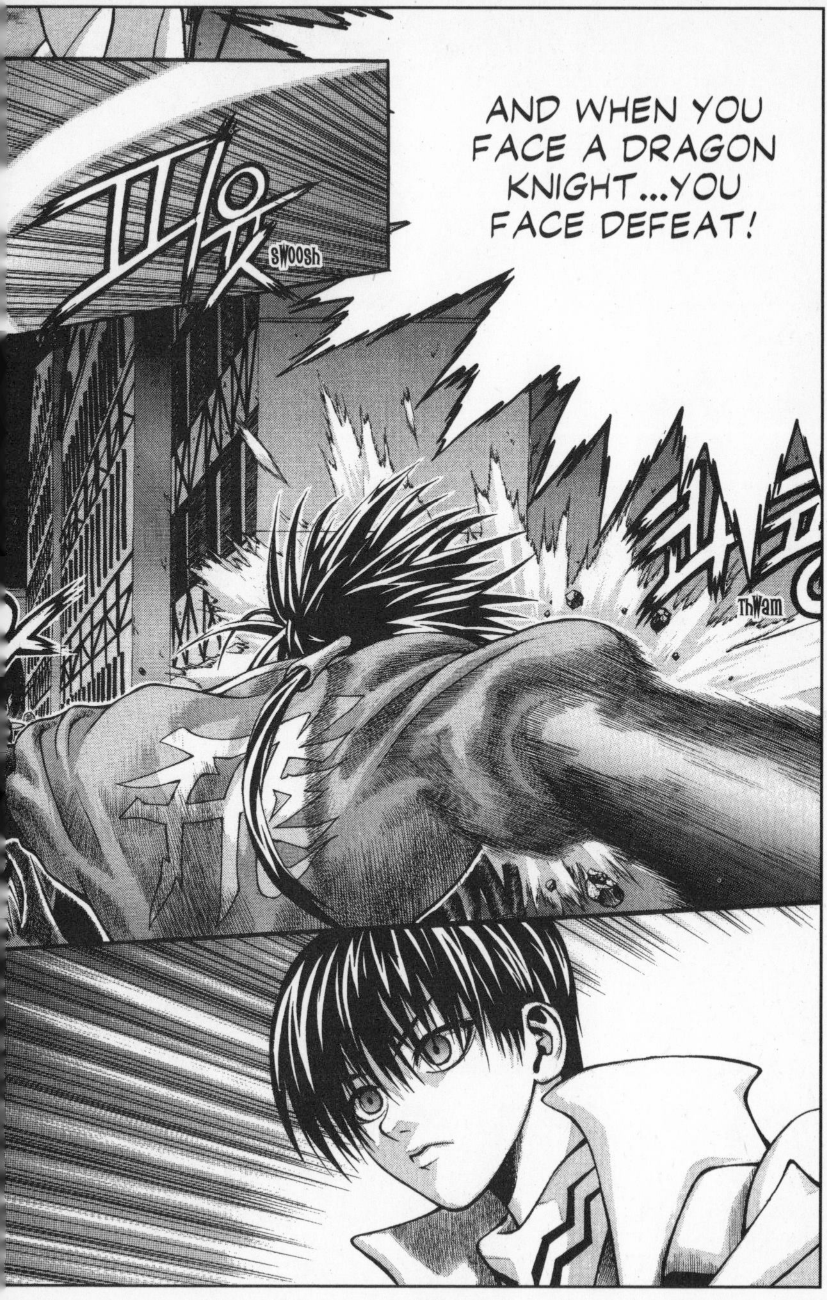
AND WHEN YOU FACE A DRAGON KNIGHT...YOU FACE DEFEAT!
SWOOSH
THWAM

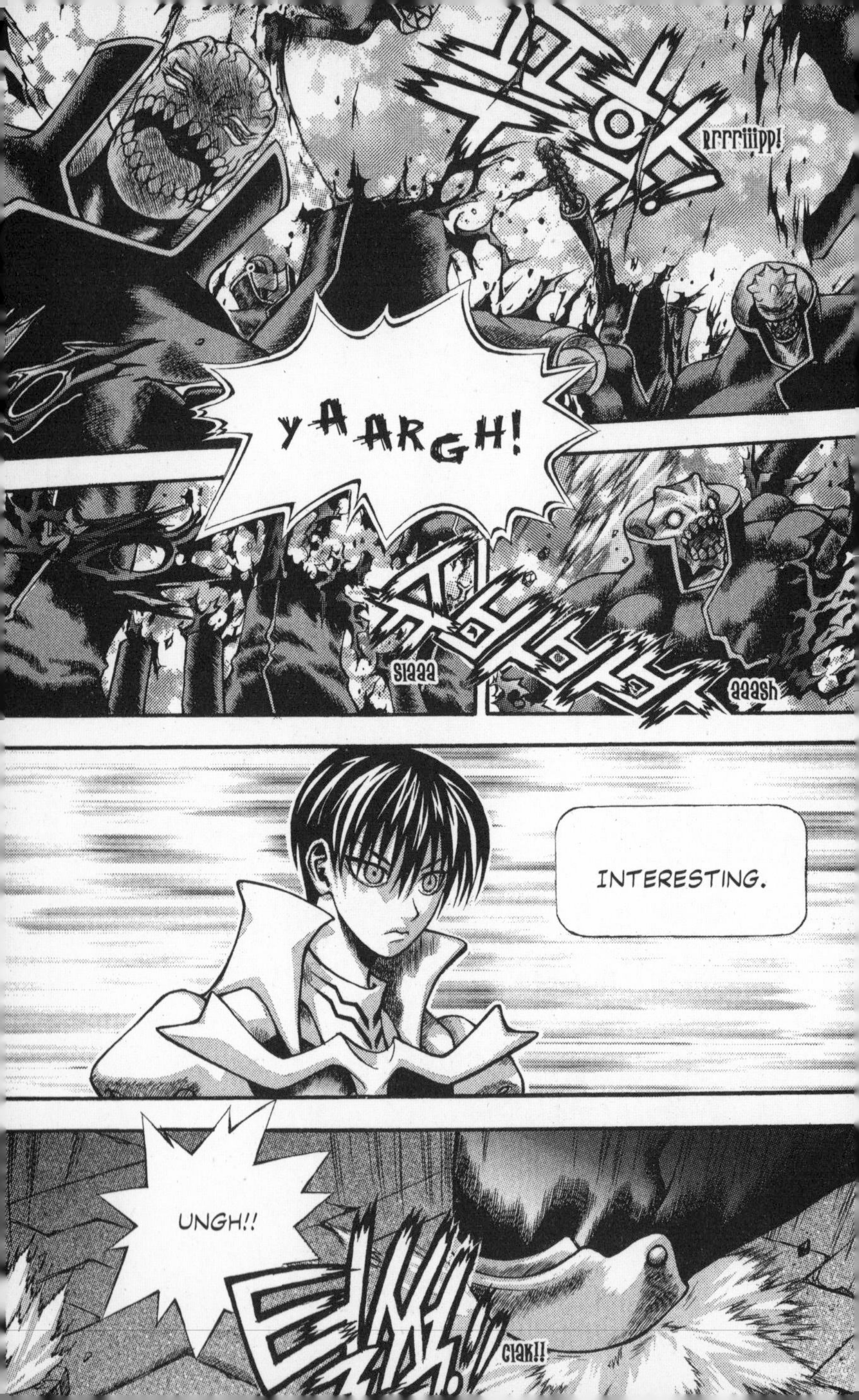
Rrrriiipp!
YAARGH!
slaaa
aaash
INTERESTING.
UNGH!!
clak!!

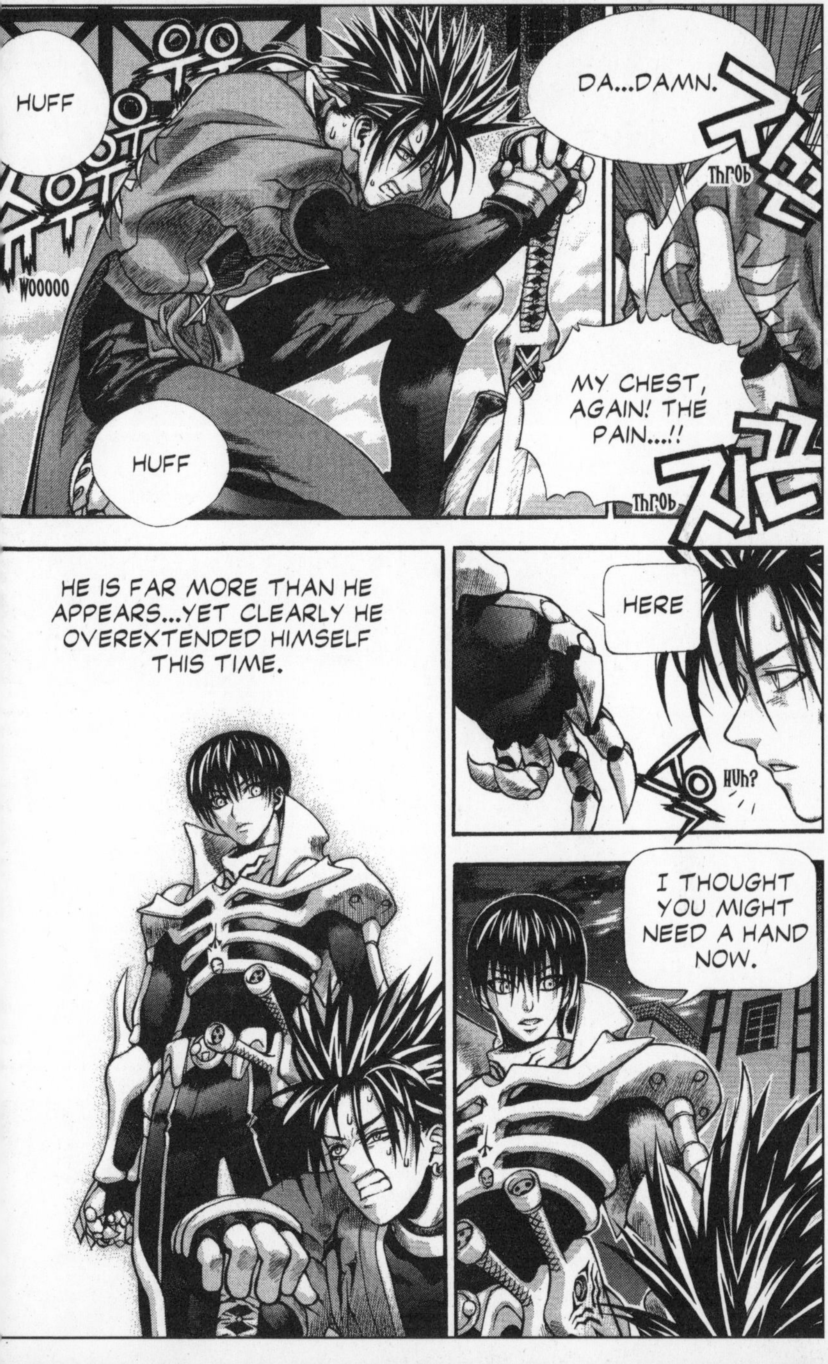
HUFF
WOOOOO
HUFF
DA...DAMN.
Throb
MY CHEST, AGAIN! THE PAIN...!!
Throb
HE IS FAR MORE THAN HE APPEARS...YET CLEARLY HE OVEREXTENDED HIMSELF THIS TIME.
HERE
HUh?
I THOUGHT YOU MIGHT NEED A HAND NOW.

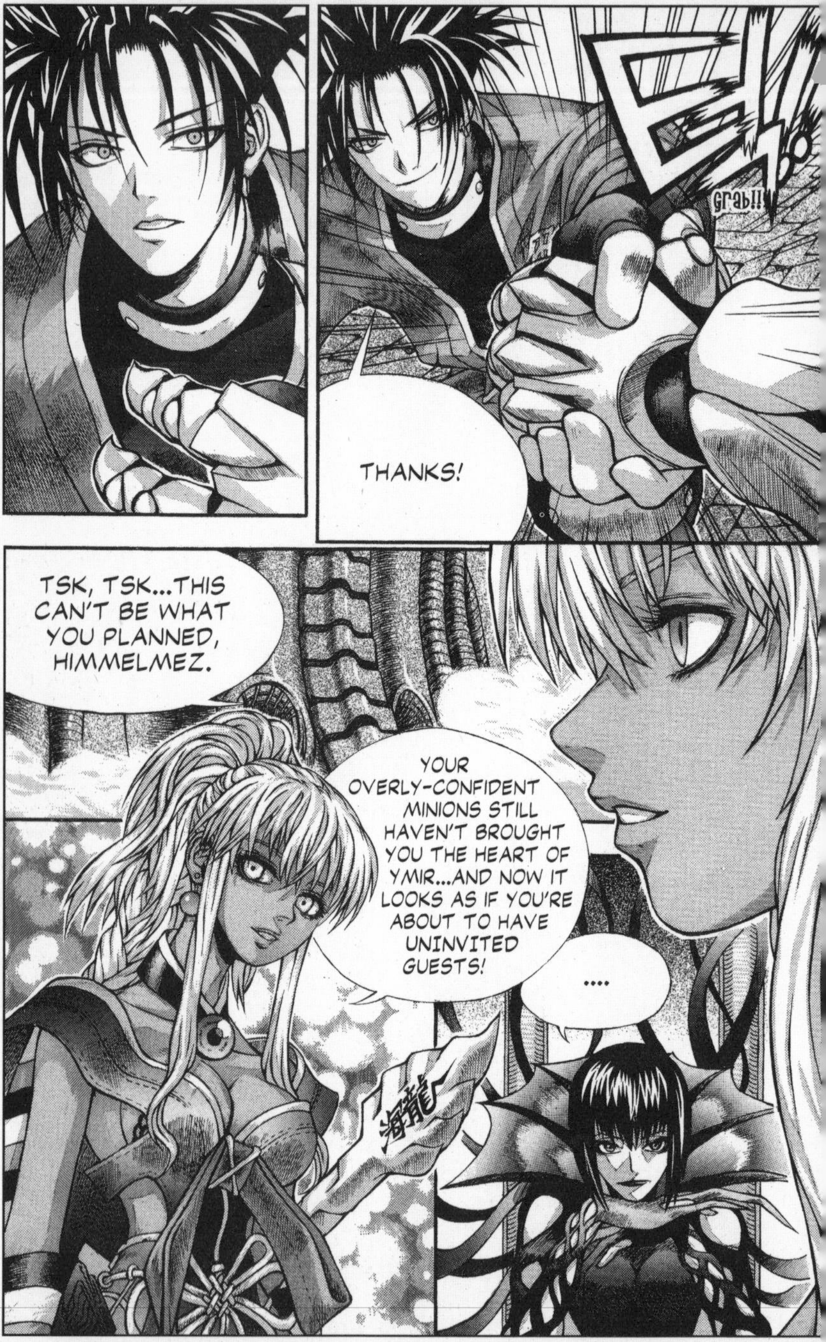
GRAB!!
THANKS!
TSK, TSK...THIS CAN'T BE WHAT YOU PLANNED, HIMMELMEZ.
YOUR OVERLY-CONFIDENT MINIONS STILL HAVEN'T BROUGHT YOU THE HEART OF YMIR...AND NOW IT LOOKS AS IF YOU'RE ABOUT TO HAVE UNINVITED GUESTS!
....
海龍

RAGNAROK
라그나로크
IN TO THE ABYSS

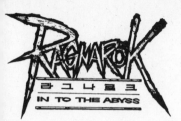

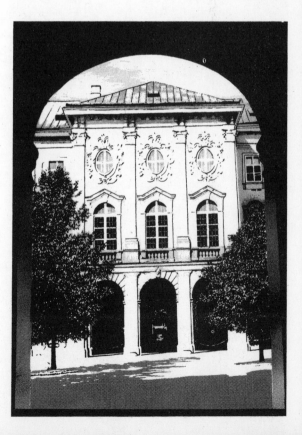

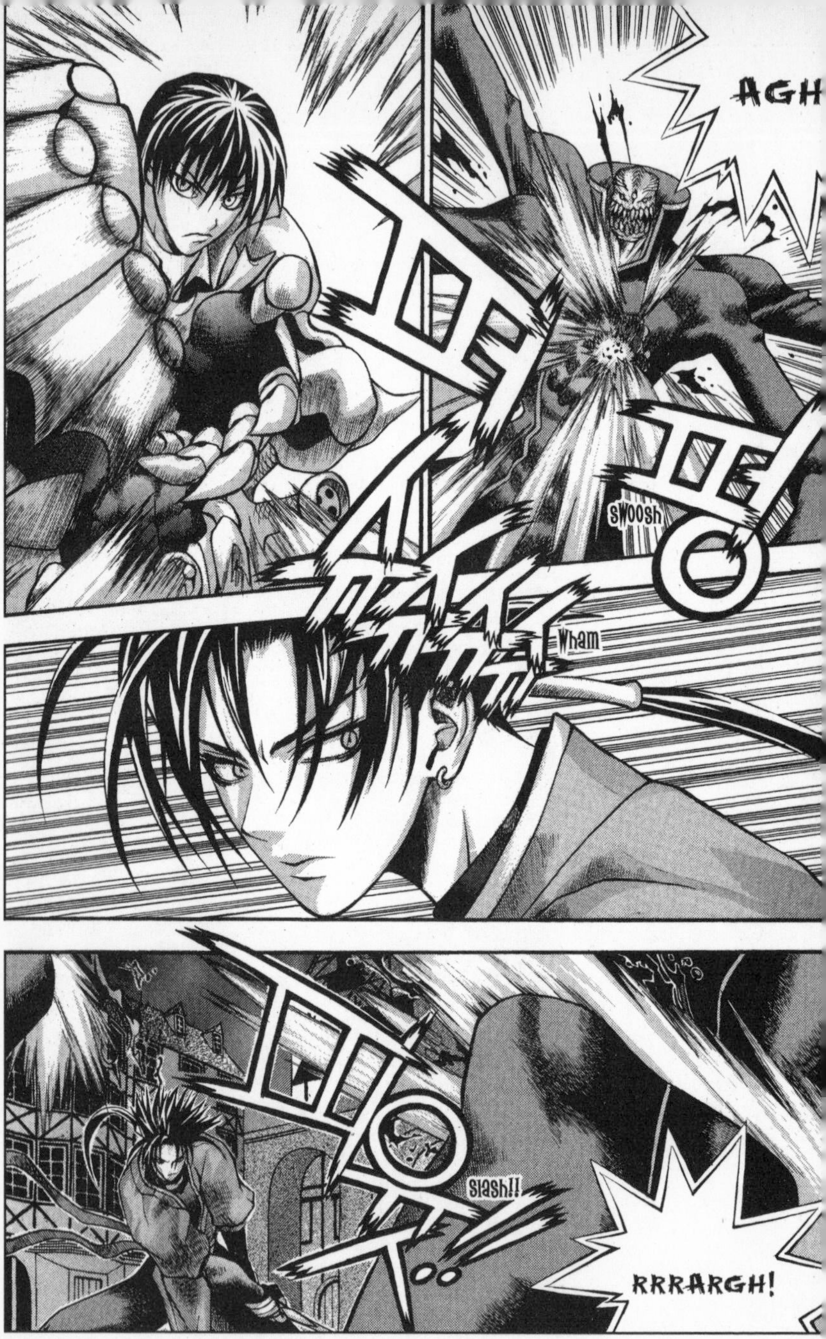
AGH
SWOOSH
Wham
slash!!
RRRARGH!

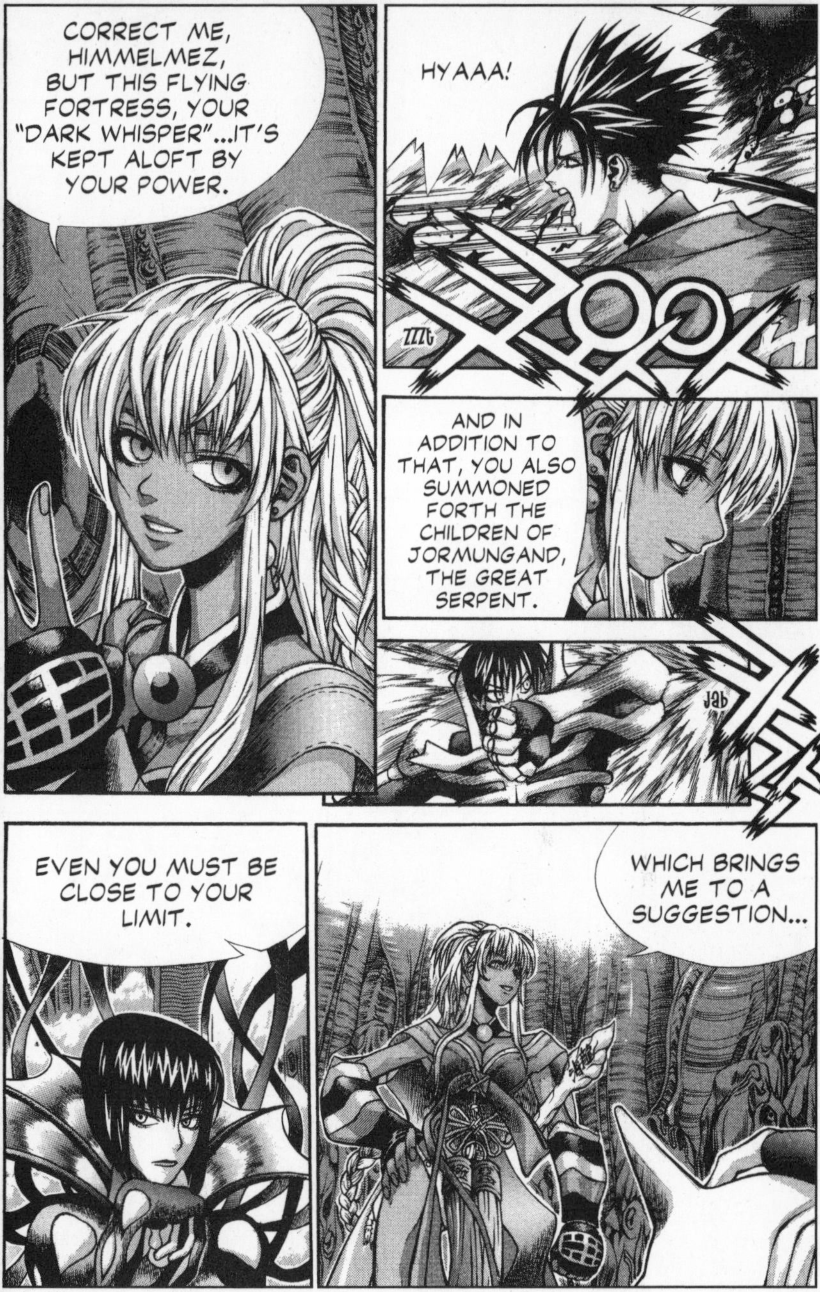
CORRECT ME, HIMMELMEZ, BUT THIS FLYING FORTRESS, YOUR "DARK WHISPER"...IT'S KEPT ALOFT BY YOUR POWER.
HYAAA!
ZZZT
AND IN ADDITION TO THAT, YOU ALSO SUMMONED FORTH THE CHILDREN OF JORMUNGAND, THE GREAT SERPENT.
JAB
EVEN YOU MUST BE CLOSE TO YOUR LIMIT.
WHICH BRINGS ME TO A SUGGESTION...

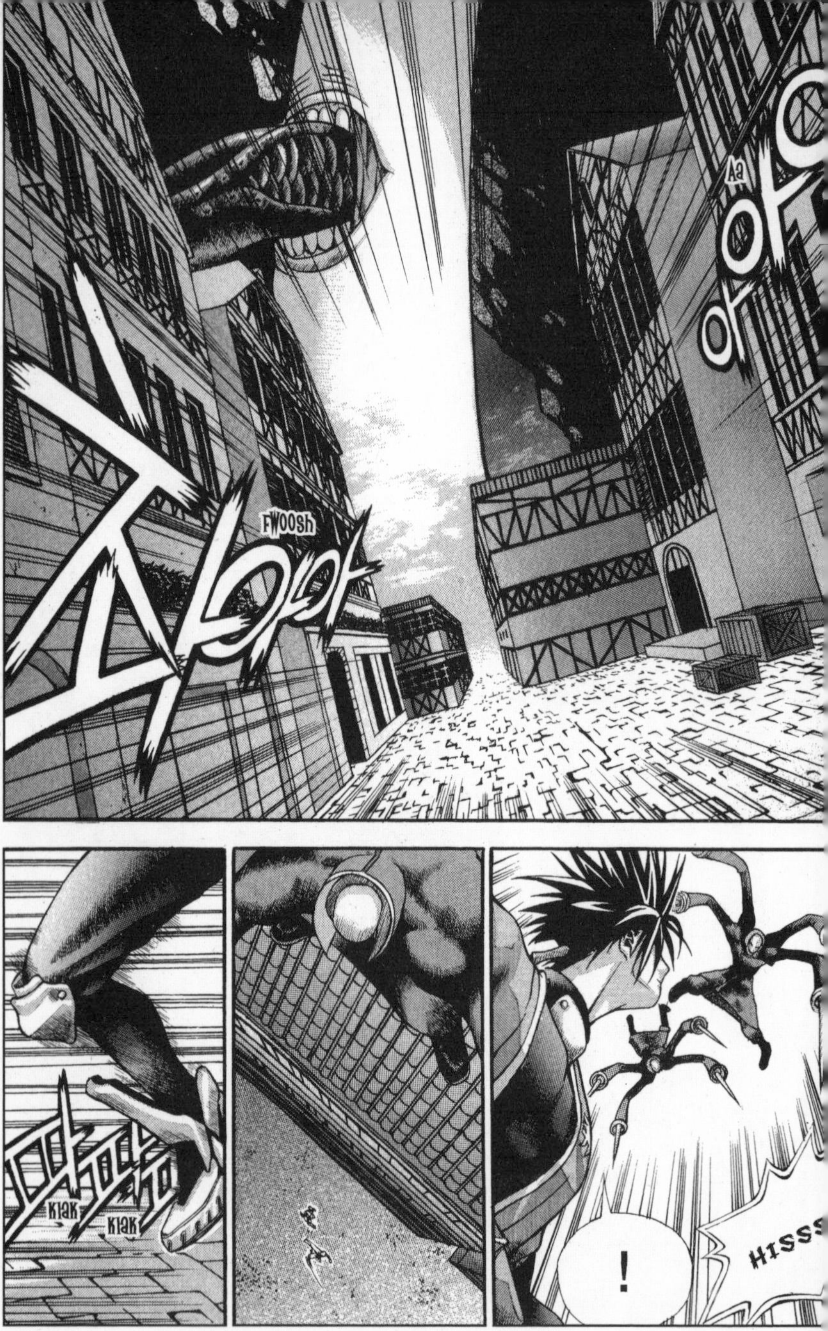
Aa
FWOOSH
KlAK
KlAK
!
HISSS

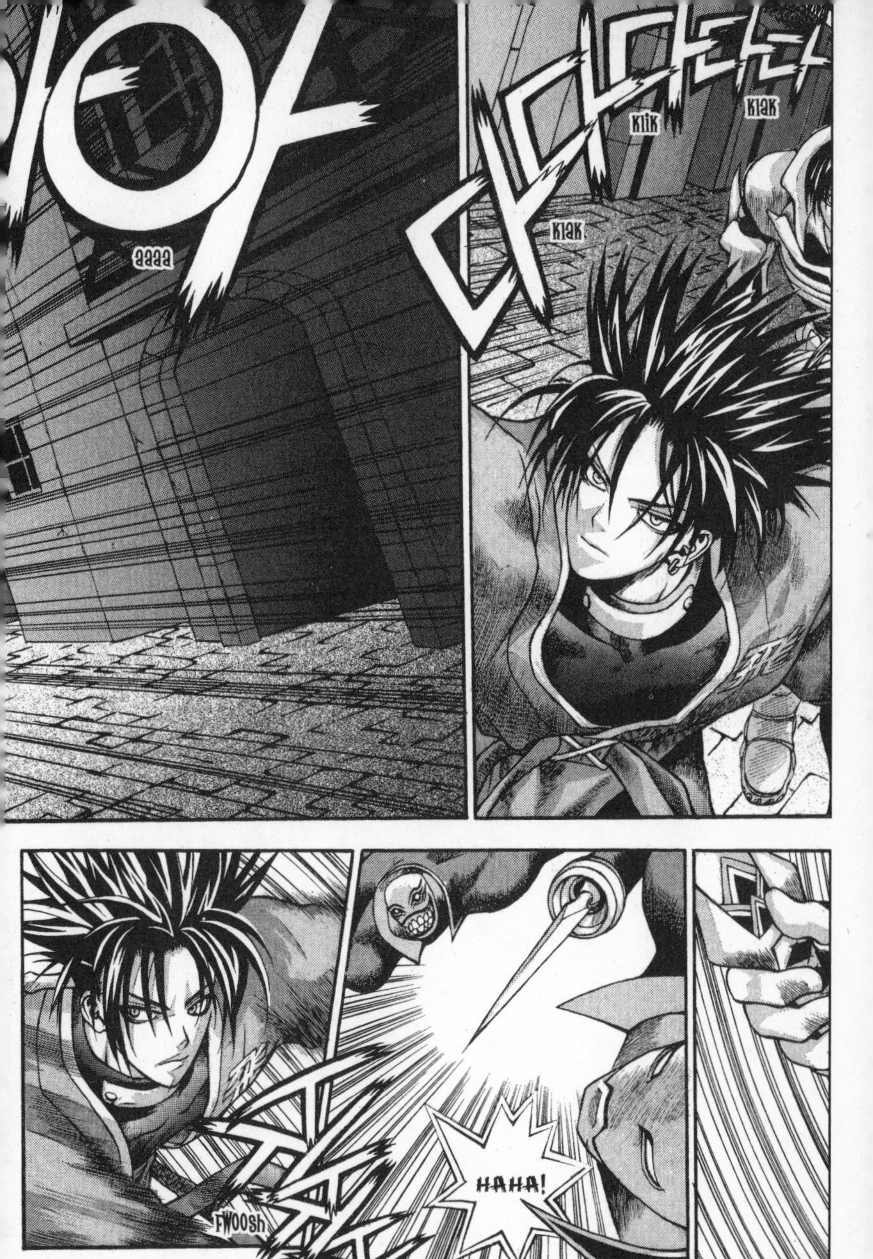
aaaa
Klik
Klak
Klak
fwoosh
HAHA!

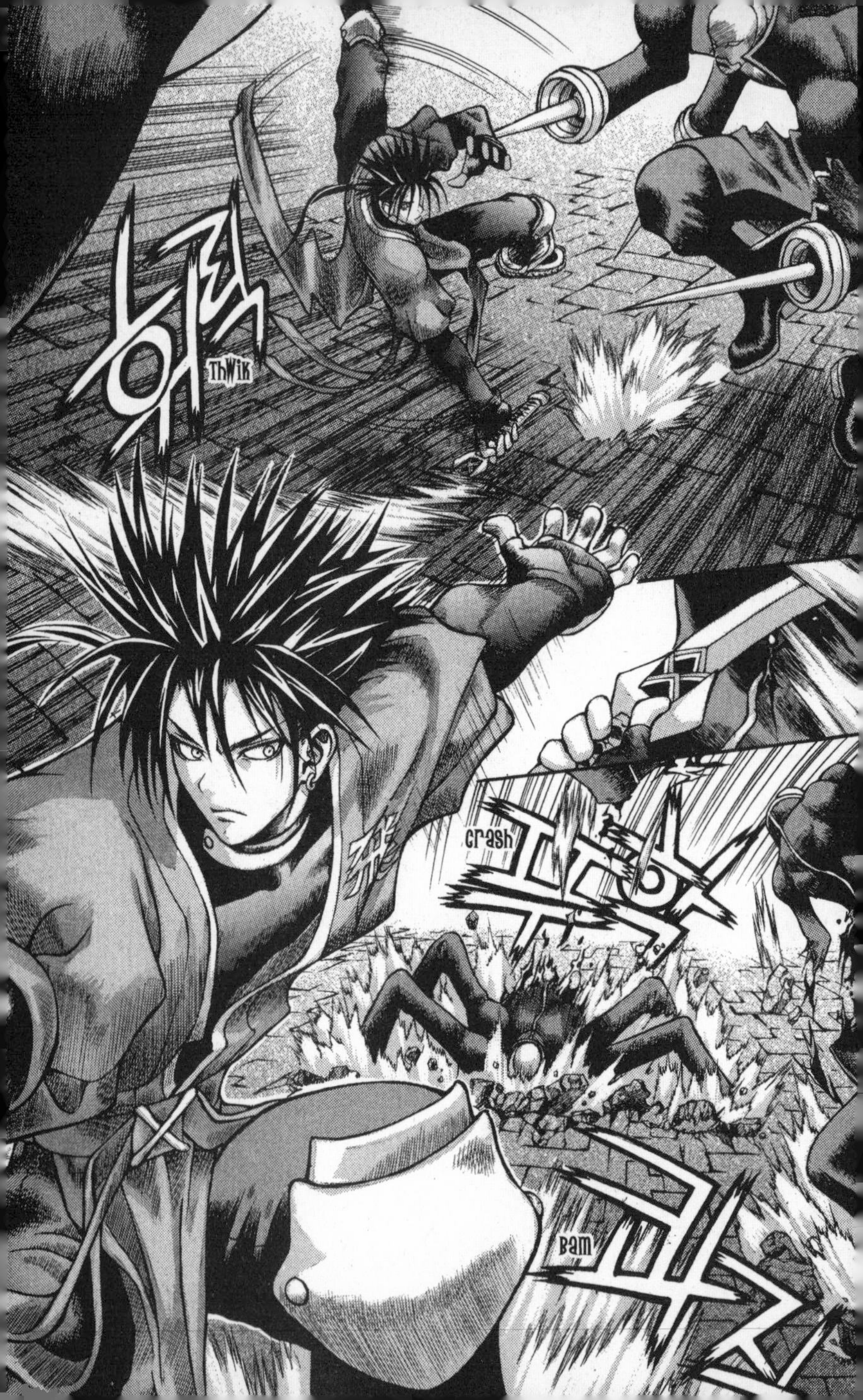
ThWiK
Crash
Bam

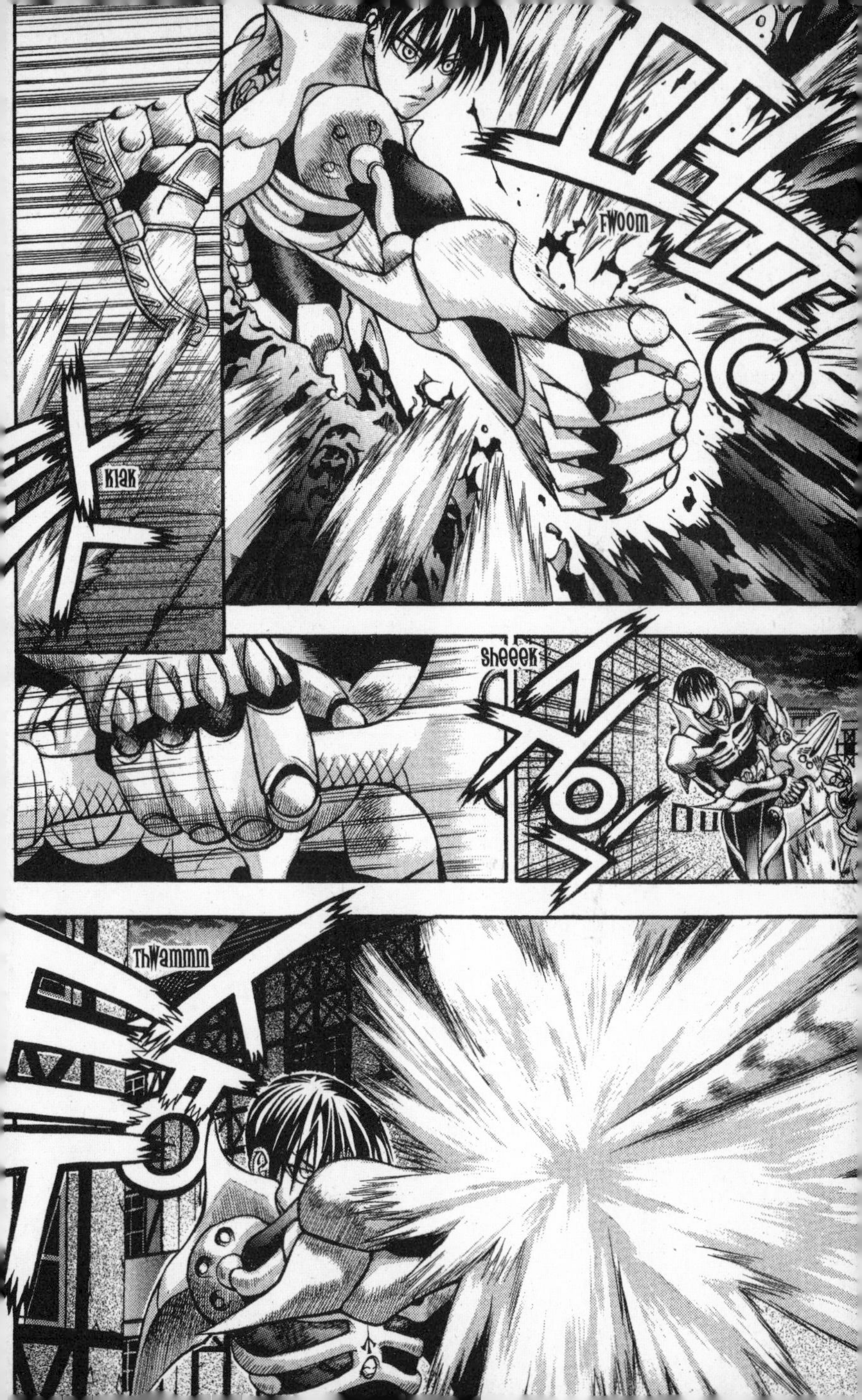
KLAK
FWOOM
SHEEEK
THWAMMM

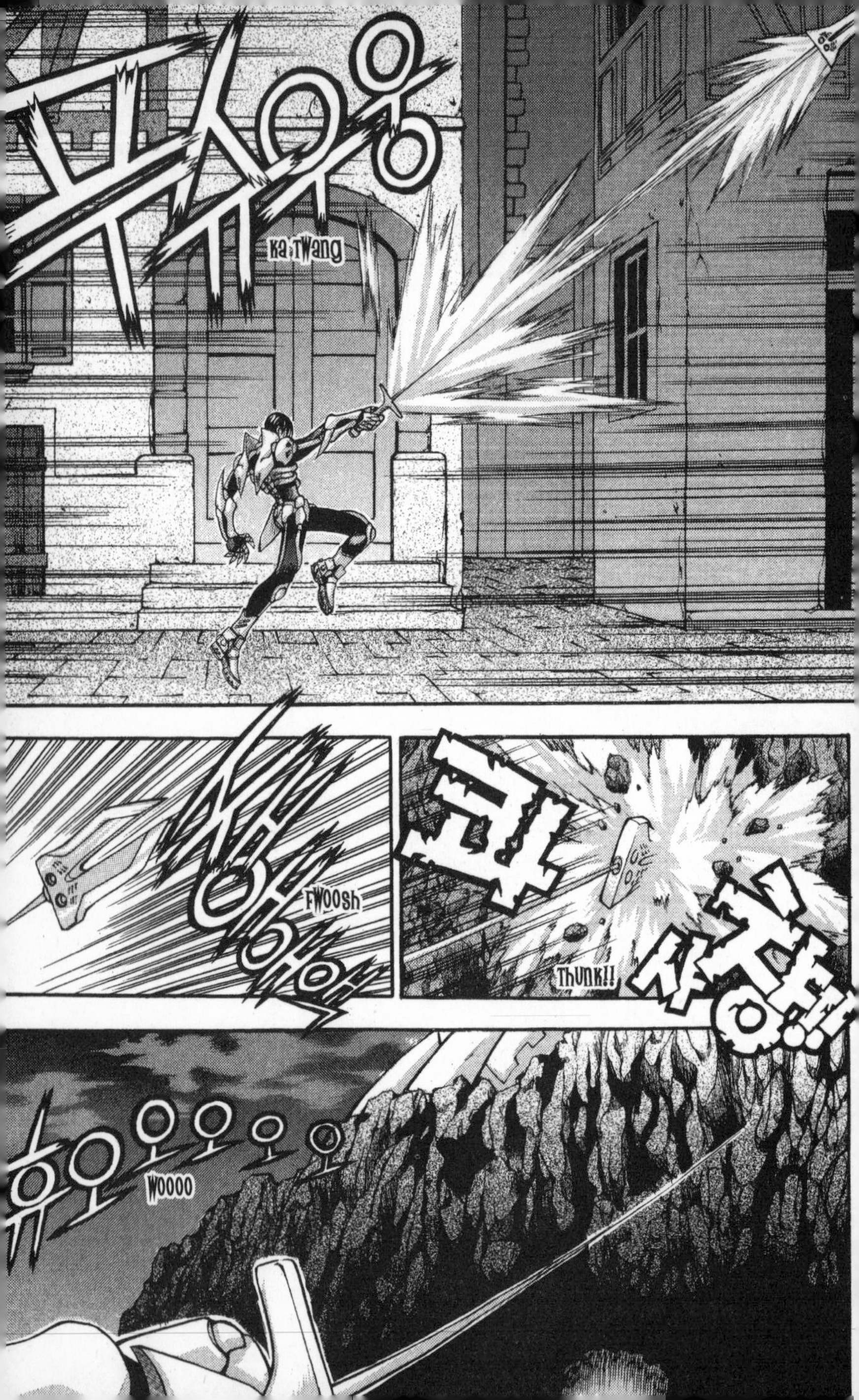
KA-TWANG
FWOOSH
THUNK!!
WOOOO

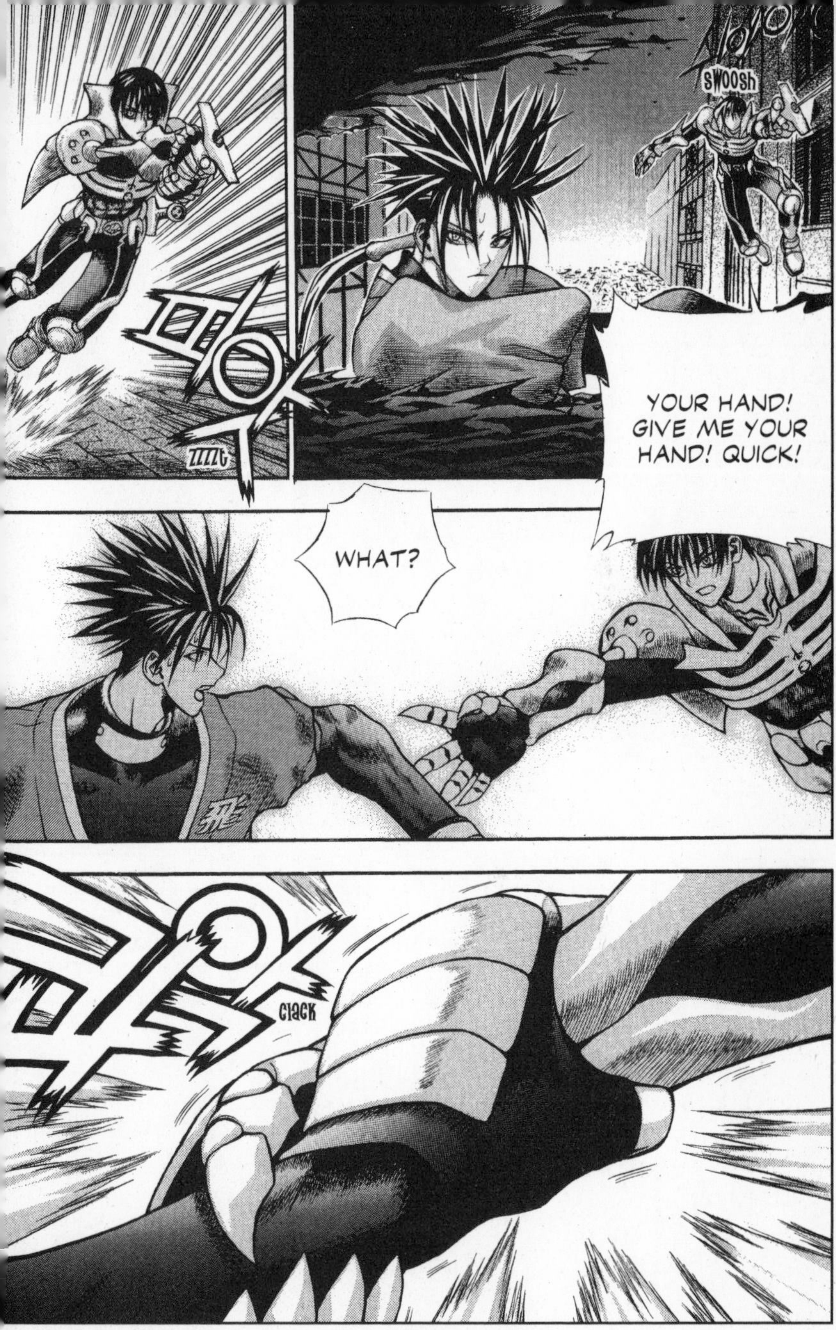

ZZZZt
SWOOSh
YOUR HAND! GIVE ME YOUR HAND! QUICK!
WHAT?
clack

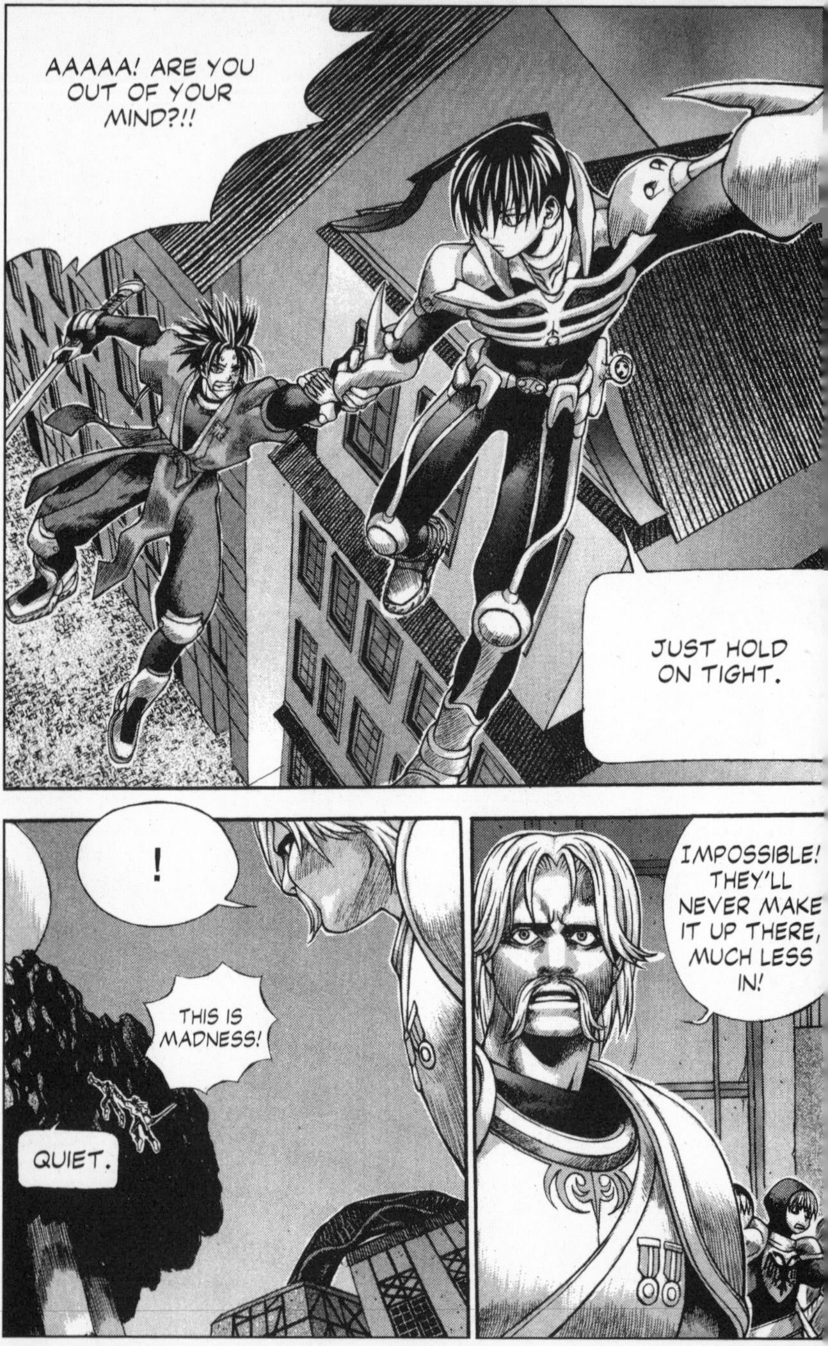
AAAAA! ARE YOU OUT OF YOUR MIND?!!
JUST HOLD ON TIGHT.
!
THIS IS MADNESS!
QUIET.
IMPOSSIBLE! THEY'LL NEVER MAKE IT UP THERE, MUCH LESS IN!

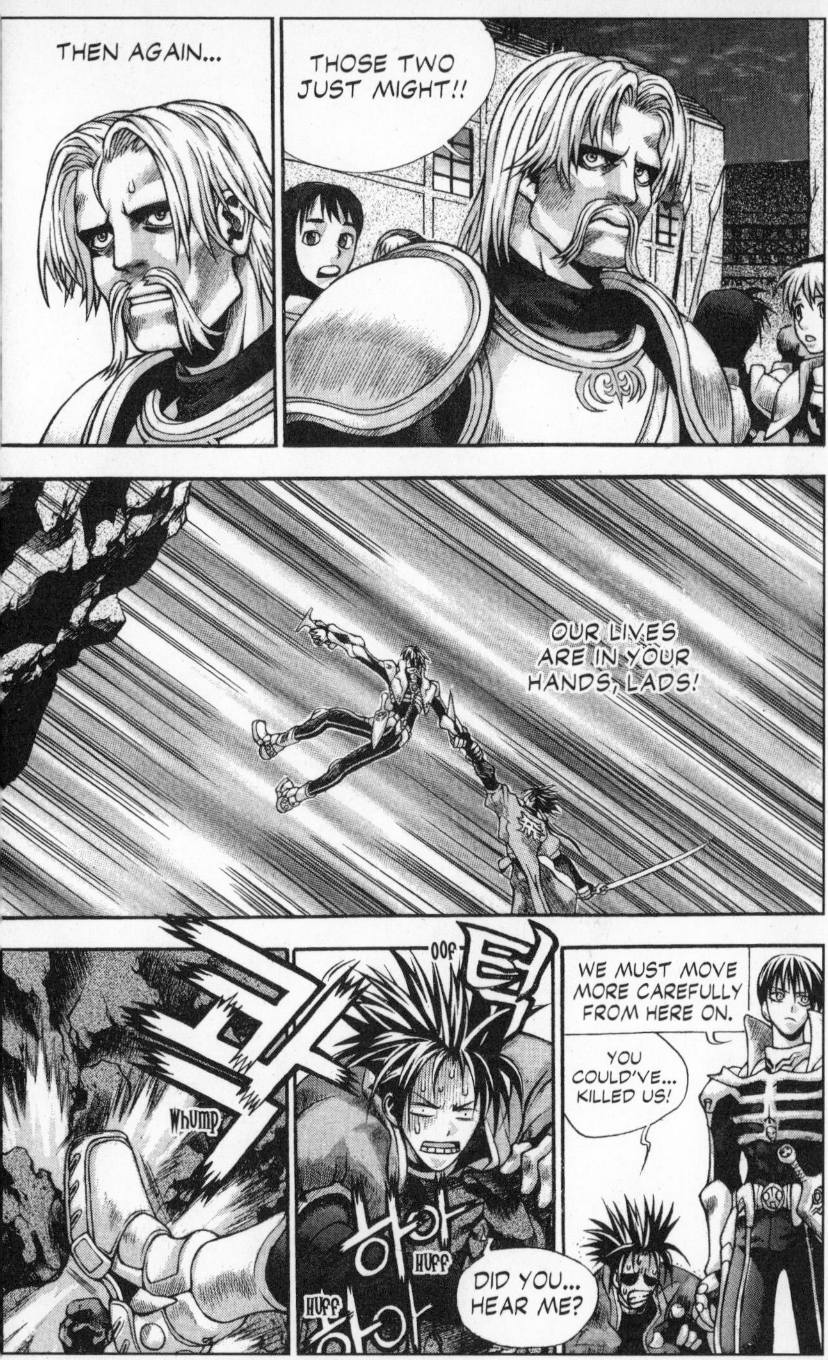
THEN AGAIN...
THOSE TWO JUST MIGHT!!
OUR LIVES ARE IN YOUR HANDS, LADS!
Whump
OOF
HUFF
HUFF
DID YOU... HEAR ME?
WE MUST MOVE MORE CAREFULLY FROM HERE ON.
YOU COULD'VE... KILLED US!

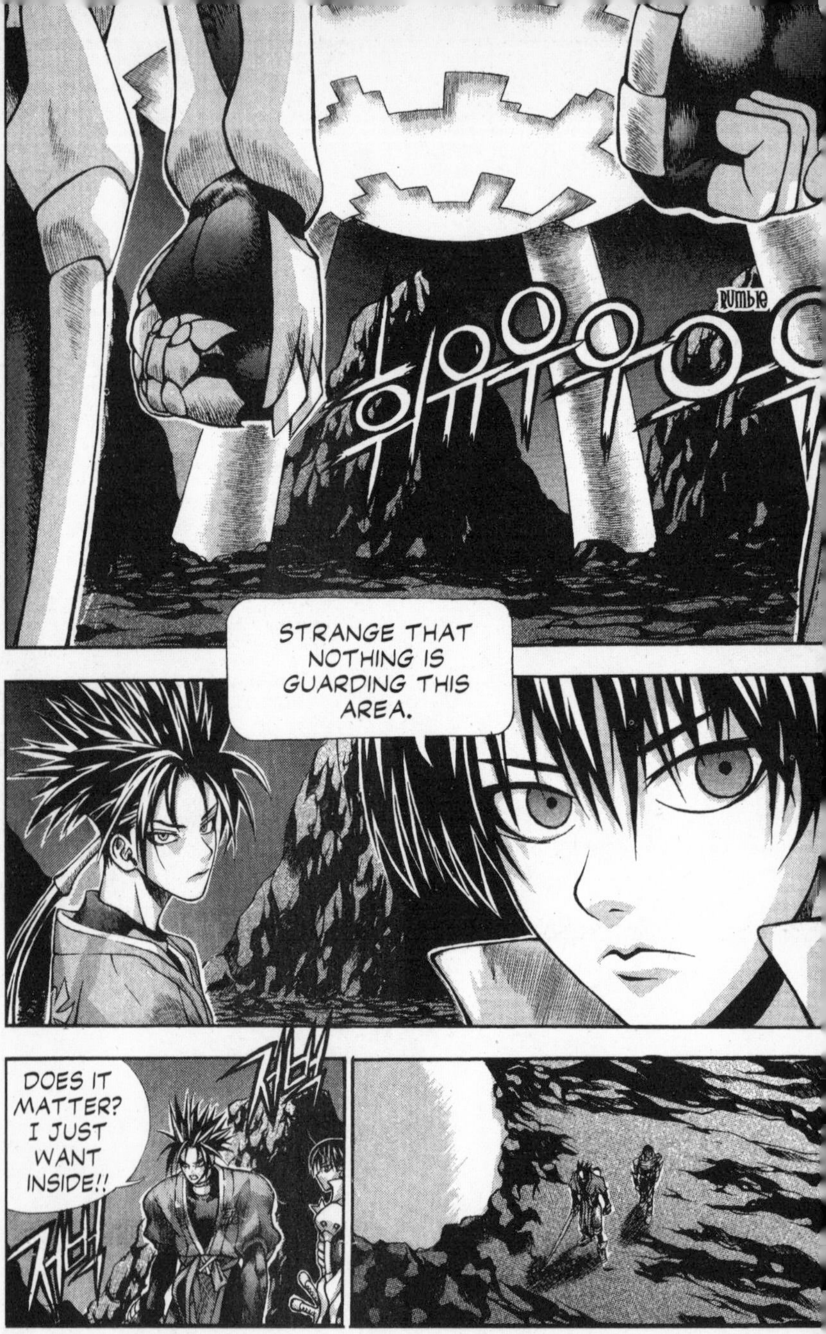
RUMBLE
STRANGE THAT NOTHING IS GUARDING THIS AREA.
DOES IT MATTER? I JUST WANT INSIDE!!

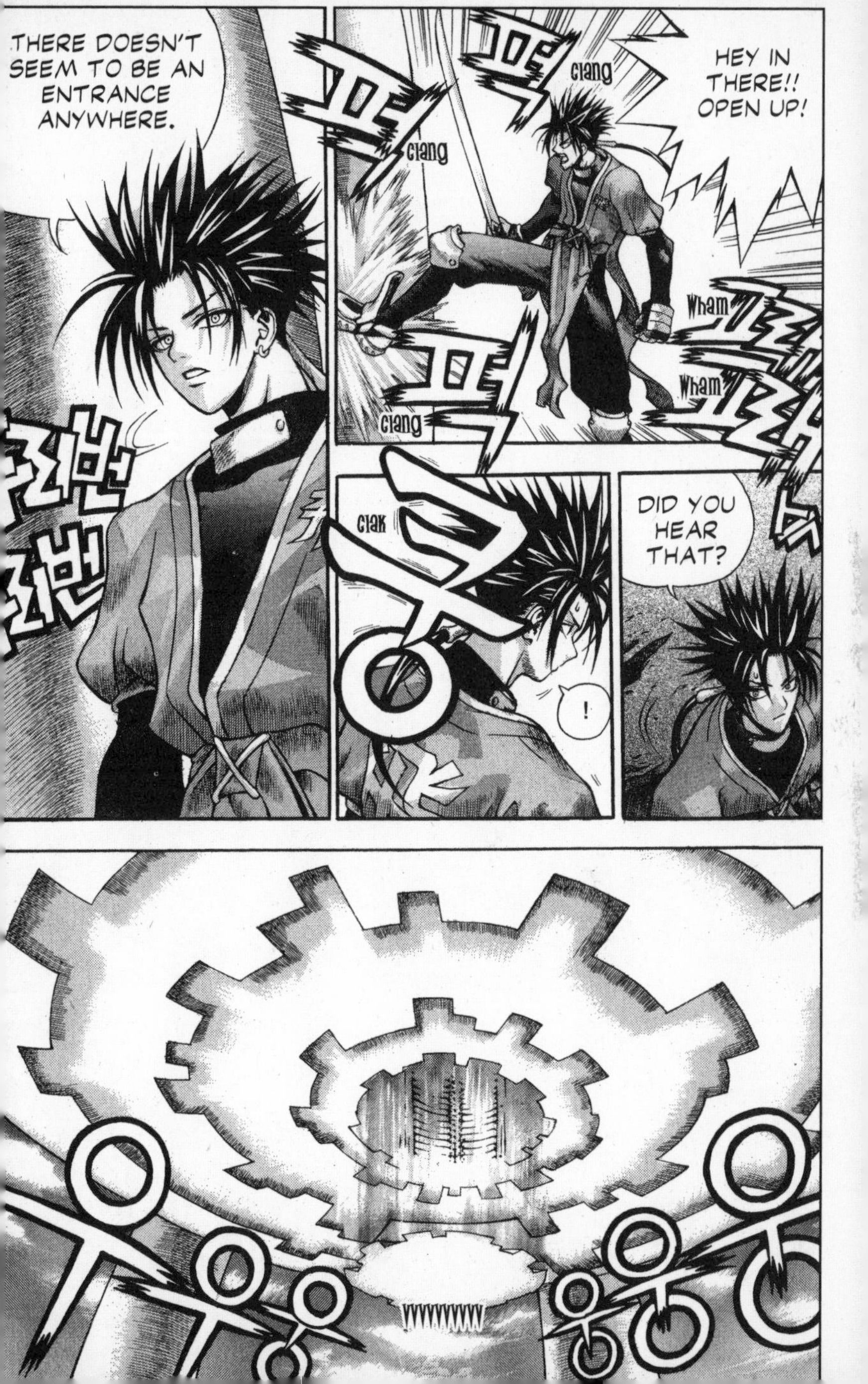
THERE DOESN'T SEEM TO BE AN ENTRANCE ANYWHERE.
clang
clang
HEY IN THERE!! OPEN UP!
Wham
Wham
clang
clak
!
DID YOU HEAR THAT?

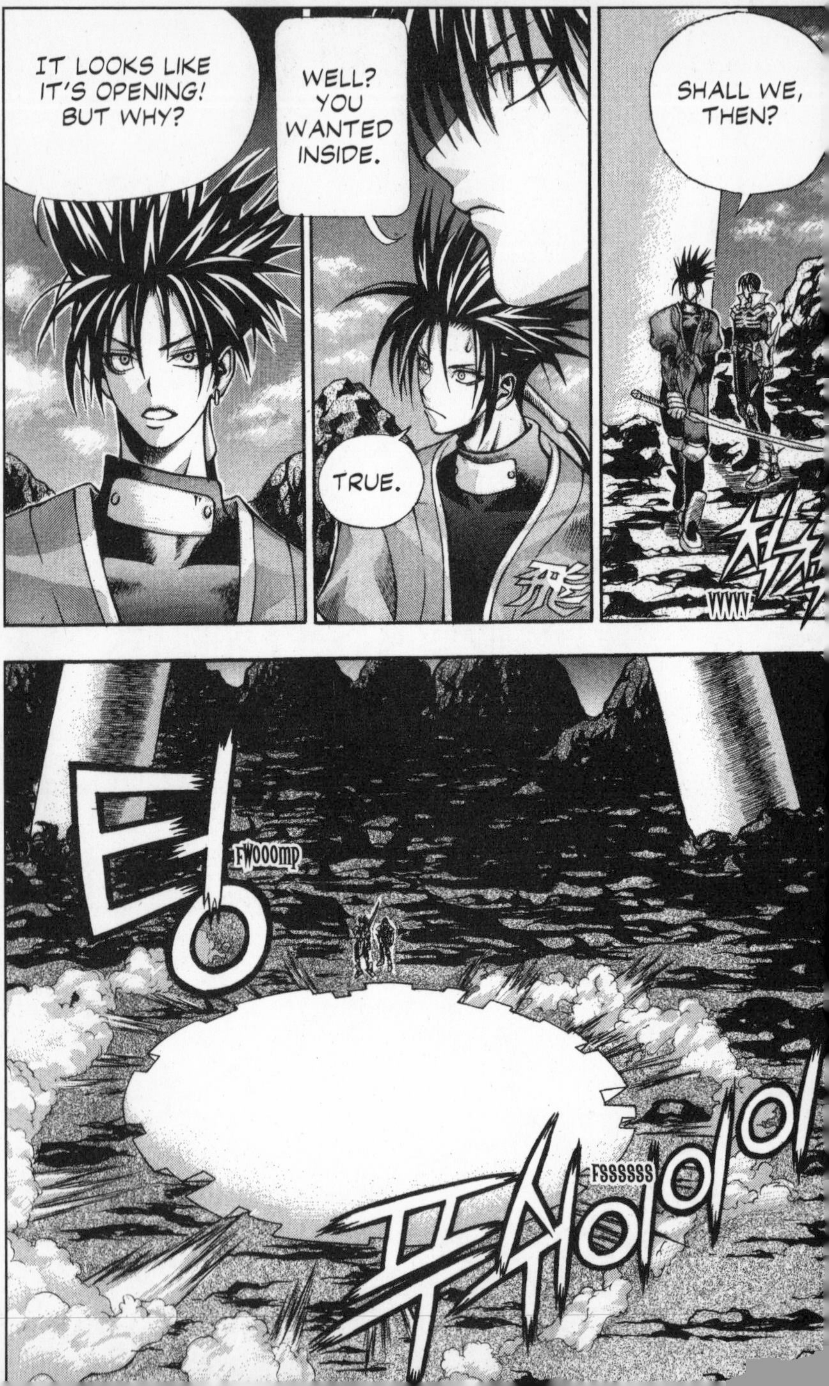
IT LOOKS LIKE IT'S OPENING! BUT WHY?
WELL? YOU WANTED INSIDE.
TRUE.
SHALL WE, THEN?
VVVVV
FWOOOMP
FSSSSSS

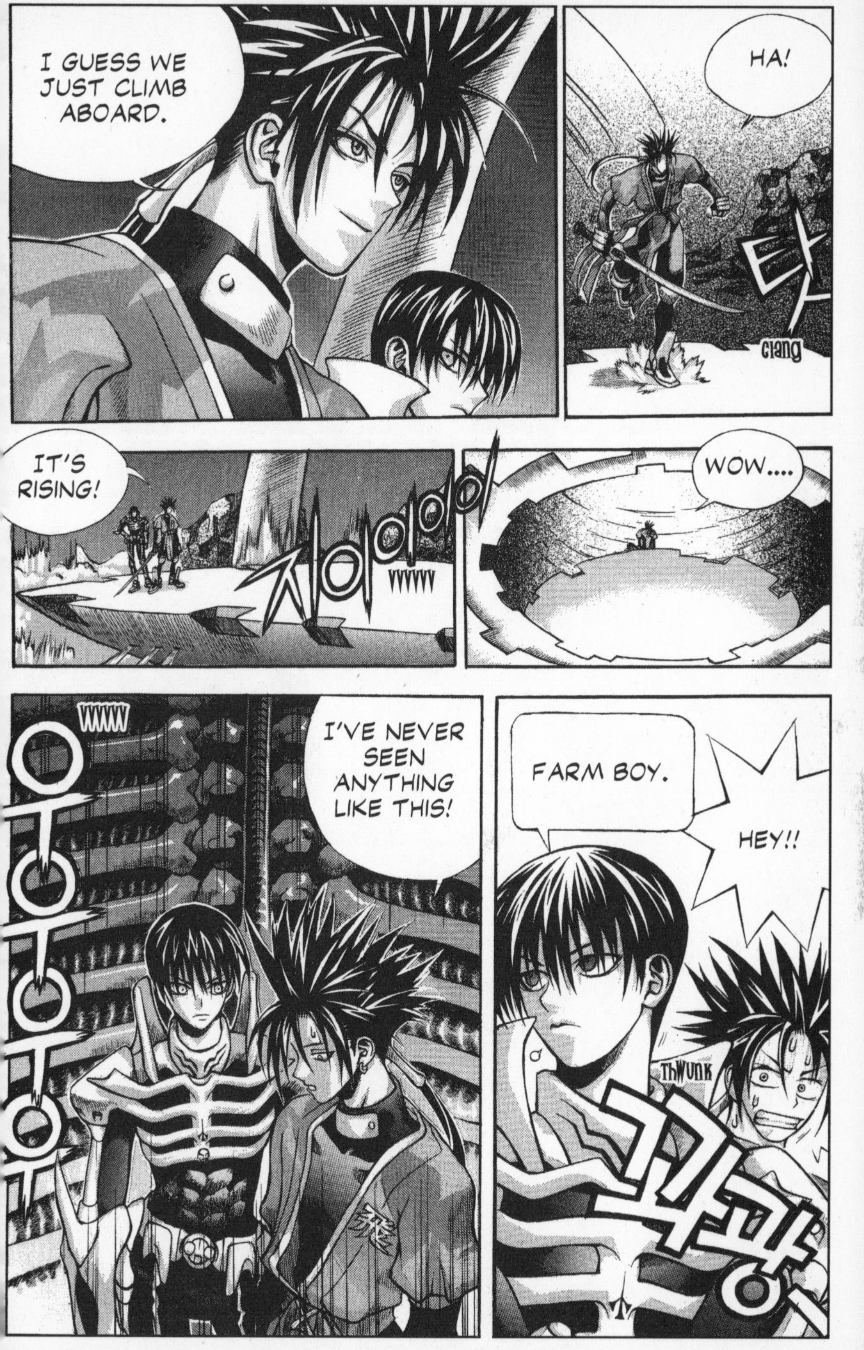
I GUESS WE JUST CLIMB ABOARD.
HA!
Clang
IT'S RISING!
VVVVVV
WOW....
WWWW
I'VE NEVER SEEN ANYTHING LIKE THIS!
FARM BOY.
HEY!!
ThWUNK

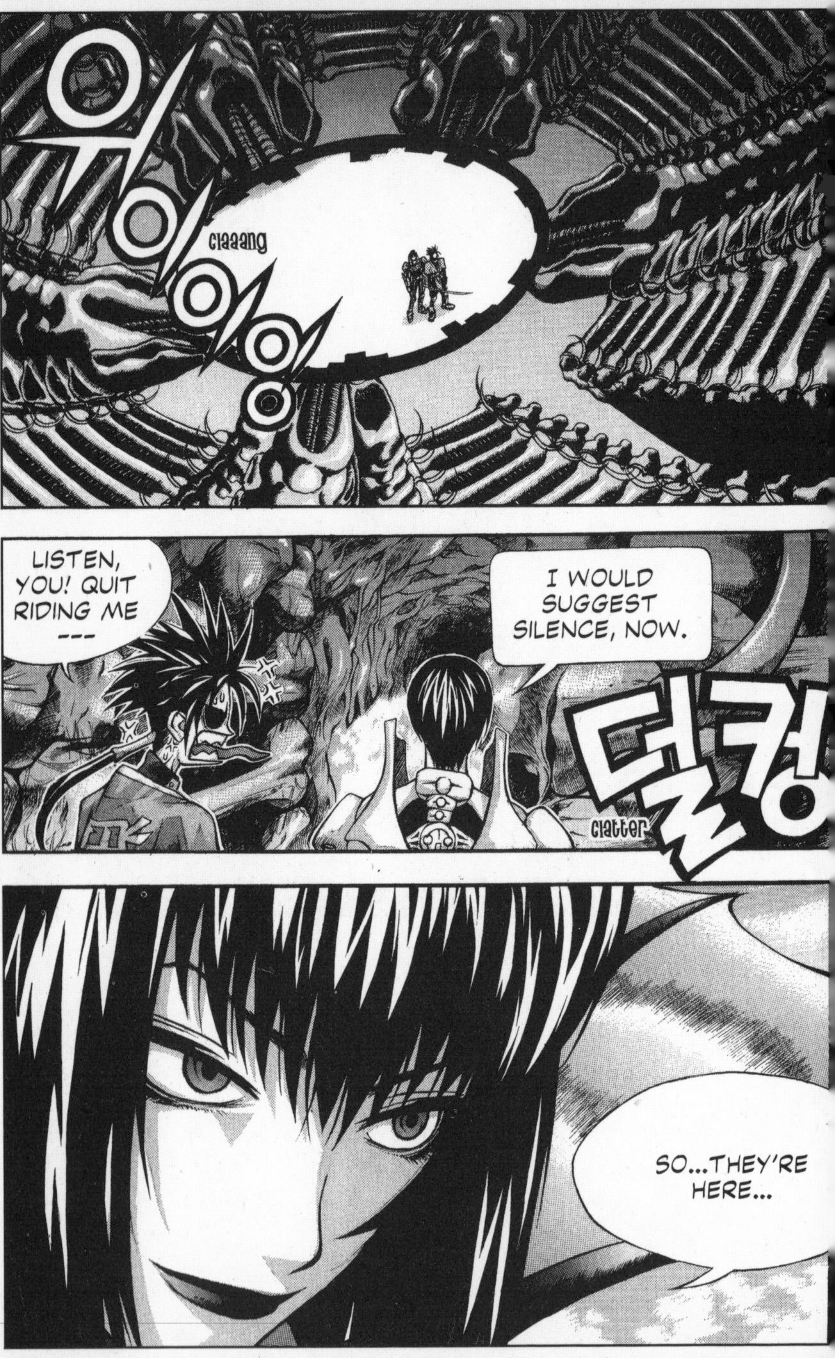
claaang
LISTEN, YOU! QUIT RIDING ME ---
I WOULD SUGGEST SILENCE, NOW.
clatter
덜컹!
SO...THEY'RE HERE...

RAGNAROK
라그나로크
IN TO THE ABYSS

海龍

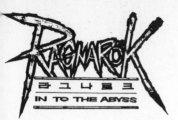

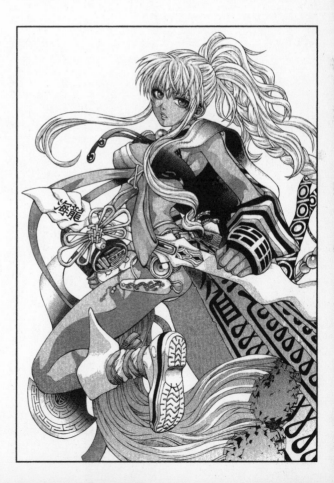

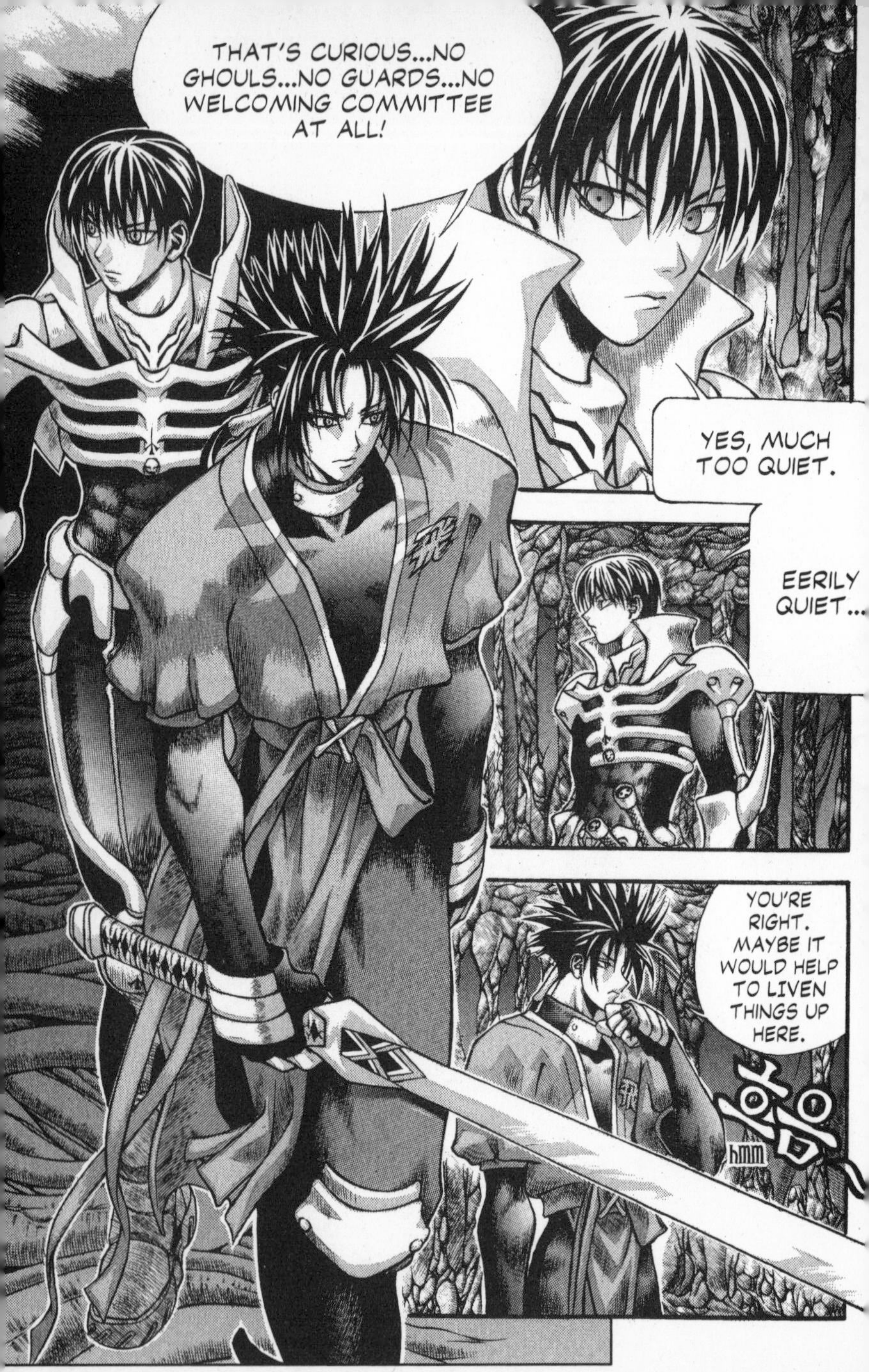
THAT'S CURIOUS...NO GHOULS...NO GUARDS...NO WELCOMING COMMITTEE AT ALL!
YES, MUCH TOO QUIET.
EERILY QUIET...
YOU'RE RIGHT. MAYBE IT WOULD HELP TO LIVEN THINGS UP HERE.
흠
hmm

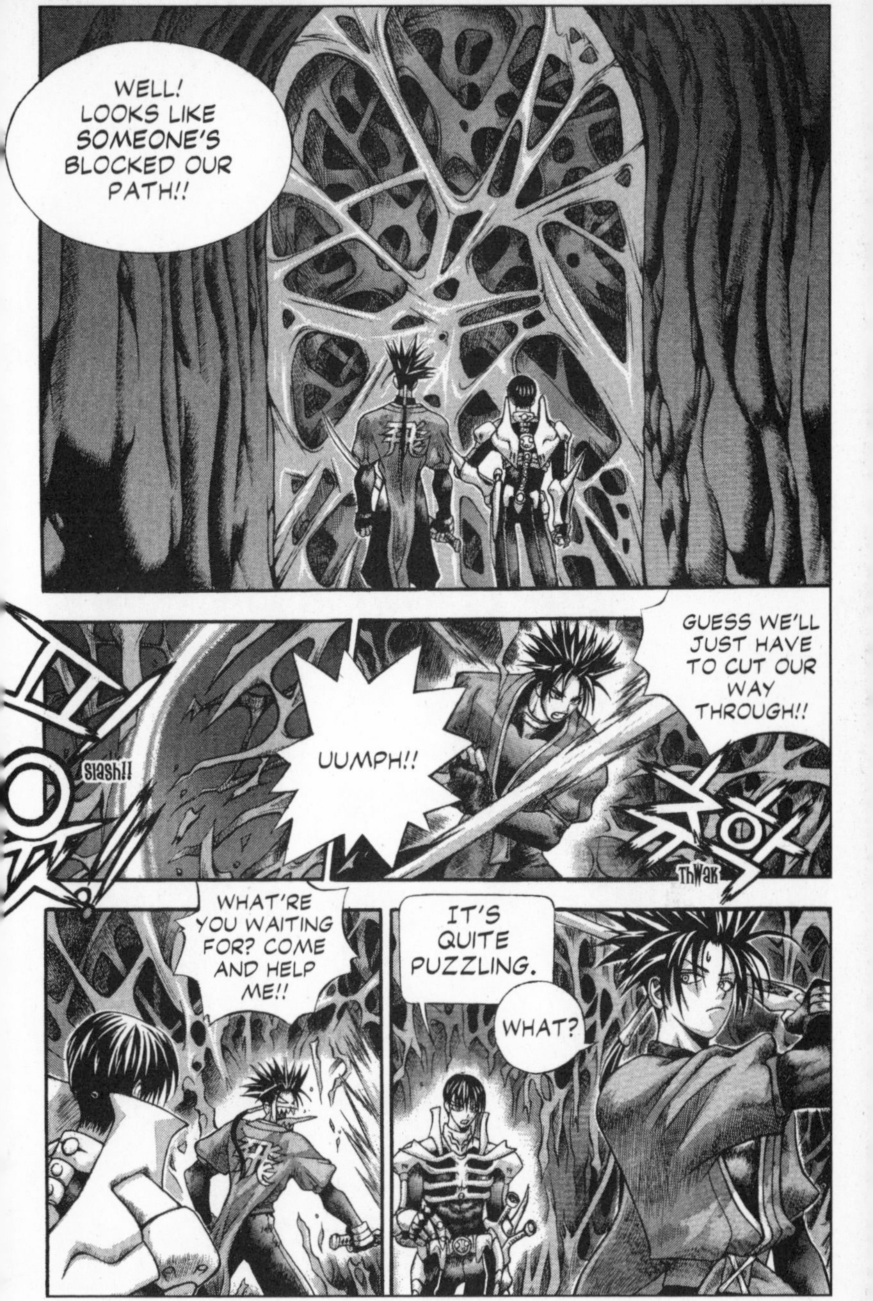

WELL! LOOKS LIKE SOMEONE'S BLOCKED OUR PATH!!
SLASH!!
UUMPH!!
GUESS WE'LL JUST HAVE TO CUT OUR WAY THROUGH!!
THWAK
WHAT'RE YOU WAITING FOR? COME AND HELP ME!!
IT'S QUITE PUZZLING.
WHAT?

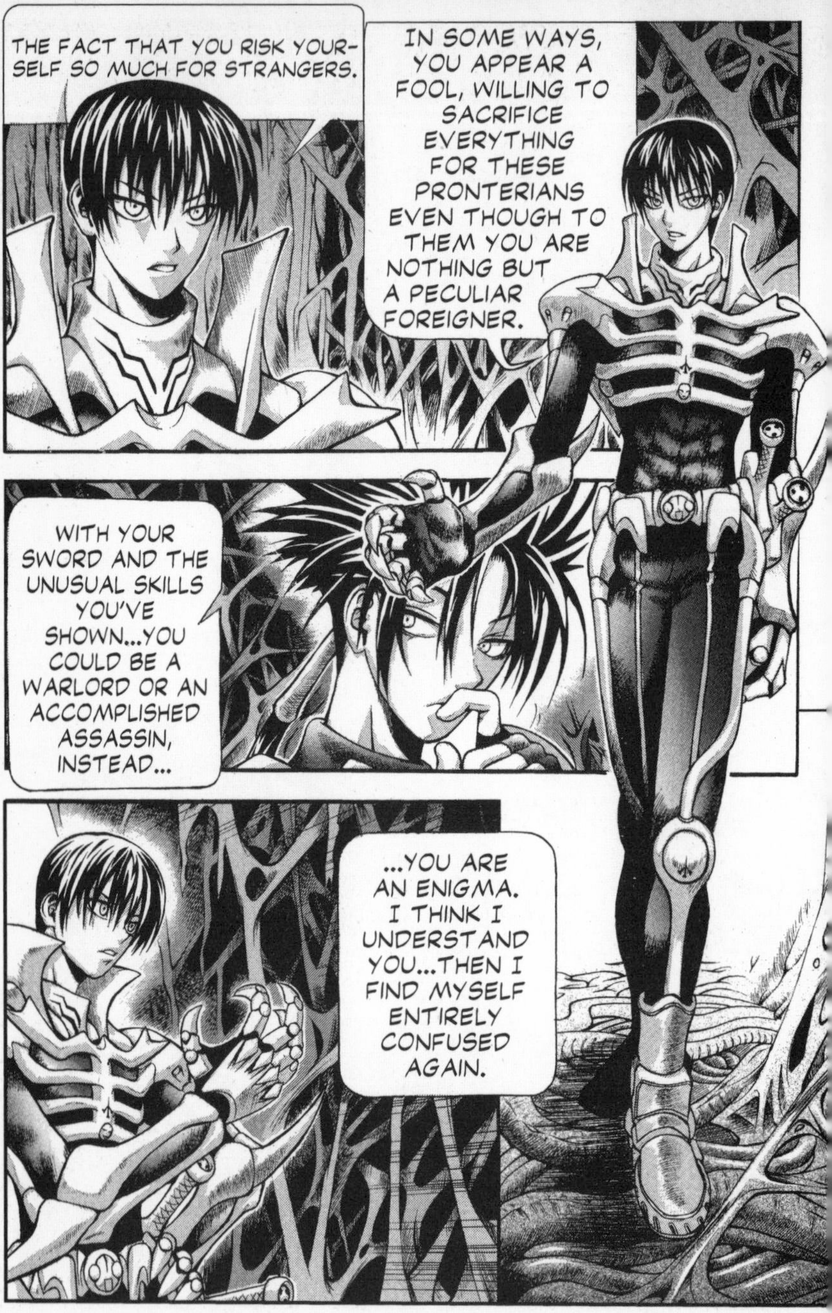
THE FACT THAT YOU RISK YOURSELF SO MUCH FOR STRANGERS.
IN SOME WAYS, YOU APPEAR A FOOL, WILLING TO SACRIFICE EVERYTHING FOR THESE PRONTERIANS EVEN THOUGH TO THEM YOU ARE NOTHING BUT A PECULIAR FOREIGNER.
WITH YOUR SWORD AND THE UNUSUAL SKILLS YOU'VE SHOWN...YOU COULD BE A WARLORD OR AN ACCOMPLISHED ASSASSIN, INSTEAD...
...YOU ARE AN ENIGMA. I THINK I UNDERSTAND YOU...THEN I FIND MYSELF ENTIRELY CONFUSED AGAIN.

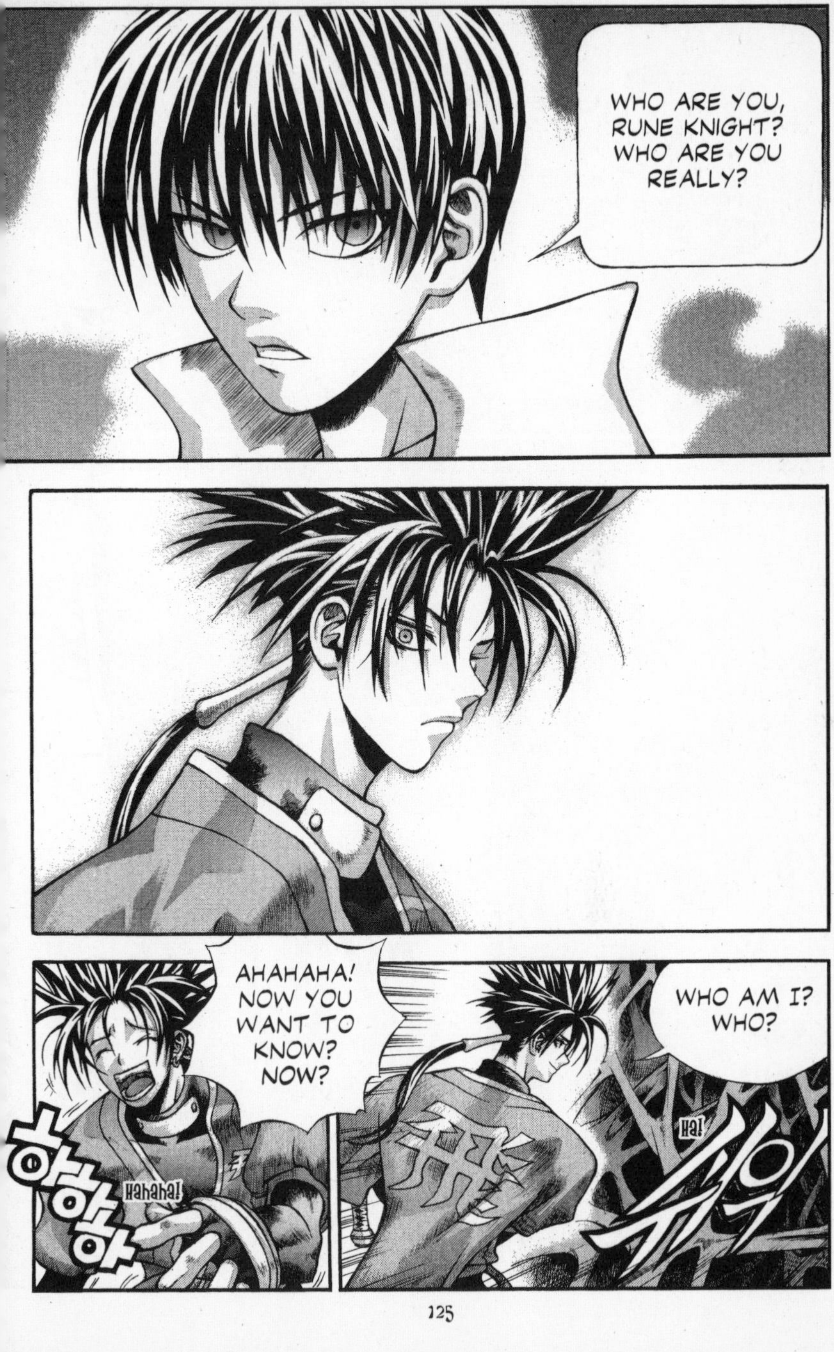
WHO ARE YOU, RUNE KNIGHT? WHO ARE YOU REALLY?
AHAHAHA! NOW YOU WANT TO KNOW? NOW?
Hahaha!
WHO AM I? WHO?
HA!

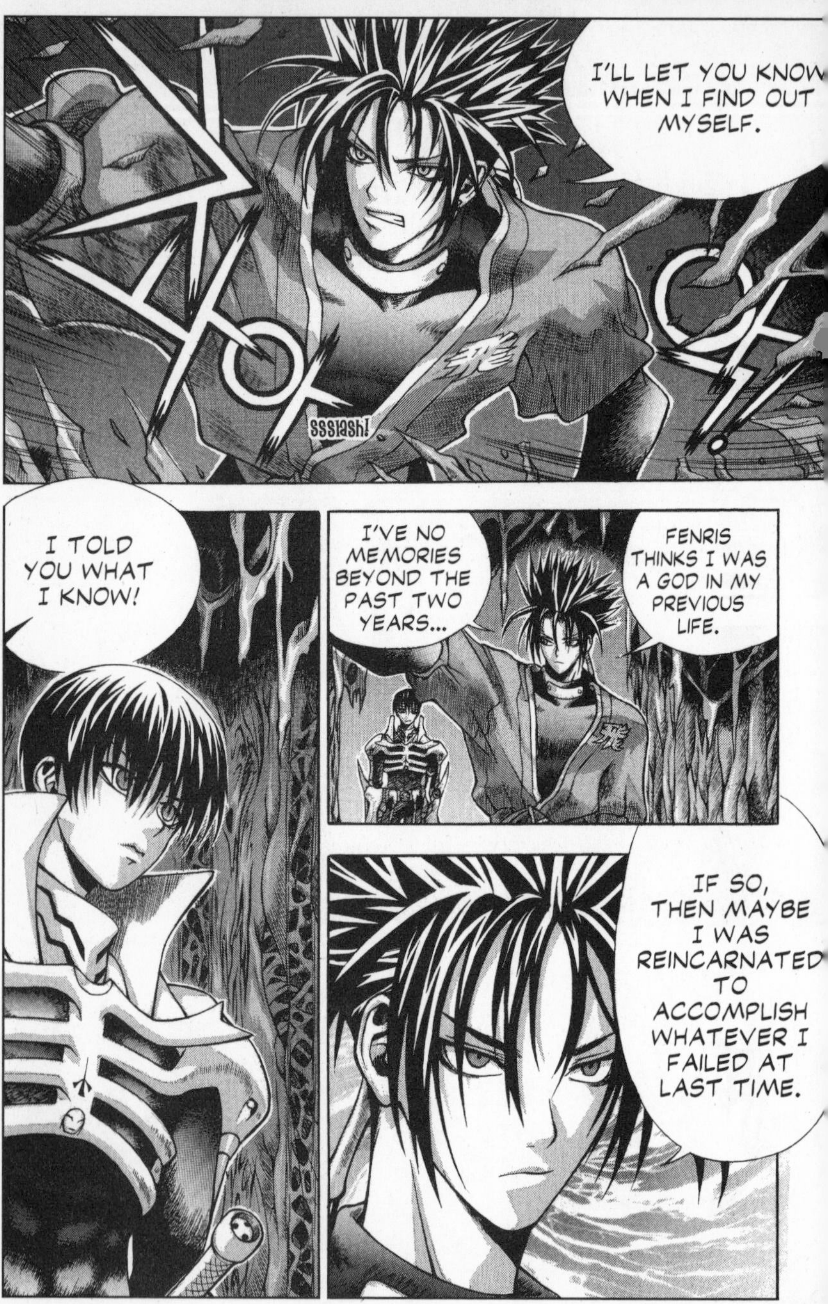
I'LL LET YOU KNOW WHEN I FIND OUT MYSELF.
SSSLASH!
I TOLD YOU WHAT I KNOW!
I'VE NO MEMORIES BEYOND THE PAST TWO YEARS...
FENRIS THINKS I WAS A GOD IN MY PREVIOUS LIFE.
IF SO, THEN MAYBE I WAS REINCARNATED TO ACCOMPLISH WHATEVER I FAILED AT LAST TIME.

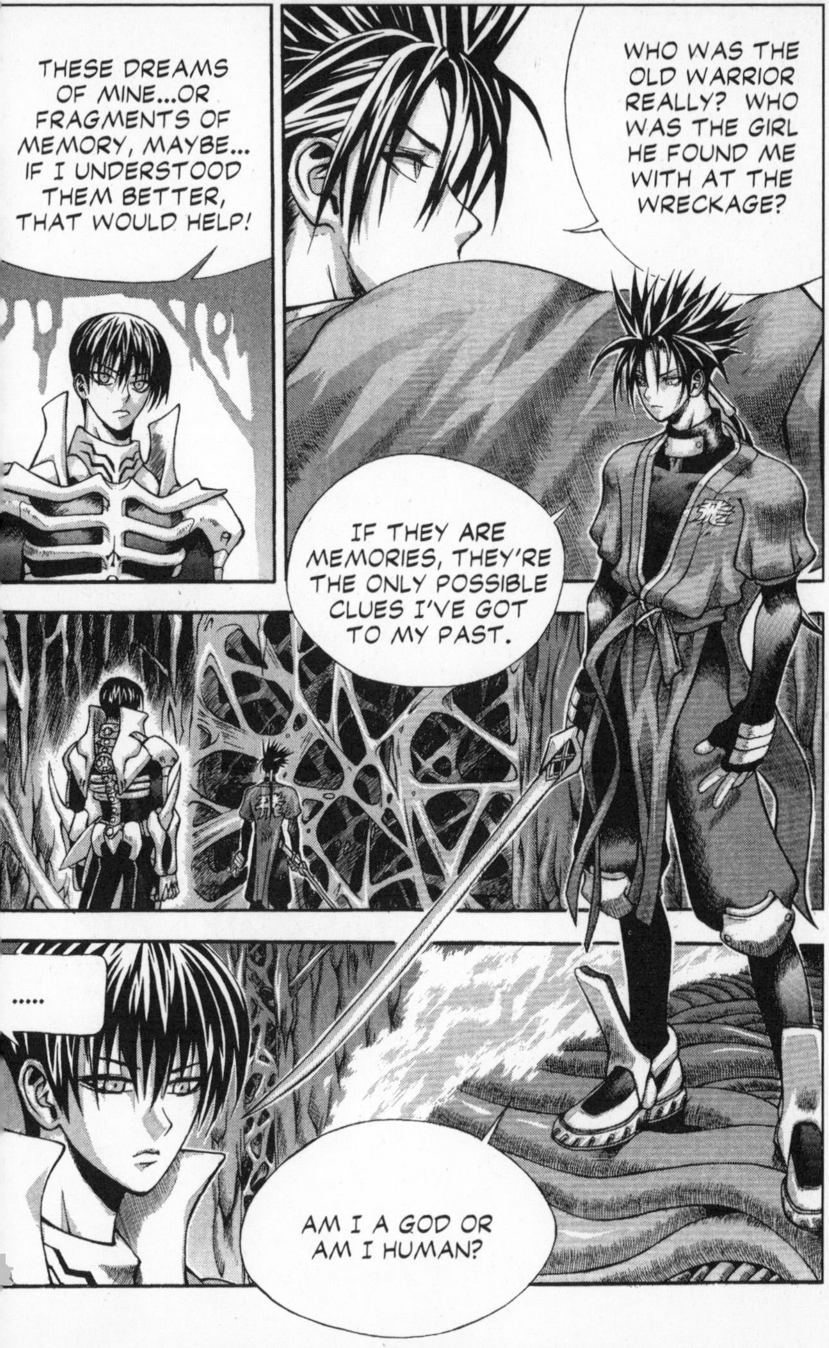
THESE DREAMS OF MINE...OR FRAGMENTS OF MEMORY, MAYBE... IF I UNDERSTOOD THEM BETTER, THAT WOULD HELP!
WHO WAS THE OLD WARRIOR REALLY? WHO WAS THE GIRL HE FOUND ME WITH AT THE WRECKAGE?
IF THEY ARE MEMORIES, THEY'RE THE ONLY POSSIBLE CLUES I'VE GOT TO MY PAST.
.....
AM I A GOD OR AM I HUMAN?

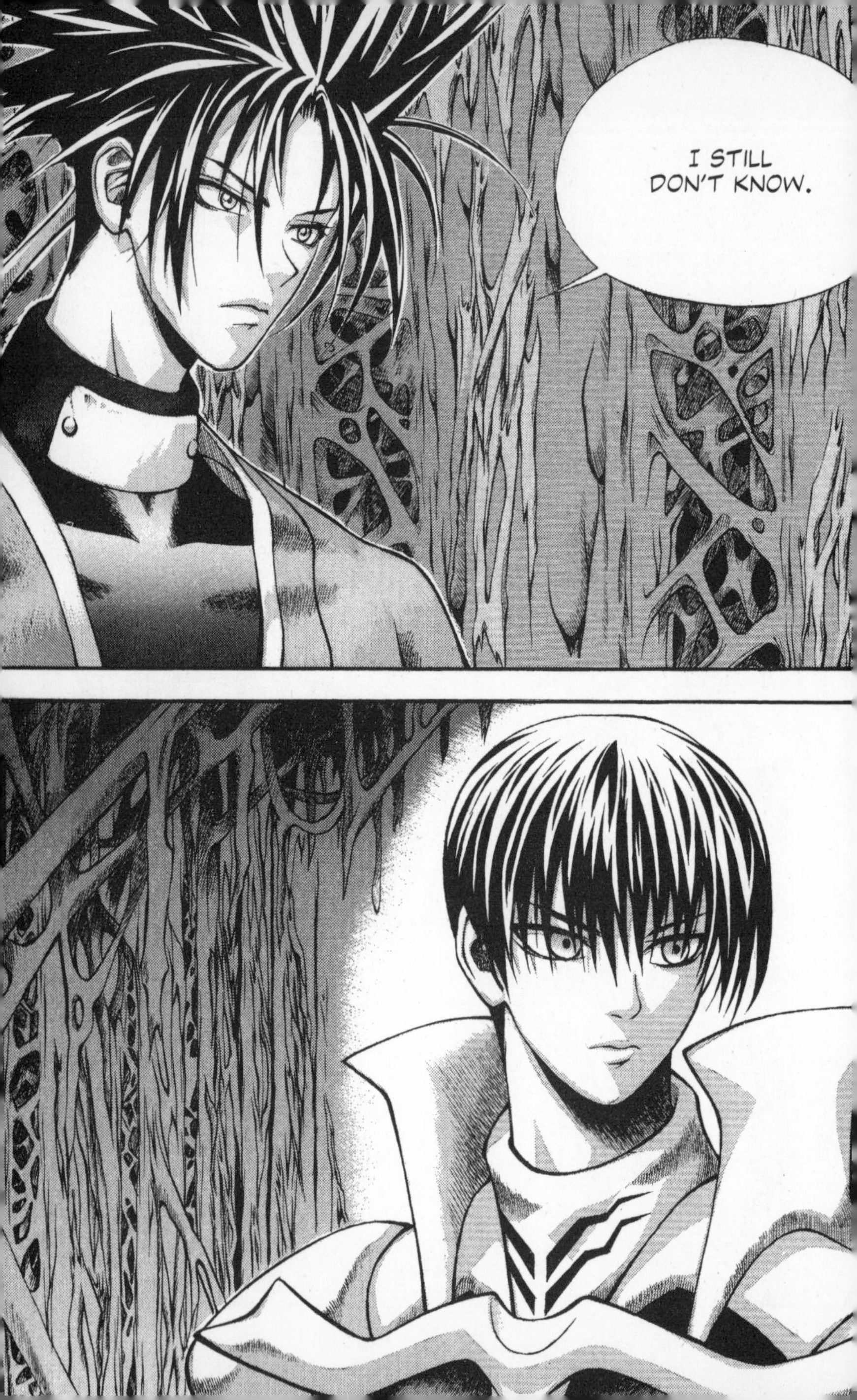
I STILL DON'T KNOW.

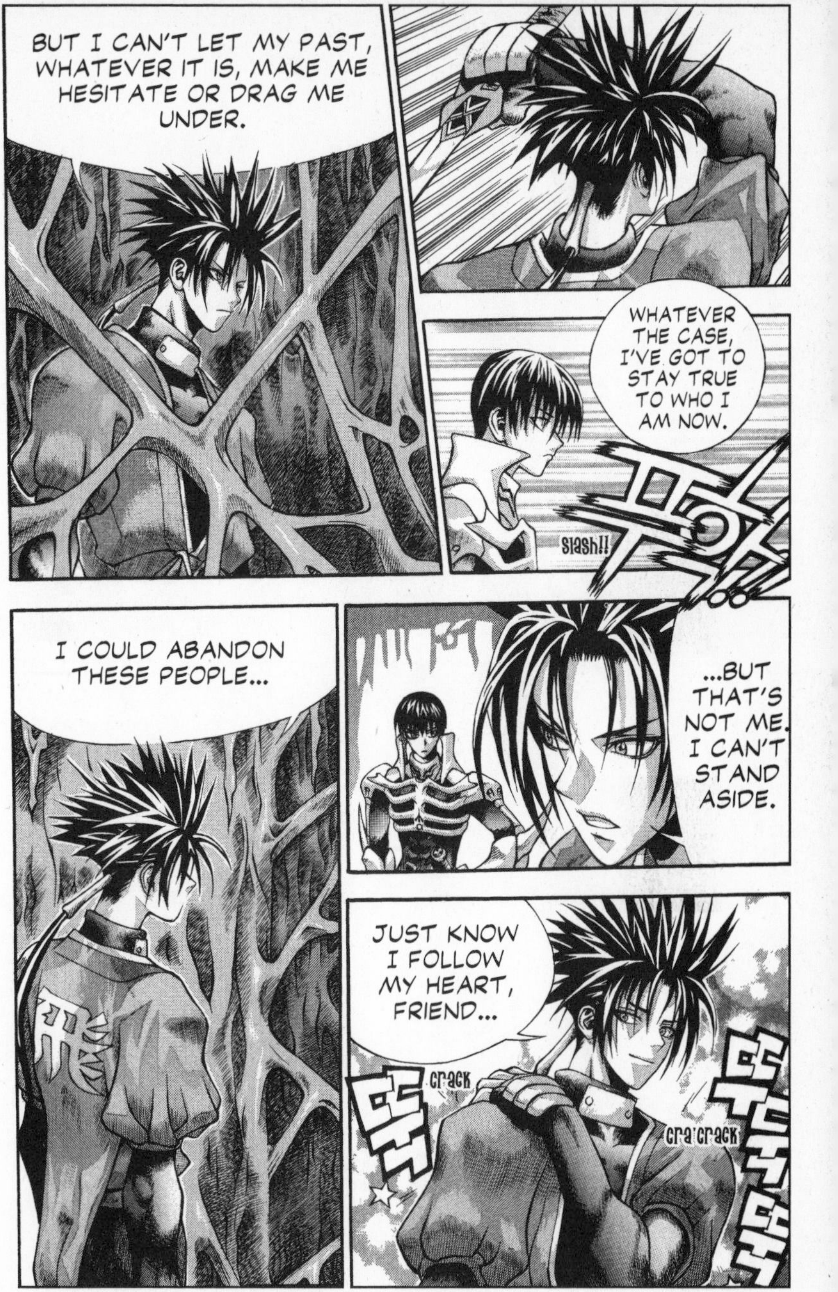
BUT I CAN'T LET MY PAST, WHATEVER IT IS, MAKE ME HESITATE OR DRAG ME UNDER.
WHATEVER THE CASE, I'VE GOT TO STAY TRUE TO WHO I AM NOW.
SLASH!!
I COULD ABANDON THESE PEOPLE...
...BUT THAT'S NOT ME. I CAN'T STAND ASIDE.
JUST KNOW I FOLLOW MY HEART, FRIEND...
CRACK
CRA'CRACK

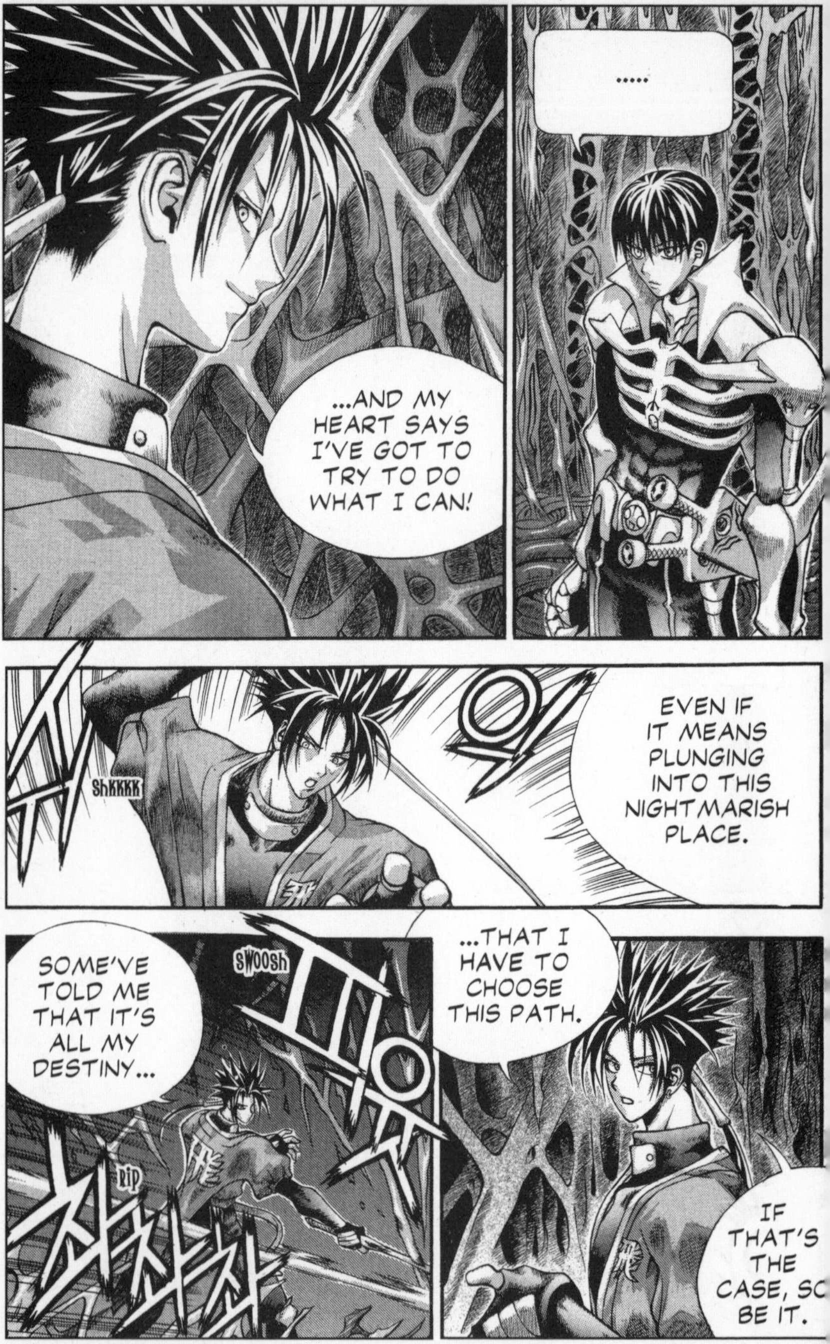

...AND MY HEART SAYS I'VE GOT TO TRY TO DO WHAT I CAN!
......
ShKKKK
EVEN IF IT MEANS PLUNGING INTO THIS NIGHTMARISH PLACE.
SOME'VE TOLD ME THAT IT'S ALL MY DESTINY...
SWOOSh
RIP
...THAT I HAVE TO CHOOSE THIS PATH.
IF THAT'S THE CASE, SO BE IT.

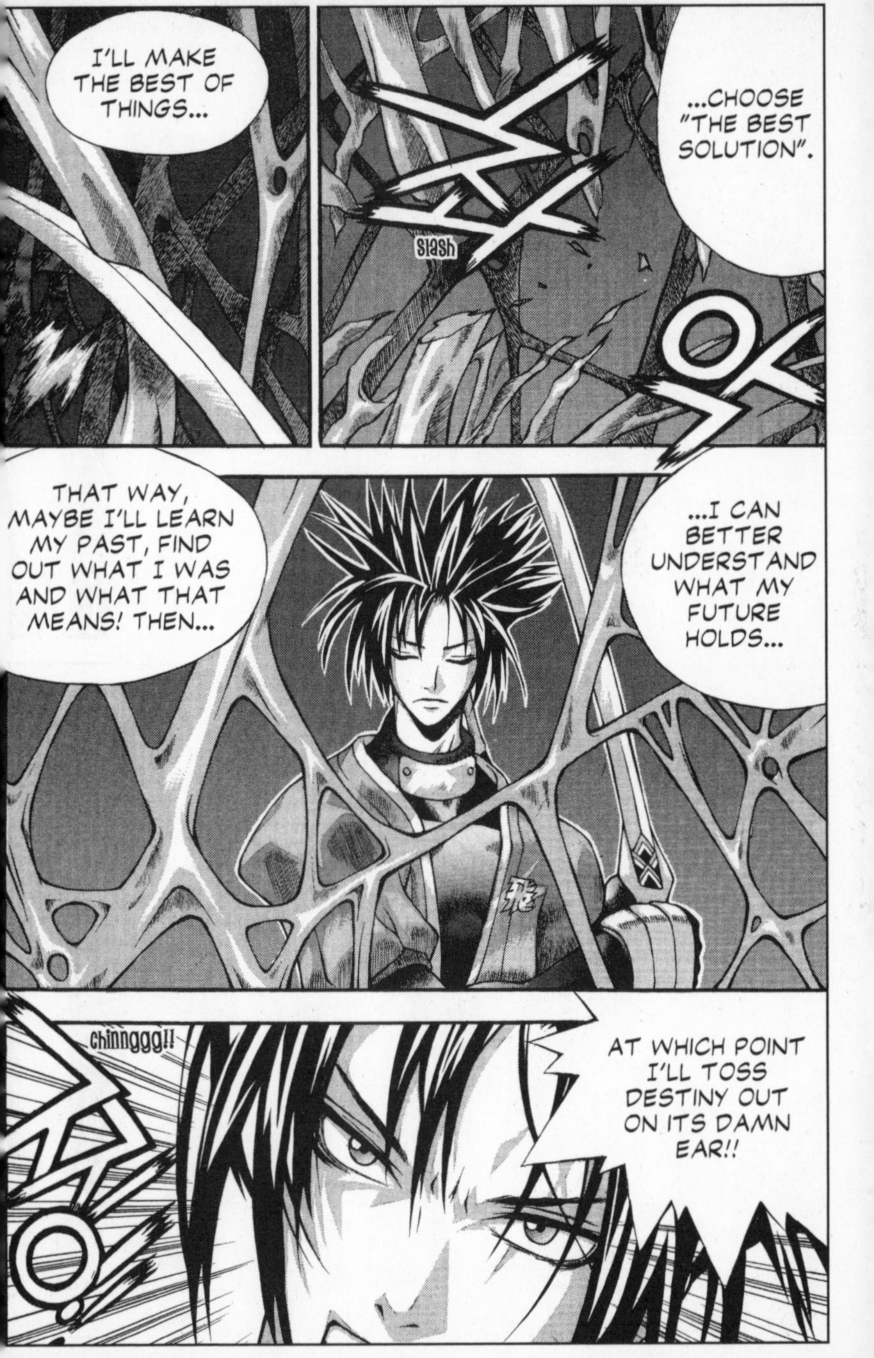
I'LL MAKE THE BEST OF THINGS...
slash
...CHOOSE "THE BEST SOLUTION".
THAT WAY, MAYBE I'LL LEARN MY PAST, FIND OUT WHAT I WAS AND WHAT THAT MEANS! THEN...
...I CAN BETTER UNDERSTAND WHAT MY FUTURE HOLDS...
chinnggg!!
AT WHICH POINT I'LL TOSS DESTINY OUT ON ITS DAMN EAR!!

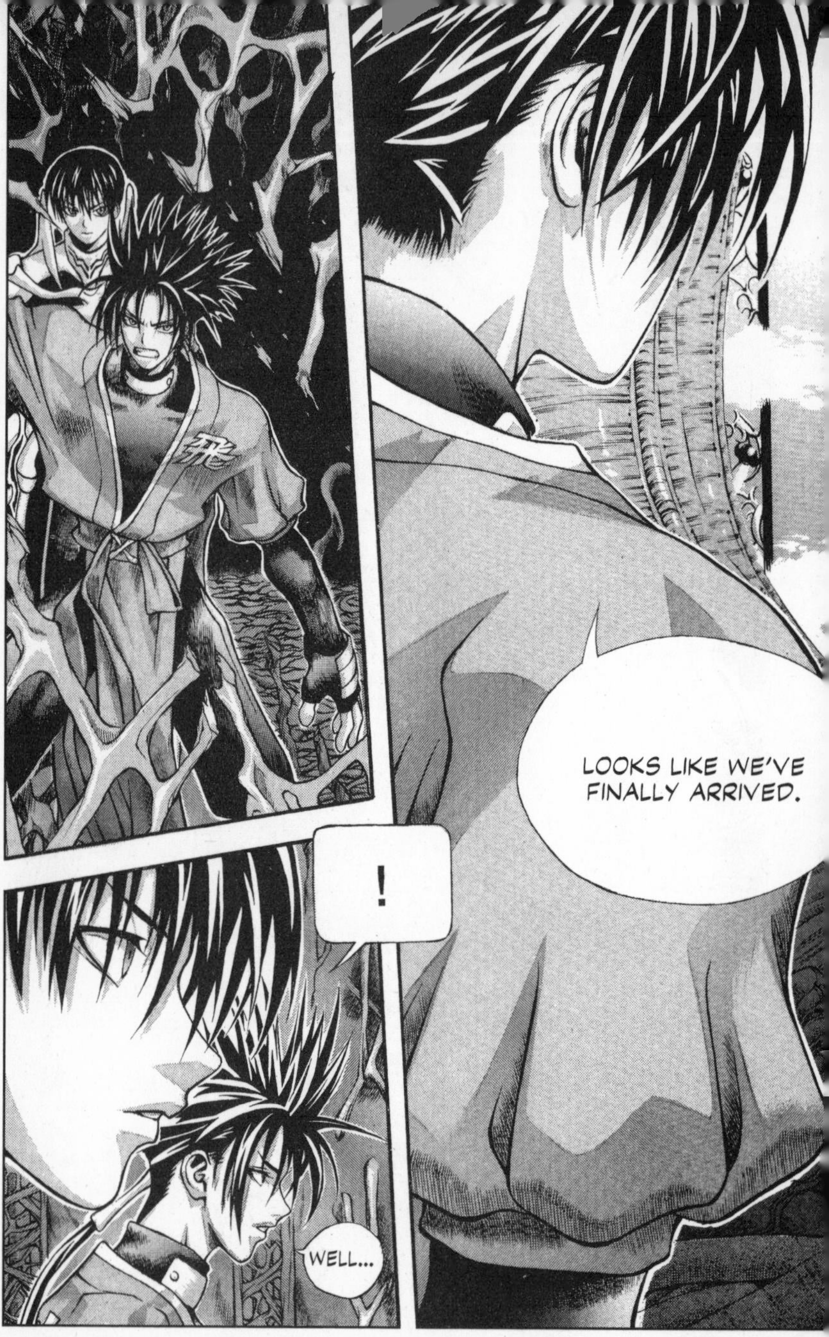
!
WELL...
LOOKS LIKE WE'VE FINALLY ARRIVED.

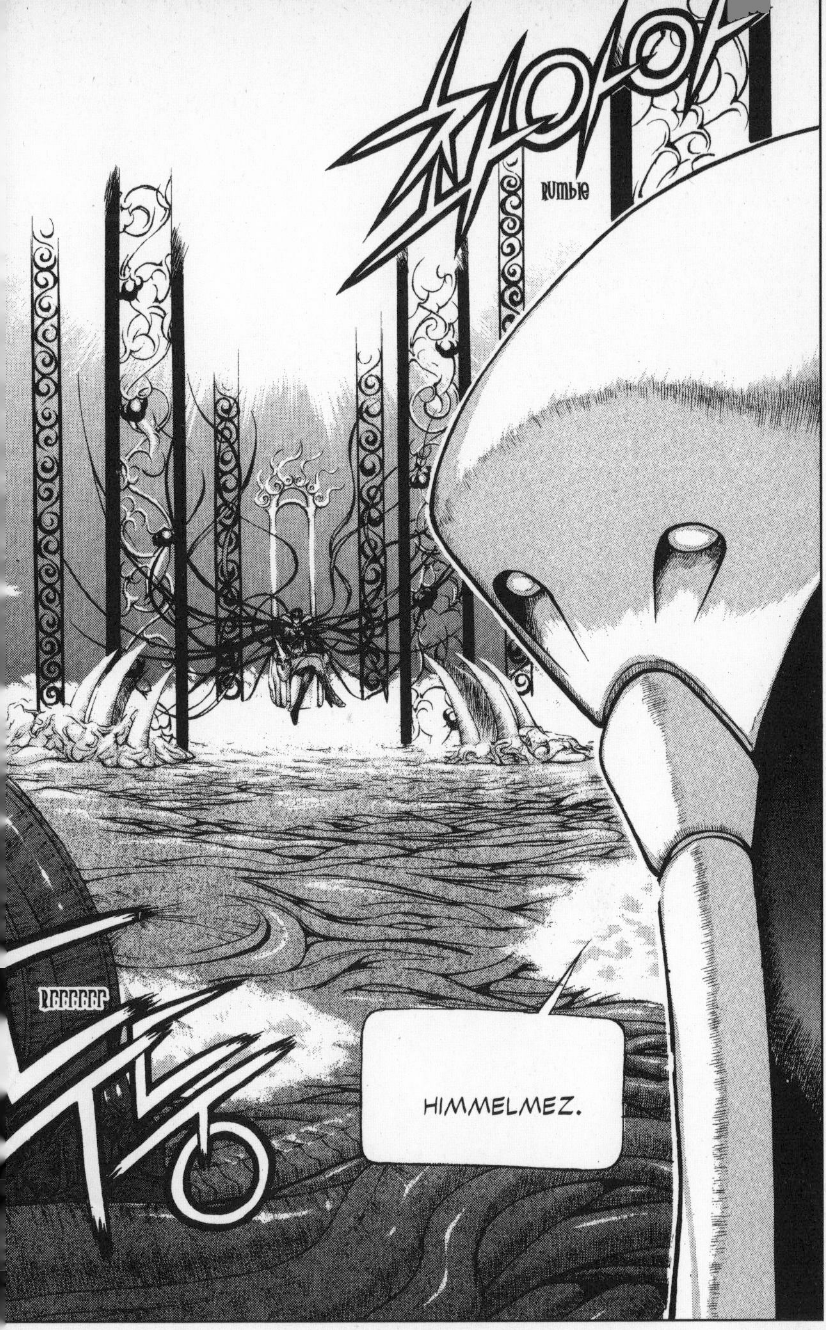
RUMBLE
RGGGGGR
HIMMELMEZ.

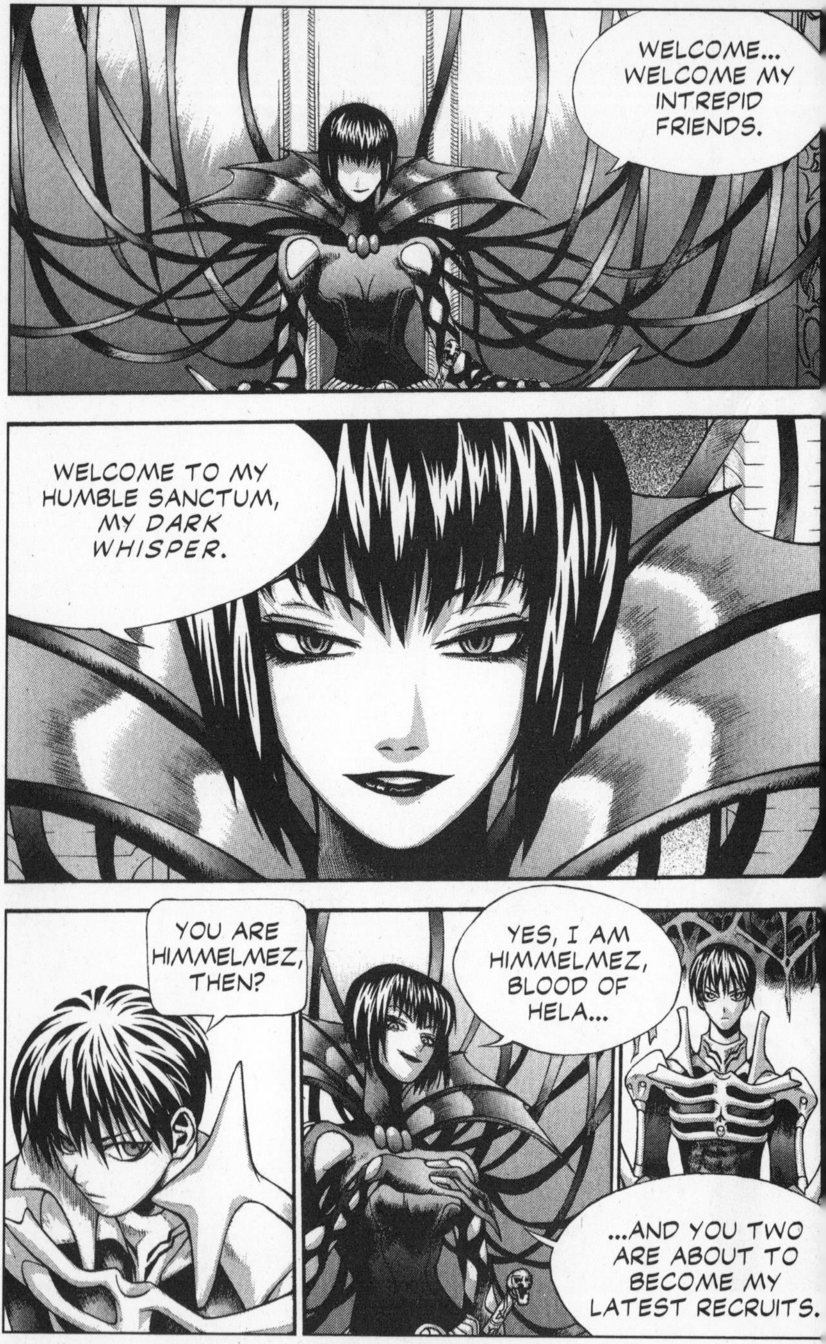
WELCOME... WELCOME MY INTREPID FRIENDS.
WELCOME TO MY HUMBLE SANCTUM, MY *DARK WHISPER*.
YOU ARE HIMMELMEZ, THEN?
YES, I AM HIMMELMEZ, BLOOD OF HELA...
...AND YOU TWO ARE ABOUT TO BECOME MY LATEST RECRUITS.

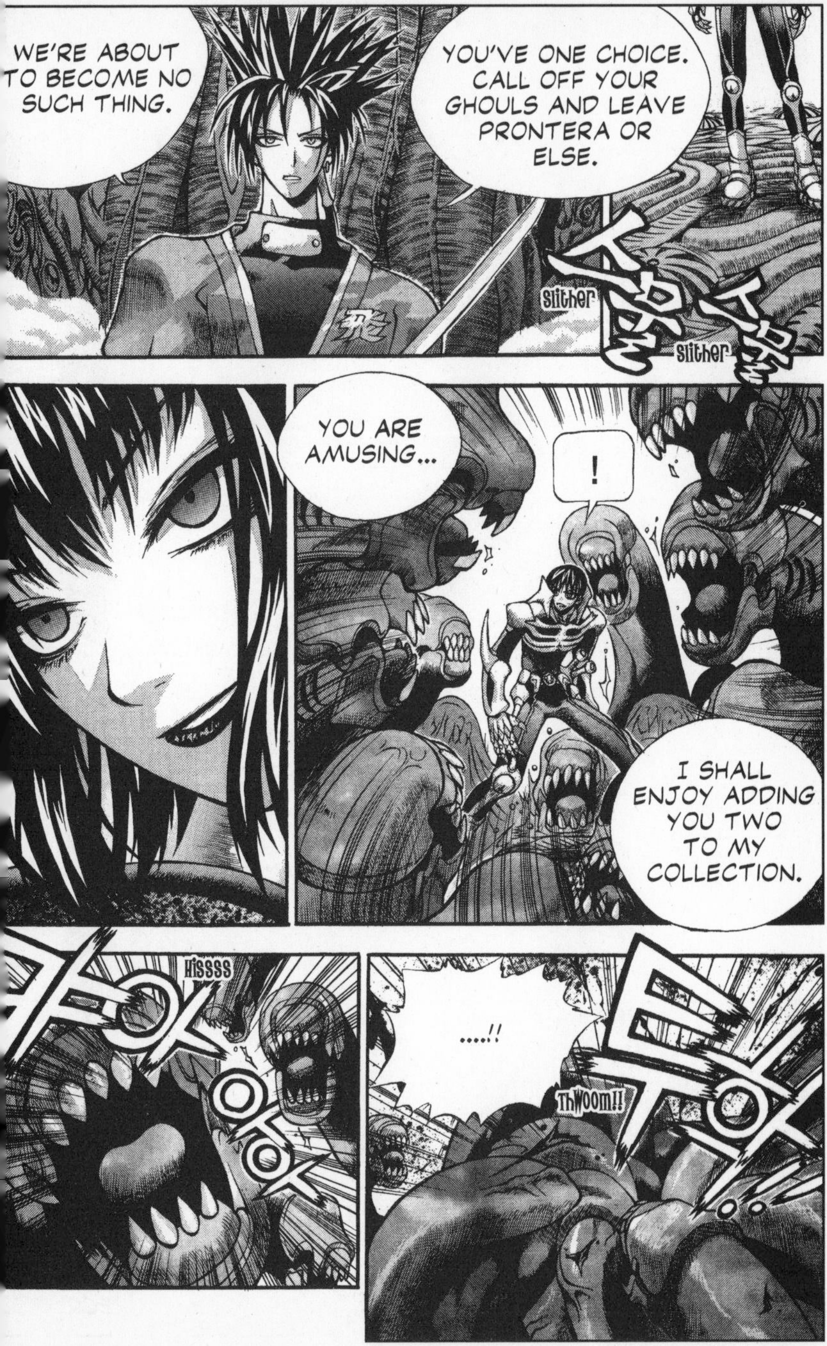
WE'RE ABOUT TO BECOME NO SUCH THING.
YOU'VE ONE CHOICE. CALL OFF YOUR GHOULS AND LEAVE PRONTERA OR ELSE.
Slither
Slither
YOU ARE AMUSING...
!
I SHALL ENJOY ADDING YOU TWO TO MY COLLECTION.
Hissss
.....!!
ThWoom!!

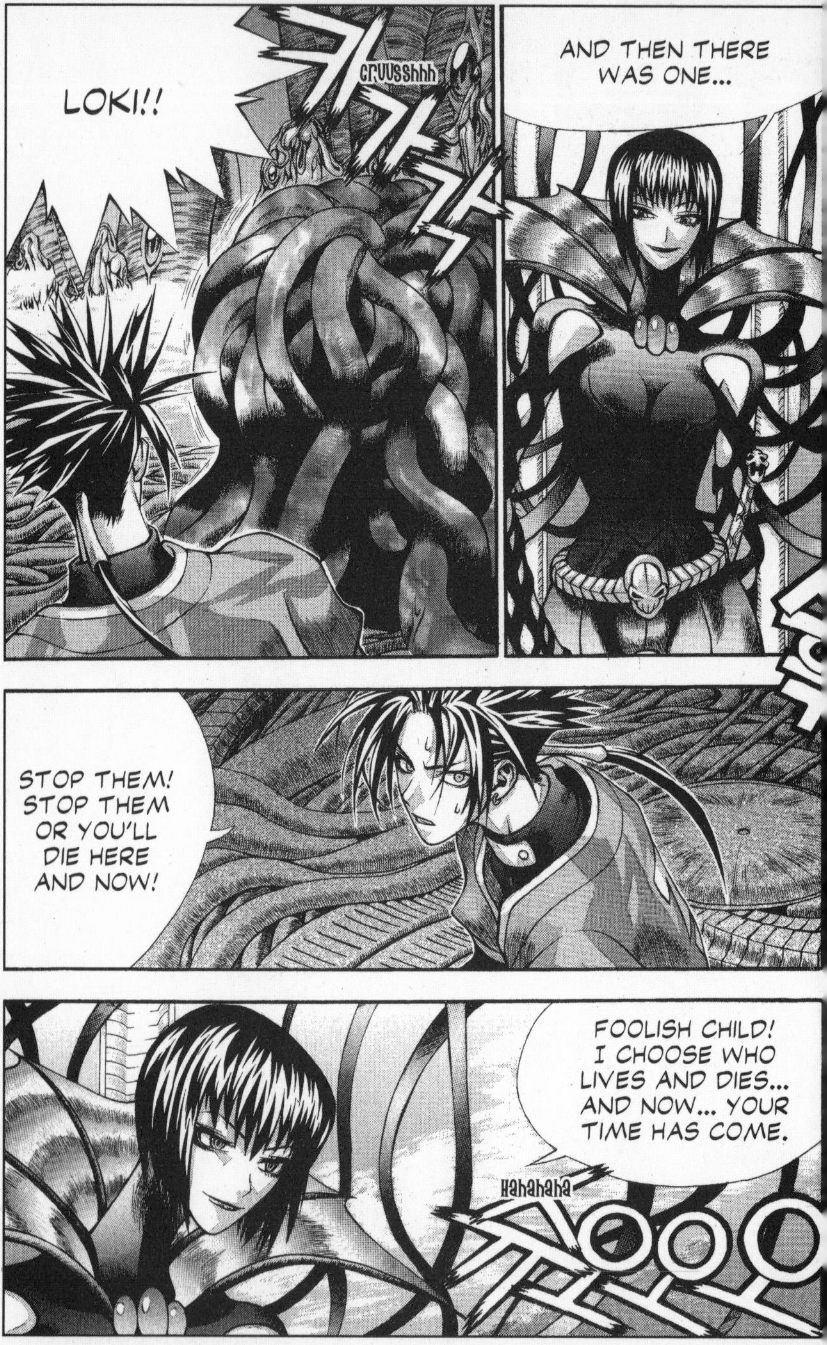
LOKI!!
cruusshhh
AND THEN THERE WAS ONE...
STOP THEM! STOP THEM OR YOU'LL DIE HERE AND NOW!
FOOLISH CHILD! I CHOOSE WHO LIVES AND DIES... AND NOW... YOUR TIME HAS COME.
Hahahaha

RAGNAROK
라그나로크
IN TO THE ABYSS

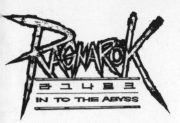

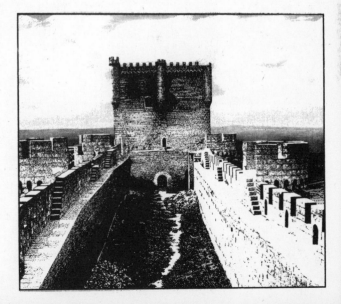

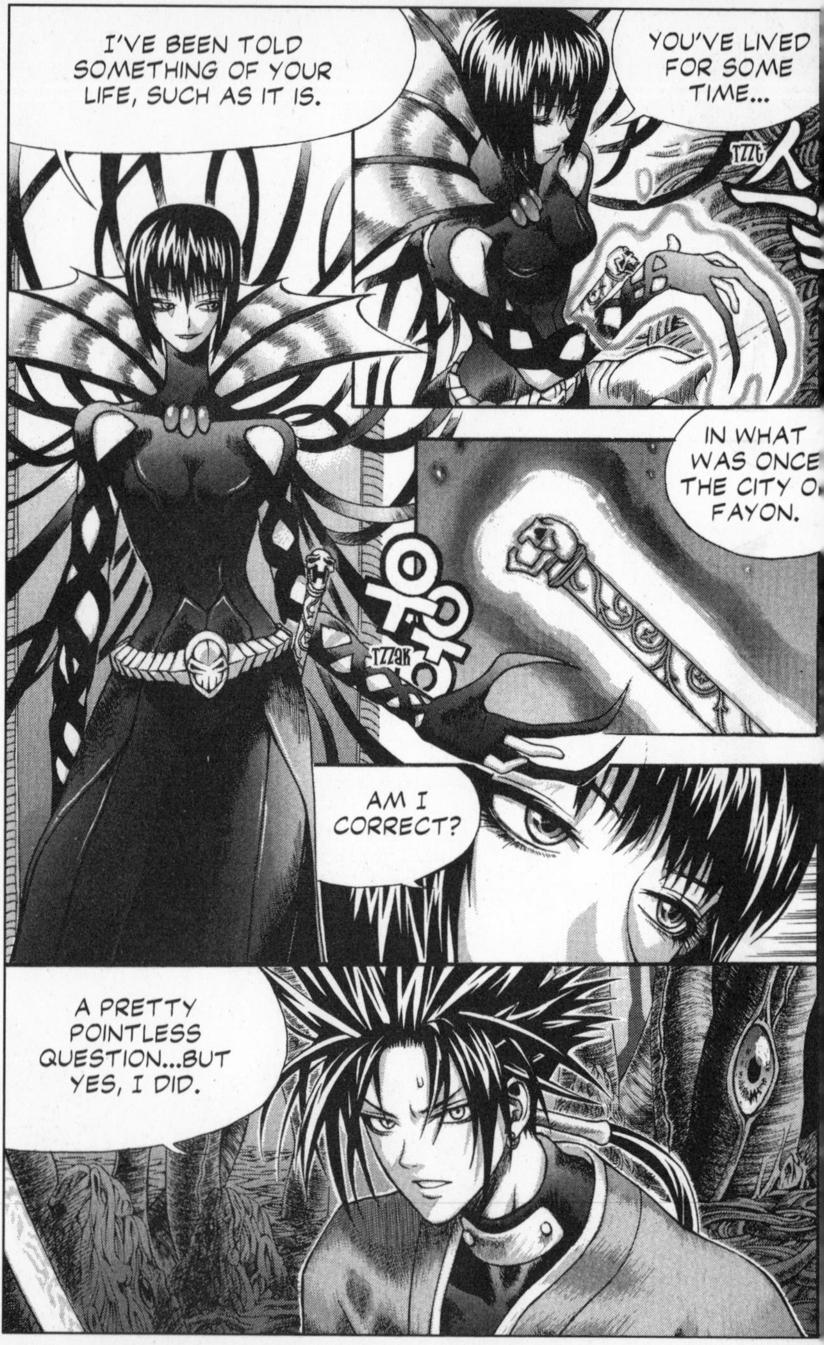
I'VE BEEN TOLD SOMETHING OF YOUR LIFE, SUCH AS IT IS.
YOU'VE LIVED FOR SOME TIME...
TZZT
IN WHAT WAS ONCE THE CITY O FAYON.
TZZAK
AM I CORRECT?
A PRETTY POINTLESS QUESTION...BUT YES, I DID.

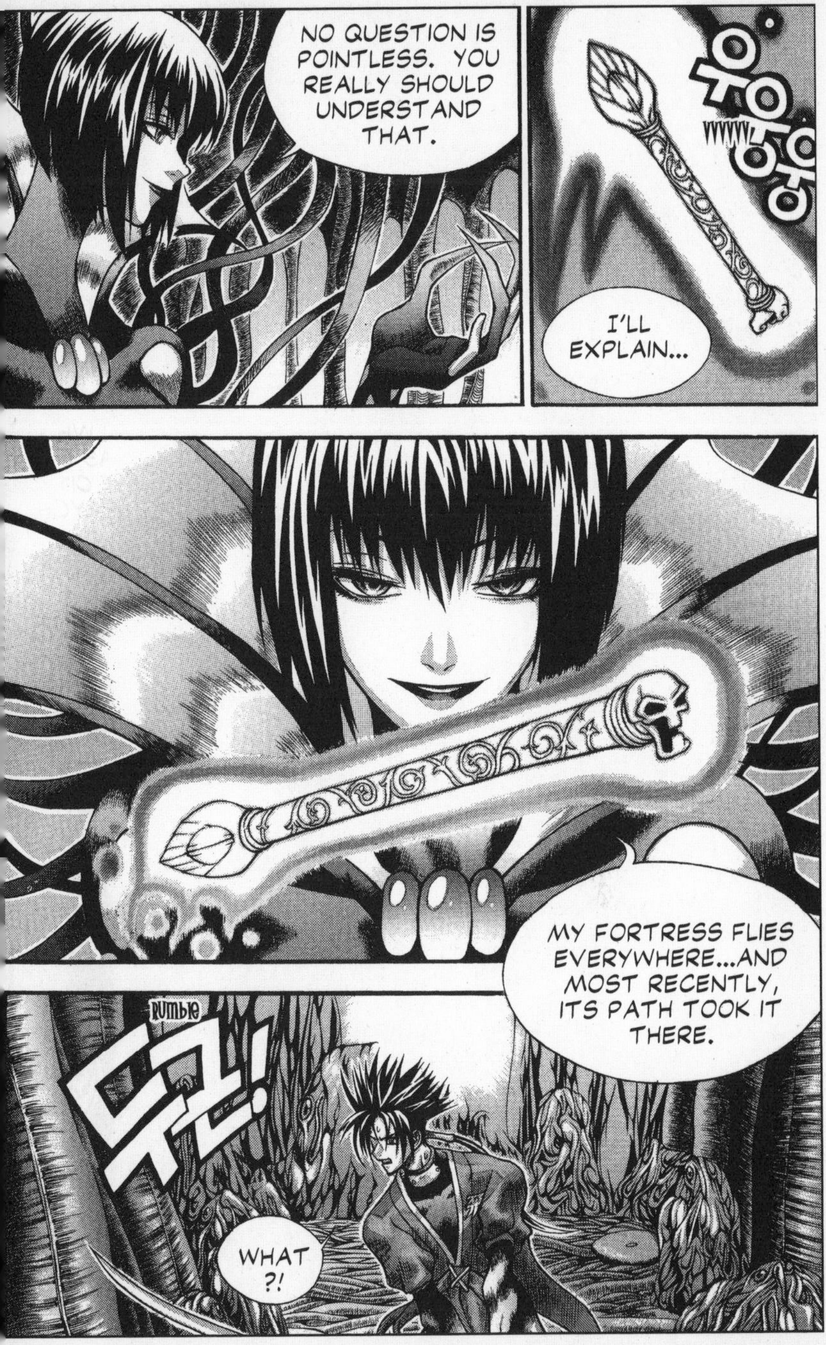
NO QUESTION IS POINTLESS. YOU REALLY SHOULD UNDERSTAND THAT.
I'LL EXPLAIN...
MY FORTRESS FLIES EVERYWHERE...AND MOST RECENTLY, ITS PATH TOOK IT THERE.
RUMBLE
WHAT ?!

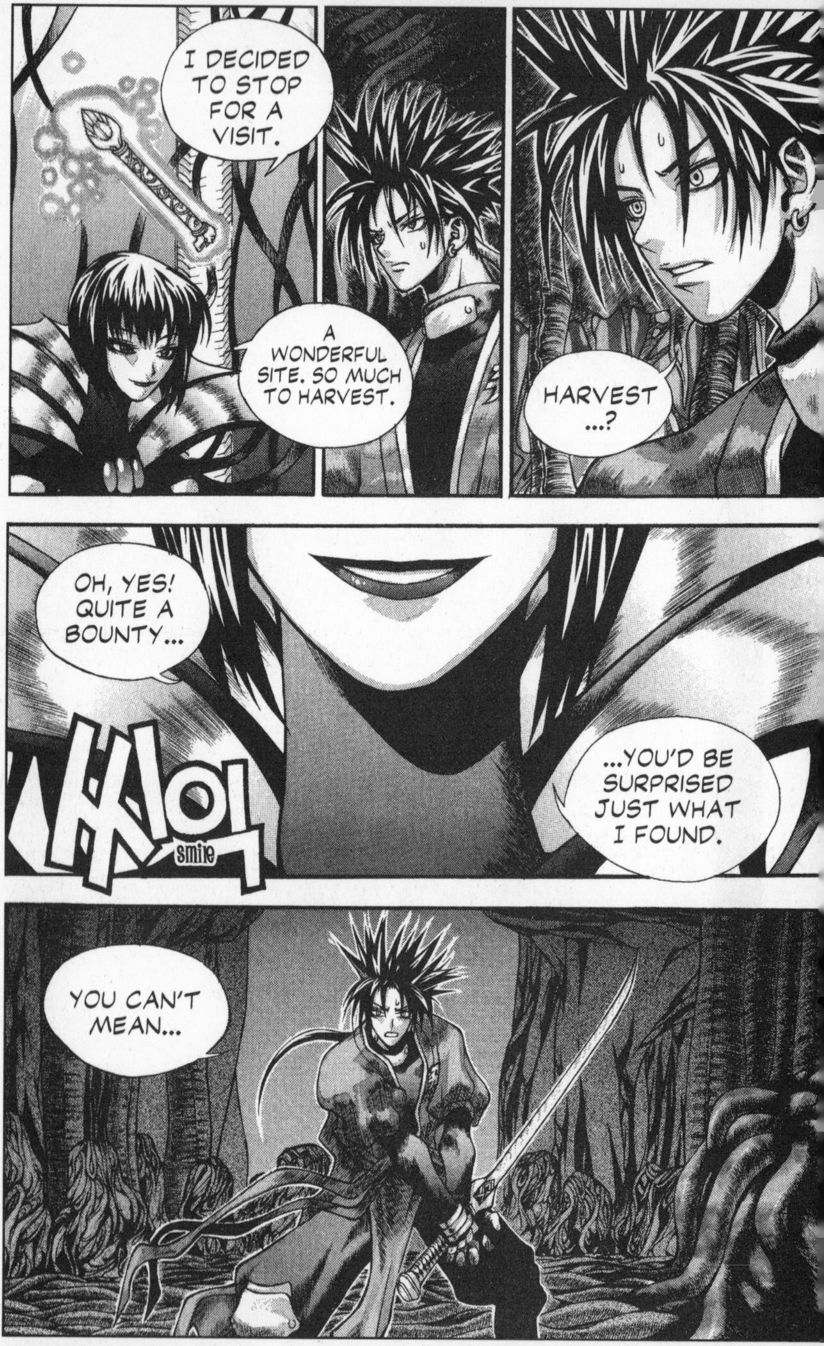
I DECIDED TO STOP FOR A VISIT.
A WONDERFUL SITE. SO MUCH TO HARVEST.
HARVEST ...?
OH, YES! QUITE A BOUNTY...
smile
...YOU'D BE SURPRISED JUST WHAT I FOUND.
YOU CAN'T MEAN...

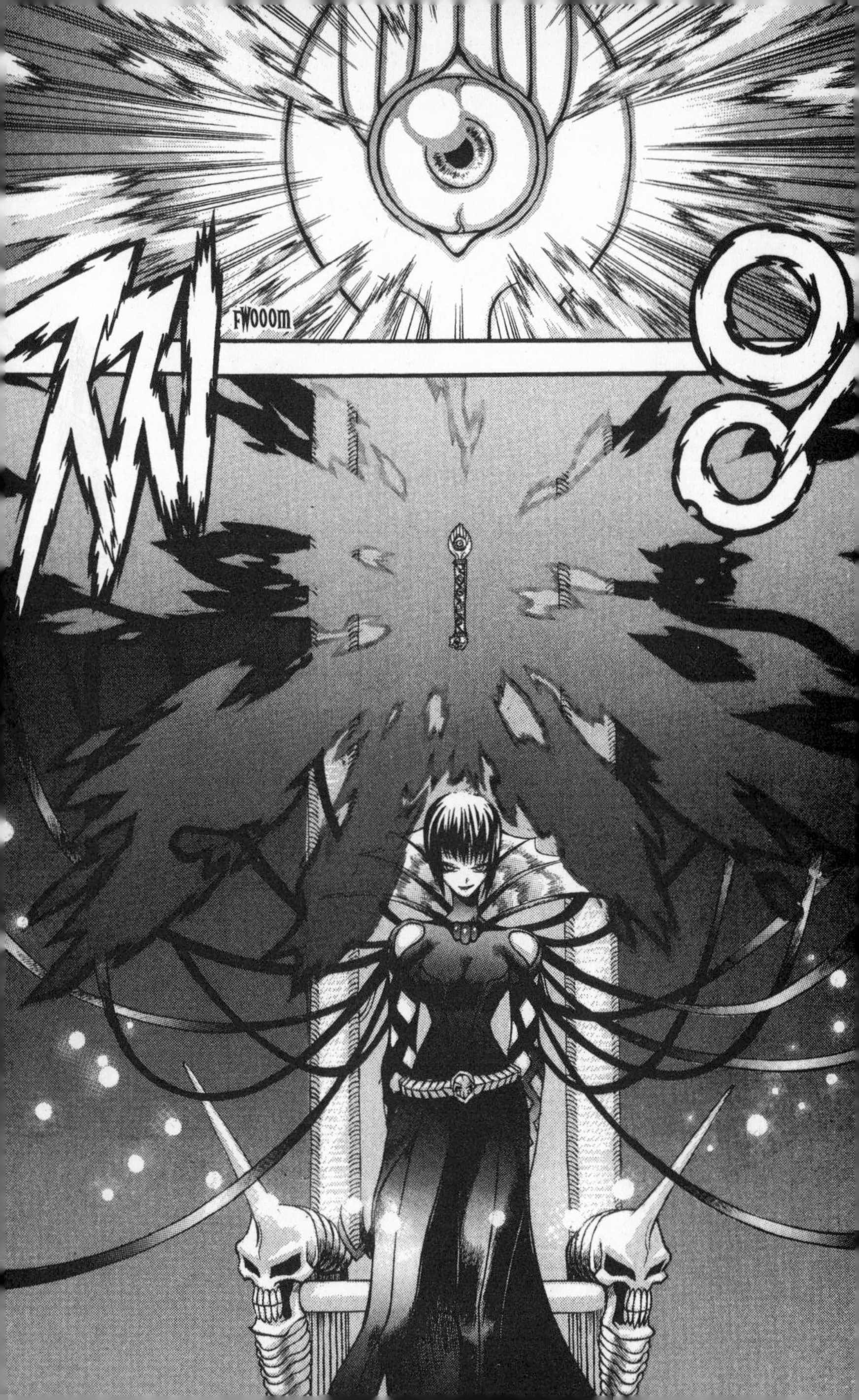
FWOOOM

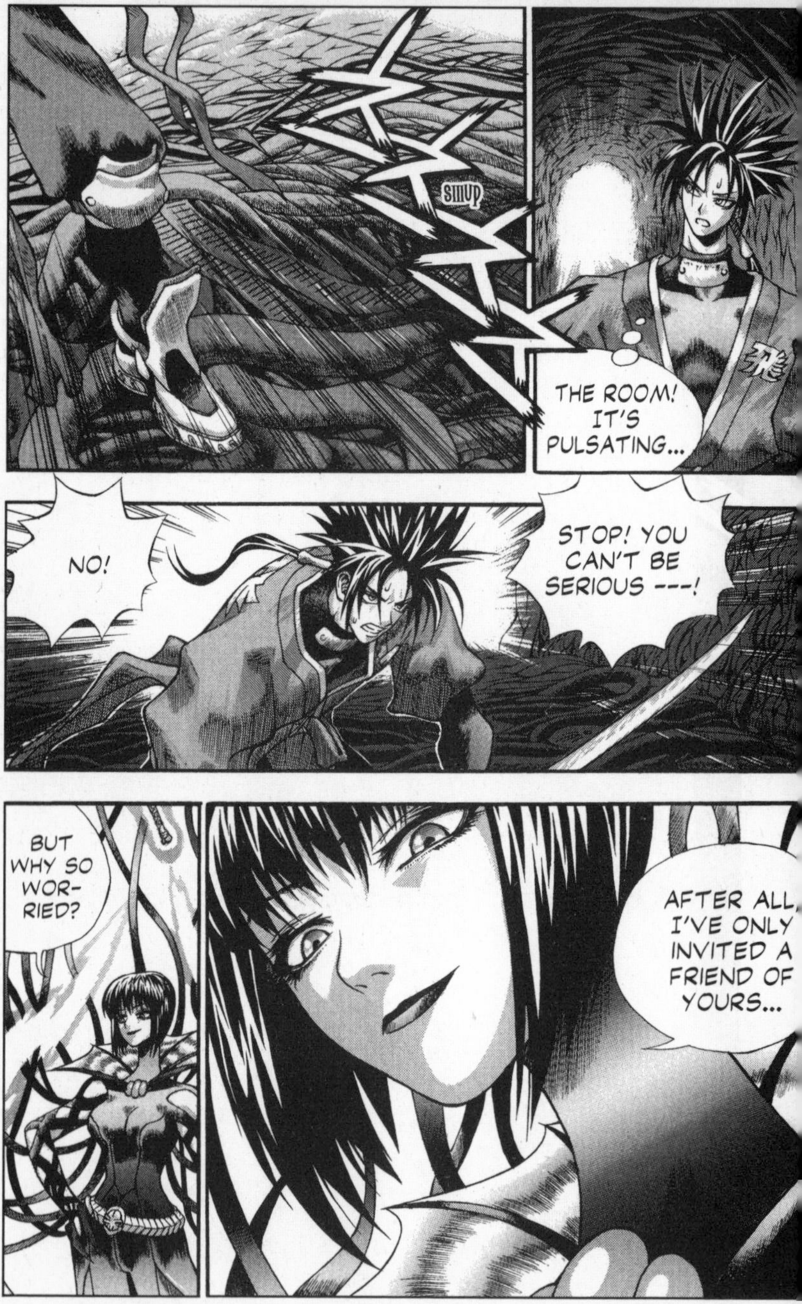
SHUP
THE ROOM! IT'S PULSATING...
NO!
STOP! YOU CAN'T BE SERIOUS ---!
BUT WHY SO WOR-RIED?
AFTER ALL, I'VE ONLY INVITED A FRIEND OF YOURS...

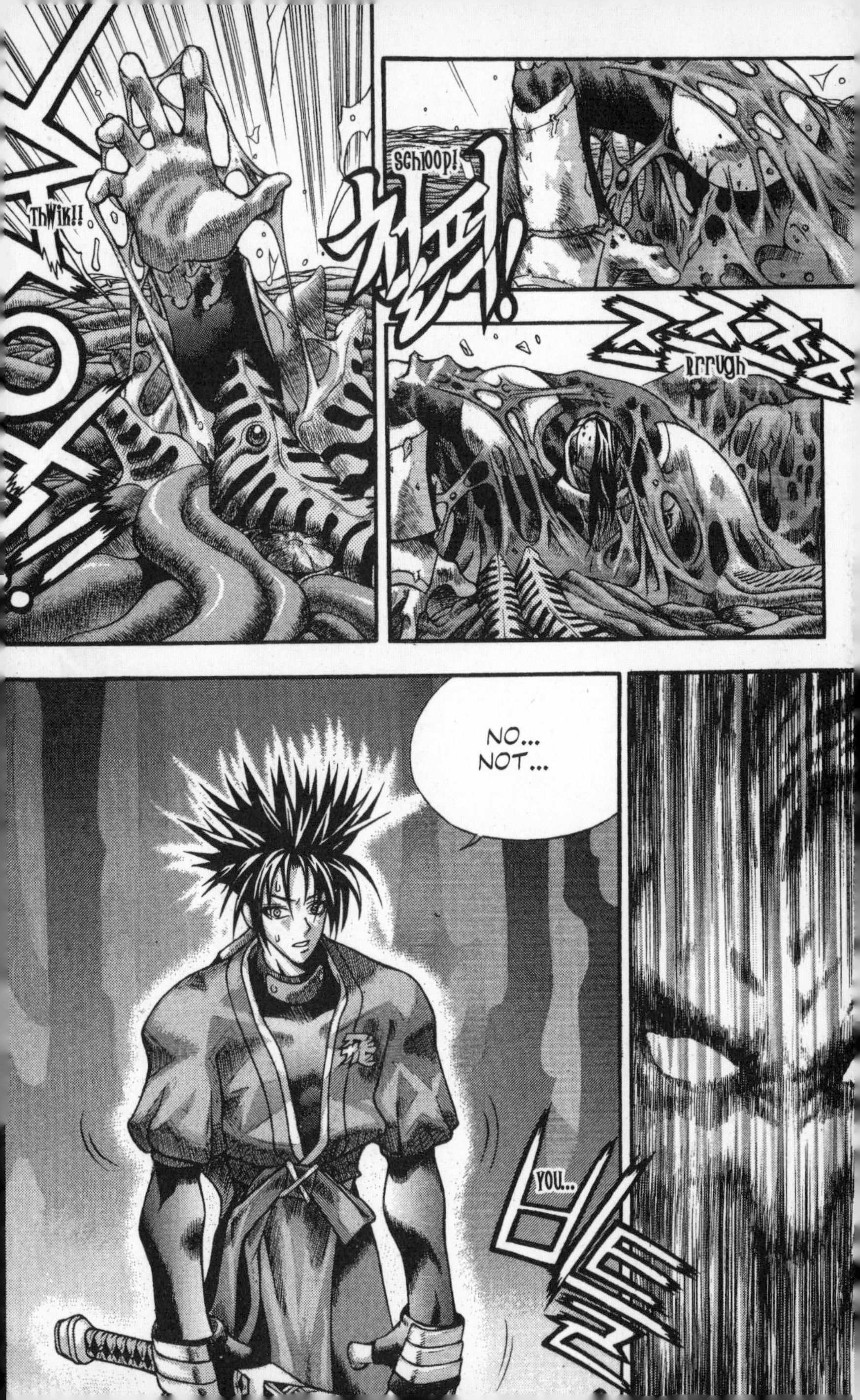
ThWiK!!
SCHLOOP!
RRRUGH
NO... NOT...
YOU...

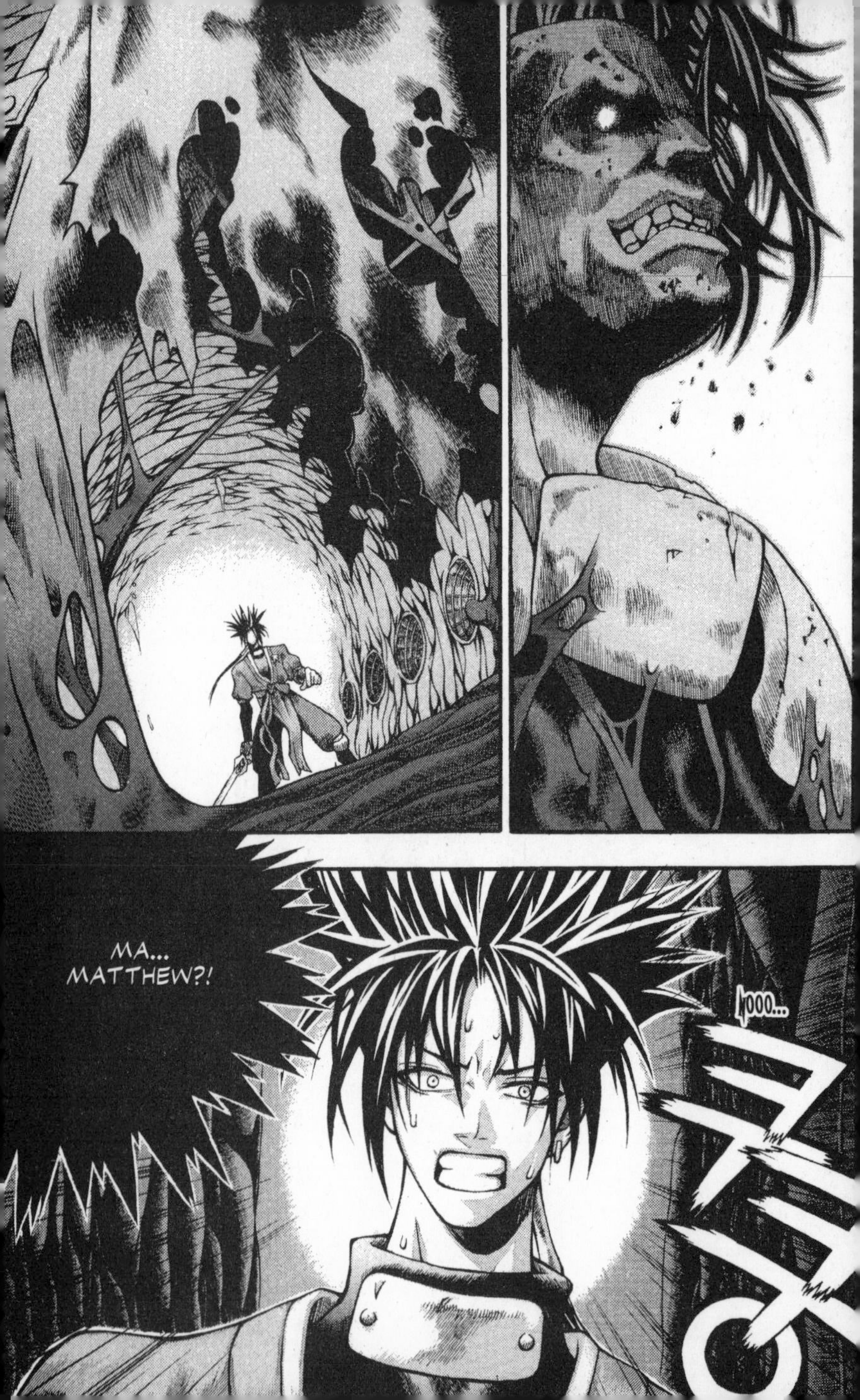
MA... MATTHEW?!
kooo...

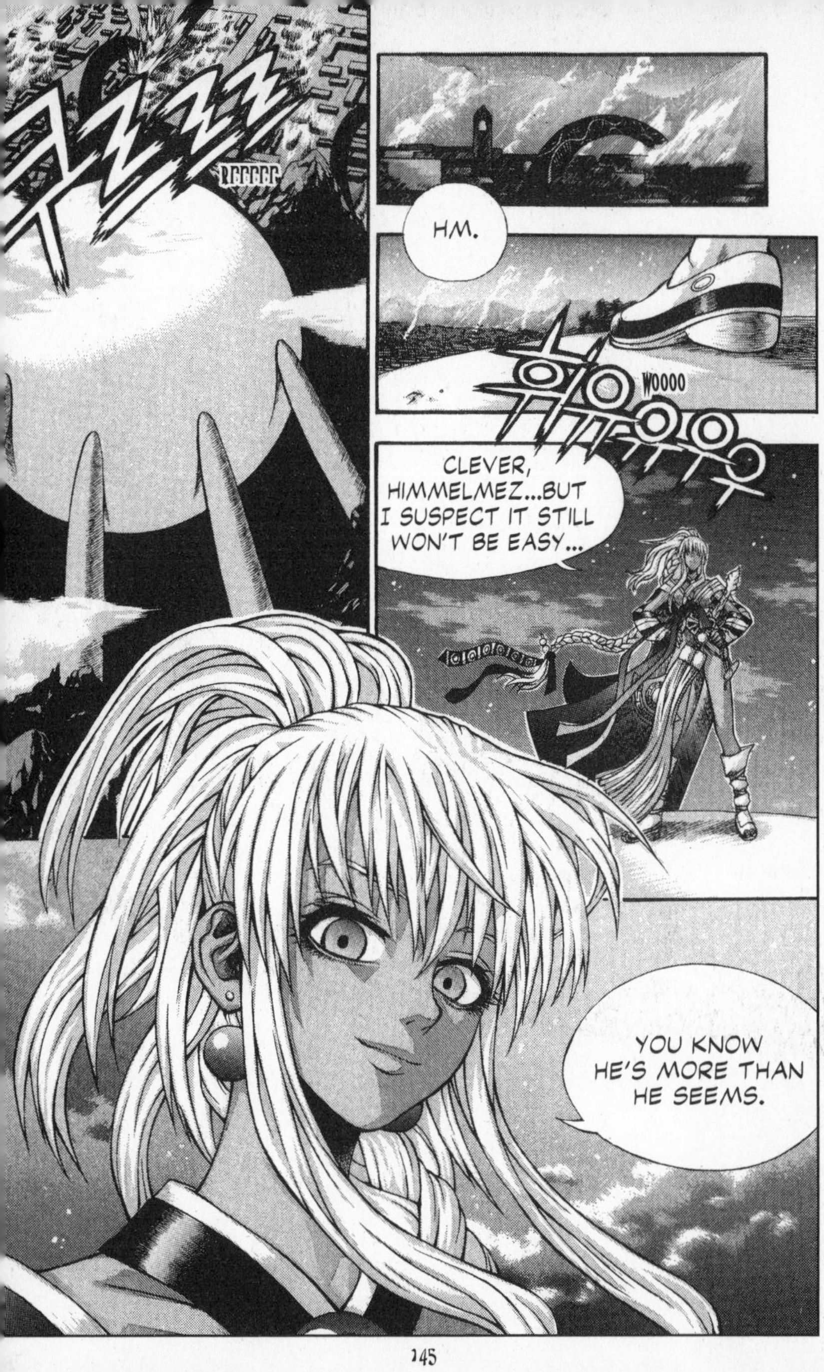
RRRRRR
HM.
WOOOO
CLEVER, HIMMELMEZ...BUT I SUSPECT IT STILL WON'T BE EASY...
YOU KNOW HE'S MORE THAN HE SEEMS.

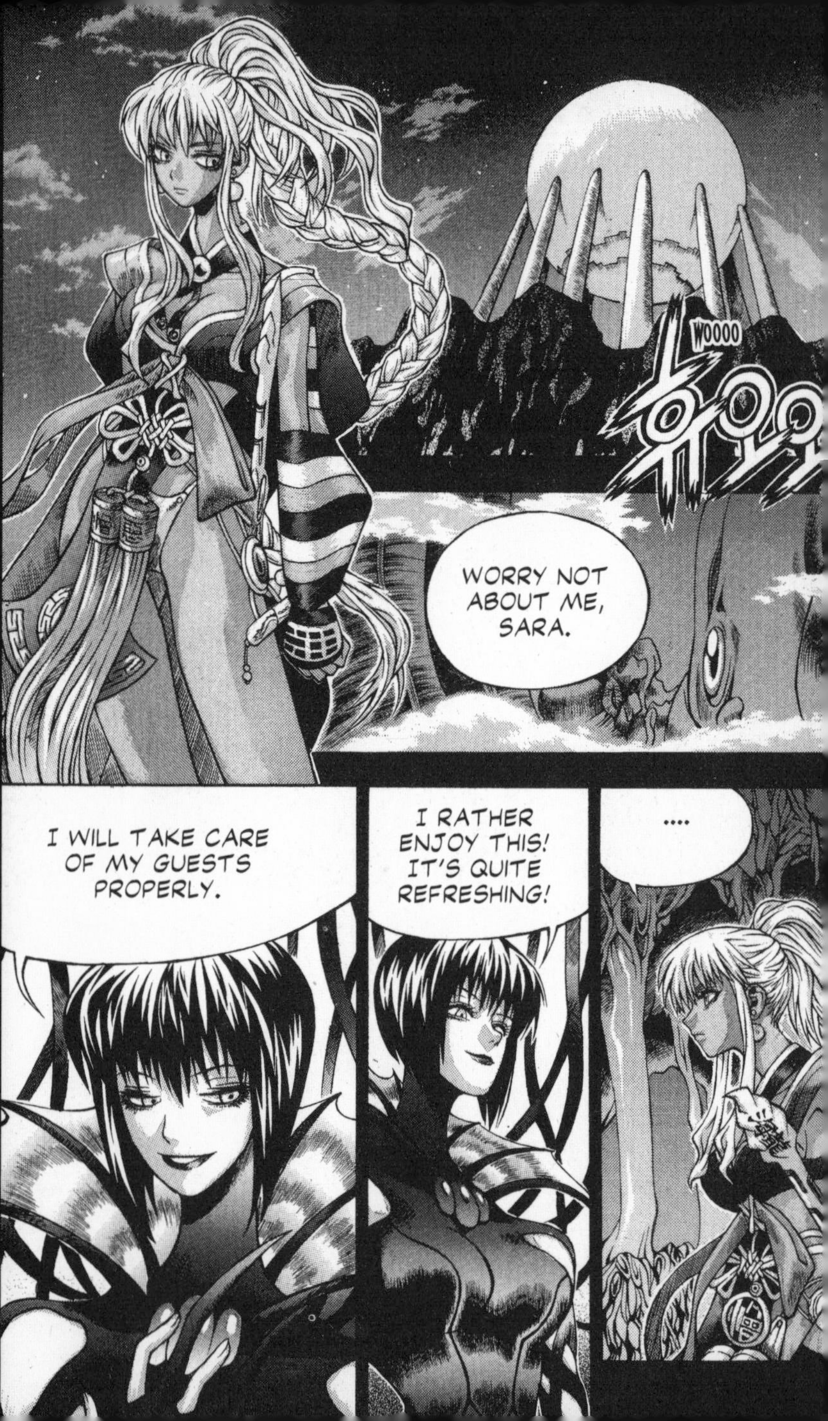
WOOOO
WORRY NOT ABOUT ME, SARA.
I WILL TAKE CARE OF MY GUESTS PROPERLY.
I RATHER ENJOY THIS! IT'S QUITE REFRESHING!
....

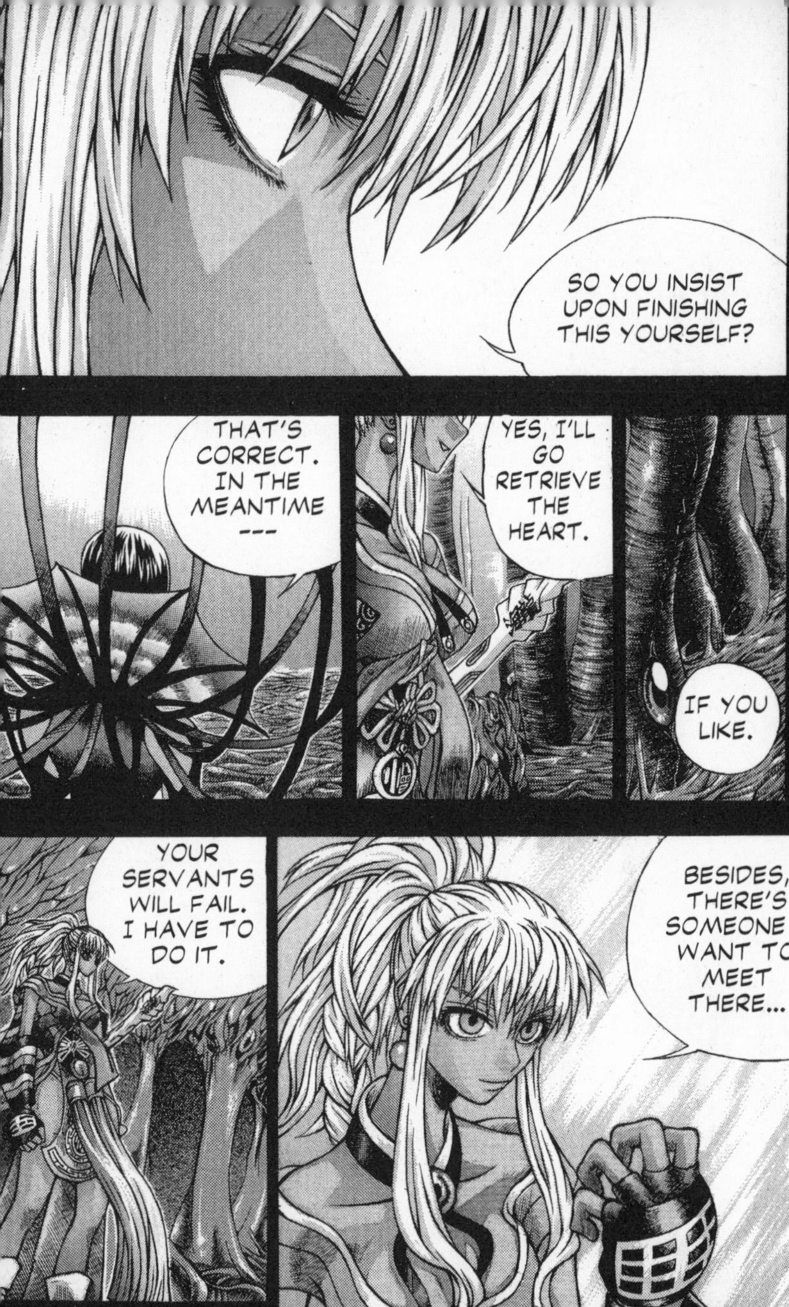
SO YOU INSIST UPON FINISHING THIS YOURSELF?
THAT'S CORRECT. IN THE MEANTIME ---
YES, I'LL GO RETRIEVE THE HEART.
IF YOU LIKE.
YOUR SERVANTS WILL FAIL. I HAVE TO DO IT.
BESIDES, THERE'S SOMEONE I WANT TO MEET THERE...

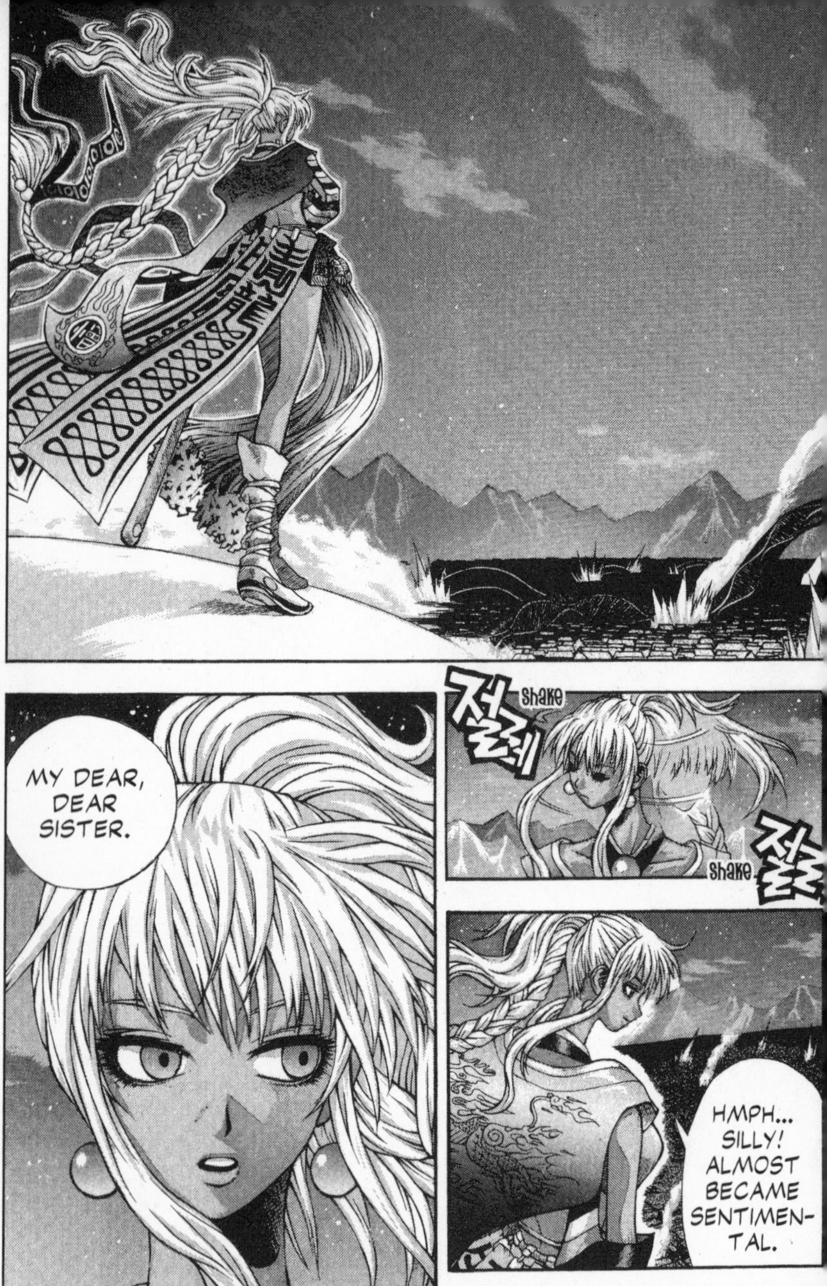
MY DEAR, DEAR SISTER.
절레
shake
shake
절레
HMPH... SILLY! ALMOST BECAME SENTIMEN-TAL.

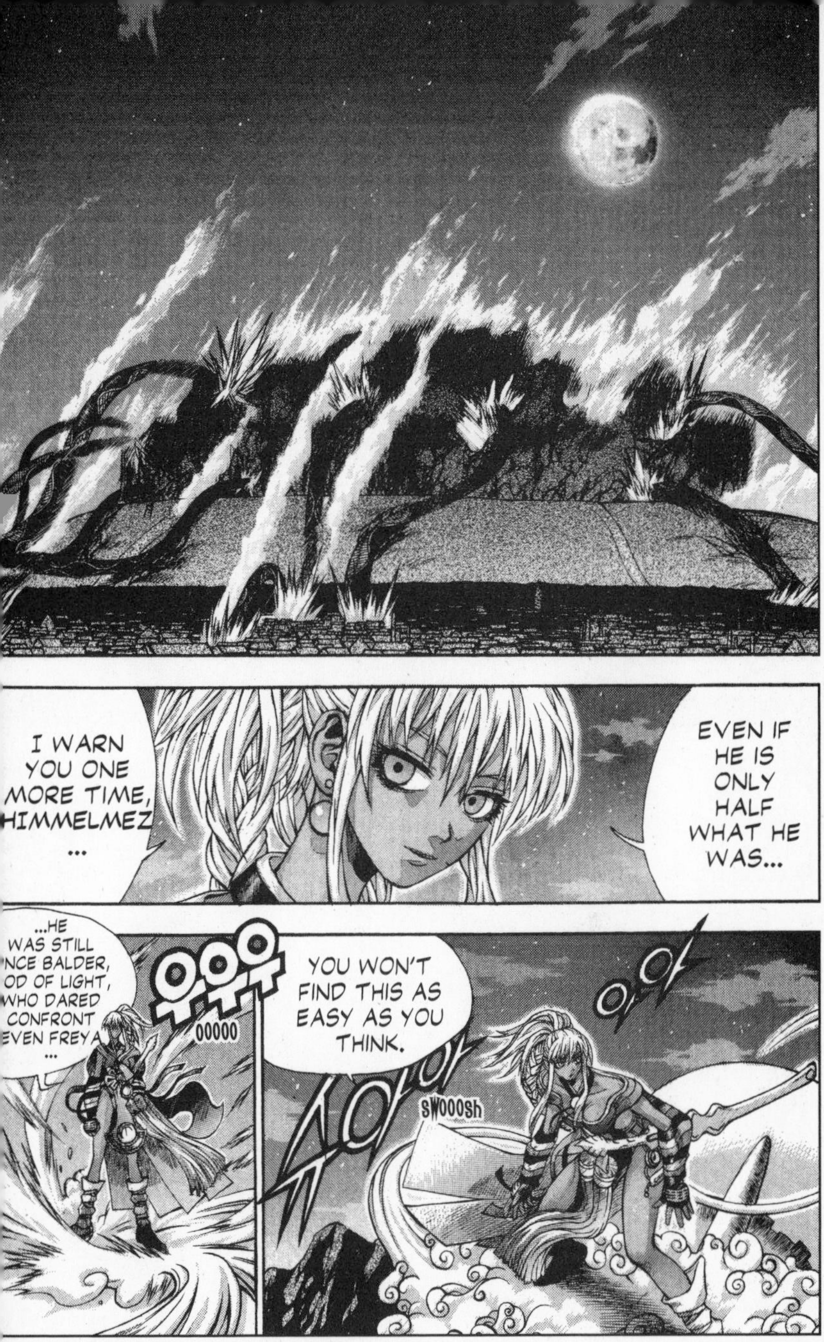

I WARN YOU ONE MORE TIME, HIMMELMEZ ...
EVEN IF HE IS ONLY HALF WHAT HE WAS...
...HE WAS STILL NCE BALDER, OD OF LIGHT, WHO DARED CONFRONT EVEN FREYA ...
OOOOO
YOU WON'T FIND THIS AS EASY AS YOU THINK.
SWOOOSH

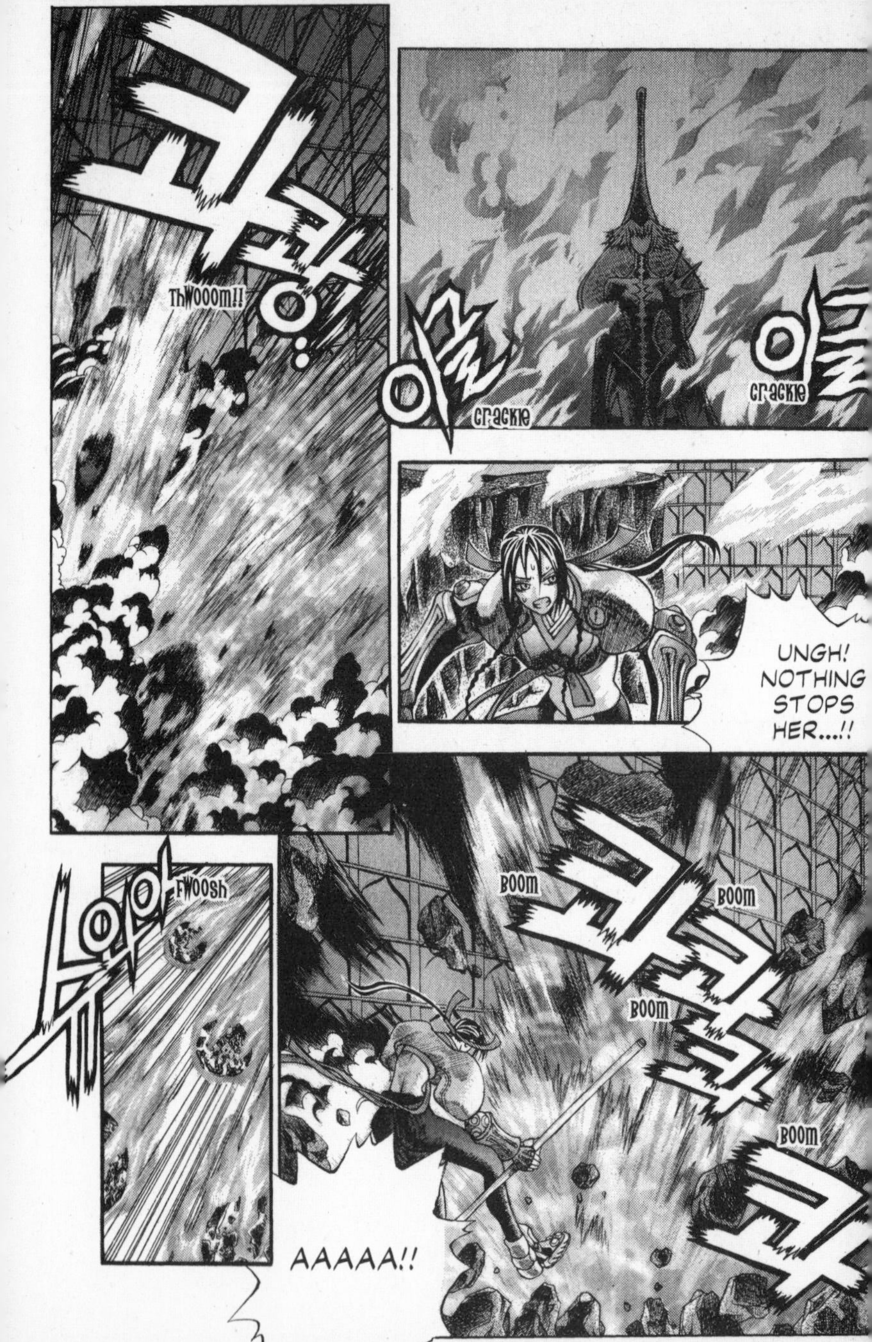
ThWOOOM!!
CRACKLE
CRACKLE
UNGH! NOTHING STOPS HER...!!
FWOOSh
BOOM
BOOM
BOOM
BOOM
AAAAA!!

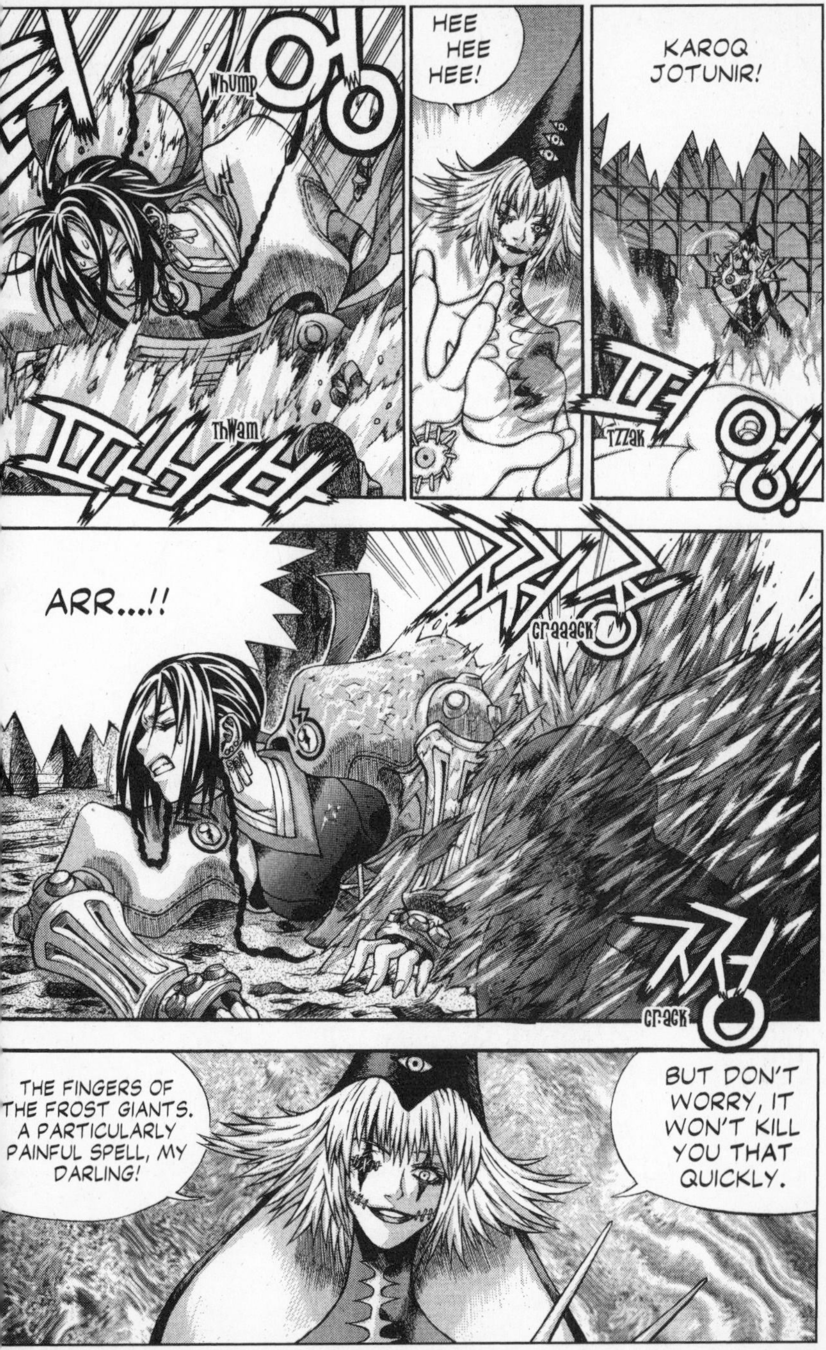

Whump
Thwam
HEE HEE HEE!
KAROQ JOTUNIR!
Tzzak
ARR...!!
Craaack
Crack
THE FINGERS OF THE FROST GIANTS. A PARTICULARLY PAINFUL SPELL, MY DARLING!
BUT DON'T WORRY, IT WON'T KILL YOU THAT QUICKLY.

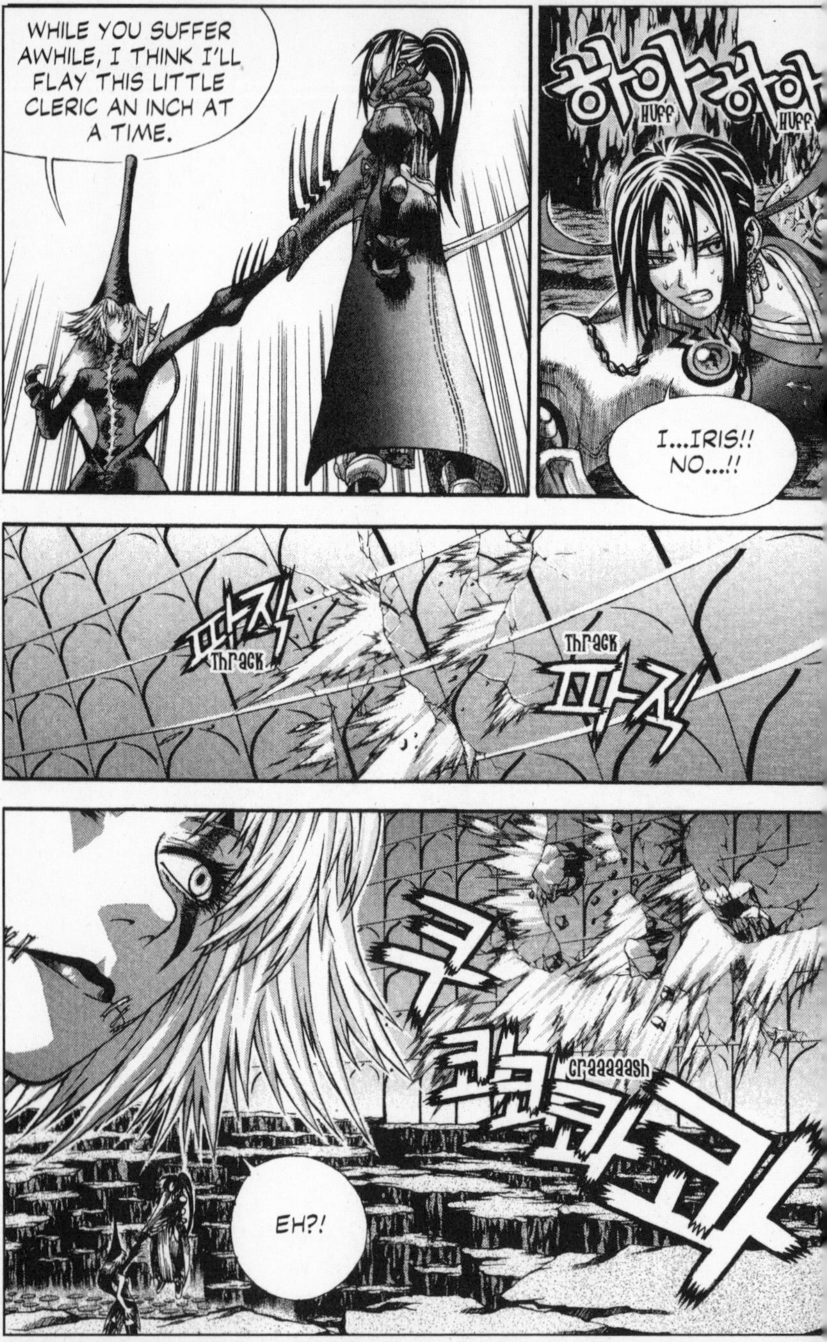
WHILE YOU SUFFER AWHILE, I THINK I'LL FLAY THIS LITTLE CLERIC AN INCH AT A TIME.
HUFF
HUFF
I...IRIS!! NO...!!
Thrack
Thrack
Craaaaash
EH?!

RAGNAROK
라그나로크
IN TO THE ABYSS

STUDIO
DTCS

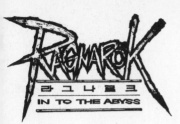

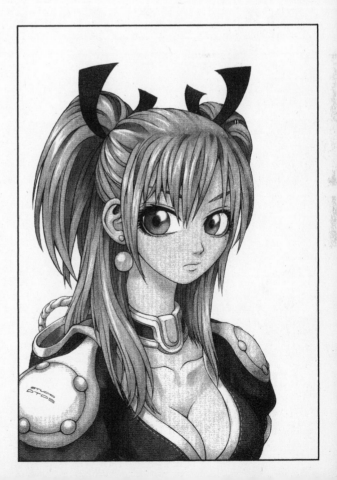

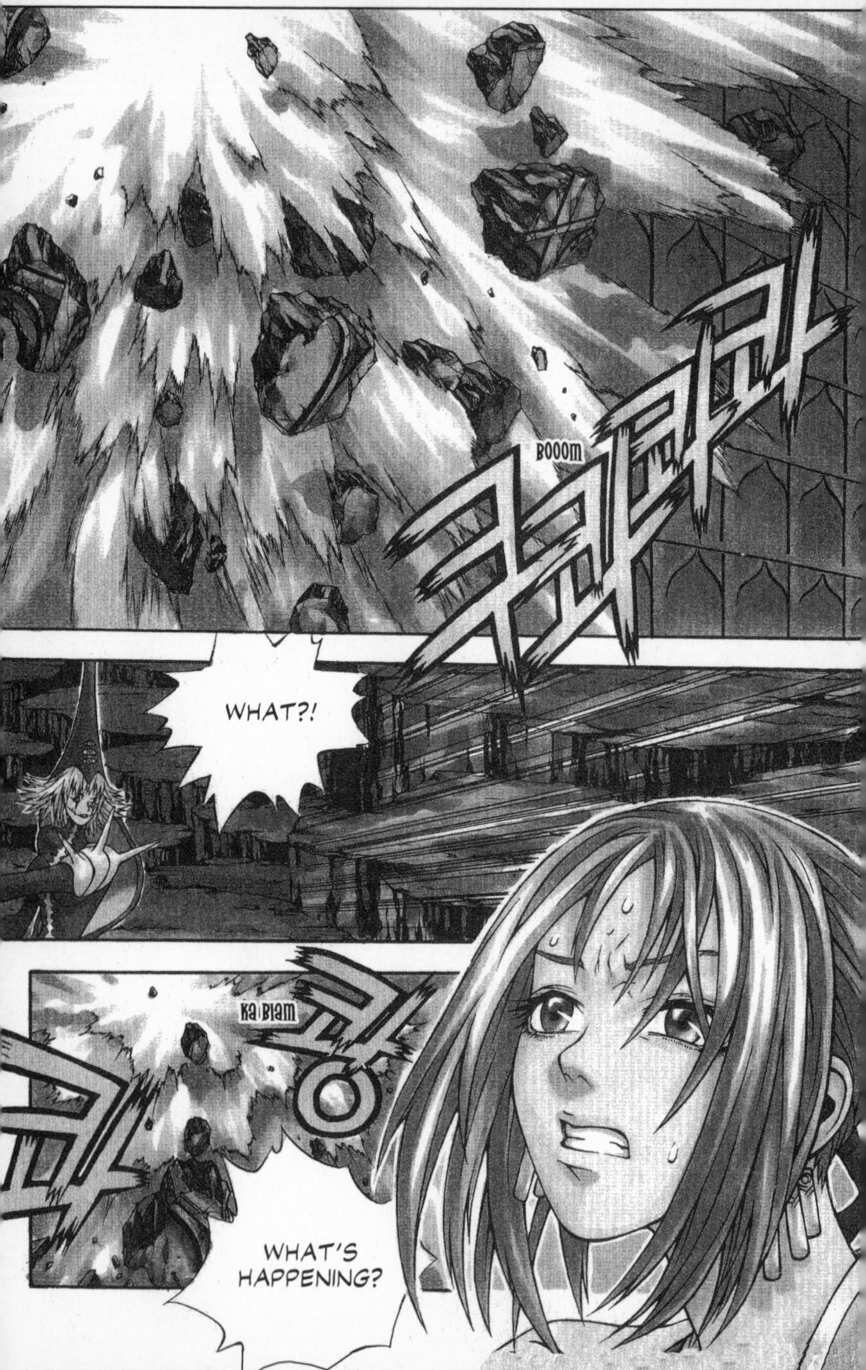
BOOOM
WHAT?!
KA-BLAM
WHAT'S HAPPENING?

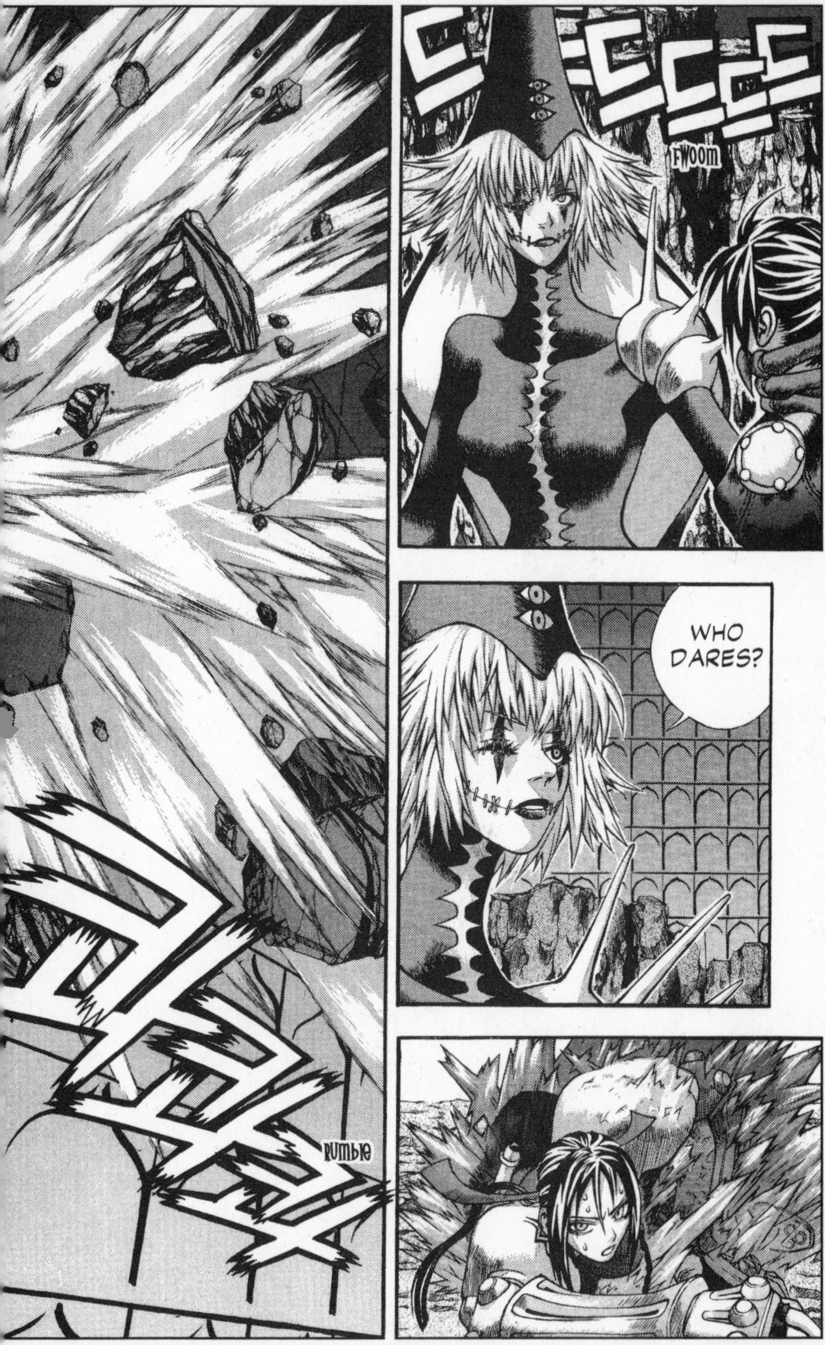
RUMBLE
FWOOM
WHO DARES?

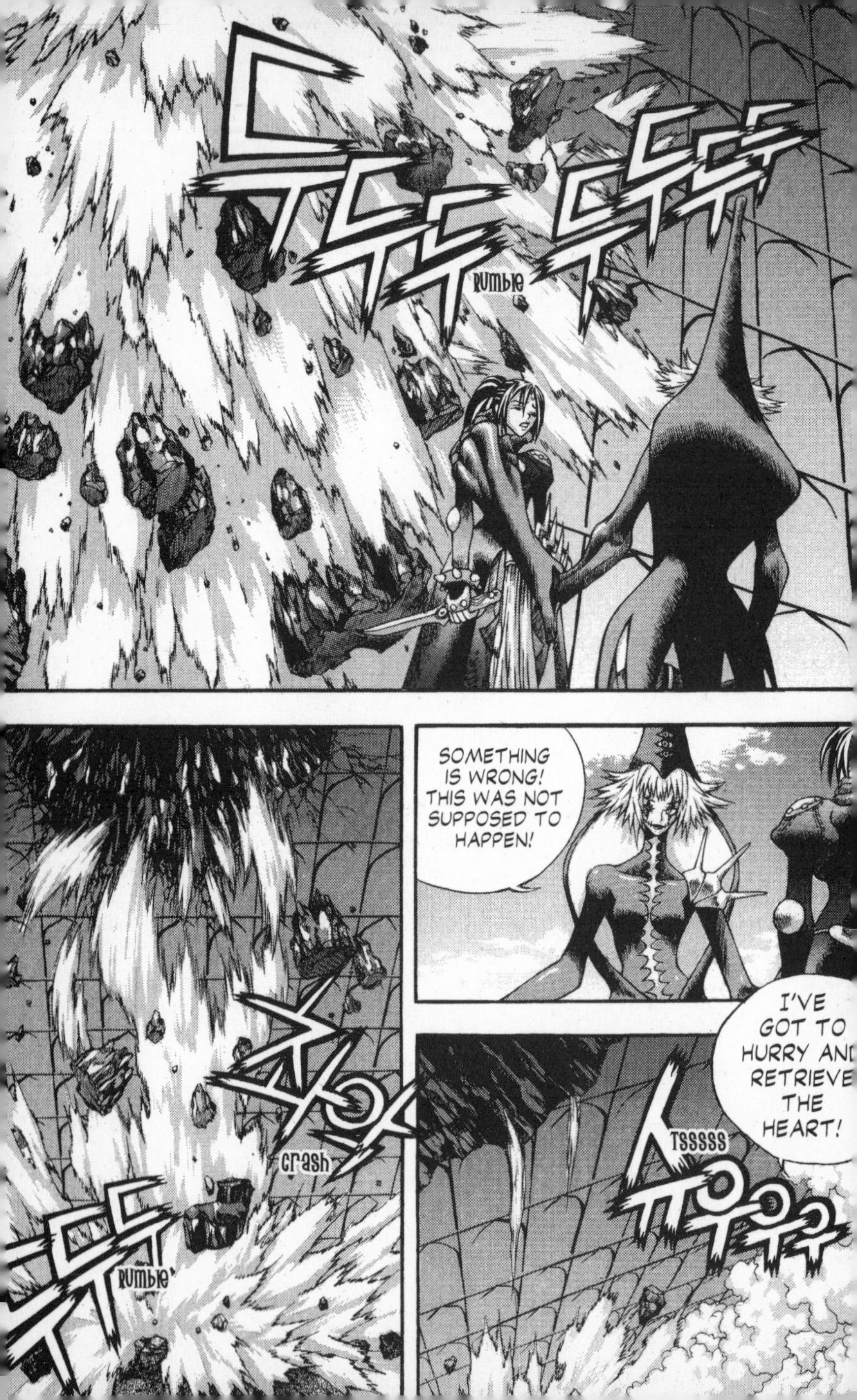
RUMBLE
SOMETHING IS WRONG! THIS WAS NOT SUPPOSED TO HAPPEN!
CRASH
RUMBLE
I'VE GOT TO HURRY AND RETRIEVE THE HEART!
TSSSSS

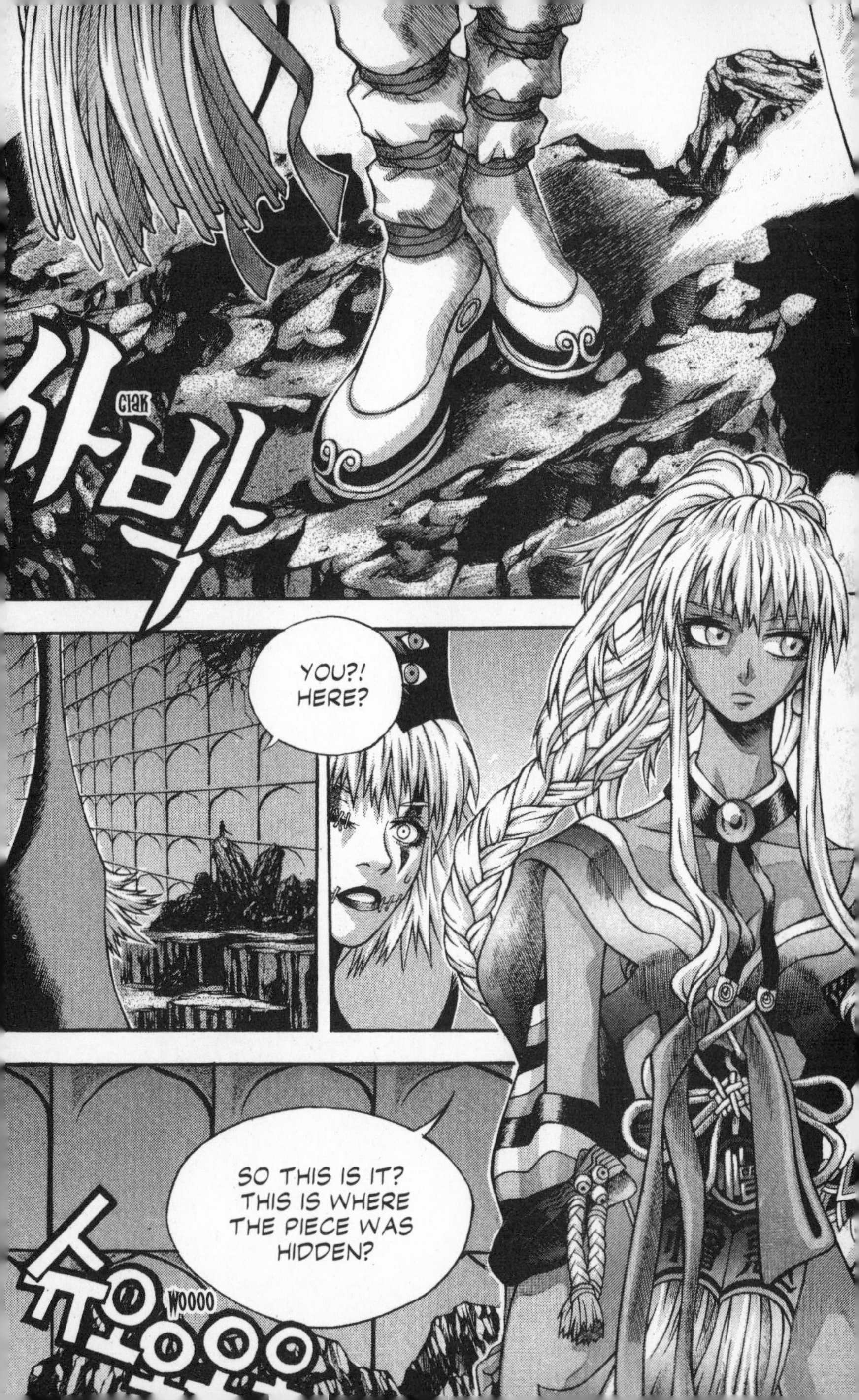

착
CIAK
YOU?! HERE?
SO THIS IS IT? THIS IS WHERE THE PIECE WAS HIDDEN?
슈우ㅇㅇㅇ
WOOOO

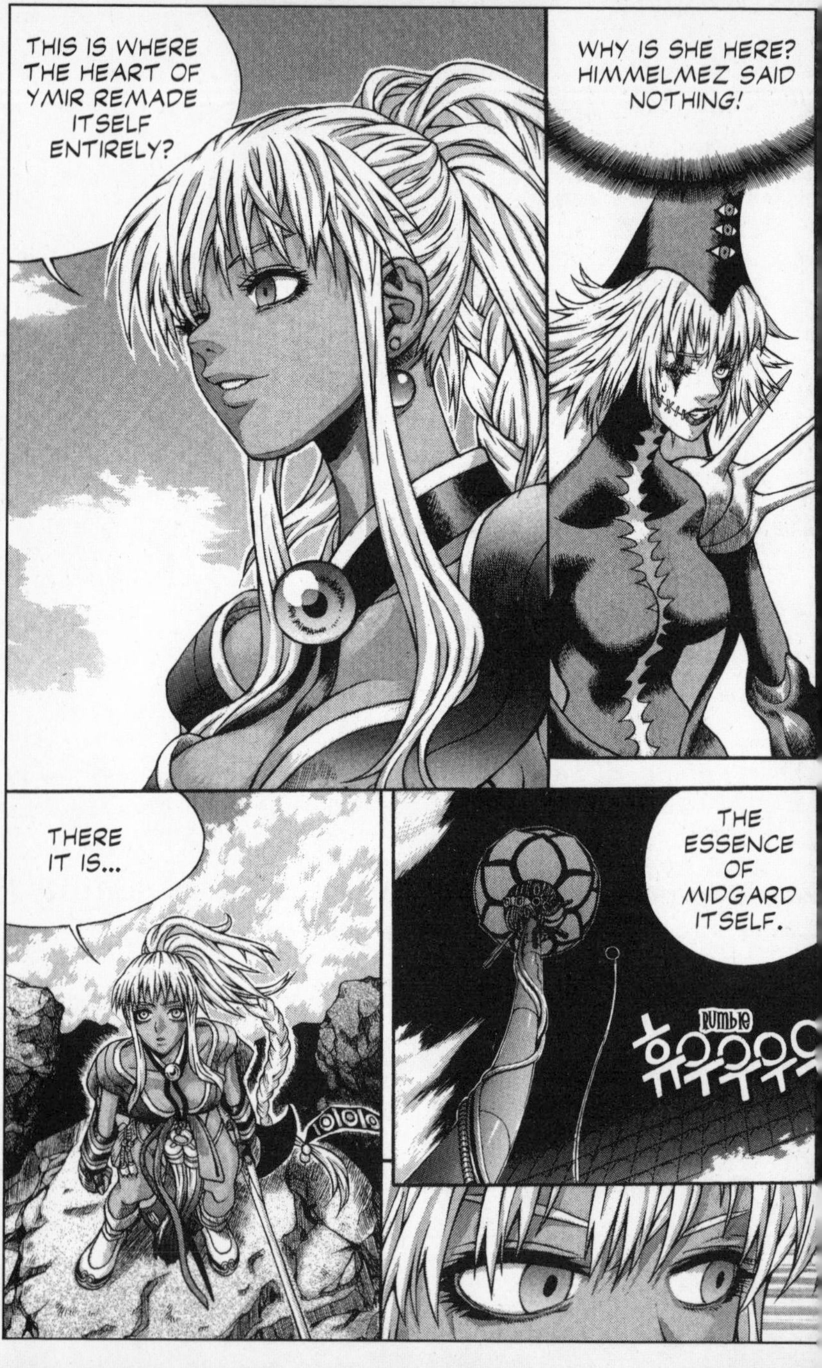
THIS IS WHERE THE HEART OF YMIR REMADE ITSELF ENTIRELY?
WHY IS SHE HERE? HIMMELMEZ SAID NOTHING!
THERE IT IS...
THE ESSENCE OF MIDGARD ITSELF.
RUMBLE
휴우우우

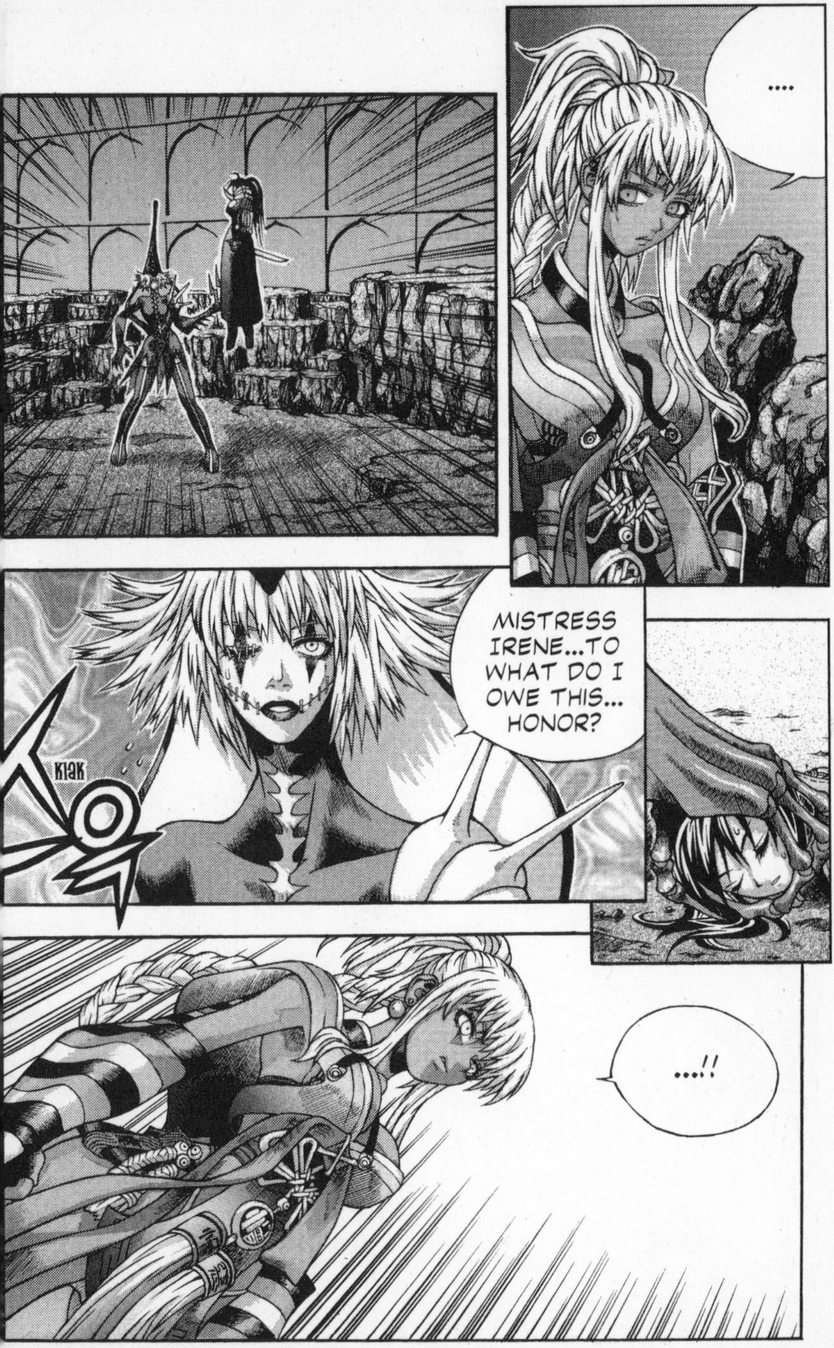
....
KIAK
MISTRESS IRENE...TO WHAT DO I OWE THIS... HONOR?
...!!

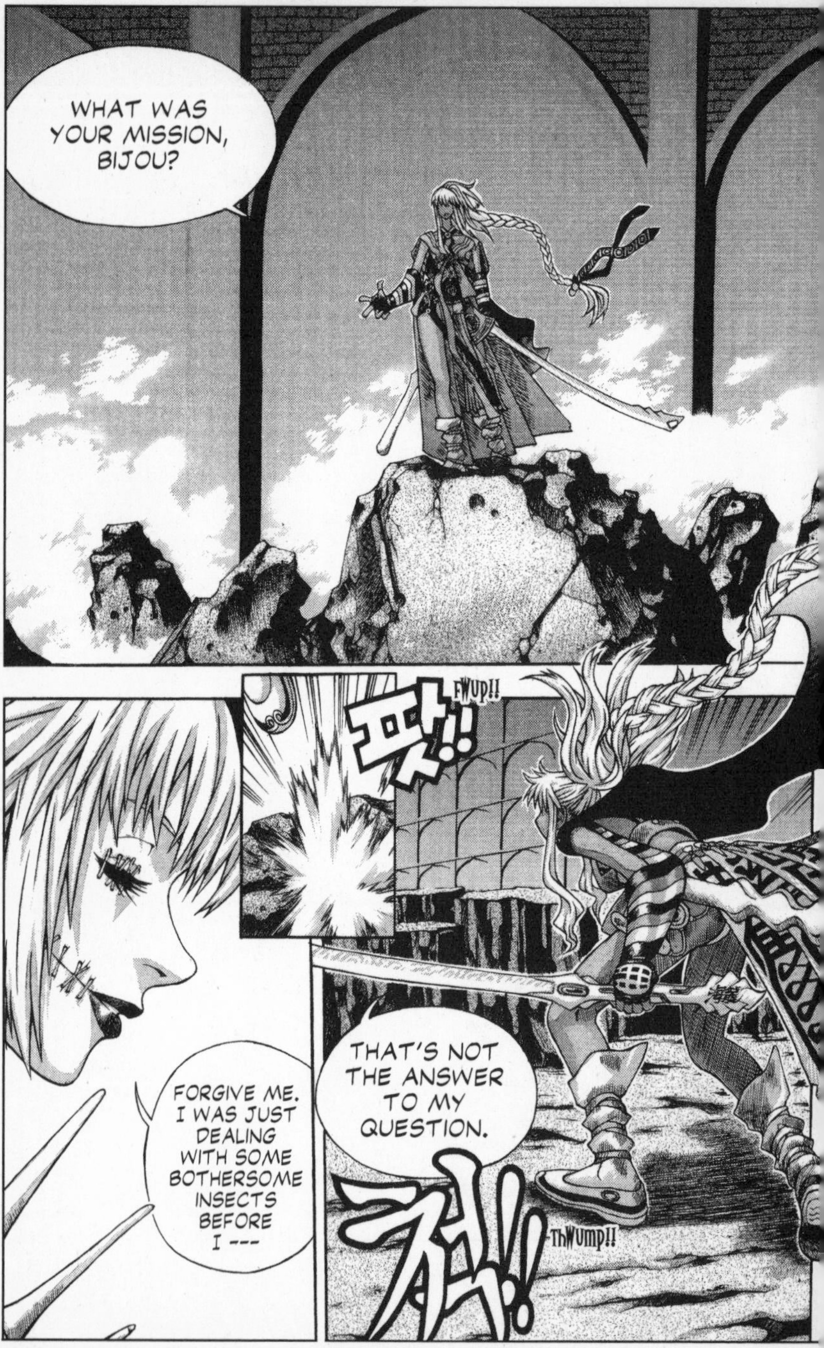
WHAT WAS YOUR MISSION, BIJOU?
FORGIVE ME. I WAS JUST DEALING WITH SOME BOTHERSOME INSECTS BEFORE I ---
FWUP!!
THAT'S NOT THE ANSWER TO MY QUESTION.
ThWump!!

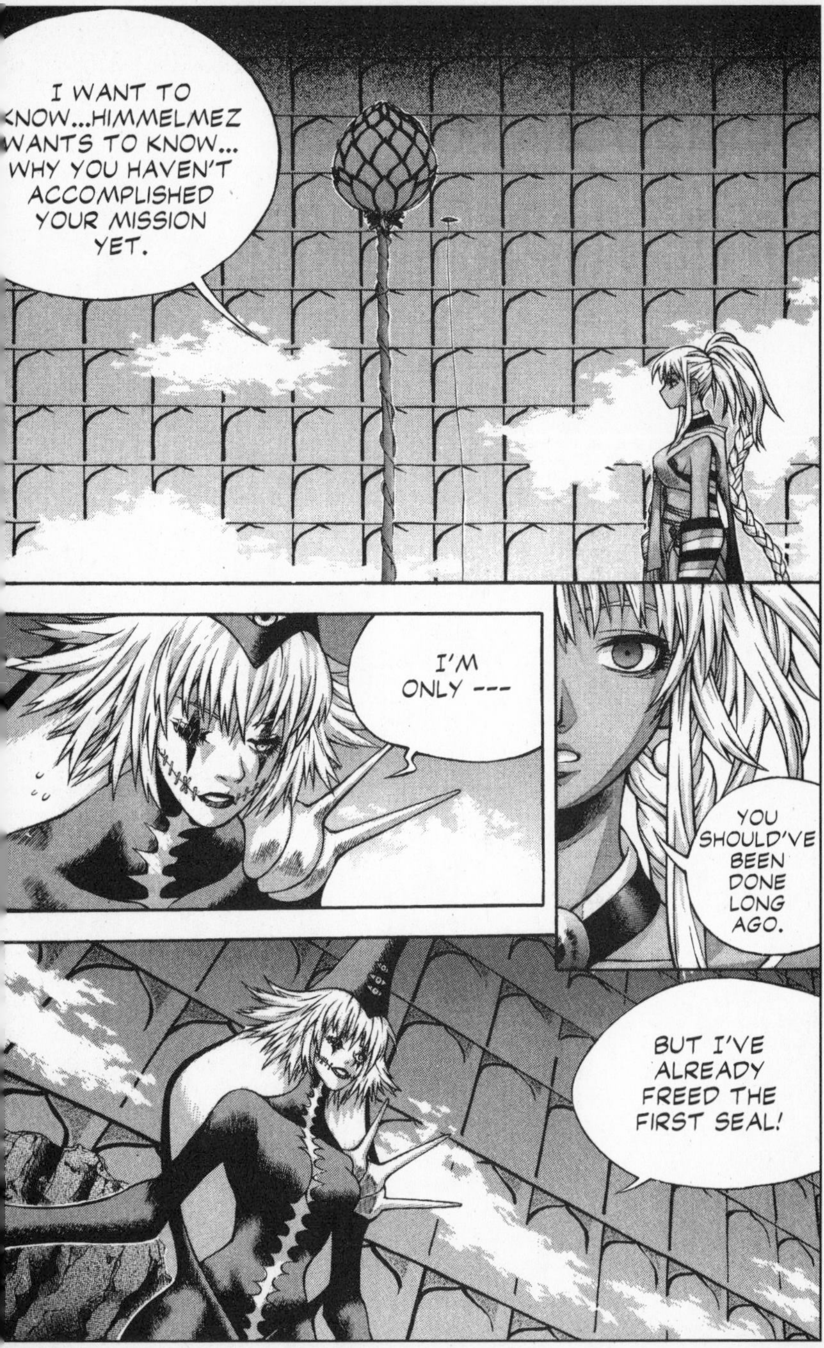
I WANT TO KNOW...HIMMELMEZ WANTS TO KNOW... WHY YOU HAVEN'T ACCOMPLISHED YOUR MISSION YET.
I'M ONLY ---
YOU SHOULD'VE BEEN DONE LONG AGO.
BUT I'VE ALREADY FREED THE FIRST SEAL!

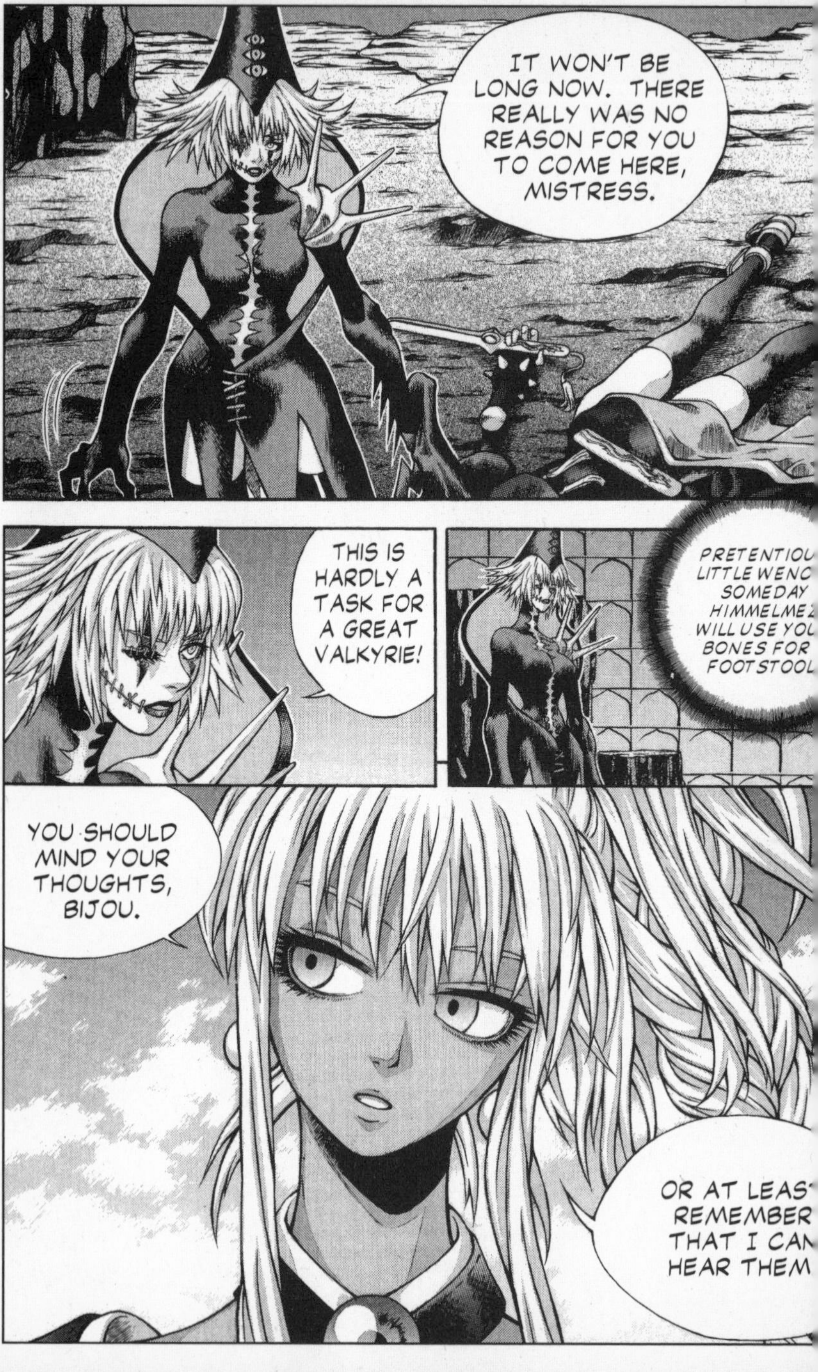
IT WON'T BE LONG NOW. THERE REALLY WAS NO REASON FOR YOU TO COME HERE, MISTRESS.
THIS IS HARDLY A TASK FOR A GREAT VALKYRIE!
PRETENTIOU LITTLE WENC SOMEDAY HIMMELME WILL USE YOU BONES FOR FOOTSTOOL
YOU SHOULD MIND YOUR THOUGHTS, BIJOU.
OR AT LEAS REMEMBER THAT I CAN HEAR THEM

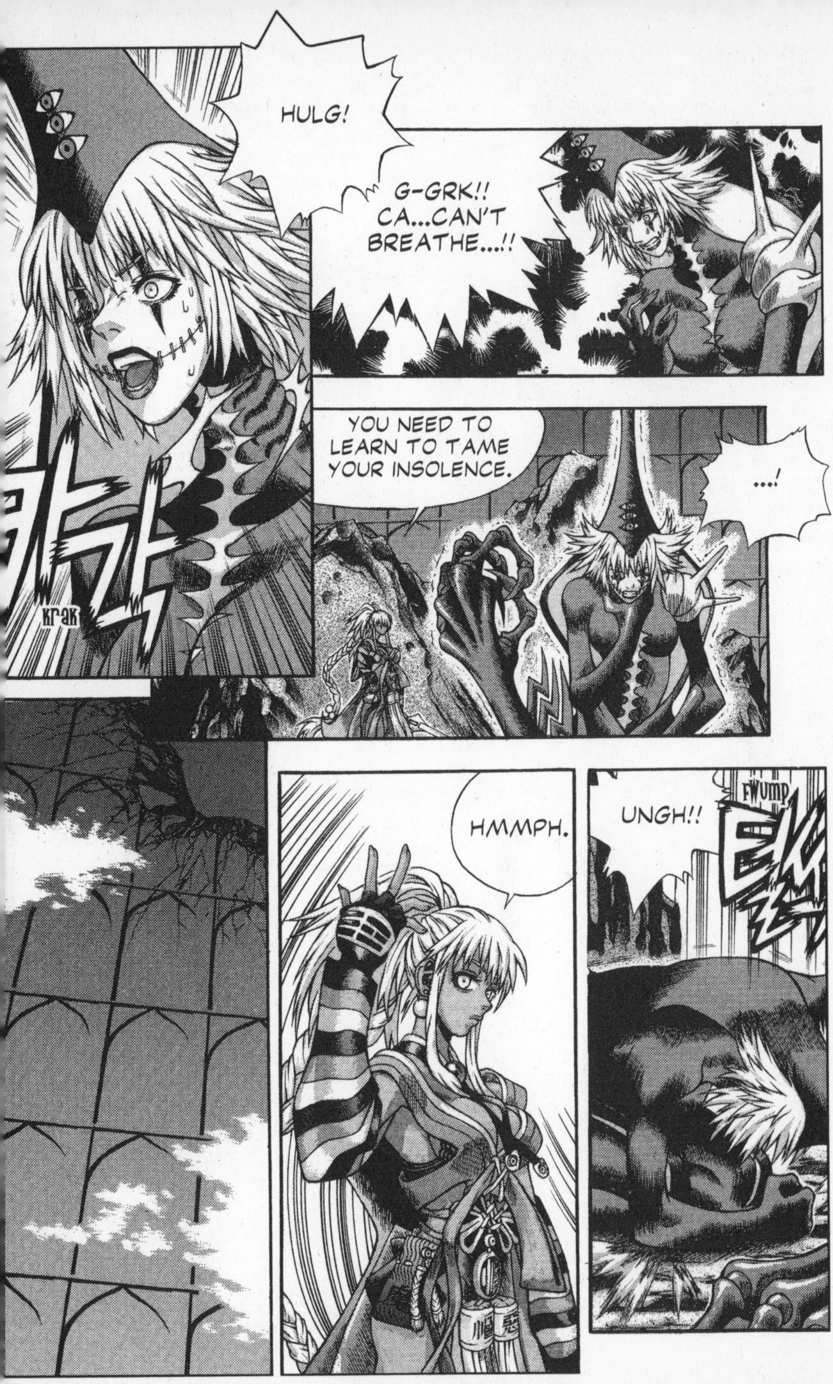
HULG!
KRAK
G-GRK!! CA...CAN'T BREATHE...!!
YOU NEED TO LEARN TO TAME YOUR INSOLENCE.
...!
HMMPH.
UNGH!!
FWUMP

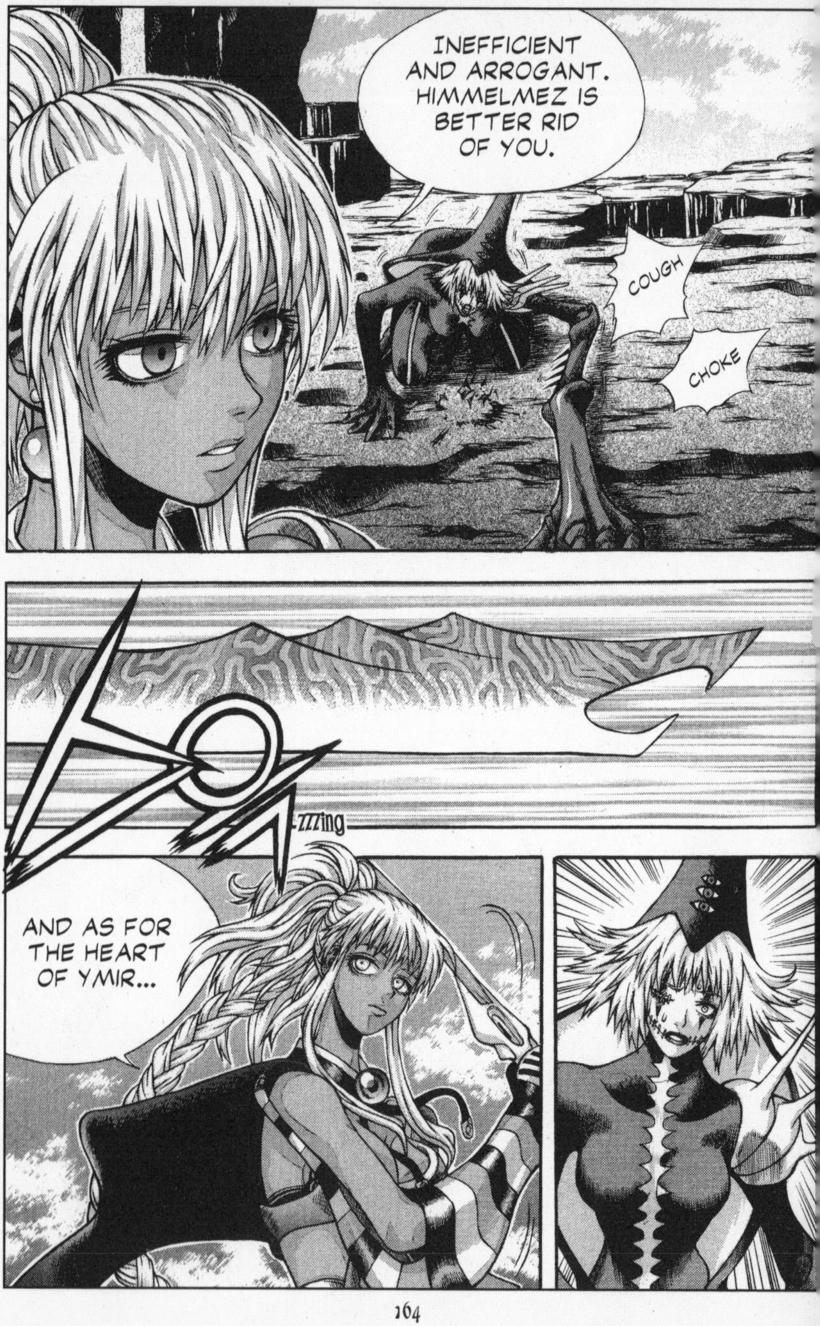
INEFFICIENT AND ARROGANT. HIMMELMEZ IS BETTER RID OF YOU.
COUGH
CHOKE
ZZZing
AND AS FOR THE HEART OF YMIR...

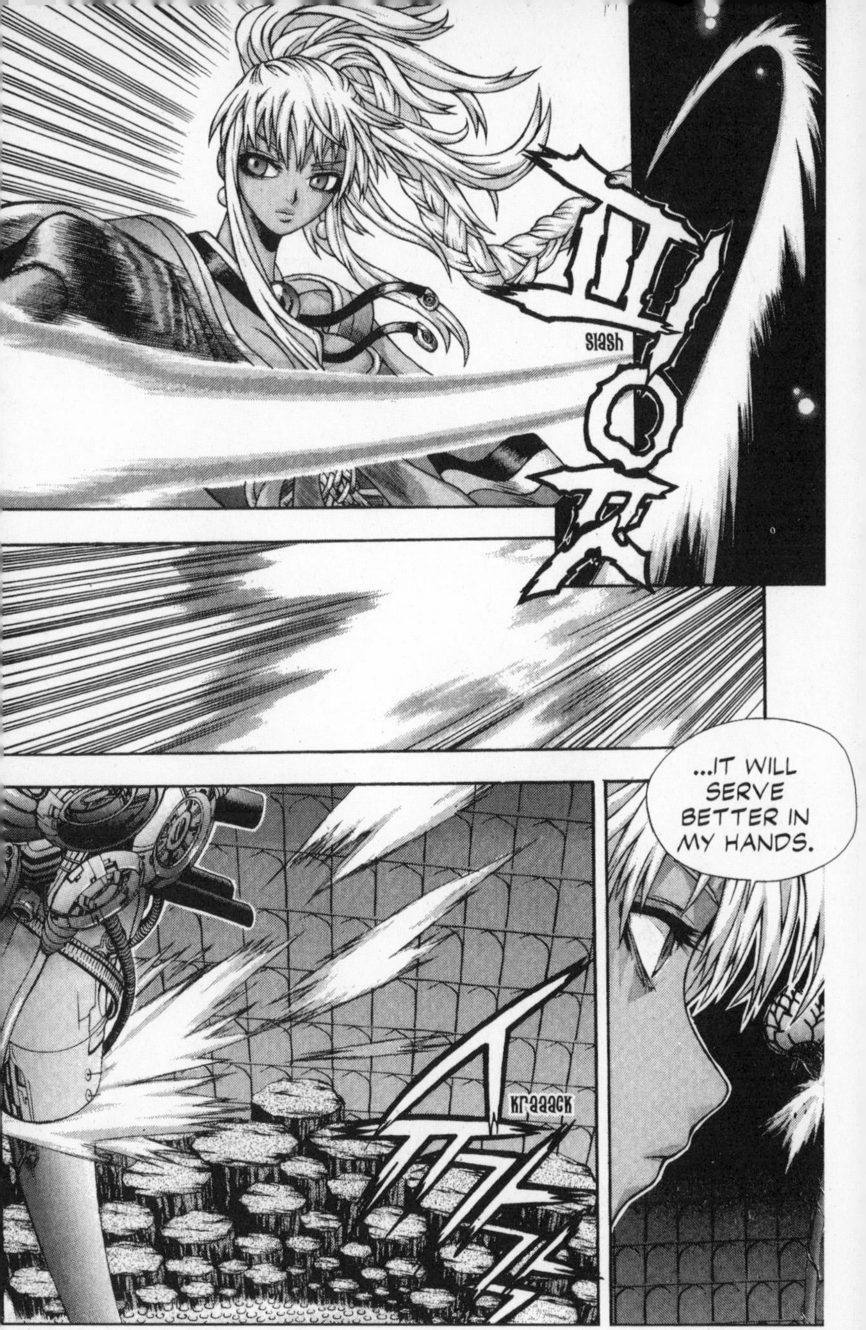
slash
kraaack
...IT WILL SERVE BETTER IN MY HANDS.

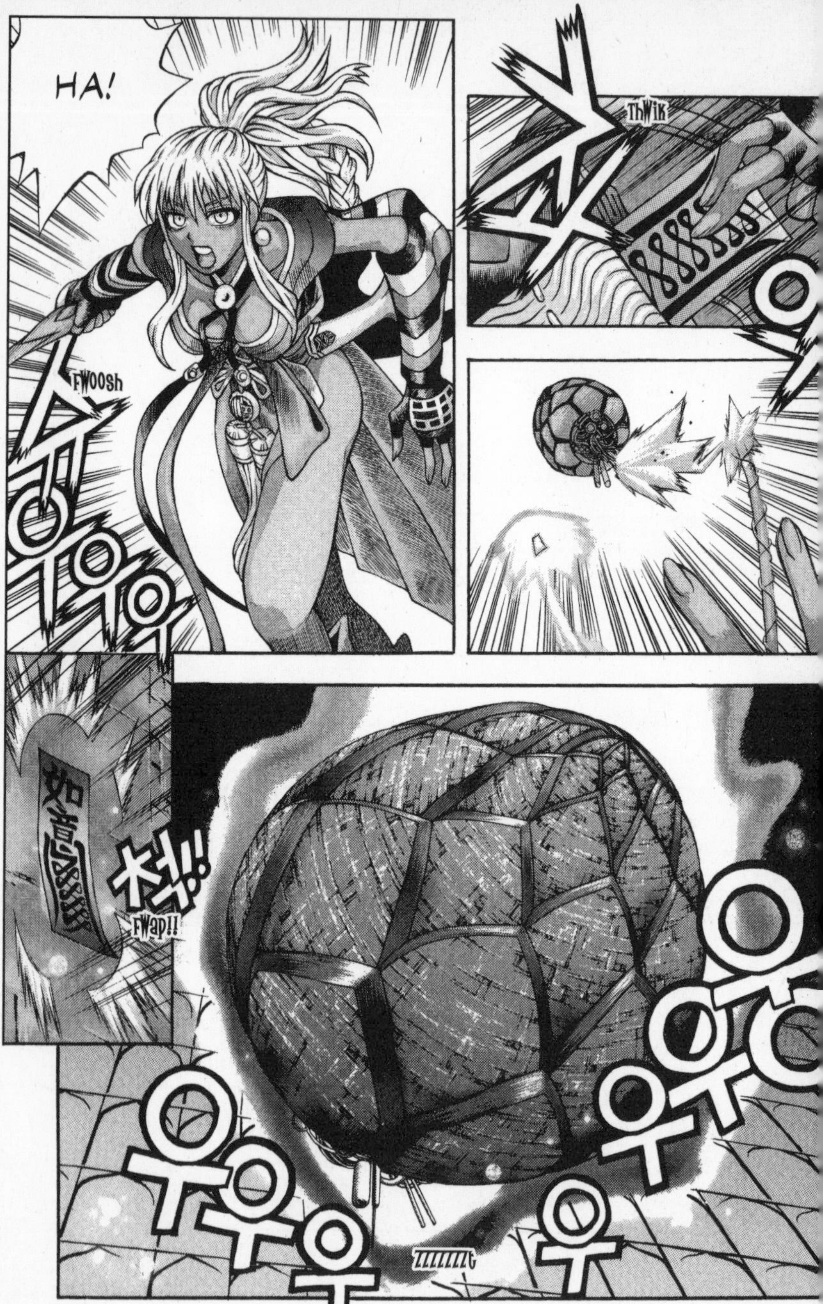
HA!
FWOOSH
THWIK
如意
FWAP!!
ZZZZZZZG

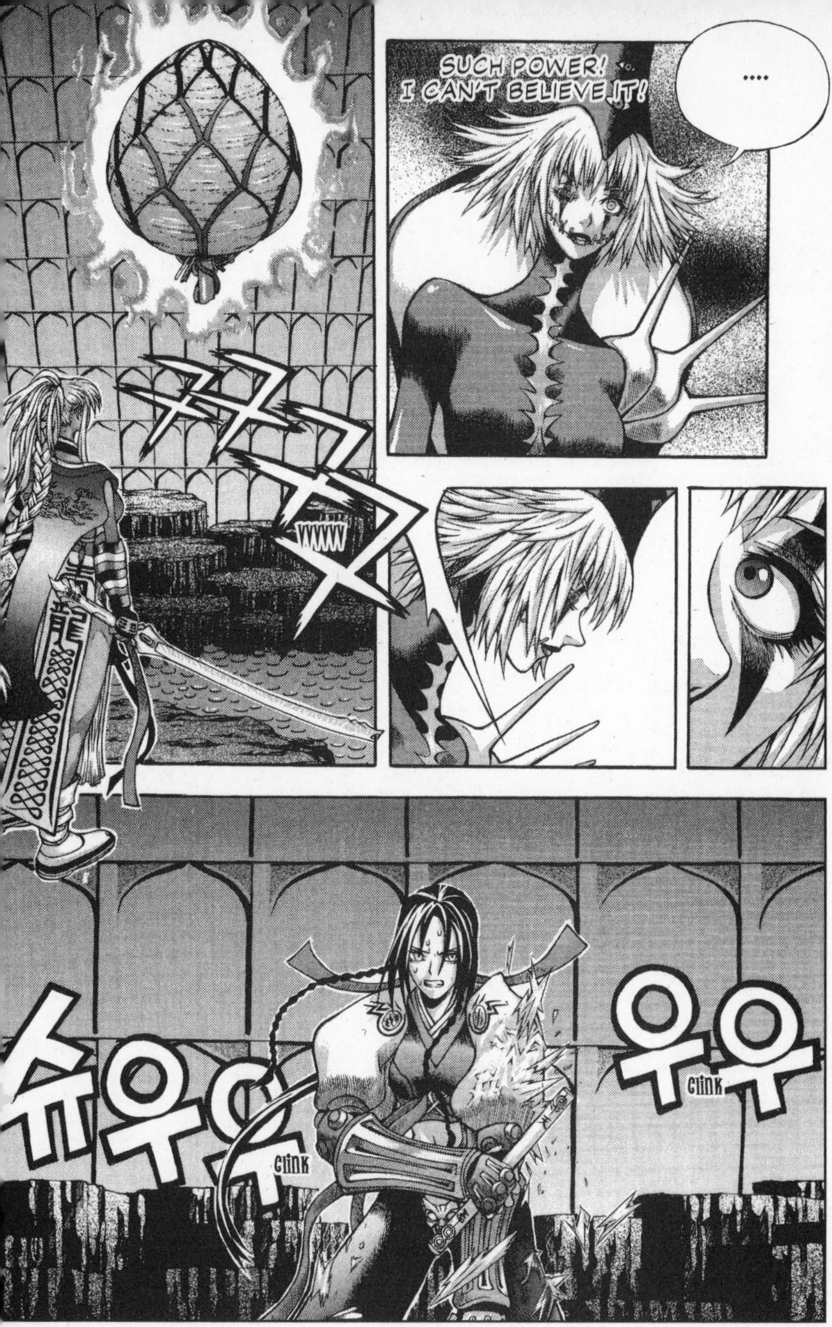
VVVVVV
SUCH POWER! I CAN'T BELIEVE IT!
....
CLINK
CLINK

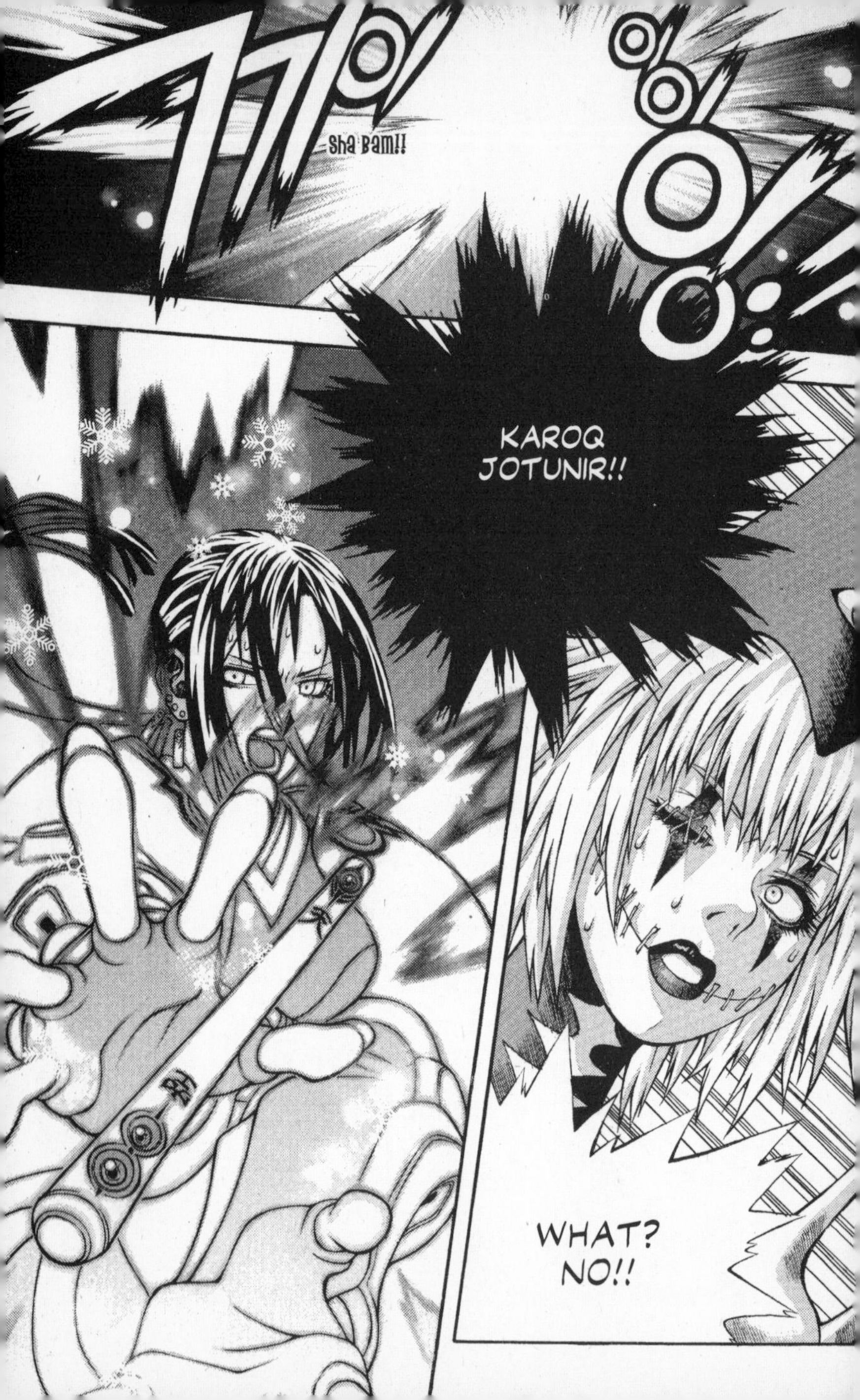
Sha Bam!!
KAROQ JOTUNIR!!
WHAT? NO!!

RAGNAROK
라그나로크
IN TO THE ABYSS

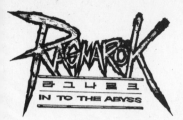

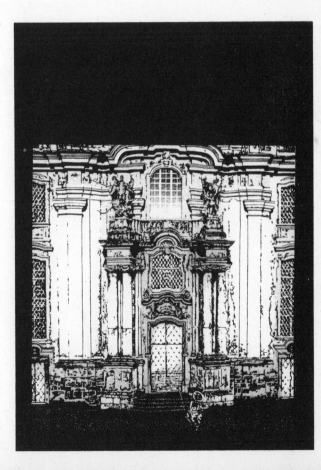

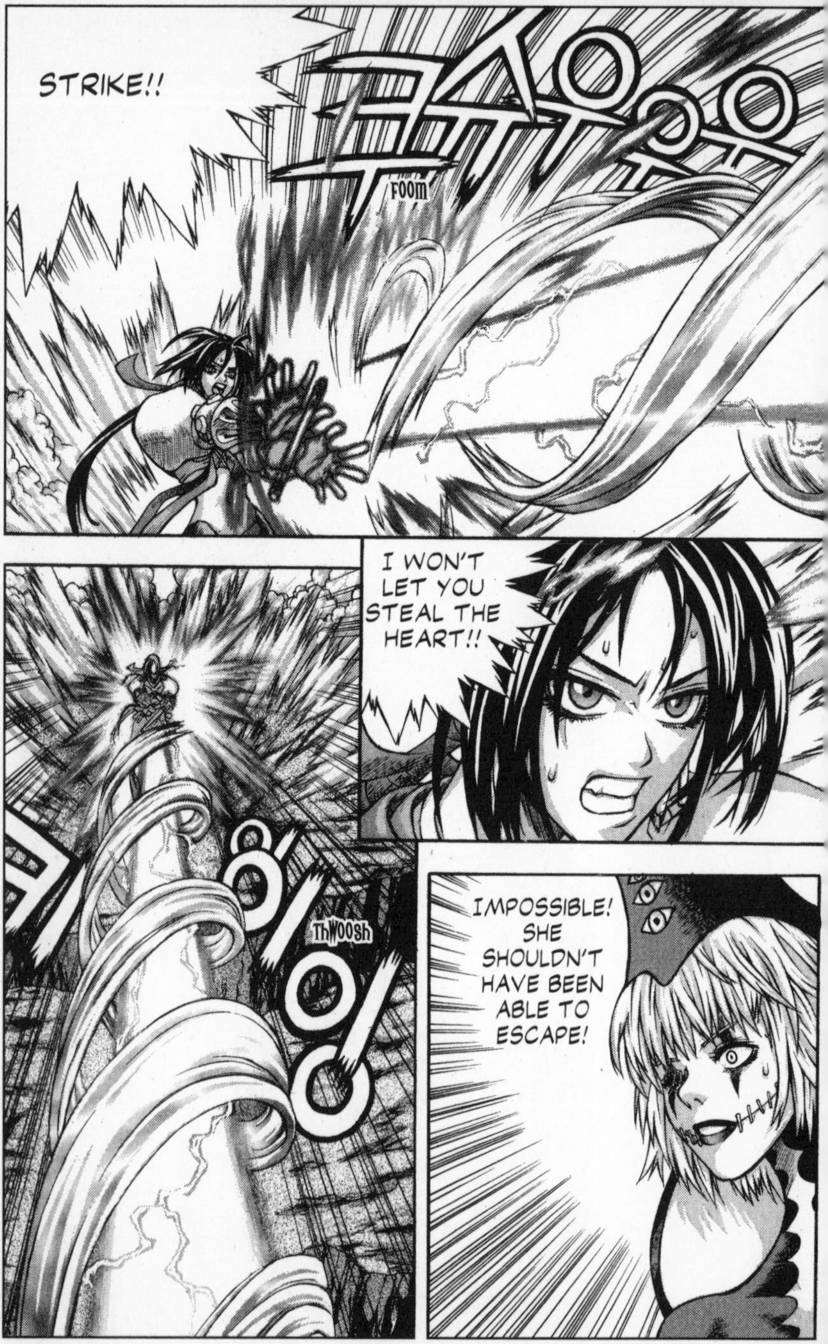
STRIKE!!
FOOM
I WON'T LET YOU STEAL THE HEART!!
ThWOOSh
IMPOSSIBLE! SHE SHOULDN'T HAVE BEEN ABLE TO ESCAPE!

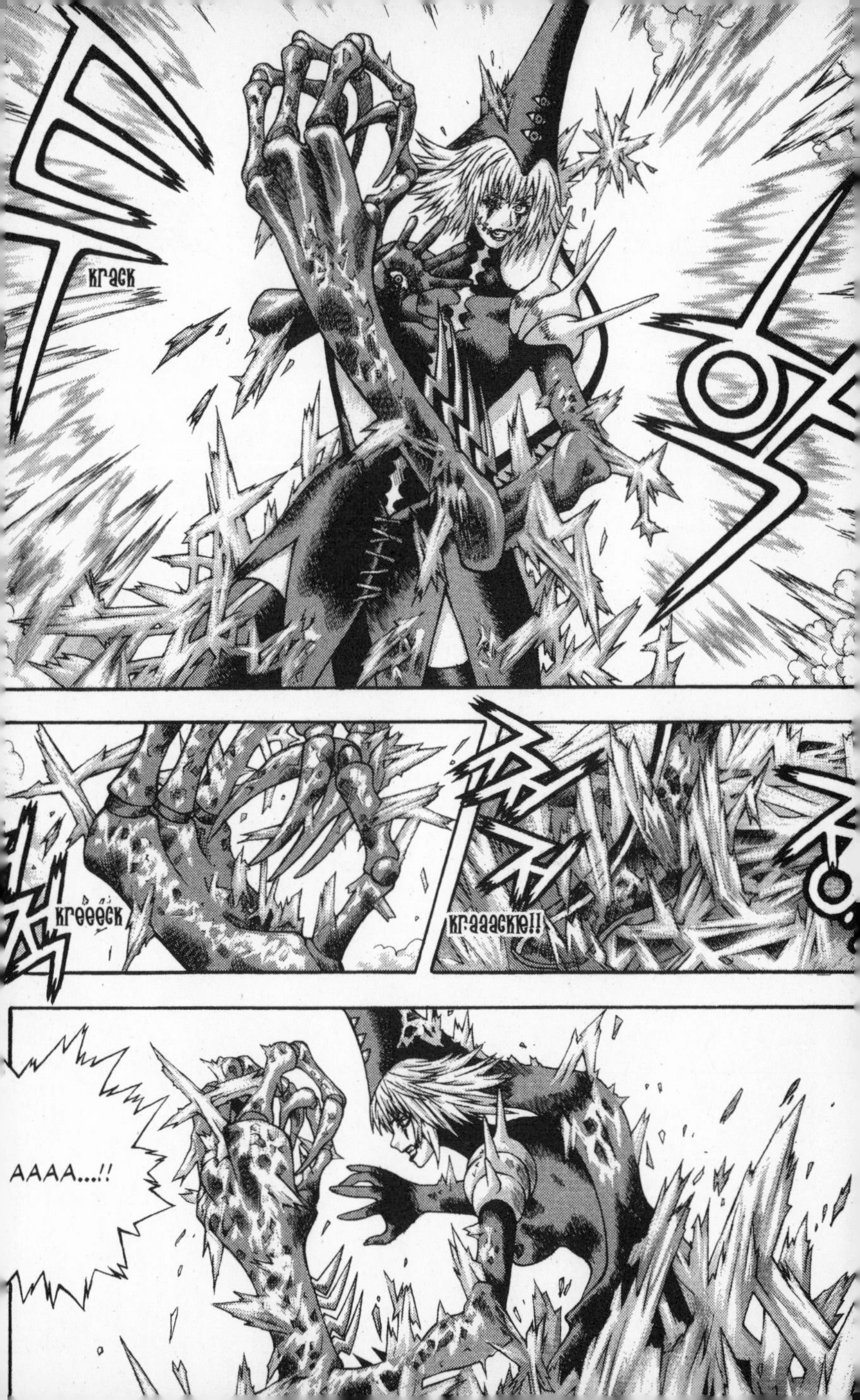
KRACK
KREEECK
KRAAACKLE!!
AAAA...!!

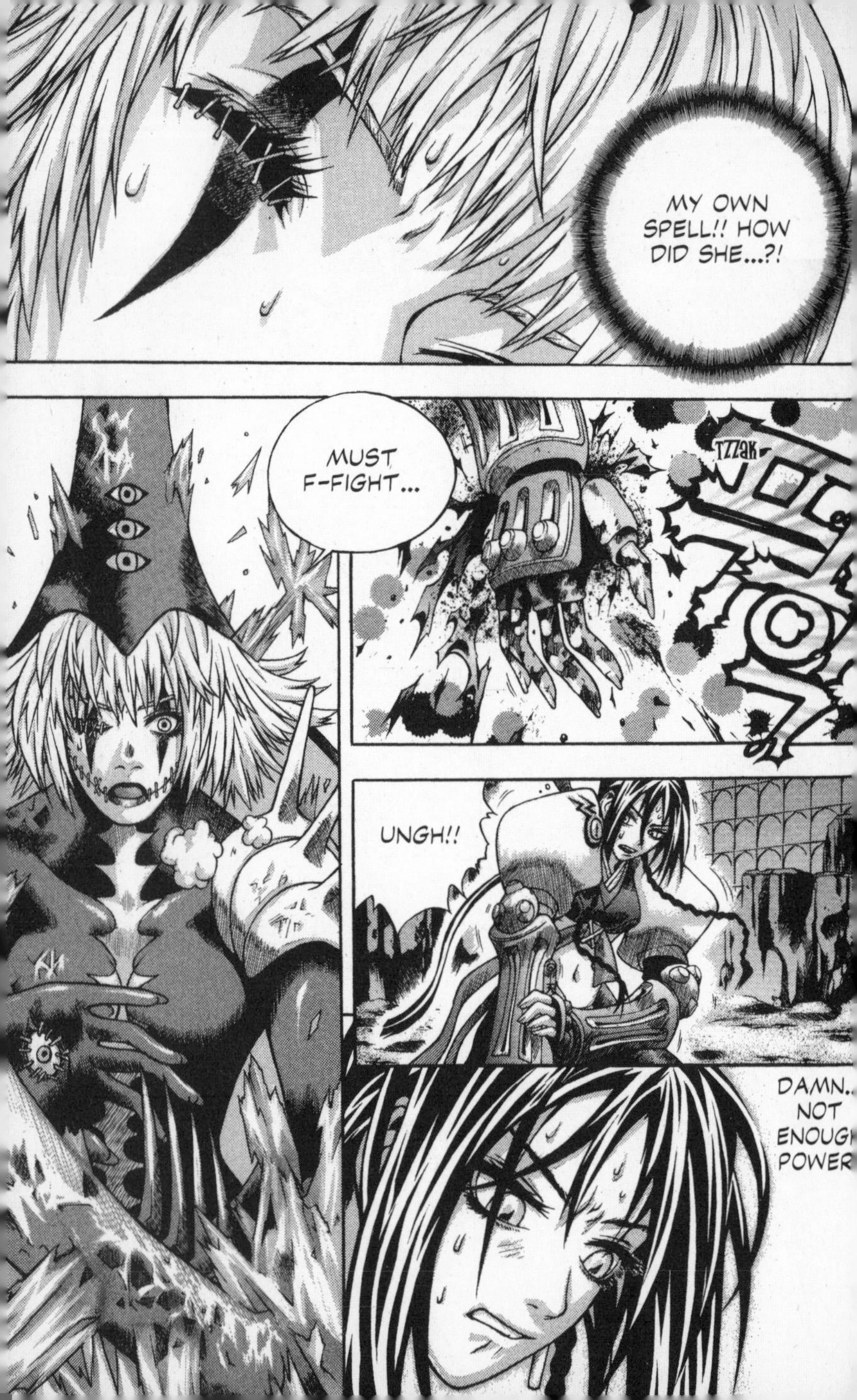
MY OWN SPELL!! HOW DID SHE...?!
MUST F-FIGHT...
TZZAK
UNGH!!
DAMN.. NOT ENOUG POWER

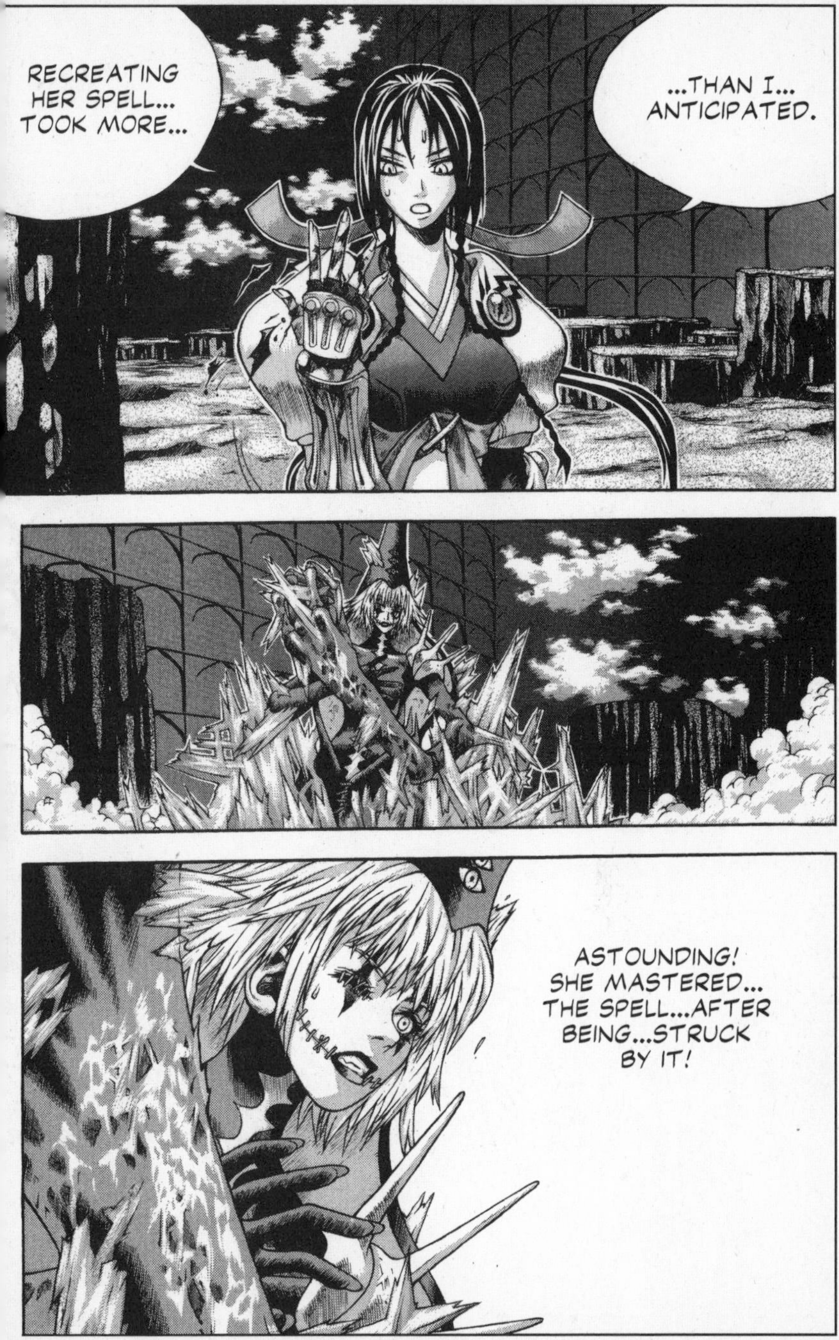
RECREATING HER SPELL... TOOK MORE...
...THAN I... ANTICIPATED.
ASTOUNDING! SHE MASTERED... THE SPELL...AFTER BEING...STRUCK BY IT!

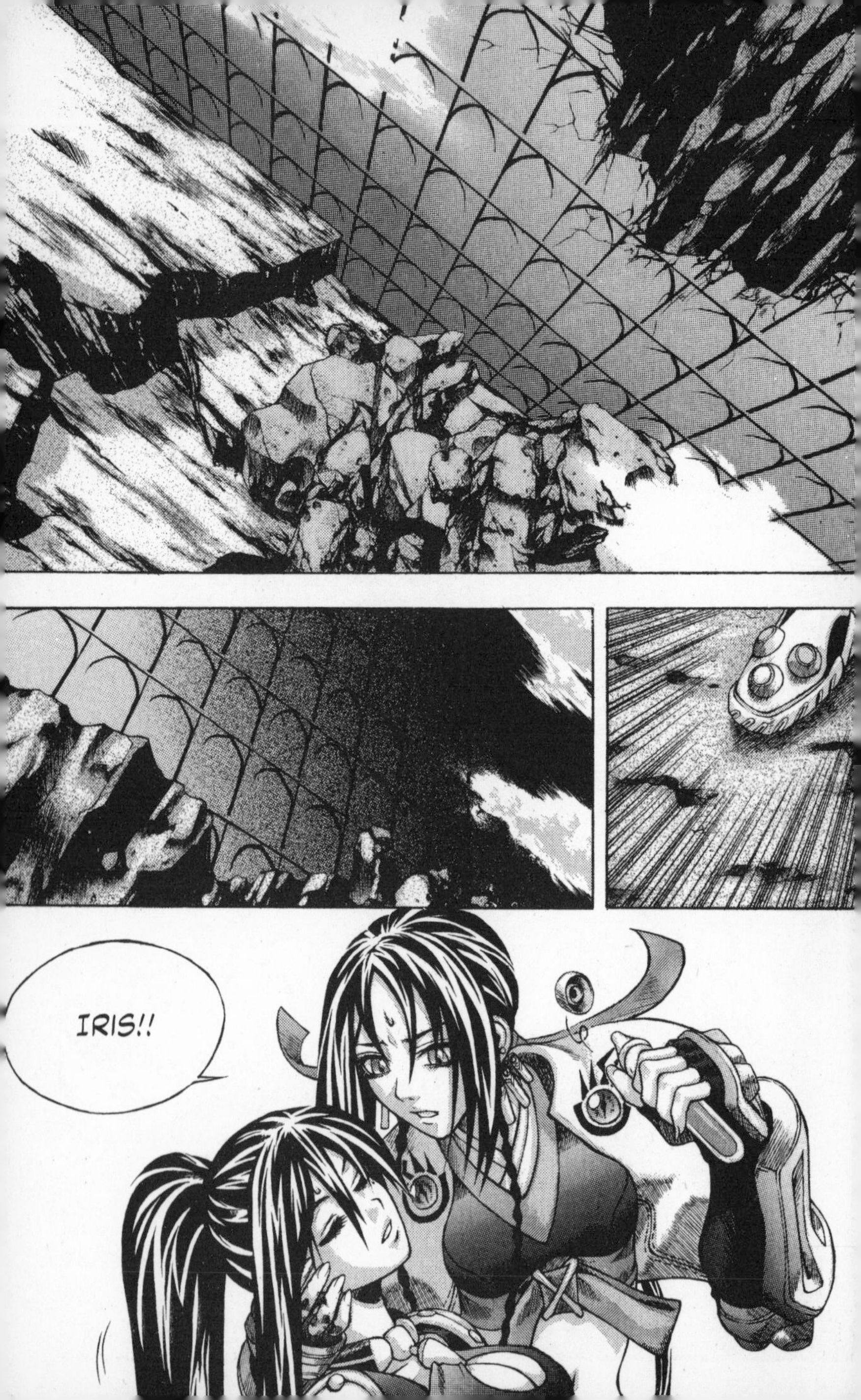
IRIS!!

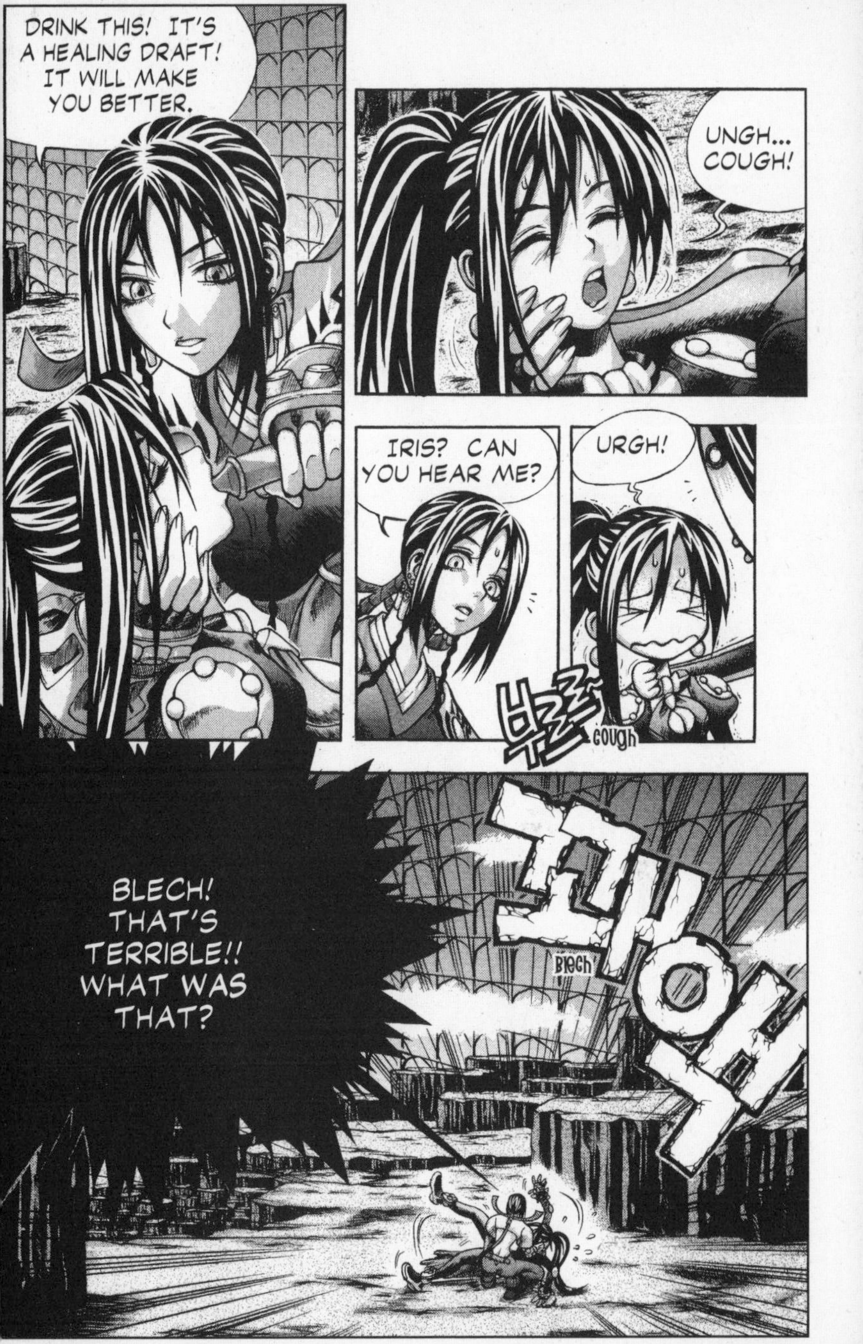
DRINK THIS! IT'S A HEALING DRAFT! IT WILL MAKE YOU BETTER.
UNGH... COUGH!
IRIS? CAN YOU HEAR ME?
URGH!
COUGH
BLECH! THAT'S TERRIBLE!! WHAT WAS THAT?
BLECH

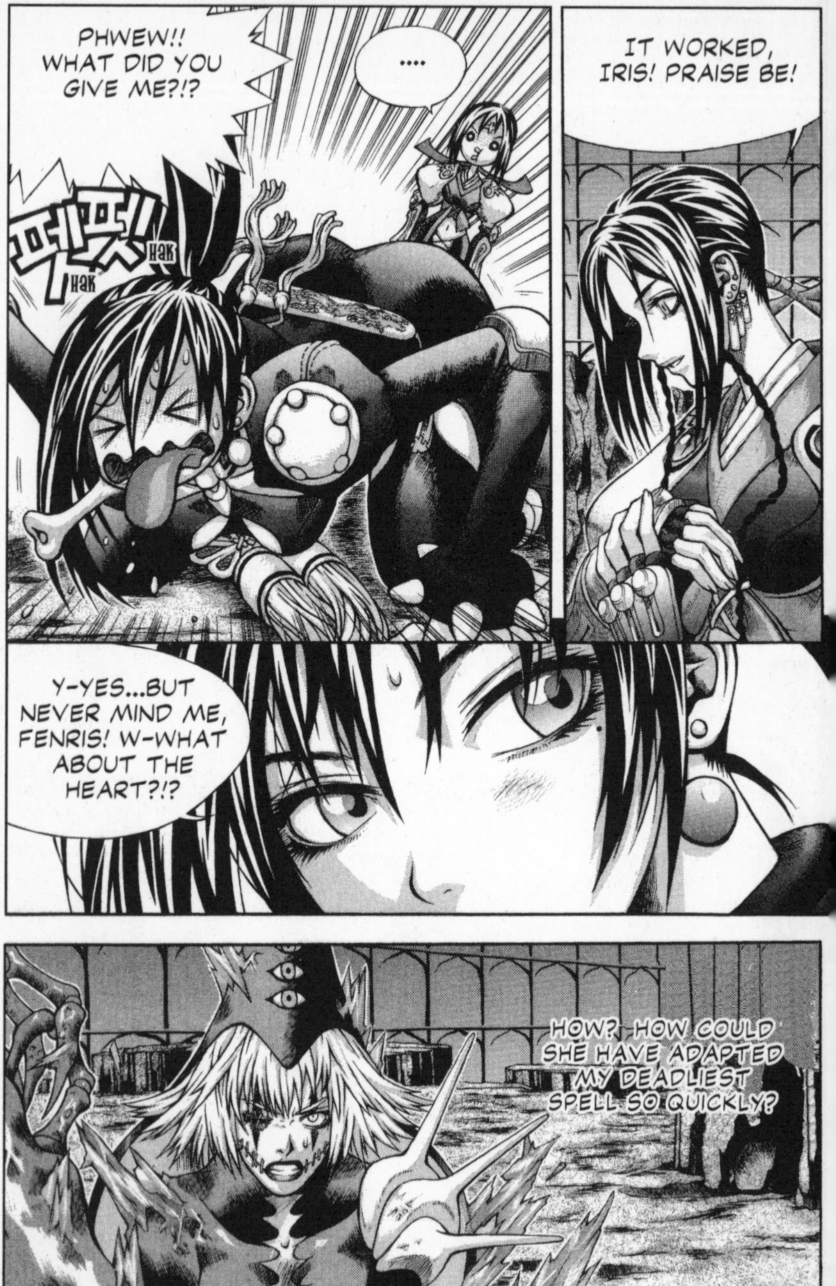
PHWEW!! WHAT DID YOU GIVE ME?!?
....
HAK
HAK
IT WORKED, IRIS! PRAISE BE!
Y-YES...BUT NEVER MIND ME, FENRIS! W-WHAT ABOUT THE HEART?!?
HOW? HOW COULD SHE HAVE ADAPTED MY DEADLIEST SPELL SO QUICKLY?

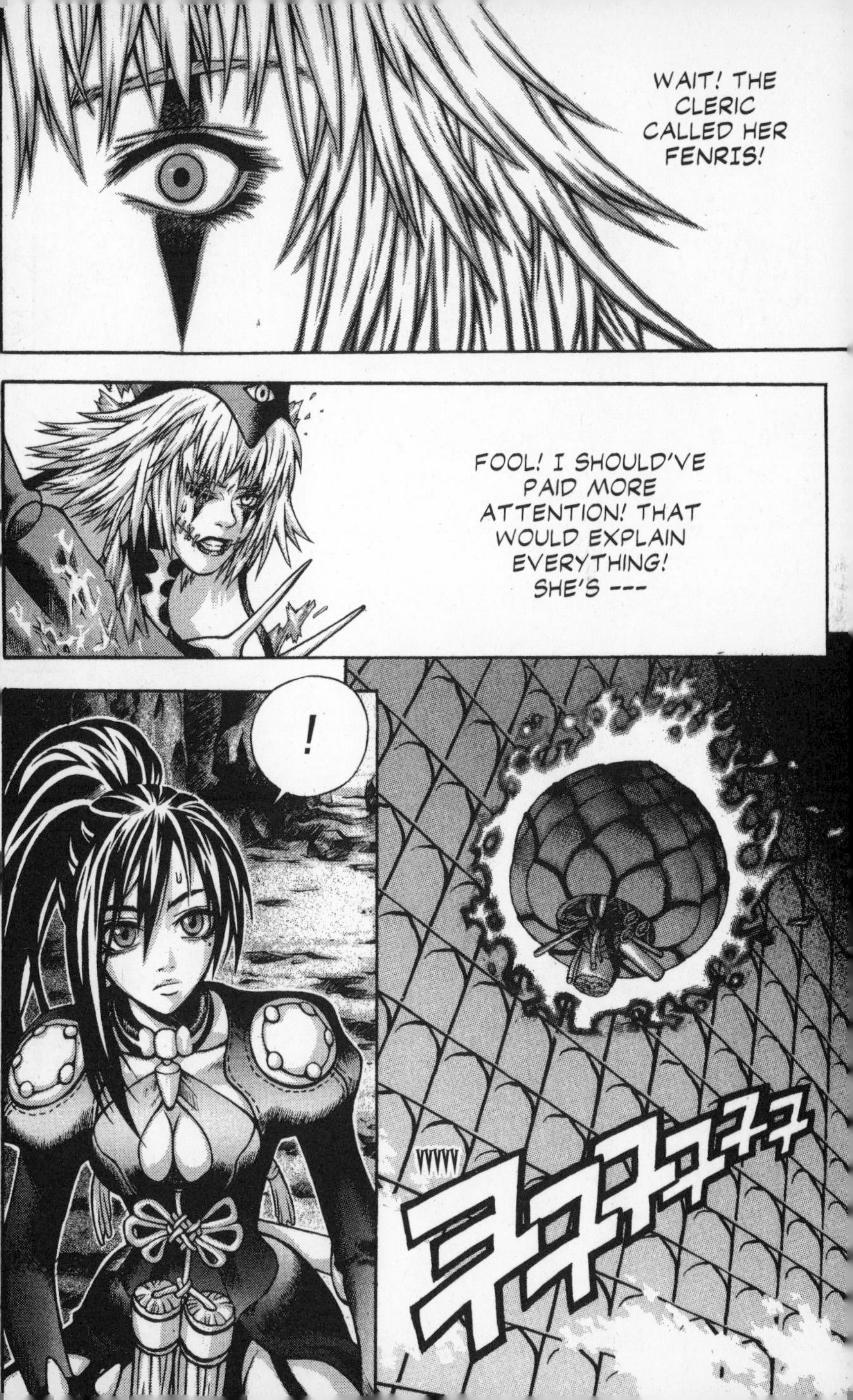
WAIT! THE CLERIC CALLED HER FENRIS!
FOOL! I SHOULD'VE PAID MORE ATTENTION! THAT WOULD EXPLAIN EVERYTHING! SHE'S ---
!
VVVVV

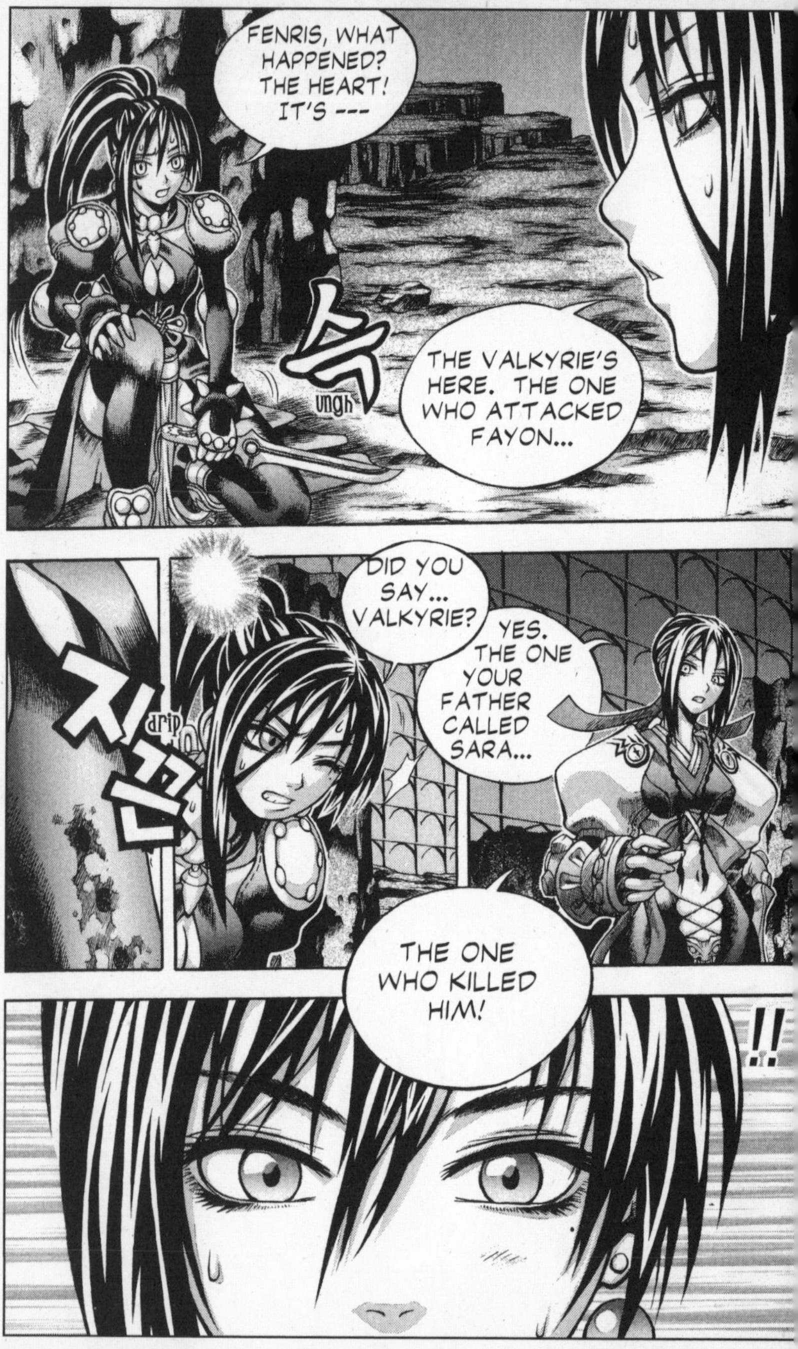
FENRIS, WHAT HAPPENED? THE HEART! IT'S ---
ungh
THE VALKYRIE'S HERE. THE ONE WHO ATTACKED FAYON...
drip
DID YOU SAY... VALKYRIE?
YES. THE ONE YOUR FATHER CALLED SARA...
THE ONE WHO KILLED HIM!
!!

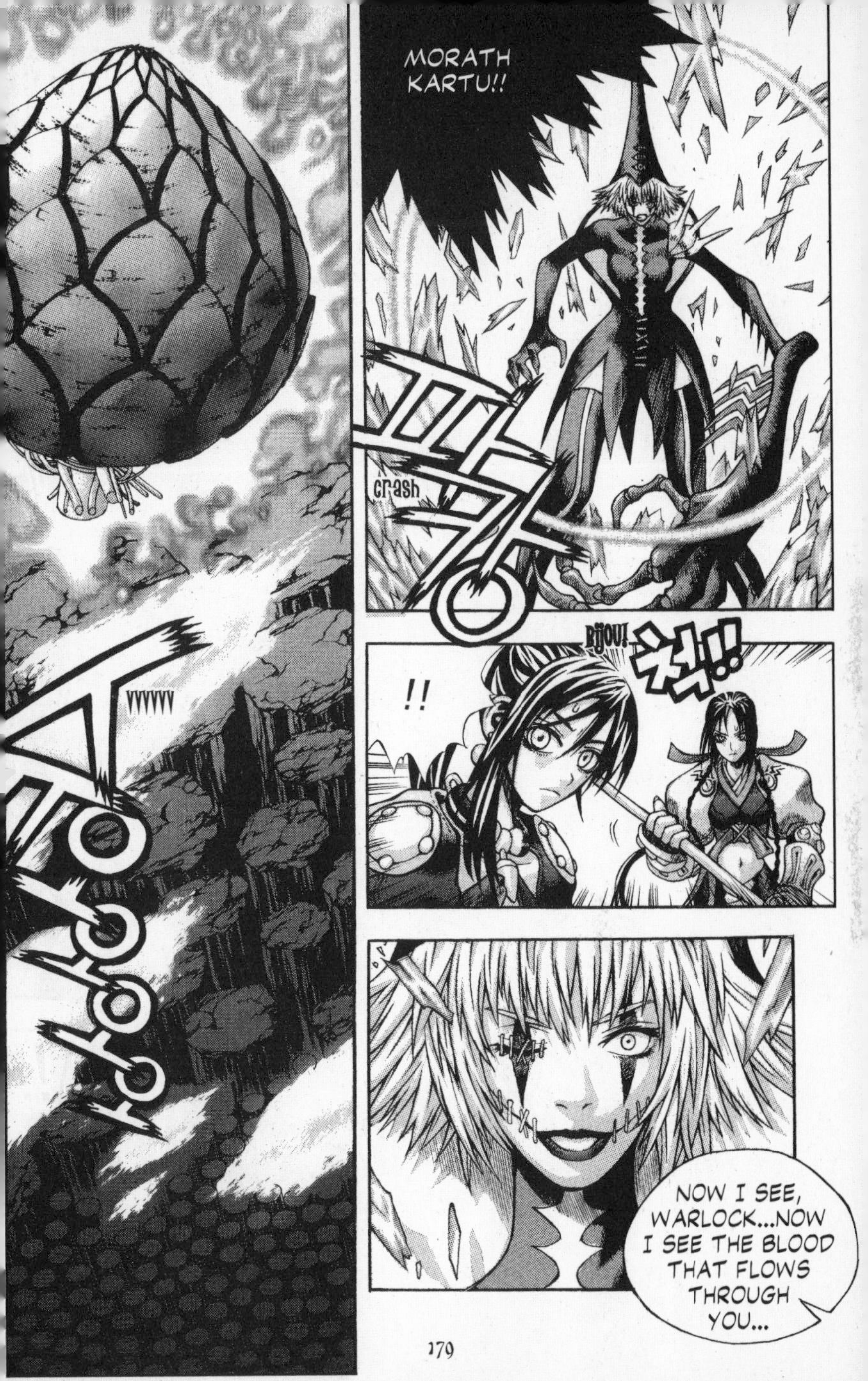
VVVVVV
MORATH KARTU!!
crash
BIJOU!
!!
NOW I SEE, WARLOCK...NOW I SEE THE BLOOD THAT FLOWS THROUGH YOU...

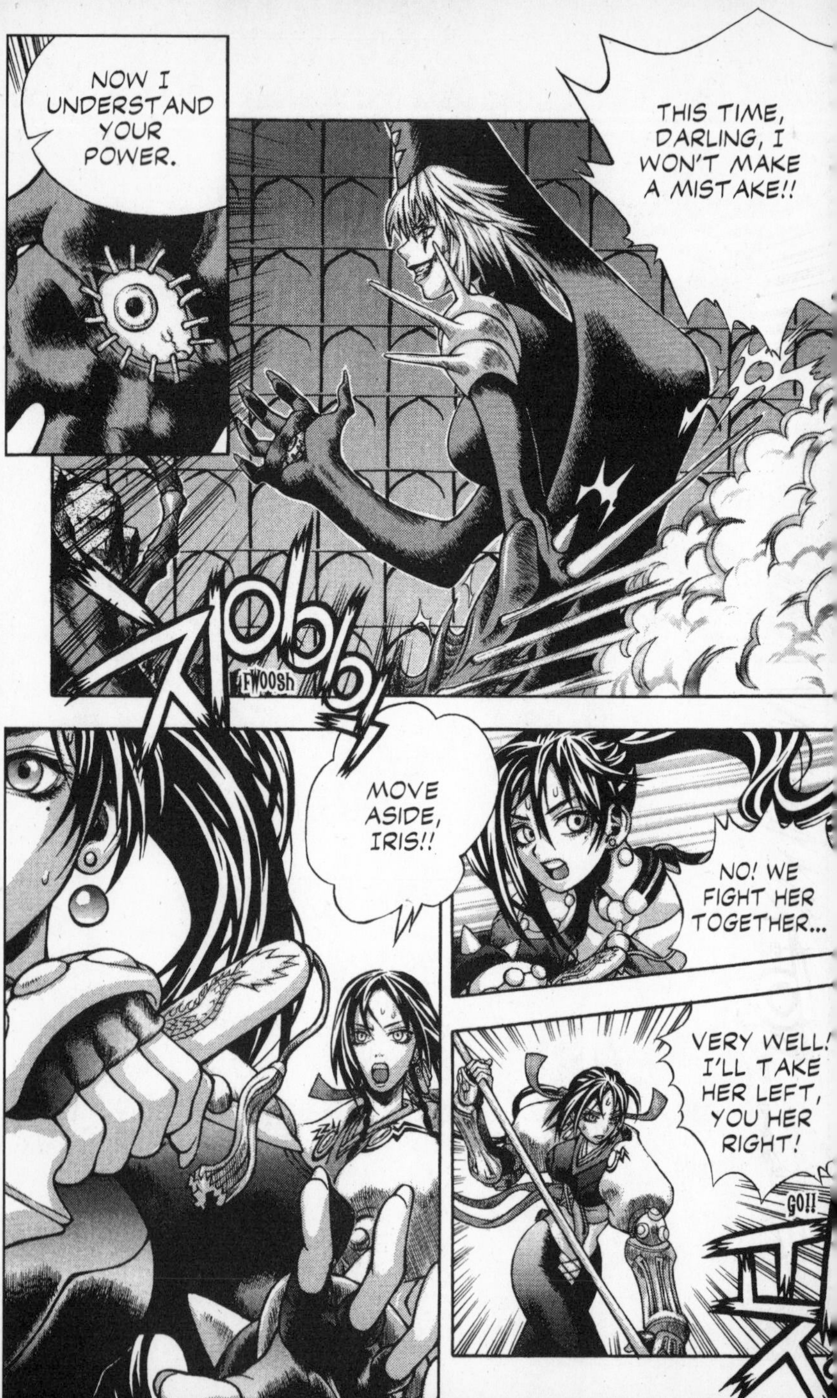
NOW I UNDERSTAND YOUR POWER.
THIS TIME, DARLING, I WON'T MAKE A MISTAKE!!
FWOOSh
MOVE ASIDE, IRIS!!
NO! WE FIGHT HER TOGETHER...
VERY WELL! I'LL TAKE HER LEFT, YOU HER RIGHT!
GO!!

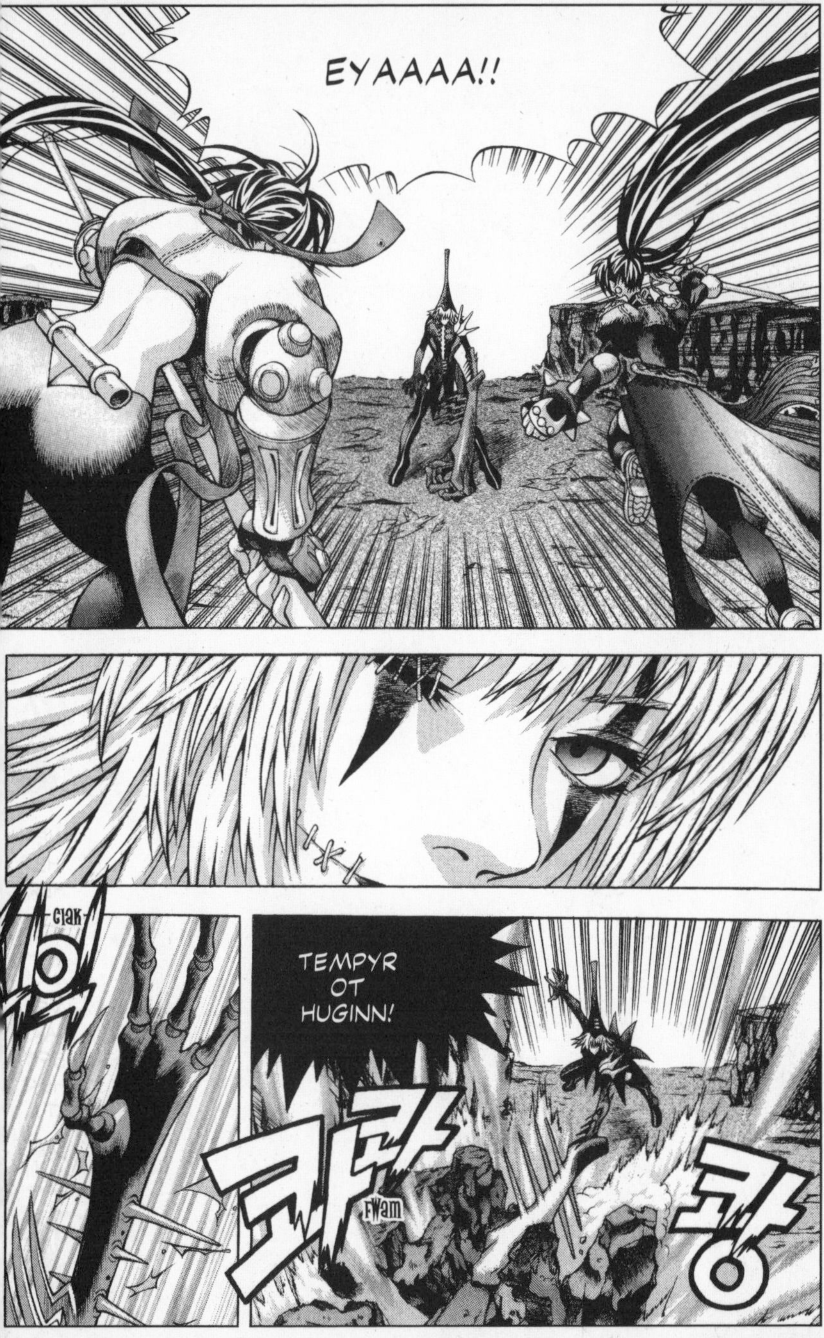
EYAAAA!!
CLAK
TEMPYR OT HUGINN!
FWAM

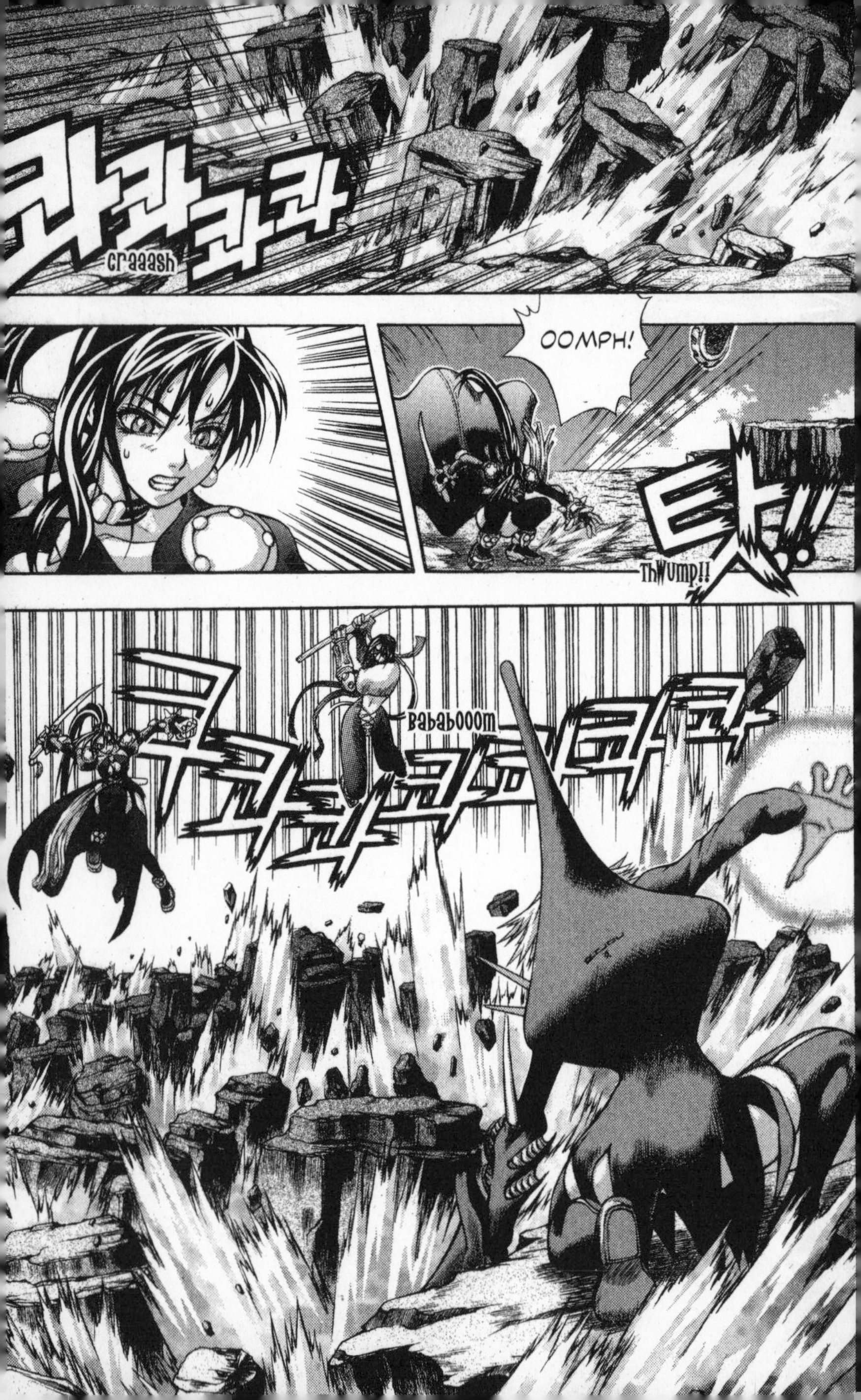
Craaash
OOMPH!
ThWump!!
Bababoom

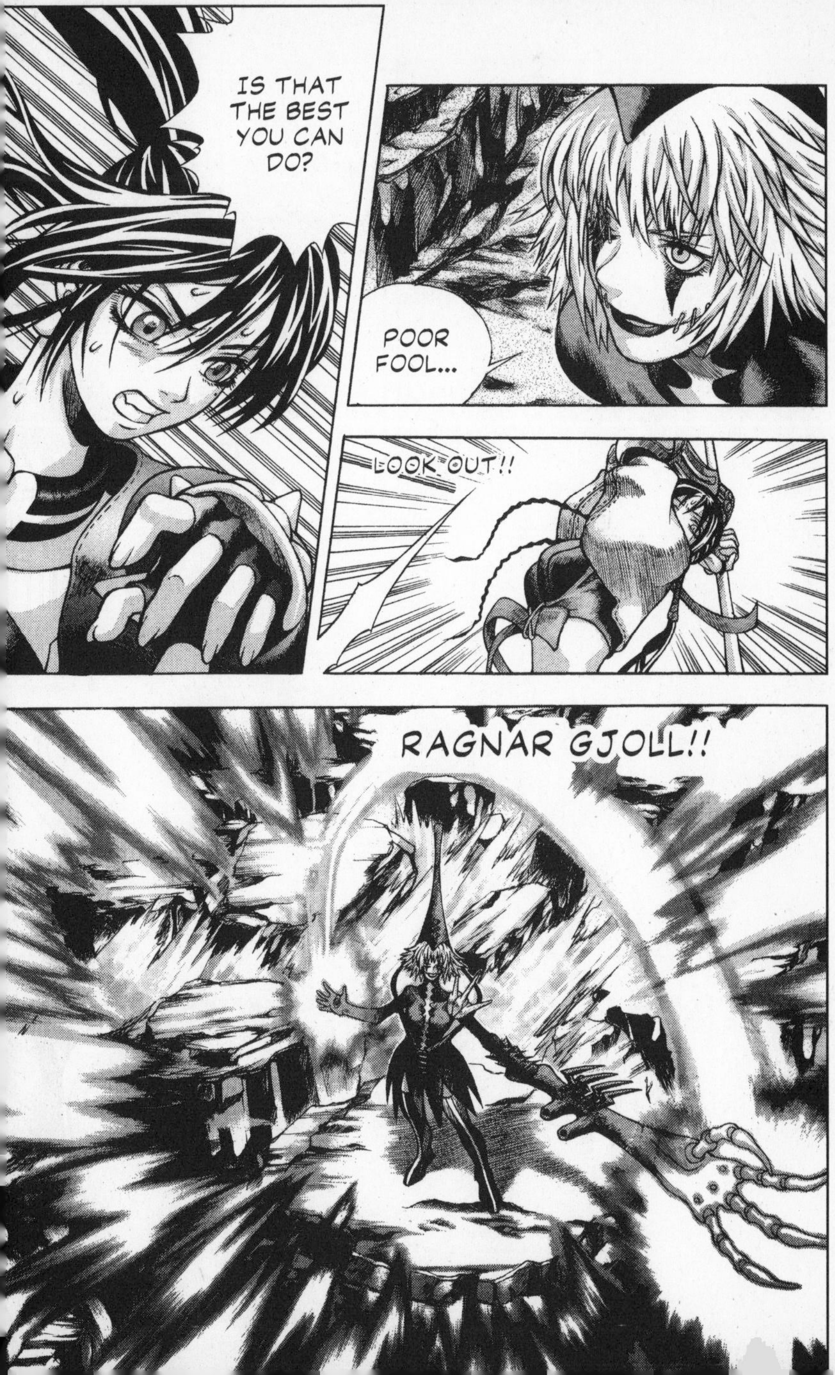
IS THAT THE BEST YOU CAN DO?
POOR FOOL...
LOOK OUT!!
RAGNAR GJOLL!!

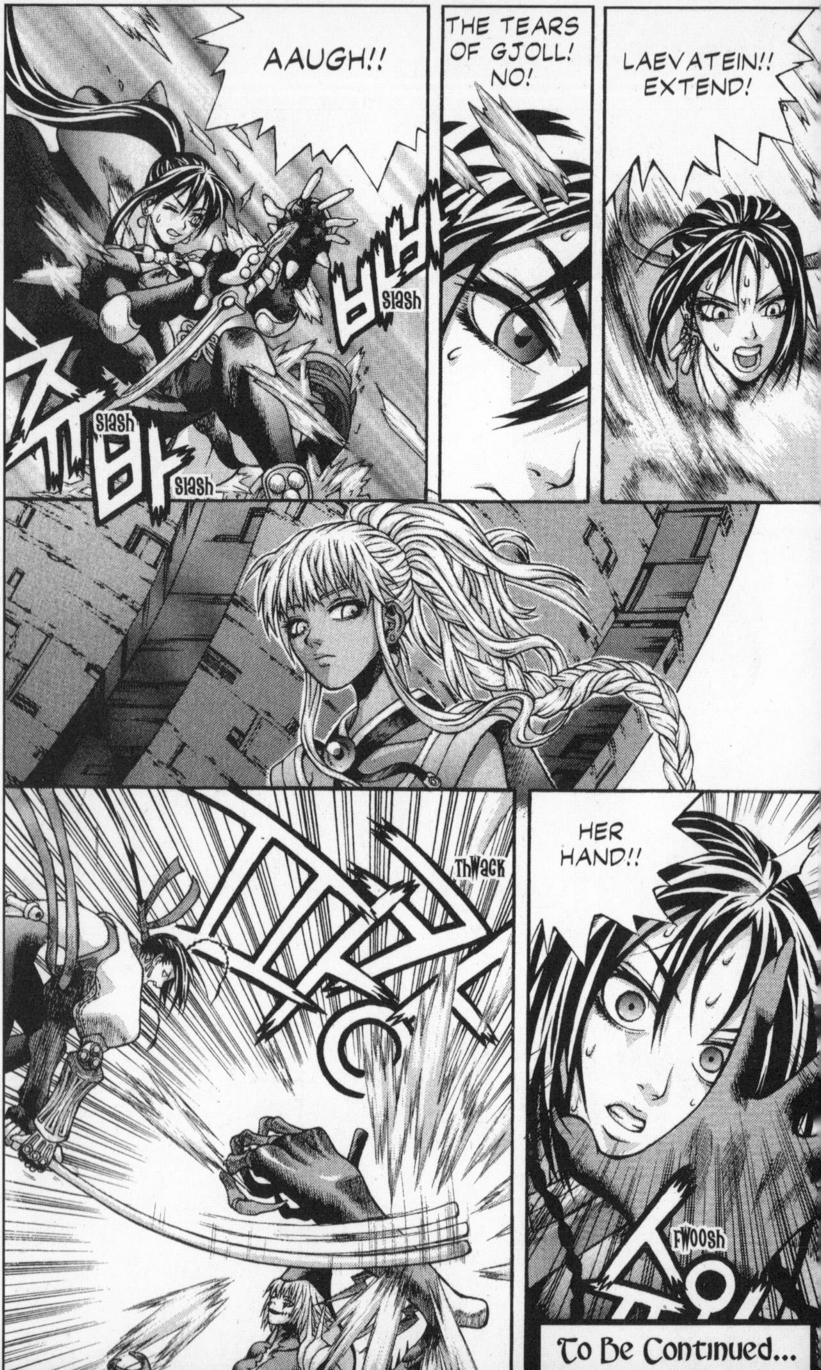

AAUGH!!
SLASH
SLASH
SLASH
THE TEARS OF GJOLL! NO!
LAEVATEIN!! EXTEND!
THWACK
HER HAND!!
FWOOSH
To Be Continued...

FENRIS FENRIR

THE WARLOCK VER.02

The Great Costume Overhaul!

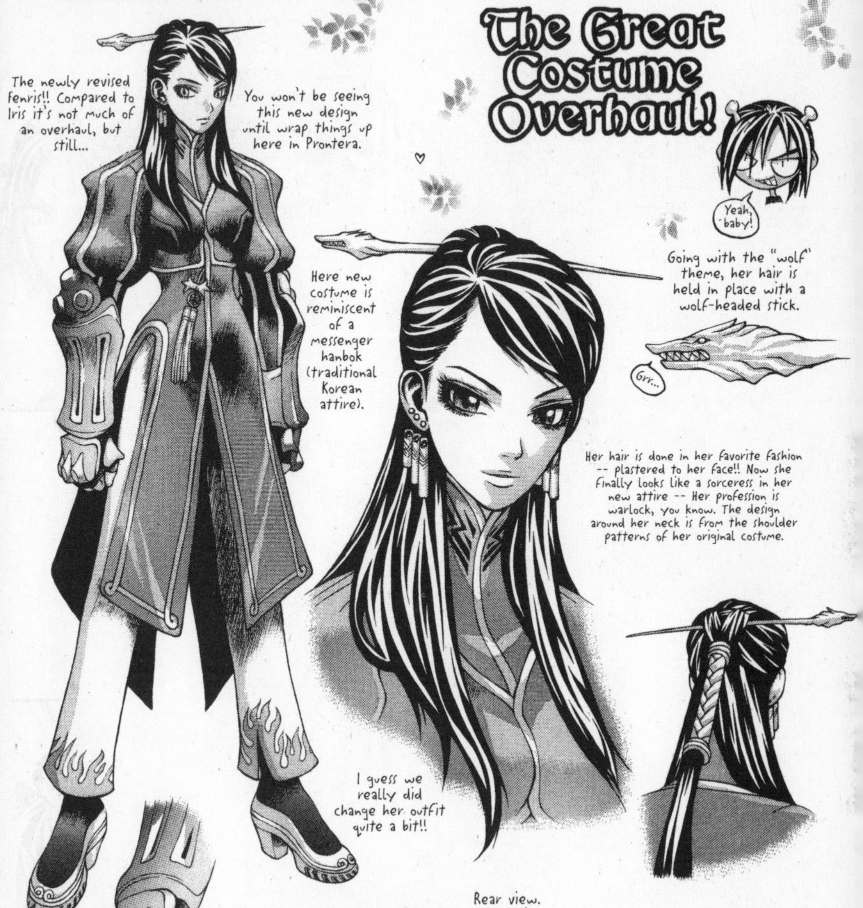

The newly revised fenris!! Compared to Iris it's not much of an overhaul, but still...
You won't be seeing this new design until wrap things up here in Prontera.
Yeah, baby!
Here new costume is reminiscent of a messenger hanbok (traditional Korean attire).
Going with the "wolf" theme, her hair is held in place with a wolf-headed stick.
Grr...
Her hair is done in her favorite fashion -- plastered to her face!! Now she finally looks like a sorceress in her new attire -- Her profession is warlock, you know. The design around her neck is from the shoulder patterns of her original costume.
I guess we really did change her outfit quite a bit!!

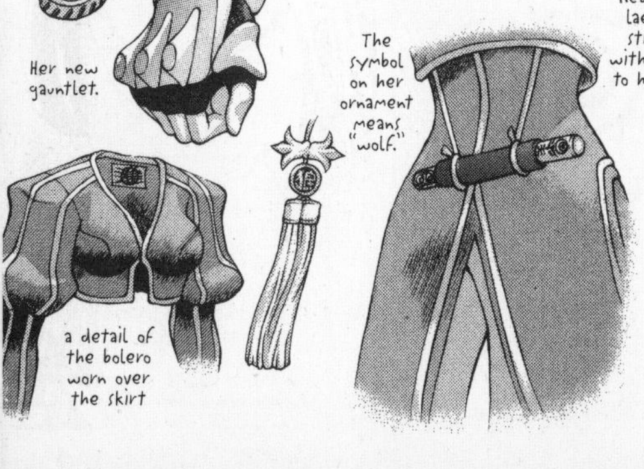

Her new gauntlet.
The symbol on her ornament means "wolf."
Rear view. laevatein strapped with leather to her back.
a detail of the bolero worn over the skirt

A brief note about Fenris Fenrir

In a way, Fenris is the most tragic of our heroes. In her past life she was in love with Balder and ultimately sacrificed her life for him. But now, reborn 1000 years later, she finally tracks down the man she loves, only to find beside him a charming girl who obviously loves him. In spite of this Fenris remains true to the man she loved and follows Chaos, even to the end of the Earth. May the spirits watch over her.

Iris Irine

The Cleric Ver.04

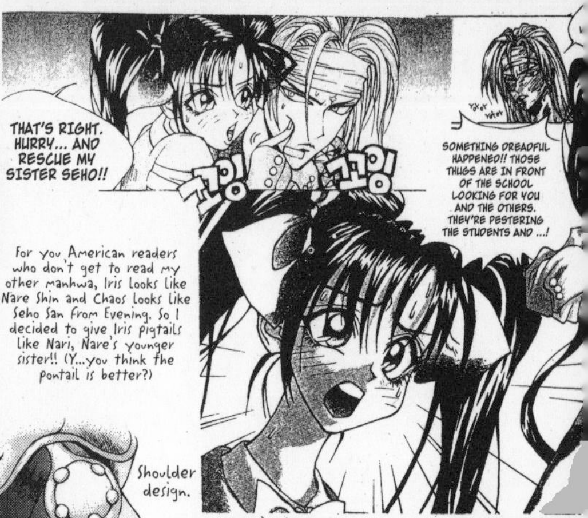
THAT'S RIGHT. HURRY... AND RESCUE MY SISTER SEHO!!
SOMETHING DREADFUL HAPPENED!! THOSE THUGS ARE IN FRONT OF THE SCHOOL LOOKING FOR YOU AND THE OTHERS. THEY'RE PESTERING THE STUDENTS AND ...!

That's right...from the 9th volume of evening.

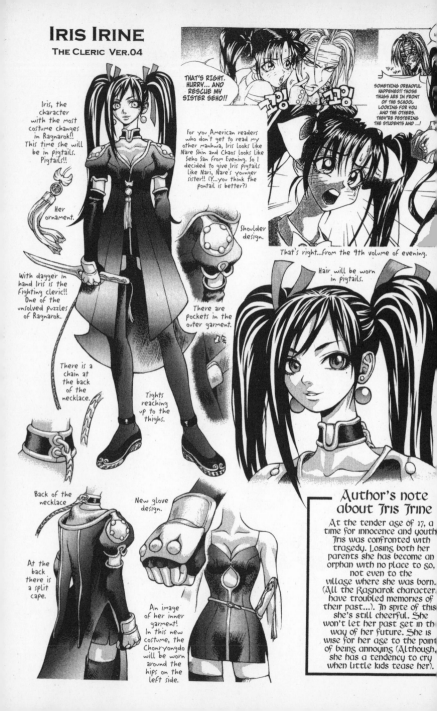

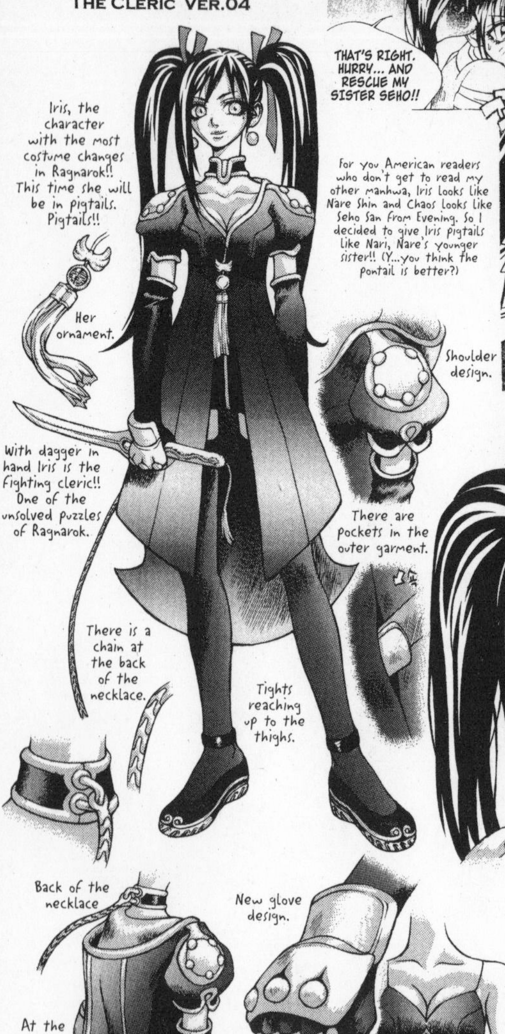
Iris, the character with the most costume changes in Ragnarok!! This time she will be in pigtails. Pigtails!!
For you American readers who don't get to read my other manhwa, Iris looks like Nare Shin and Chaos looks like Seho San from Evening. So I decided to give Iris pigtails like Nari, Nare's younger sister!! (Y...you think the pontail is better?)
Her ornament.
Shoulder design.
With dagger in hand Iris is the fighting cleric!! One of the unsolved puzzles of Ragnarok.
There are pockets in the outer garment.
There is a chain at the back of the necklace.
Tights reaching up to the thighs.
Back of the necklace
New glove design.
At the back there is a split cape.
An image of her inner garment! In this new costume, the Chonryongdo will be worn around the hips on the left side.

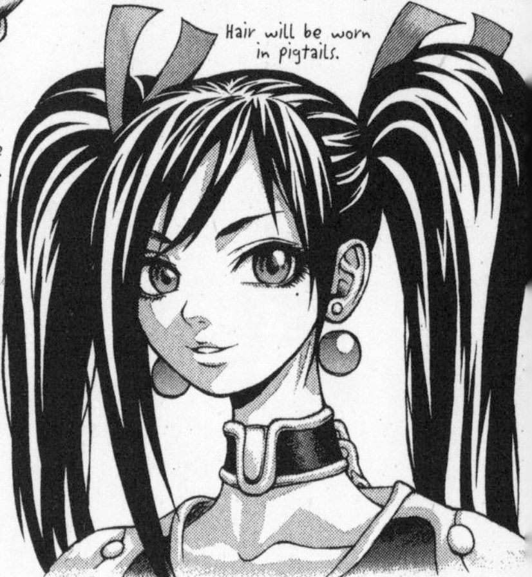
Hair will be worn in pigtails.

Author's note about Iris Irine

At the tender age of 17, a time for innocence and youth Iris was confronted with tragedy. Losing both her parents she has become an orphan with no place to go, not even to the village where she was born. (All the Ragnarok character have troubled memories of their past...). In spite of this she's still cheerful. She won't let her past get in th way of her future. She is wise for her age to the point of being annoying (Although, she has a tendency to cry when little kids tease her).

RAGNAROK BONUS 4-PANEL STRIPS!

Peko
Gangpyo Shin

KIM JIRO

SEHUN

KURO.

Four Ragnarok assistants from our DIVE TO DREAM SEA studio came up with the following comic scenarios. Their dreams are of becoming famous comic manhwa writers of their own. Okay then, let's DIVE into the sea of dreams!!

Lonely Assassin

by PEKO

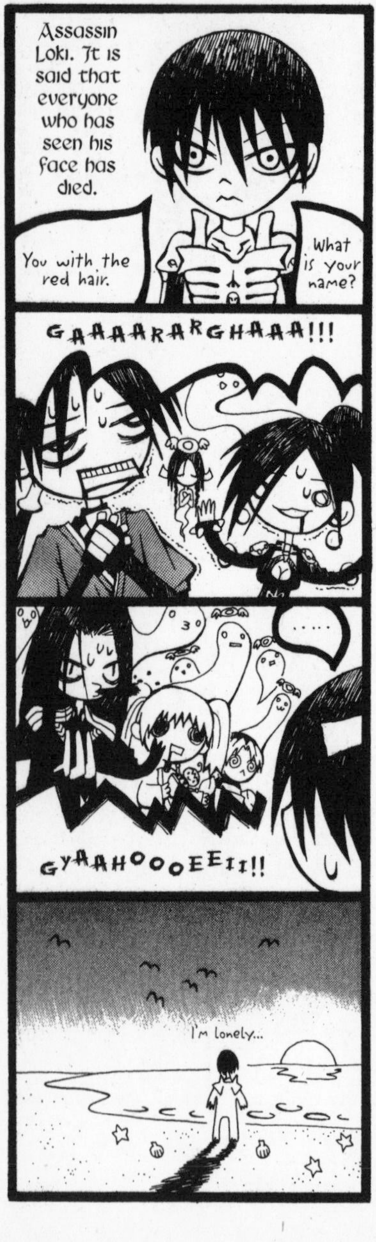
Assassin Loki. It is said that everyone who has seen his face has died.
You with the red hair.
What is your name?
GAAAARARGHAAAA!!!
.....
GYAAHOOOOEEII!!
I'm lonely...

Pain in the Neck

by KIM JIRO

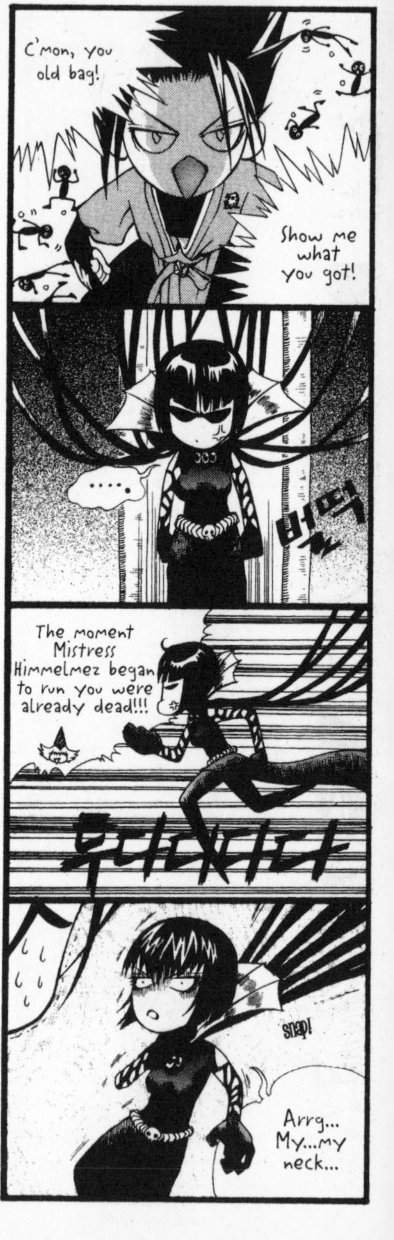
C'mon, you old bag!
Show me what you got!
.....
벌떡
The moment Mistress Himmelmez began to run you were already dead!!!
SNAP!
Arrg... My...my neck...

No Mercy!

by SEYHUN

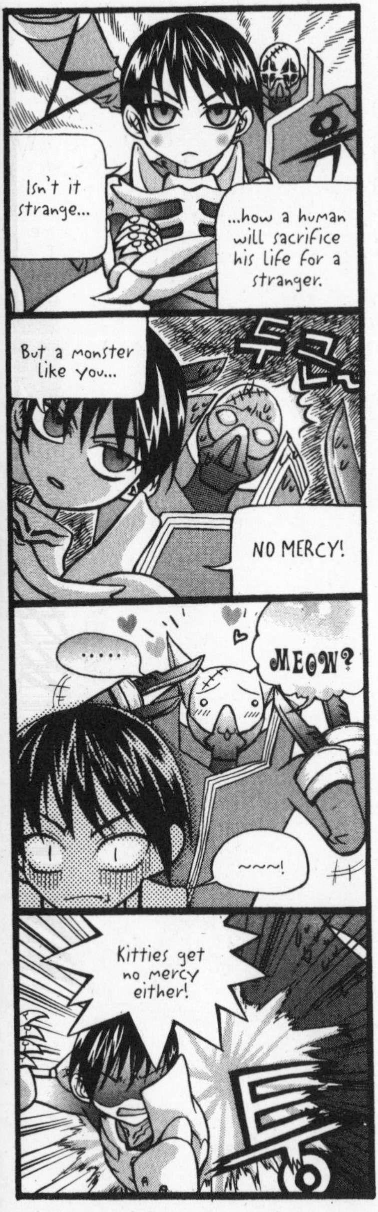
Isn't it strange...
...how a human will sacrifice his life for a stranger.
But a monster like you...
NO MERCY!
......
MEOW?
~~~!
Kitties get no mercy either!

Tricks of the Trade

by KURO

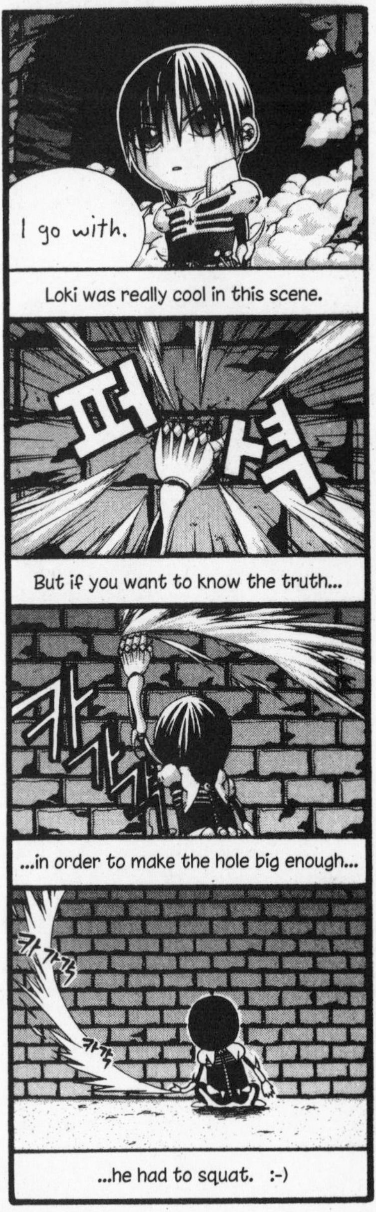
I go with.
Loki was really cool in this scene.
But if you want to know the truth...
...in order to make the hole big enough...
...he had to squat. :-)
~~~

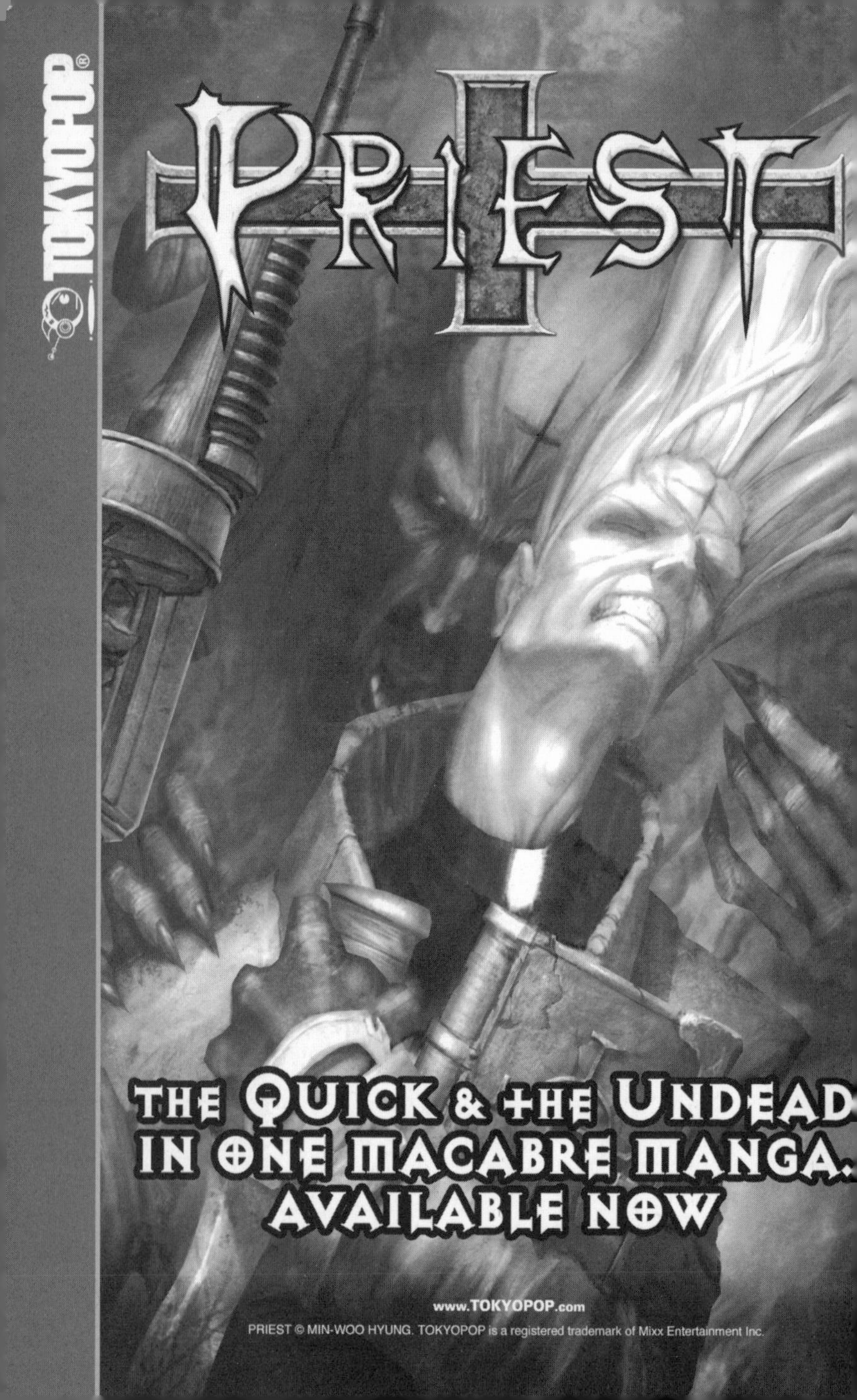
TOKYOPOP
PRIEST
THE QUICK & THE UNDEAD
IN ONE MACABRE MANGA.
AVAILABLE NOW
www.TOKYOPOP.com
PRIEST © MIN-WOO HYUNG. TOKYOPOP is a registered trademark of Mixx Entertainment Inc.